DISCERNING
SPIRITS

A Volume in the Series

CONJUNCTIONS OF RELIGION & POWER IN THE MEDIEVAL PAST
Edited by BARBARA H. ROSENWEIN

A full list of titles in the series appears at the end of the book.

DISCERNING SPIRITS

DIVINE AND DEMONIC

POSSESSION

IN THE MIDDLE AGES

NANCY CACIOLA

Cornell University Press

Ithaca and London

First published 2003 by Cornell University Press
First printing, Cornell Paperbacks, 2006

Printed in the United States of America

Library of Congress Cataloging-in-Publication Data

Caciola, Nancy, 1963–
    Discerning spirits : divine and demonic possession in the Middle Ages / Nancy Caciola.
        p.   cm. — (Conjunctions of religion & power in the medieval past)
    Includes bibliographical references and index.
    ISBN-13: 978-0-8014-4084-7 (cloth : alk. paper)
    ISBN-10: 0-8014-4084-X (cloth : alk. paper)
    ISBN-13: 978-0-8014-7334-0 (pbk. : alk. paper)
    ISBN-10: 0-8014-7334-9 (pbk. : alk. paper)
        1. Discernment of spirits—History of doctrines—Middle Ages, 600–1500.
    2. Women in Christianity—History—Middle Ages, 600–1500.   I. Title.   II. Series.
    BR253.C33   2003
    235'.2'082—dc21

                                                                                    2003005454

Cornell University Press strives to use environmentally responsible suppliers and mate-rials to the fullest extent possible in the publishing of its books. Such materials include vegetable-based, low-VOC inks and acid-free papers that are recycled, totally chlorine-free, or partly composed of nonwood fibers. For further information, visit our website at www.cornellpress.cornell.edu.

Cloth printing   10 9 8 7 6 5 4 3 2 1
Paperback printing   10 9 8 7 6 5 4 3 2

For Richard

CONTENTS

ILLUSTRATIONS

PREFACE

In finishing this book, I have found myself in the somewhat unusual position of arguing against my first conception for it. Initially, I intended to tell the tale of flowering religious life among laywomen in the twelfth century and beyond, of rising veneration for these figures within their communities, followed by a clerical backlash that took the form of discernment of spirits literature. By the middle of the fifteenth century, I imagined, the trend of forming saints' cults for contemporary laywomen had been reversed as these individuals increasingly fell under suspicion.

I now believe that important elements within this narrative are wrong. In the spring of 1998 I was teaching an undergraduate seminar titled "Topics in Medieval History: Saints in Social Context." Preparing for a class on André Vauchez's *Sainthood in the Middle Ages*, I noticed a numerical figure that had not previously caught my attention: only four laywomen were canonized during the period covered by that monumental study, from 1198 to 1431. This number surprised me, since I often had read that women constituted 55.5 percent of all laity canonized throughout the Middle Ages and 71.4 percent of laity canonized after 1305. I suddenly realized that these percentages, also derived from Vauchez and widely cited, were somewhat misleading, and that the vast majority of the women described in recent studies as "saints" were not in fact saints at all. Further research revealed that many of the women lionized by medieval hagiographers either had no public cults or else very restrained ones. Finally, of the four laywomen canonized in the Middle Ages, only one, Brigit of Sweden, was a visionary or "mystic" of the kind that dominates current historiography (though to Brigit may be added Catherine of Siena, canonized in 1461, three decades after the end of the period Vauchez studied).

This series of new realizations forced me to rethink my approach to the medieval discernment of spirits. I became convinced that the process of debate and dissent about laywomen's religiosity began much earlier than I initially had thought and that it formed an integral part of their public careers from the earliest decades of the "women's religious movement." I began to see these women as divisive figures within their communities who elicited scalding controversy, rather than as unifying figures who attracted broad veneration. Seeking to triangulate my evidence, I extended my documentary base outward from hagiographies to include hostile depictions of "inspired women" drawn from chronicles, exempla, exorcisms, and polemical texts. These sources often described women who acted very similarly to the ones portrayed in hagiographies, while interpreting them in diametrically opposite ways. Finally, the labels themselves—"saint," "demoniac," "faker"—began to seem saturated with a religious ideology incompatible with the historical project at hand. I thus decided to abandon these categorizations altogether in my discussion of particular individuals, in order to preserve the sense of indeterminacy these people represented for their communities. Foregoing these ossified categories allowed me to better understand the emergent richness and fluidity of medieval religious life. My work as presented here is a tale of conflictual interpretations and shifting reinterpretations, of hopes for a celestial civic patron coupled with tests for fraud and fears of demonic deception.

It is always a pleasure to acknowledge scholarly debts, particularly in the case of a project which, like this one, has evolved substantially over time. My institutional debts are many. As a doctoral candidate I benefited from the financial support of several fellowship organizations, including generous grants from the Andrew Mellon Foundation, the Charlotte Newcombe Foundation, and the Horace H. Rackham School of Graduate Studies at the University of Michigan. In subsequent years, I was granted time away from my teaching schedule through a President's Research Fellowship in the Humanities from the University of California Regents and through a Humanities Fellowship and a Chancellor's Summer Faculty Fellowship, both from the University of California, San Diego. I also owe thanks to the staffs of the Archivio Segreto Vaticano, the Biblioteca Vaticana, the Bibliothèque Nationale de France, and the Bäyerische Staatsbibliothek, who generously provided me with a surfeit of exorcisms and other unusual manuscripts. The staff at the Rare Book and Manuscript collection of the Carl Kroch Library at Cornell University were likewise kind and helpful. Finally, the Interlibrary Loan office here at the University of California, San Diego has responded with swift grace to a relentless barrage of requests; and Sam Dunlop, our European Bibliographer, last year brought forth the miracle of the electronic Patrologia Latina and Acta Sanctorum. I also would like to take this opportunity to thank the Medieval Academy of America and the Berkshire Conference of Women Historians for their encouragement and recognition of previously published work.

Many individuals helped me to refine my thinking as this project progressed. I would like to express my appreciation to Barbara Rosenwein, whose trenchant insights on an early draft have improved this book immeasurably. An anonymous reader for Cornell University Press also offered perceptive comments that helped me to reformulate certain portions, as did John Ackerman, my editor at Cornell. Philippe Buc also read the entire manuscript and offered helpful suggestions. Patrick Geary, among his many kindnesses, led me to reevaluate my use of the word "mystic," an adjustment that significantly reoriented my presentation of ideas. Lester K. Little has been a paragon of generosity and encouragement to a young scholar in all ways; I have benefited from conversations with him about maledictions, exorcisms, and false saints of all kinds. I also thank Gàbor Klaniczay for sharing his stimulating work and for inviting me to speak at the 1999 conference in Budapest on "Demons, Spirits, Witches: Christian Demonology and Popular Mythology," a meeting that helped me draw together certain ideas about trance states, discernment, and witchcraft. A very special debt of gratitude and admiration is reserved for Diane Owen Hughes, who taught me so much. Diane remains for me the embodiment of a humane intellectual, and I hope someday to live up to her example as a creative scholar, international citizen, and fantastic mentor. I also would like to acknowledge the generosity of Bernice Cohen, David Cohen, James B. Given, Jack A. Greenstein, Michele Greenstein, William Chester Jordan, Richard Kieckhefer, John Marino, Barbara Newman, Eliot Wirshbo, and Robert Westman. Thanks also to the participants in the California Medieval History Seminar in the fall of 1999, who were kind enough to comment on earlier writing related to this work.

My mother, Eve Caciola, has offered me love and support throughout the long gestation of this project—and though she might have preferred me to gestate in other ways, I appreciate her forbearance. Susan J. Valcic has been both a sounding board for ideas and my best friend: thanks, Suze, for your intelligence and love. Illych was for twenty years the presiding *daimon* of my higher education, from its very beginnings until the completion of this manuscript, and I would like to remember him here.

My greatest acknowledgment goes to Richard Cohen, whose perseverance—in photographing demons, reading the manuscript, suggesting references, and arguing with me about religious categories—is just the beginning of his contribution. Our lives have now been entwined for over twenty years, and his love for me has been a source of continual sustenance and warmth. As a token of my own love for Richard, I dedicate this book to him.

ABBREVIATIONS

AASS *Acta Sanctorum, quotquot toto orbe coluntur, vel a Catholicis Scripto-ribus celebrantur.* Ed. Société des Bollandistes. 68 vols. Brussels and Antwerp, 1863–87.

  ASV Archivio Segreto Vaticano, Vatican City.

  BN Bibliothèque Nationale, Paris.

  BS Bäyerische Staatsbibliotek, Munich.

  BV Biblioteca Vaticana, Vatican City.

  CJ Carol du Plessis d'Argentre, ed. *Collectio Judiciorum de Novis Er-roribus.* 3 vols. Paris, 1728.

CPCS M. H. Laurent, ed. "Il Processo Castellano." In *Fontes Vitae S. Catharinae Senensis Historicae,* vol. 9. Milan, 1942.

De Ap. Thomas of Cantimpré. *Bonum universale de apibus.* Douai, 1627.

  DM Caesarius of Heisterbach. *Dialogus miraculorum.* Ed. Joseph Strange. 2 vols. Cologne, 1851.

  DS Henry of Langenstein. *De discretione spirituum.* In Thomas Hohmann, ed., *Heinrichs von Langenstein: "Unterscheidung der Geister," Lateinisch und Deutsch: Texte und Untersuchungen zu Übersetzungsliteratur aus der Wiener Schule.* Zurich and Munich, 1977.

DVVF Jean Gerson. *De distinctione verarum visionum a falsis.* In Palemon Glorieux, ed., *Jean Gerson: Oeuvres Complètes,* 3:36–56. Paris, 1962.

  ED Jean Gerson. *De examinatione doctrinarum.* In Palemon Glorieux, ed., *Jean Gerson: Oeuvres Complètes,* 9:458–660. Paris, 1973.

E de B Étienne de Bourbon. *Librum seu tractatum de diversis materiis praedicabilibus . . . secundum dona Spiritus Sancti.* In A. Lecoy de la Marche, ed., *Anecdotes historiques, légendes et apologues tirés du recueil inédit d'Étienne de Bourbon.* Paris, 1877.

  F Johannes Nider. *Formicarius.* N.p., 1516 or 1517; published by Johannes Knoblouch and Paul Götz.

J de V   Jacques de Vitry. *The Exempla of Jacques de Vitry*. Ed. Thomas Crane. London, 1890.

PL   *Patrologiae cursus completus, series latina*. Ed. J. P. Migne. 221 vols. Paris, 1841–66.

PS   Jean Gerson. *De probatione spirituum*. In Palemon Glorieux, ed., *Jean Gerson: Oeuvres Complètes*, 9:177–85. Paris, 1973.

RP   Bartholomew the Englishman. *De rerum proprietatibus*. Frankfurt, 1601.

Spec. Doc.   Vincent of Beauvais. *Speculum doctrinale*. Graz, 1965.

Spec. Hist.   Vincent of Beauvais. *Speculum historiale*. Graz, 1965.

Spec. Nat.   Vincent of Beauvais. *Speculum naturale*. Graz, 1965.

VCS   Raymond of Capua. *Vita Maior Catharinae Senensis*. In AASS, April 3:853–959.

VMC   Iunctae Bevegnatis. *Legenda de vita et miraculis beatae Margaritae de Cortona*. In Fortunato Iozzelli, ed., *Biblioteca Franciscana Ascetica Medii Aevi*, vol. 13. Grottaferrata, 1997.

DISCERNING SPIRITS

INTRODUCTION

In truth, this is an effeminate age.
— HILDEGARD OF BINGEN

It was an ancient injunction: "Test the spirits, to see whether they are of God" (1 John 4:1). John's words demanded vigilance from the faithful, a constant awareness of the interplay of depth and surface. To test the spirits is to interrogate marvels, to scrutinize miracle workers, and to question the unseen. It requires skepticism not toward the possibility of wonders but toward the character of the supernatural forces that enable them. Nor was the first letter of John the only scripture to enjoin such caution. Jesus himself had predicted the rise of false prophets and false Christs after his death. The apostle Paul warned of the manifold disguises Satan and his servants adopted in order to deceive the faithful. Throughout, the New Testament is sprinkled with reminders to be on guard against the manifold deceptions of the demonic hosts and their human agents. According to the infallible logic of scripture, the most benign surface may well mask multiple layers of deceit: private motivations, possible self-deceptions, demonic ruses, collusions, and lies.

This book is about the dialectic between suspicion and lies that inheres in the imperative to test, or to discern, spirits. These synonymous phrases—the "testing of spirits" and "discernment of spirits"—designate a practice of institutionalized mistrust regarding individual claims to visionary or prophetic authority. Several conceptual categories are negotiated in the practice of discernment. On the one hand, a person encompassed by constant supernatural interventions might be defined as a divinely inspired prophet or visionary, a mouthpiece of God. Yet it was equally possible to categorize such an individual as a demoniac possessed of unclean spirits, as a false saint puffed up with pride, or as a victim of demonic delusion. Observers wondered: What spirit is inside this person and making her act in this way? Whence comes this uncanny power? Is it the Holy Spirit, infused into the most intimate recesses of her soul through union with the divine? A diabolic spirit, possessing her from within? In many cases, several competing definitions of the individual's status were successively proposed, debated, and refined by a community of observers, then supplanted by new interpretations. In short, the discernment of spirits was a long-term labor of social interpretation that sometimes never reached final resolution, even after the death of the person concerned. As one late medieval sermon phrased it, "We must beware, lest in seeking celestial patronage, we give offense by using as intercessors persons whom God hates."[1]

The chapters that follow trace how the testing of spirits was coded and recoded in response to evolving social, cultural, and religious currents of the late twelfth through fifteenth centuries. The medieval revival of John's injunction emerged as a response to the rapid proliferation of religious lifestyles that began in the late twelfth century, and it constituted a vivid expression of the mingled admiration and hostility that certain of these movements elicited. Despite attempts by the ecclesiastical hierarchy to stem the tide of new religious observances—the Fourth Lateran Council in 1215 flatly prohibited the formation of any new religious rules of life, and the Second Council of Lyons in 1274 suppressed many already existing lay mendicant orders—fresh religious movements and innovative individual gestures continued to have a galvanizing appeal for the laity, male and female alike. The *vita apostolica*, spectacular penitential acts, fire-and-brimstone preaching, anticlerical sentiments, and swiftly moving rumors of miraculous cures and charitable gestures spiraled outward from charismatic individuals to absorb the attention of broad segments of the community. The involvement of new sectors of the population in these forms of religious devotion and spectacle in turn helped diffuse new religious ideas among the laity more rapidly than ever before.

Concern about the discernment of spirits flourished in tandem with the diffusion of these new religious sensibilities among the laity. Yet the testing of spirits remained an insoluble problem. It is largely impossible for a human observer conclusively to detect a careful and accomplished liar, as the devil was believed to be. One cannot observe the interior spiritual disposition of another individual; one can only scrutinize comportment and behavior. This conundrum fueled speculation about deception and discernment for cen-

[1] CPCS, 515.

turies, and ultimately resulted in a reevaluation of the behaviors expected of the saints.

In the meantime, however, the long-term debate about discernment provides an excellent point of entry into a broader set of questions concerning social and religious epistemology in the Middle Ages. What politics of knowledge production were involved in decisions about whom to venerate as a saint and whom to reject as a demoniac? At its core, the testing of spirits is a process of constructing categories of immanent good and evil. Yet this process of construction takes place within particular social and intellectual contexts, and thus arises from broader cultural influences and priorities. This book aims to unpack both the specific content of the discernment dispute and the wider cultural tensions and ideals that it expressed.

LINGUISTIC LEITMOTIFS

Suspecting deceit or demonic interference on the part of those who claimed inspired status held an unassailable pedigree of scriptural tradition. According to tradition, Jesus had forewarned (in the so-called "Little Apocalypse" or "Synoptic Apocalypse")[2] that in the End Times, "false Christs and false prophets will arise and show signs and wonders, in order to lead astray the elect if they can" (Mark 13:22; Matt. 24:24). This fear of deception was exploited by the itinerant preacher Paul, who, in his second letter to the Corinthians, cast doubt upon the authority of his competitors—that is, other gospel preachers, presumably with different theological emphases—by denigrating them as "false apostles, cunning workmen, disguising themselves as apostles of Christ. And no wonder, for even Satan disguises himself as an angel of light. So it is no great thing if his servants also disguise themselves as servants of righteousness" (2 Cor. 11:13–15). The two letters to Timothy (now considered pseudo-Pauline but accepted as authentic in the Middle Ages) present the seductions of false spirits just before the Apocalypse as unavoidable: "The Spirit clearly teaches that in these times some people will depart from the faith, adhering to spirits of error and the doctrines of demons, through the hypocrisy of lie-speakers, those whose consciences are burned and branded" (1 Tim. 3:1–2). Second Timothy expands on the thought, describing the expected false prophets as people "who love them-

[2] Bernard McGinn, *Antichrist: Two Thousand Years of the Human Fascination with Evil* (New York, 1994), 38–41.

selves, greedy, puffed up, proud, blasphemous, disobedient to their relatives, ungrateful criminals. . . . They have the appearance of piety, but in fact they reject virtue. Avoid them! Of this kind are those who go into houses and lead captive silly women burdened down with sins, who are led by various lusts: women who always are learning, yet never reaching an understanding of the Truth" (2 Tim 3:2, 5–7). And of course, the first letter of John exhorts, "Beloved, do not believe every spirit, but test the spirits to see whether they are of God; for many false prophets have gone out into the world" (1 John 4:1).

These five passages form the main scriptural basis for the discernment of spirits and provide a basic set of linguistic idioms that medieval authors drew upon when discussing the issue.[3] Yet if the words and phrases drawn from these passages remained unchanged, their meanings evolved significantly. In the context of the first-century Jesus Movement, these passages had strongly eschatological overtones: one must beware false Christs, false prophets, and false apostles so that, in the coming cosmic conflict of good and evil, one may be sure of remaining among the righteous who will inherit the Kingdom of God. Furthermore, such caveats also targeted the fundamental question of how, and in whom, the authority and leadership of the emerging Church should be vested. The problem of false Christs, false prophets, and false apostles was one of how to recognize legitimate authority and thus stay on the side of righteousness. A person who willingly submits to an authority without "testing the spirits" risks being "led astray" by the fraudulent "signs and wonders," "cunning work," "lies," and "disguises" of those who are "servants of Satan." "Silly women burdened down with sins" are especially vulnerable, but everyone must be on guard against "false prophets" teaching the "doctrines of demons."

Despite persistent concern about the possibility of false leadership within the Church, there was no consensus in the New Testament canon about procedures for "testing the spirits." Jesus' warning about false Christs concludes with an injunction to be vigilant against deception but does not suggest any particular strategy of watchfulness. The Johannine test for ferreting out false prophets is clear, but limited: "By this you know the spirit of God: every spirit that confesses that Jesus Christ has come in the flesh is of God, and every spirit which releases Jesus from the flesh is not of God; this one is of the An-

---

[3] For more on the early history of discernment, see Fr. Dingjan, *Discretio: Les origines patristiques et monastiques de la doctrine sur la prudence chez saint Thomas d'Aquin* (Assen, 1967); Steven Kruger, *Dreaming in the Middle Ages* (Cambridge, 1992); F. Vandenbroucke, "Discernement des esprits au moyen âge," in Marcel Villier, et al., ed., *Dictionnaire de spiritualité, ascétique et mystique* (Paris, 1937–94), 3:1254–66.

tichrist" (1 John 4:2–3). Unfortunately, this advice does not account for the possibility of lying spirits, for it relies upon the testimony of the spirit itself. What of the case discussed by Paul, in which an "angel of darkness" conceals its nature, disguising itself as an "angel of light"? Or a "servant of Satan" veiled as a "servant of righteousness"? John's letter does not account for the possibility of such cunning. As for Paul, he offers no comment at all about how to test a suspected fraud, merely noting with apparent resignation that "their ends will correspond to their deeds" (2 Cor. 11:15). In an earlier letter to the community at Corinth, he had suggested that "the ability to distinguish between spirits" (1 Cor. 12:10) was a special boon available only to a few, like a gift for prophecy or miracle working. Perhaps this was why Paul neglected to instruct the community at Corinth in general guidelines for the recognition of false apostles and prophets. For Paul, the discernment of spirits was a supernatural grace rather than a human endeavor. Indeed, the Book of Revelation suggests that the seductions of false prophets are an inevitable aspect of the Last Days. Revelation 20:7–8 predicts that, as part of the unspooling chaos of the End Times, "Satan will be freed and will seduce the peoples of the four corners of the earth, Gog and Magog." The exceptionally righteous might avoid such snares through some means of testing spirits, but the wider process of universal seduction was an unavoidable element in the final battle between good and evil.

Several factors contributed to an erosion of interest in these passages as the Church grew in influence and prestige. First, the apocalyptic expectations of the earliest Christian communities, which formed part of the background context for these concerns, consistently failed to materialize. Of course, a recurrent pattern of rising apocalyptic expectation followed by a deflation of these hopes and fears, remained (and remains) an element of Christian religiosity. However, millennial ideas became increasingly marginal within Christian theology, especially after Saint Augustine argued in book 21 of *The City of God* for a strictly allegorical explication of the apocalyptic currents of scripture. Although Augustine's reading did not wholly supplant more literal interpretations, it provided a powerful alternative.[4] Moreover, as the Christian community was transformed in the fourth century from a persecuted minority to a dominant social institution, the literal passing away of the world seemed less and less a desideratum: the Church already had triumphed.

---

[4] Paula Fredriksen, "Tyconius and Augustine on the Apocalypse," in R. Emmerson and B. McGinn, eds., *The Apocalypse in the Middle Ages* (Ithaca, N.Y., 1992), 20–37; Ann Matter, "The Apocalypse in Early Medieval Exegesis," in Emmerson and McGinn, *Apocalypse*, 38–50.

Another important change that led to a decline of interest in the testing of spirits concerned authority structures within the Church. In the middle of the first century, individual preachers such as Paul relied upon their own magnetic personalities and rhetorical skills to establish a position of authority. Such a situation could not long endure as the Church expanded into more and more communities. By the second century, leadership of the churches already had begun to pass to a burgeoning ecclesiastical hierarchy of priests, deacons, sub-deacons, acolytes, readers, doorkeepers, and exorcists. In tandem with this development, the slow movement toward the recognition of a limited number of canonical scriptures worked to consolidate authority around a narrow spectrum of Christian interpretations.

As with all important theological questions in the early Church, challenges that ultimately were rejected as heterodox helped to refine the dominant position.[5] Two particular debates are directly pertinent to the discernment of spirits. The first was the Montanist question, beginning in the late second century. Montanus envisioned the leadership of the Church being vested in a cadre of inspired prophets and, especially, prophetesses who would contribute a continuing process of revelation to the faithful in the declining years of the Church before Christ's triumphant return.[6] Indeed, adherents referred to their community as the "New Prophecy," underscoring the centrality of continuing, extrabiblical inspiration as the main element of their religious belief.[7] Sources for Montanist beliefs are both few and hostile, but this description from the *Church History* of Eusebius illuminates the terms of the debate between Montanus and his ecclesiastical opponents:

> He became beside himself, and . . . raved in a frenzy and ecstasy, and began to babble and utter strange things, prophesying in a manner contrary to the constant custom of the Church handed down by tradition from the beginning. Some of those who heard his spurious utterances at that time were indignant, and rebuked him as one possessed and under

[5] J. N. D. Kelly, *Early Christian Doctrines* (San Francisco, 1978); M. Wiles and M. Santer, eds., *Documents in Early Christian Thought* (Cambridge, 1975).

[6] Christine Trevett, *Montanism: Gender, Authority, and the New Prophecy* (Cambridge, 1996). A partial reconstruction of Montanist self-understanding is Susanna Elm's "'Pierced by Bronze Needles:' Anti-Montanist Charges of Ritual Stigmatization in the Fourth-Century Context." *Journal of Early Christian Studies* 4, 4 (1996): 409–39. For broader discussion of women's religious roles in this period, including their involvement in Montanist prophecy, idem, *"Virgins of God": The Making of Asceticism in Late Antiquity* (Oxford, 1994).

[7] Trevett, *Montanism*, 2.

the control of a demon. . . . But others, imagining themselves possessed by the Holy Spirit and having a prophetic gift, were elated.[8]

There seems to have been little dispute over the fact that Montanus and his followers were possessed by a spirit. Rather, the central issue was the character of that spirit: Holy or demonic? Whereas Eusebius and his informants viewed these ecstasies and utterances as side effects of possession by a demon, Montanus himself and his followers were convinced of their own righteousness, understanding their trances and prophecies as signs of their inspiration by the Holy Spirit.

The encounter with Montanism spurred a counterreaction within the Church, now forced to examine more closely its own position on individual charisms and prophecy. By the time of Constantine's conversion in the early fourth century, individual inspiration had largely been disavowed as a basis for religious authority: the Church was to be led by priests ordained by the ecclesiastical leadership, not prophets directly inspired by the Spirit.[9] As historian of the ancient world E. R. Dodds wrote, "from the point of view of the hierarchy, the Third Person of the Trinity had outlived his primitive function."[10] Moreover, as the Church worked to locate spiritual power and prestige exclusively within ecclesiastical officeholders, it correspondingly tried to marginalize and reject leadership claims based on inspiration by the Holy Spirit. In the long run, this resolution rendered the discernment of spirits an increasingly peripheral issue within the triumphant Church. Since prophecy was now unacceptable grounds to claim leadership within the Christian community, the concern with false prophets leading people astray was attenuated.

In the ensuing centuries, the verb *discernere* took on new applications. The term gradually lost its exclusive association with false prophecy as the apocalypticism of the early Church declined, and evolved to accommodate more pressing contemporary concerns. Patristic sources invoke the idea of discernment within discussions of dreams, for instance, as part of a centuries-long effort to define the boundaries between the natural and the supernatural

[8] Eusebius, *Church History* 5.16, trans. A. McGiffert, in *Nicene and Post-Nicene Fathers*, ser. 2 (Peabody, Mass., 1999), 1:231. I have made minor emendations to the translation for the sake of clarity, cutting long paratactic constructions into more manageable units.

[9] Marie Mayeski, "'Let Women Not Despair': Rabanus Maurus on Women as Prophets," *Theological Studies* 58 (1997): 237–53; Karen King, "Prophetic Power and Women's Authority: The Case of the *Gospel of Mary* (Magdalene)," in Beverly Kienzle and Pamela Walker, eds., *Women Preachers and Prophets through Two Millennia of Christianity* (Berkeley, 1998), 21–41.

[10] E. R. Dodds, *Pagan and Christian in an Age of Anxiety* (Cambridge, 1965), 67.

worlds.[11] Book 12 of Augustine's *Literal Commentary on Genesis* dealt in depth with the theme of true and false visions, the three types of vision, and the discernment of dreams, viewed as the primary medium through which questionable visions may appear.[12] Such concerns were not merely theological but practical. Thus in 401 a local church council at Carthage complained of "the altars which are being erected everywhere by certain men because of dreams and hollow revelations, and which are altogether reprobate."[13] The Church acted to check the proliferation of these local cults of veneration, which threatened to transform the landscape into a patchwork of rustic shrines and commemorations based upon individual dreams and fantasies. The Carthaginian leaders may have had in mind altars like the one destroyed by Saint Martin in Gaul: though the locals believed the tomb contained the power-charged remains of holy martyrs, Martin discovered that the deceased was a robber.[14] Even more unrestrained was the belief, censured by the eighth-century *Little List of Superstitions*, "that the dead of any kind are saints."[15] The need to apply discernment criteria to identify the truly "very special dead" was viewed as a necessity.[16] Carolingian intellectuals like Alcuin and Agobard of Lyon continued to express fear that demonic idolatry might sneak into the Church of God through an undiscerning veneration of saints' tombs and relics, a concern also shared by the eleventh-century chronicler Ralph Glaber.[17]

Yet the discernment of spirits was never entirely divorced from questions of living, inspired leadership. As Isabel Moreira has shown in a recent study of visions in Merovingian Gaul, control over the definition of legitimate authority rested firmly with ecclesiastical authorities. The latter were able, by and large, to deal with any unwelcome intrusions into their sphere of influ-

---

[11] Kruger, *Dreaming*.

[12] Augustine, *De Genesi ad litteram* 12; quoted in Kruger, *Dreaming*, 50–53.

[13] C. Munier, ed., *Concilia Africae, a. 345–a. 525* (Turnholt, Belg., 1974). *Corpus Christianorum, series latina*, 149:204–5.

[14] Sulpicius Severus, *Vita Sancti Martini*, in *PL*, 20:166–67.

[15] "Indiculus superstitionum et paganiorum," ed. A. Boretius and V. Krause, in *Monumenta Germaniae historica, leges sectio II: Capitularia Regum Francorum*, 2 vols. (Hannover, 1883–97), 1:223.

[16] The phrase "very special dead" is from Peter Brown, *The Cult of the Saints* (Chicago, 1981).

[17] Klaus Schreiner, "'Discrimen Veri ac Falsi': Ansatze und Formen der Kritik in der Heiligen- und Reliquienverehung des Mittelalters," *Archiv für Kulturgeschichte* 48, 1 (1966): 1–53. My thanks to Philippe Buc for this reference. Rodulfus Glaber, *The Five Books of Histories*, ed. and trans. J. France (Oxford, 1989), 180–82; Edmond Marténe, *De antiquis ecclesiae ritibus libri*, 4 vols. (Hildesheim, 1967), 2:968–70, includes a ritual for testing relics by fire. On the proliferation of multiple claims to the relics of a single saint, see Patrick Geary, *Furta Sacra: Thefts of Relics in the Central Middle Ages* (Princeton, N.J., 1978).

ence.[18] An apposite example from Gregory of Tours' *History of the Franks* is the famous tale of the woodcutter from Bourges who, after an unfortunate encounter with some flies, believed himself to be Christ.[19] The man soon attracted a devoted circle of followers, including a woman called Mary who became his partner. After he was killed by an agent of the local bishop, many of the man's rustic devotees nevertheless continued to insist on his divinity. Yet Gregory swiftly dismissed the woodcutter as a false prophet, employing a predictable pun to the effect that this self-proclaimed Christ was more likely an Antichrist.[20] Similarly, an apocalyptic visionary named Thiota, who in 847 gained a following among both laity and clergy, could be summarily silenced with a whipping imposed by an episcopal court.[21] While discernment cases remained infrequent in the West before the twelfth century, when they did arise the ecclesiastical authorities were able to respond with lean efficiency.

IMITATIO CHRISTI? OR PSEUDO-CHRISTI?

Toward the end of the twelfth century, the testing of spirits took on renewed life against a background of significant cultural revival. Indeed, the twelfth century has come to be regarded as a renaissance period in which medieval culture was reinvigorated and social life was transformed in far-reaching ways.[22] Driving many of these changes was the rebirth of cities for the first time since the decline of Rome. The growth of urban environments occurred first in Italy and the Low Countries in the late eleventh century, eventually spreading to other parts of Western Europe. With their dense population, new forms of community solidarity, and rising middle class, cities altered social intercourse in ways that touched on every facet of culture, including relations of power, local and translocal economies, intellectual life, and the forms of religious existence.

[18] Isabel Moreira, *Dreams, Visions, and Spiritual Authority in Merovingian Gaul* (Ithaca, N.Y., 2000).

[19] Gregory of Tours, *Historia Francorum* 10.25, in *PL*, 71:556–57.

[20] In addition to Moreira, *Dreams*, see John Kitchen, *Saints' Lives and the Rhetoric of Gender: Male and Female in Merovingian Hagiography* (Oxford, 1998); Raymond Van Dam, *Saints and Their Miracles in Late Antique Gaul* (Princeton, N.J., 1993), Aron Gurevich, *Medieval Popular Culture* (Cambridge, 1988), 58–73.

[21] *Annales Fuldenses*, ed. F. Kurze, in *Monumenta Germaniae historica* (Hannover, 1891), 37.

[22] The classic treatment is Charles Haskins, *The Renaissance of the Twelfth Century* (New York, 1966). A recent, global treatment of how some of these changes came about is R. I. Moore, *The First European Revolution, c. 970–1215* (Oxford, 2000).

Cities quickly became sites for specialized skills and manufacture that opened new avenues of exchange distinct from the "closed" economy of the manor that had prevailed earlier. The new middle class, fostering trade and artisanal production, ultimately shifted the economy toward a monetary basis. Currency henceforth began to compete with land as the main measure of wealth.[23] Guilds, confraternities, and neighborhood associations within the urban parish structure provided new forms of association and standards of professionalization for bourgeois tradesmen. Eventually, the middle class sought to rule themselves through the institution of the commune, a sworn association of men demanding greater rights and freedoms from their traditional lord. Universities, another product of urbanization, emerged when early cathedral schools expanded and began to attract increasing numbers of students.[24] Theology remained the most prestigious discipline, and, beginning in the twelfth century, Greek philosophy, Arab science, and Jewish exegesis all were mined by Christian intellectuals for new perspectives on God and His creation. This juxtaposition of different worldviews prompted vigorous new intellectual forms such as public debate and the development of the scholastic mode of argumentation. However, even as Europe was expanding its cultural horizons, it also was becoming increasingly concerned about the maintenance of the religious and social purity of the Christian community. The persecution of religious minorities, of heretics, and of other marginal groups such as lepers and prostitutes took on new life beginning in the twelfth century, as definitions of acceptable belief and behavior narrowed.[25]

These broad social and intellectual changes formed the background to alterations in the religious landscape that are central to this study, most notably the laicization of religious life. Suddenly, exemplars of fervent devotion were spilling onto urban plazas and streets, as well as into domestic spaces and local churches, rather than remaining cloistered behind remote

[23] See Moore, *First European Revolution*; Georges Duby, *The Early Growth of the European Economy: Warriors and Peasants from the Seventh to the Twelfth Century*, trans. H. Clarke (Ithaca, N.Y., 1974); Jacques Le Goff, *Time, Work, and Culture in the Middle Ages*, trans. A. Goldhammer (Chicago, 1980).

[24] Jacques Le Goff, *Intellectuals in the Middle Ages*, trans. T. Fagan (Oxford, 1992); M.-D. Chenu, *Nature, Man, and Society in the Twelfth Century*, trans. J. Taylor and L. Little (Toronto, 1997); Giles Constable, *Three Studies in Medieval Religious and Social Thought* (Cambridge, 1995).

[25] There currently exists a debate in the historiographical literature about the significance of these changes in patterns of persecution. For two opposing viewpoints, see R. I. Moore, *The Formation of a Persecuting Society* (Oxford, 1987); David Nirenberg, *Communities of Violence: Persecution of Minorities in Medieval Europe* (Princeton, N.J., 1996).

monastery walls. Religious intensity was no longer confined to a cadre of elite monastic specialists set apart from the daily rhythms of mundane existence, but was immanent within the life of the town, as the new mendicant orders grew in numbers and enlarged their preaching ambits.[26] The rapid growth of interest in the *vita apostolica*—direct imitation of the life of Christ and the apostles, played out within the worldly sphere—engaged the laity with religious ideals with an immediacy that had been rare in preceding generations. The new urban environment and monetary economy fostered these movements, which were strongest in precisely those areas that urbanized earliest: the Low Countries and Italy. Mendicant ("begging") orders dedicated to voluntary poverty, like the Franciscans and the Dominicans, were sustained in their formative years by offerings from members of the new middle class whom they encountered in city streets and plazas. New female-dominated religious movements, such as the Beguines in northern Europe and tertiaries in the Mediterranean regions, supported themselves through the generosity of urban patrons and by work in trades such as cloth production or midwifery. Moreover, these new religious groups also drew heavily from the middle classes for membership, providing a place for those who were unable, or unwilling, to live as householders. Changes in family structure fostered this association. Around this time families were moving toward an ever more firmly patrilineal and male-centered self-definition, a change that had important repercussions in the options available for a large portion of the adult population. In most parts of Europe, bilateral descent reckoning gave way to patrilineal emphases; the morning gift was replaced with an increasingly inflated dowry; and primogeniture was instituted in place of partible inheritance.[27] These changes tended to marginalize daughters and younger sons within the family economy in all but the very wealthiest families, creating a permanent class of persons for whom marriage was an impossibility. Indeed, the most distinctive forms of religious life of the later Middle Ages were

[26] See Herbert Grundmann, *Religious Movements in the Middle Ages*, trans. S. Rowan (Notre Dame, Ind., 1995); Lester K. Little, *Religious Poverty and the Profit Economy* (Ithaca, N.Y., 1978); André Vauchez, *Sainthood in the Middle Ages*, trans. J. Birrell (Cambridge, 1997); idem, *Ordini mendicanti e società italiana XIII–XV secolo* (Milan, 1990).

[27] For background on family changes, see Suzanne Wemple, *Women in Frankish Society: Marriage and the Cloister, 500–1000* (Philadelphia, 1981); Christiane Klapisch-Zuber, *Women, Family, and Ritual in Renaissance Italy*, trans. L. Cochraine (Chicago, 1985); Diane Owen Hughes, "From Brideprice to Dowry in Mediterranean Europe," *Journal of Family History* 3 (1978): 262–96; David Herlihy, *Medieval Households* (Cambridge, Mass., 1985); Georges Duby, *Medieval Marriage: Two Models from Twelfth-Century France*, trans. E. Forster (Baltimore, 1978).

highly interdependent with the secular order.[28] The proliferation of new religious movements occurred largely at the margins of the ecclesiastical sphere, in the shadow of the Church yet on the public streets of the secular world.

In turn, admiration for these movements encouraged a novel and, to some, disturbing phenomenon: the formation of new cults of saintly veneration for near contemporaries. In the ninth century, Adrevald of Fleury had felt a need to apologize for daring to compose a hagiography of an individual who lived a mere two hundred years earlier.[29] The Carolingians tended to regard saints as historical figures shrouded in a venerable past. Beginning in the late eleventh century, however, cults for "new" saints began to multiply, centering around charismatic contemporary figures such as Robert of Arbrissel.[30] The cult of veneration for Saint Francis spread rapidly even before his death. The growing attraction to these saints was nourished by their personal magnetism and very public careers.

Yet this novel reenactment of the life of Christ and the apostles—with its emphasis on public penitence and its tendency to attract sensational personalities surrounded by a tumultuous aura of the supernatural—inevitably raised the possibility of false prophets, false apostles, and false Christs once again. Indeed, the late twelfth century also witnessed a rebirth of interest in theorizing the demonic and in calculating the advent of the Apocalypse, when demons and pseudo-prophets would abound. Thus, while at the start of the century the problem of evil was largely attenuated within the culture of the intelligentsia, the success of the dualistic theology of the Cathars (a group that became a fully alternate Church in southern France and northern Italy and that taught the irreconcilable duality of spirit and flesh as emanations of a good and an evil cosmic principle respectively) spurred the university culture to interrogate the place of evil and the demonic within the world.[31] The earliest official definition of demons pronounced by the Church, at the Fourth Lateran Council in 1215, was couched as a direct response to the Cathar threat.[32] The earliest demonological compendium was

---

[28] For documents and background, see G. G. Meersseman, *Dossier de l'ordre de la pénitence au XIIIe siècle* (Fribourg, 1982).

[29] Thomas Head, *Hagiography and the Cult of the Saints: The Diocese of Orléans, 800–1200* (Cambridge, 1990), 40–41.

[30] Head, *Hagiography*, 4; Vauchez, *Sainthood*, 13–26.

[31] Raoul Manselli, *Il secolo XII: Religione popolare ed eresia* (Rome, 1983), 13.

[32] Paul Quay, "Angels and Demons: The Teaching of IV Lateran," *Theological Studies* 42, 1 (1981): 20–45. See also Alan Bernstein, "Teaching and Preaching Confession in Thirteenth-Century Paris," in Alberto Ferreiro, ed., *The Devil, Heresy, and Witchcraft in the Middle Ages: Essays in Honor of Jeffrey B. Russell* (Leiden, 1998), 111–30.

produced soon after, in the 1230s. William of Auvergne devoted book 3 of his *On the Universe* to an extended treatment of the demonic forces, including discussions of demonic intelligence, demonic temptation, and demonic illusion.[33] William wished to demonstrate both that the "miracles" of demons often were illusory and that those who willingly trafficked with unclean forces did so at the risk of their salvation. This third book of *On the Universe* sometimes was copied separately from books 1 and 2, circulating as an independent treatise titled *On Evil Spirits*.[34] In turn, the elite ideas of intellectuals were disseminated to a broad audience through various media. Public preaching, for instance, drew upon collections of exempla that popularized contemporary university ideas, while encyclopedias like the *Universal Mirror*, by the Dominican Vincent of Beauvais, and *On the Properties of Things*, by the Franciscan Bartholomew the Englishman, were partly or entirely translated into several vernacular languages and became wildly popular.

Developing in tandem with the fascination with evil was the heightening of eschatological consciousness that occurred largely through the dissemination of the ideas of Joachim of Fiore (d. 1202).[35] Though often called a prophet, Joachim did not consider himself as such and emphasized that his predictions for the future were based upon close interpretation of the Old and New Testaments rather than on visionary illumination. Joachim's exegetical "principle of concordance," which served as the basis for his theology of history, grew out of his belief that the mystery of the Trinity—three persons, one Godhead—was woven into the fabric of history itself. His view of history was melioristic: the crown and culmination of history is evolution toward greater spiritual "intelligence" or understanding, on the one hand, and greater contemplation or spiritual attainment, on the other. The Church, according to Joachim, will be purified after the tribulations of the Apocalypse, when the world will be transformed and society perfected. Though Joachim himself declined to set a date for the Apocalypse, his followers saw clues in his writings that set the day of wrath for 1260.

[33] William of Auvergne, *De universo*, in *Guillelmi Alverni Opera Omnia*, 2 vols. (Paris, 1674; reprint, Frankfurt-am-Main, 1963).

[34] BV ms. Vat. Lat. 4867, ff. 1r–66v, is a fifteenth-century version titled *De spiritibus malignis* and lacking authorial attribution.

[35] Marjorie Reeves, *The Influence of Prophecy in the Later Middle Ages* (Notre Dame, Ind., 1969); idem, *Joachim of Fiore and the Prophetic Future* (New York, 1976); Marjorie Reeves and Morton Bloomfield, "The Penetration of Joachimism into Northern Europe," *Speculum* 29, 4 (1954): 772–93; Delno West and Sandra Zimdars-Swartz, *Joachim of Fiore* (Bloomington, Ind., 1983); Roberto Rusconi, *Profezia e profeti alla fine del Medioevo* (Rome, 1999); Robert Lerner, "Antichrist and Antichrists in Joachim of Fiore," *Speculum* 60, 3 (1985): 553–70; idem, "The Black Death and Western European Eschatological Mentalities," *American Historical Review* 86, 3 (1981): 533–52.

The growth in the numbers of new saints' cults, combined with the recently heightened concern about demons and the Last Days, was a potent combination. Against this background, Pope Innocent III (1198–1216) asserted an exclusively papal right to determine the supreme exemplars of Christian righteousness.[36] In so doing, Innocent arrogated to the Papacy the unique prerogative to discern spirits in the case of potential saints, separating out the false heralds of the Antichrist. Indeed, Innocent's very first bull of canonization in 1199 explicitly invoked the testing of spirits, echoing the classic scriptural passages: "Satan transfigures himself into an angel of light and there are some who seek, by their works, human glory. . . . Pharaoh's magicians performed marvels in times past, and Antichrist will work wonders to lead into error even the elect."[37]

As André Vauchez has noted, Innocent's reign "marked a decisive turning-point in the history of attitudes to the supernatural."[38] This was so not only on a juridical level, but also in terms of his foregrounding of the testing of spirits in considering the field of the miraculous. Henceforth, no individual's supernatural powers or visions could be accepted as divine in origin without rigorous investigation. Reports of miracles increasingly became sources of suspicion rather than celebration. Wondrous events or supernatural boons, which traditionally had elicited spontaneous responses of awe, joy, or reverence from the community, were henceforth to be subjected to a lengthy process of juridical authentication and discernment of spirits before they could be acclaimed as marks of divine favor.

AN EFFEMINATE AGE?

A significant number of those laying claim to positions of leadership based upon oracular and visionary prerogatives were women. Medieval people themselves noticed this trend in which the "fragile sex" suddenly was made adamantine-strong. Hildegard of Bingen, for example, attributed her own inspiration by the Holy Spirit to a broader cultural change, the entry of Christendom into a new stage of religious history. Her century—the twelfth—had entered into an "effeminate age" marked by a failure of masculine leadership

[36] Vauchez, *Sainthood*; E. W. Kemp, *Canonisation and Authority in the Western Church* (Oxford, 1948).

[37] Bull for canonization of Homobonus of Cremona, in O. Hagenender and A. Haidacher, eds., *Die Register Innocenz III, Pontifikatsjahr 1198/99* (Graz, 1964), 762.

[38] Vauchez, *Sainthood*, 36.

that left women like herself as their own best guides.[39] Hildegard was an astute observer; the elaboration of uniquely feminine, highly visionary forms of religious life during this time period is well attested.[40] We know that these women exhibited a particular set of behaviors that constituted a startlingly new idiom of religious devotion. A profile of the "typical" medieval religious woman has emerged as deeply ascetic, highly ecstatic, and devoted to meditation upon the events of Jesus' life on earth. The result of such devotional practices was an experience of identification with the suffering body of the human Christ so intense that it often was said to be somatically manifested in the woman's own body. Paramystical transformations such as immobile and insensible trances, reception of the stigmata, or uncontrollable fits and crying (the "gift of tears") were commonly reported of women visionaries, and were understood by them as the physical side effects of their spiritual union with the divine. However, these forms of devotion inspired heated controversy as well. For this new cultural idiom—with its emphasis upon union with God through the interior penetration of his spirit into the body—provided a uniquely apt parallel to the already existing concept of demonic invasion and possession.[41]

[39] Hildegard of Bingen, letter 49, in *PL*, 197:256. For the timing, see Barbara Newman, *Sister of Wisdom: St. Hildegard's Theology of the Feminine* (Los Angeles, 1987), 239; André Vauchez, "Le Prophétisme médiéval d'Hildegarde de Bingen à Savanarole," in *Saints, prophètes et visionnaires: Le pouvoir surnaturel au Moyen Age* (Paris, 1999), 114–33.

[40] To cite only the most influential studies: Caroline Bynum, *Holy Feast and Holy Fast: The Religious Significance of Food to Medieval Women* (Berkeley, 1987); idem, *Jesus as Mother: Studies in the Spirituality of the High Middle Ages* (Berkeley, 1982); idem, *Fragmentation and Redemption: Essays on Gender and the Human Body in Medieval Religion* (New York, 1991); Vauchez, *Sainthood*; idem, *Saints, prophètes et visionnaires*; Barbara Newman, *From Virile Woman to WomanChrist: Studies in Medieval Religion and Literature* (Philadelphia, 1995); Jeffrey Hamburger, *The Visual and the Visionary: Art and Female Spirituality in Late Medieval Germany* (New York, 1998); Elizabeth Petroff, *Body and Soul: Essays on Medieval Women and Mysticism* (Oxford, 1994); Ulrike Wiethaus, ed., *Maps of Flesh and Light: The Religious Experience of Medieval Women Mystics* (Syracuse, 1993); Renate Blumenfeld-Kosinski and Timea Szell, eds., *Images of Sainthood in Medieval Europe* (Ithaca, N.Y., 1991); John Nichols and Lillian Shank, eds., *Distant Echoes: Medieval Religious Women* (Kalamazoo, 1984); idem, *Peace Weavers: Medieval Religious Women* (Kalamazoo, 1987); Anna Benvenuti Papi, *"In castro poenitentiae:" Santità e società femminile nell' Italia medievale* (Rome, 1990); Gabriella Zarri, *Le sante vive: Profezie di corte e devozione femminile tra '400 e '500* (Turin, 1990); Daniel Bornstein and Roberto Rusconi, eds., *Women and Religion in Medieval and Renaissance Italy* (Chicago, 1996); Maiju Lehmijoki-Gardner, *Worldly Saints: Social Interaction of Dominican Penitent Women in Italy, 1200–1500* (Helsinki, 1999); Catherine Mooney, ed., *Gendered Voices: Medieval Saints and their Interpreters* (Philadelphia, 1999).

[41] Study of this phenomenon has taken on momentum recently. A chronological listing of important contributions is: Marcello Craveri, *Sante e streghe: Biografie e documenti dal XIV al XVII secolo* (Milan, 1980); Gabriella Zarri, ed., *Finzione e santità tra medioevo ed*

The medieval debate over the testing of spirits focused with particular intensity on women. The rapid proliferation of female claims to divine inspiration was rife with ambivalences, and laywomen were particularly vulnerable. The sheer visibility of laywomen involved in the penitential religious life rendered them significantly more liable than their protected, cloistered counterparts to charges of demonic possession or false sanctity. Although nuns were not immune from inquiry into their behavior and reported revelations,[42] female conventuals already were subordinated within the traditional male authority structure of the *cura monialium*.[43] By contrast, most lay religious women lived their lives in ways that were only loosely subject to direct masculine control, usually being both unmarried and uncloistered.[44] Their main source of male supervision was their confessor, who often acted more as a willing chief devotee than as a stern spiritual director. This pattern seemed to some observers to be an inversion of the natural order of the sexes, and the perception that the world had entered into an effeminate age, in which women were usurping traditionally male avenues of authority, could lead to bitter recriminations. Indeed, religious laywomen sometimes were viewed by clergy and theologians as sources of malign influence, since as public penitents they were free to interact with other laity and offer religious ad-

---

età moderna (Turin, 1991); Nancy Caciola, "Discerning Spirits: Sanctity and Possession in the Later Middle Ages" (PhD diss., University of Michigan, 1994); Richard Kieckhefer, "The Holy and the Unholy: Sainthood, Witchcraft, and Magic in Late Medieval Europe," *Journal of Medieval and Renaissance Studies* 24 (1994): 355–85; Peter Dinzelbacher, *Heilige oder Hexen? Schicksale auffalliger Frauen im Mittelalter und Frühneuzeit* (Zurich, 1995); Barbara Newman, "Possessed by the Spirit: Devout Women, Demoniacs, and the Apostolic Life in the Thirteenth Century," *Speculum* 73, 3 (1998): 733–70; Rosalynn Voaden, *God's Words, Women's Voices: The Discernment of Spirits in the Writings of Late Medieval Women Visionaries* (York, 1999), devoted to Brigit of Sweden and Margery Kempe; Nancy Caciola, "Mystics, Demoniacs, and the Physiology of Spirit Possession in Medieval Europe," *Comparative Studies in Society and History* 42, 2 (2000): 268–306; Deborah Fraioli, *Joan of Arc: The Early Debate* (Suffolk, 2000). The most recent entrant into this conversation is Dyan Elliott, "Seeing Double: John Gerson, the Discernment of Spirits, and Joan of Arc," *American Historical Review* 197, 1 (2002): 26–54.

[42] Barbara Newman, "Hildegard of Bingen: Visions and Validation," *Church History* 54, 2 (1985): 163–75.

[43] John Freed, "Urban Development and the '*Cura Monialium*' in Thirteenth-century Germany," *Viator* 3 (1972): 311–26; Sally Thompson, "The Problem of Cistercian Nuns in the Twelfth and Early Thirteenth Centuries," in D. Baker, ed., *Medieval Women* (Oxford, 1978), 227–52; Brenda Bolton, "*Vitae Matrum*: A Further Aspect of the Frauenfrage," in Baker, *Medieval Women*, 253–74.

[44] This tension is discussed by Katherine Gill, "*Scandala*: Controversies concerning *Clausura* and Women's Religious Communities in Late Medieval Italy," in S. Waugh and P. Diehl, eds., *Christendom and Its Discontents: Exclusion, Persecution, and Rebellion, 1000–1500* (Cambridge, 1996), 177–203.

vice. The exquisitely public character of a laywoman's religiosity—played out before a local community that likely knew her family, witnessed her harsh asceticism, judged her trances, and debated reports of her miracles—fostered an intense interpretive interplay between the individual and her audience. Given this state of controversy, it is hardly surprising that the "women's religious movement" never gained the prestige of institutional approval granted by ecclesiastical authorities. Indeed, the imprimatur of the Papacy was notably withheld from these groups. While the later Middle Ages is associated with a swift efflorescence of hagiographies arguing for the saintliness of many individual laywomen, very few of these hagiographies were associated with public cults; even fewer were forwarded to Rome for consideration for canonization; and only two visionary laywomen actually became saints during the medieval period: Brigit of Sweden (canonized in 1391, 1415, and 1419) and Catherine of Siena (canonized in 1460).[45] Both cases succeeded only after lengthy disputes and dissensions, treatises and countertreatises, at the highest levels of the hierarchy.

Although laymen also were deeply involved in the *vita apostolica*, the discernment question seldom was posed in relation to male figures, whose authority as prophets and religious leaders clearly seemed more natural to medieval people. Indeed, one statistical study of saints' cults in medieval and early modern Europe suggests that of those figures "perceived by some contemporaries as bizarre or deviant," fully two-thirds were female.[46] When religious men became targets of controversy, the debate about them usually was encoded in different terms.[47] Whereas disputes over female inspiration tended to juxtapose true inspiration with either diabolic possession or deception, debates about controversial males more frequently were couched in terms of doctrinal error or heresy. For example, Robert Lerner has analyzed the spread of what he dubs the "ecstasy defense" among apocalyptic and spiritual Franciscan circles beginning in the thirteenth century, demonstrating

---

[45] For further discussion of this point, see Caciola, "Mystics, Demoniacs," 269–71.

[46] Donald Weinstein and Rudolph Bell, *Saints and Society: Christendom, 1000–1700* (Chicago, 1982), 123. This figure would significantly increase if several different kinds of sources were utilized, rather than just those most partial of texts, hagiographies. See also Jean-Michel Sallmann, "Esiste una falsa santità maschile?" in Zarri, *Finzione e santità*, 19–28.

[47] There are exceptions: see the case reported by Thomas of Apulia in his *History of the University of Paris*, concerning a man who preached that he was sent by the Holy Spirit. The man initially was suspected of an organic dementia and examined by doctors. When the doctors judged him sane, he was imprisoned for life (*CJ*, 1:151). Caesarius of Heisterbach tells of "a certain man filled with the Devil, who publicly preached at Troyes that he was the Holy Spirit" (*DM*, 1:307).

linkages between melioristic views of spiritual intelligence and claims of ecstatic and prophetic status.[48] Thus figures as diverse as Rupert of Deutz,
Joachim of Fiore, and Arnold of Villanova (among others) all attempted to
authorize their teachings and prophecies by rooting them in involuntary ecstatic experiences.[49] Yet, however hot the friction surrounding these men,
the charges levied against them were always seen as errors, not deceits.[50]
And, in a further reversal of the typical female pattern, these men's trances
became their best defense, rather than the object of contentious scrutiny in
themselves. Theologians and ecclesiastics usually were willing to give men
the benefit of the doubt, to judge them by their intellectual productions
rather than their relationships with spirits. Indeed, in some cases men who
appeared to border on demonic possession were granted greater consideration and deference precisely because they were in orders and learned. Consider, for example, how the anonymous continuator of Guillame de Nangis's
Chronicle defends the Franciscan John of Rupescissa: "He predicted many future events as if through a prophetic spirit, and many people doubted
whether he was deceiving, or telling lies, or was speaking with a python or
an evil spirit. However, this man lived a holy life, sober and honest, and was
a cleric learned in scripture and in the texts of the sacred canon."[51] The proof

---

[48] Robert Lerner, "Ecstatic Dissent," *Speculum* 67, 1 (1992): 33–57.

[49] For background on these thinkers, see the citations in note 35, this chapter, and in
addition, Clifford Backman, "The Reception of Arnau de Vilanova's Religious Ideas," in
Waugh and Diehl, *Christendom and Its Discontents*, 112–31. David Burr, *Olivi and Franciscan Poverty: The Origins of the* Usus Pauper *Controversy* (Philadelphia, 1989); idem, *Olivi's
Peaceable Kingdom: A Reading of the Apocalypse Commentary* (Philadelphia, 1993); idem, *The
Spiritual Franciscans: From Protest to Persecution in the Century after Saint Francis* (University Park, Pa., 2001); Raoul Manselli, "L'Apocalisse da Pietro di Giovanni Olivi a S.
Bernardino da Siena," in D. Maffei and P. Nardi, eds., *Atti del simposio internazionale Cater-
niano-Bernardiniano, Siena 17–20 Aprile 1980* (Siena, 1982), 631–38; Bernard McGinn,
ed., *Apocalyptic Spirituality* (New York, 1989); Robert Lerner, *The Powers of Prophecy: The
Cedar of Lebanon Vision from the Mongol Onslaught to the Dawn of the Enlightenment* (Berkeley, 1983); L. Oliger, *De secta spiritus libertatis in Umbria, sec. XIV* (Rome, 1943), includes
documents relating to Arnold of Villanova and the spiritual Franciscans.

[50] The issue of human error, rather than supernatural interference, also was central
Salimbene's presentation of three male lay "false saints" in his chronicle. Albert of Villa
d'Ogna was derided by Salimbene as an immoral man who appealed only to an ignorant
populace. Salimbene, *The Chronicle of Salimbene de Adam*, trans. Joseph Baird et al. (Binghamton, 1986), 512–13. Lester K. Little is currently conducting research on the cult for
Albert, and I have benefited from attending his talk "Choosing Poverty" delivered at the
conference "Poverty in the Middle Ages," Claremont Graduate School, November 9,
2000. The two other laymen who attracted cults of which Salimbene disapproved were
Anthony the Pilgrim, venerated in Padua, and Armanno Pungilupo or Punzilovo, venerated in Ferrara. For the former, see *Vita Antonii Peregrini*, in C. de Smedt et al., eds.,
Analecta Bollandia 13 (1894): 417–25; for the latter, Salimbene, *Chronicle*, 514.

[51] *CJ*, 1:374–75.

of John's orthodoxy was his scriptural learning and clerical status—both the special prerogatives of men.

To look at this set of patterns in another way, one could assert that males were granted more integrity and responsibility for their ideas, whether good or evil, whereas women more often were perceived as conduits for supernatural spirits, whether good or evil. Though these statements are simplifications of very complex data, they help convey the gender dimensions of the discernment debate. On the one hand, the "fragile sex" was thought to be more susceptible to the depredations of demons, and thus more likely to mistake possession by an angel of darkness for the inspiration of an angel of light. On the other hand, given the strong differential in status between women and men, medieval people suspected—quite correctly—that women had more to gain from a conscious affectation of saintliness than did men. As many scholars have pointed out, the growth in lay female claims to divine illumination was intricately linked to issues of prestige. If such claims were accepted as authentic, a woman could gain a position of relative influence within her locale and perhaps even farther afield. Her authority as a religious expert would be secured; her pronouncements and advice would be taken seriously; she would gain admiration and respect from contemporaries who rarely accorded deference to a *muliercula*—a term of opprobrium designating a poor or silly woman, little worthy of attention. Medieval people were well aware of the potential advantages that a claim of divine possession held for women's low status. Hence it is not surprising if, on the one hand, women in particular might be drawn to make claims of divine possession and, on the other, their neighbors might suspect them of lying precisely because of their sex.

A NOTE ON LANGUAGE AND METHODOLOGY

Many of the individuals discussed in this book traditionally are referred to as mystics. This book avoids the term "mystic," preferring the phrases "divinely inspired" or "divinely possessed" instead. There are several reasons for this choice of language. A foremost reason is that these locutions closely mirror indigenous, medieval notions of the phenomenon under discussion. An emphasis upon a penetrative, interiorizing union with the divine is a central element in texts about medieval religious women. Moreover, the rhetorical parallelism inherent in the juxtaposition of divine possession with demonic possession is helpful in highlighting similarities between the two categories.

In addition, I have refrained from using the word "mystic" because it privileges internal, subjective experiences over external behaviors.[52] As William James opined, "personal religious experience has its root and center in mystical states of consciousness."[53] Because mysticism classically has been defined as an intensely private and individualistic sense of connection to God, it has been placed in opposition to public and collective aspects of religious life, such as ritual or worship. This opposition often has been viewed hierarchically, as when one scholar juxtaposed the "vitality" of mysticism as an expression of "true religion" to the "cold formality and religious torpor" of institutional religious forms.[54] This focus on mysticism as a highly charged private experience prioritizes the internal and emotional aspects of religious devotion over external behaviors or observances.

Yet as Richard King writes, "the privatized and narrowly experiential conception of the mystical results in a peculiar preoccupation in academic literature on the subject with indescribable and largely inaccessible experiences of an extraordinary nature."[55] This is an important insight, for medieval discussions of how to discern spirits always pulse back and forth between the two poles of interior and exterior. How can an exterior observer understand what takes place inside the body of another person? How can a community understand the intensely private, internal experience of possession and test the character of the penetrating spirit? Thus *Discerning Spirits* adopts an approach that consciously fans out from the level of individual experience to focus on behaviors and community reception.[56] In short, the following

---

[52] The word "mystic" is not a medieval usage. The study of mysticism began at the end of the nineteenth century, in line with a growing interest in the academic study of religions. The abstract English usage "mysticism" dates from the same period and is derived from the French *la mystique*, a word with roots in the seventeenth century and originally associated with Orientalist discourses. Richard King, *Orientalism and Religion: Postcolonial Theory, India, and "The Mystic East"* (New York, 1999), 7. As nineteenth-century intellectuals began to experiment with the idea, "mysticism" came to be applied retroactively to Western texts in order to create and historicize the category of *Christian* mysticism as a parallel to mystical traditions within Eastern religious contexts: "already existing writings were termed 'mystic' and a mystic tradition was fabricated" (Michel de Certeau, *Heterologies: Discourses on the Other* [Manchester, 1986], 82; quoted in King, *Orientalism and Religion*, 18). See also Michel de Certeau, *The Mystic Fable*, vol. 1, *The Sixteenth and Seventeenth Centuries*, trans. M. Smith (Chicago, 1992), 79–112.

[53] William James, *The Varieties of Religious Experience* (New York, 1958), 292.

[54] Margaret Smith, "The Nature and Meaning of Mysticism," in R. Woods, ed., *Understanding Mysticism* (London, 1980), 20; quoted in King, *Orientalism and Religion*, 7.

[55] King, *Orientalism and Religion*, 8, 24.

[56] Joan Scott, "Experience," in J. Butler and J. Scott, eds., *Feminists Theorize the Political* (New York, 1992), 22–40; Robert Scharf, "Experience," in M. Taylor, ed., *Critical Terms for Religious Studies* (Chicago, 1998), 94–116; idem, "Buddhist Modernism and the Rhetoric of Meditative Experience," *Numen* 42 (1995): 228–83; Timothy Fitzgerald, "Experience," in W. Braun and R. McCutcheon, eds., *Guide to the Study of Religion* (London,

analysis attempts to bridge the gap between the internal devotions and self-representations of the women, on the one hand, and the external evaluations of their careers on the part of their communities and representatives of the Church, on the other.

Aside from questions of language, a few comments on sources and methodology may provide a helpful framework for my approach. What sources are available for the study of possessed women, and how may they be interpreted? I offer three guidelines in this regard. The first concerns how to read hagiographical evidence; the second addresses what should count as evidence beyond hagiographies; and the third involves the use of categories in historical writing about religious identities.

Hagiographies, once vilified as fabulous narratives with little historical value, have recently been recognized as superb sources for the study of medieval religious mentalities.[57] Indeed, hagiographical sources have now become a dominant evidentiary base for the study of medieval society and culture, particularly as applied to questions of gender. These sources must be used carefully, however, for they are highly conventional and even tendentious. As Thomas Head has noted, hagiographies are products of the author's "act of interpretation": their authors are partisan, their goals propagandistic, and their language conventional.[58] It is in the nature of a hagiography to be a "creator of universality *a posteriori*,"[59] that is, to present their subjects as transparently saintly. Yet a careful reading of medieval vitae shows that they are not monolithic in their details. A close analysis "against the grain" can elicit much previously unnoticed information about negative receptions of women's claims to divine inspiration.

Aside from hagiographies, what other kinds of evidence are available that discuss women who avow supernatural powers or revelations? The vitae can be supplemented with a variety of other texts that discuss responses to

2000); and King, *Orientalism and Religion*, 7–34. For an attempt to recover the category of experience from such critiques, see Thomas Csordas, ed., *Embodiment and Experience: The Existential Ground of Culture and Self* (Cambridge, 1994); Hamburger, *Visual and Visionary*, 13–34.

[57] For a history of this textual genre, see Felice Lifschitz, "Beyond Positivism and Genre: Hagiographical Texts as Historical Narrative," *Viator* 25 (1994): 96–113; Patrick Geary, "Saints, Scholars, and Society: The Elusive Goal," in *Living with the Dead in the Middle Ages* (Ithaca, N.Y., 1994), 9–29. In addition see Thomas Heffernan, *Sacred Biography: Saints and Their Biographers in the Middle Ages* (Oxford, 1988); Kitchen, *Saints' Lives*; Head, *Hagiography*. For a positivist approach, see Aviad Kleinberg, *Prophets in their Own Country: Living Saints and the Making of Sainthood in the Later Middle Ages* (Chicago, 1992).

[58] Head, *Hagiography*, 14; see also Caciola, "Mystics, Demoniacs."

[59] Hughes Neveux, "Les lendemains de la mort dans les croyances occidentales (vers 1250–vers 1300)," *Annales E.S.C.* 34 (1979): 249.

women credited with miraculous powers. Inquisitorial proceedings, preaching handbooks, encyclopedias, demonologies, and scholastic treatises can offer us alternative viewpoints. Indeed, all these sources describe quite similar individuals from different perspectives. All supply tales about laywomen exhibiting the same set of possessed behaviors, sometimes interpreting them as divinely inspired, sometimes as demonically instigated. Multiplying the types of sources consulted has the prismatic effect of revealing a fuller spectrum of responses to these colorful individuals. I have avoided making this a study about "holy women" and instead sought to examine the ambiguity of this category and to take seriously its juxtaposition with categories such as demonic possession or fraud. Hence, in order to equalize the positive and negative poles of the inquiry, it is imperative to counterbalance hagiographies with sources portraying demoniacs, pseudo-prophets, simulated sanctity, and exorcisms.

Not only does this approach elicit more information, but a juxtaposition of hostile and laudatory sources also enables a broader perspective on the questions at hand, for it effectively de-essentializes the received definitions of particular women as "saints/visionaries/holy women" or as "heretics/frauds/demoniacs." Indeed, I would suggest that it is precisely the application of these highly charged word-clusters that requires investigation. This is my third methodological point: I believe it is time for historians to rethink the way we appropriate medieval categories about religious identity. Peter Brown has noted that "the supernatural becomes the depository of the objectified values of the group."[60] If saints and demoniacs, heretics and fakers, may all be considered as categories of the supernatural, then we must ask ourselves whether, when we apply these words to specific individuals, we are adopting the objectified values of medieval ecclesiastics and theologians. My underlying premise in raising this issue is that these categories are not self-evident and natural; they are social products. Moreover, though these categories arose within, and represent the ideology of, a particular historical group, they masquerade as universal judgments.[61] The authoritative quality of individual categorizations depends on the degree to which these labels come to seem natural, thus obscuring the processes of negotiation and accommodation by which they were produced.[62] As Ernesto Laclau has noted,

[60] Peter Brown, *Society and the Holy in Late Antiquity* (Berkeley, 1982), 318.

[61] A point underlined by Head, *Hagiography*.

[62] My thoughts in this area have been aided by Jacques Berlinerblau, "Toward a Sociology of Heresy, Orthodoxy, and *Doxa*," *History of Religions* 40, 4 (2001): 327–51; Bruce Lincoln, *Authority: Construction and Corrosion* (Chicago, 1994); Arthur Droge, "Retro-

"the process of representation itself creates retroactively the entity to be represented."[63]

If we refocus our view of the evidence, we can begin to see that many women categorized variously as holy persons, demoniacs, heretics, or fakers actually fall into a loosely unified data set that has been split into separate categories according to medieval theological preoccupations—preoccupations that do not necessarily accord with the objectives of the modern secular academic. While it is important to try to understand the cultural content of these categories (as I do in chapter 1), attaching them to particular individuals at the outset of a discussion obscures more than it illuminates. In fact, an individual woman could be all of these things at the same time to different people: putative saints were rejected and insulted, apparent demoniacs were venerated, so-called frauds excited admiring gossip, and some labeled heretics were lauded as martyrs. To pilfer a sentence from Patrick Geary, "Instead of attaching labels, scholars must attempt to understand how various elements—actions, objects, practices, articulations—form a unity or, conversely, coexist in a state of dissonance."[64] A finely textured history of medieval women and religion tells a tale of conflictual interpretations and shifting reinterpretations; of hopes for a celestial civic patron coupled with tests for fraud and fears of demonic deception.

PLAN OF THE BOOK

Research on the testing of spirits in the Middle Ages has required synthesis of many types of evidence. Explicit treatises devoted to theories of discernment were few in the Middle Ages, and were produced at the very end of the period. Thus, these texts actually form only a small percentage of my evidentiary base. Most of the chapters trace the history of discernment

---

fitting/Retiring 'Syncretism,'" *Historical Reflections/Reflexions Historiques* 27, 3 (2001): 375–87; Joan Scott, "Gender: A Useful Category of Historical Analysis," *American Historical Review* 91, 5 (1986): 1053–75, particularly pages 1066–75; Mark Vessey, "The Forging of Orthodoxy in Latin Christian Literature: A Case Study," *Journal of Early Christian Studies* 4, 4 (1996): 495–513.

[63] Judith Butler, Ernesto Laclau, and Slavoj Žižek, *Contingency, Hegemony, Universality: Contemporary Dialogues on the Left* (London, 2000).

[64] Patrick Geary, "The Uses of Archaeological Sources for Religious and Cultural History," in *Living with the Dead*, 33.

through a variety of other sources, such as hagiographies, exempla and chronicle accounts, theological works, medical textbooks, images, and exorcisms. All translations of these sources are my own unless otherwise noted. For images, I have preferred to analyze public works, such as frescoes and altarpieces, rather then artwork produced for private viewing.

The first part of the book is entitled "A Protracted Disputation" after a quotation from the canonization inquiry for Catherine of Siena that describes a contentious quarrel between Catherine and some cardinals over the source of her inspiration. This segment of the book discusses the contours of the late medieval discernment dispute and the broad cultural debates it engendered. Thus chapter 1, "Possessed Behaviors," explores the twinned cultural categories of demonic and divine possession, highlighting similarities in the behaviors associated with each. Both the divinely and the demonically possessed were likely to be female, both were viewed as having incorporated foreign spirits into the body, and both were reported to manifest identical supernatural actions such as trances, prophesying, rigidity, bloating, levitation, and so forth. Yet, however indistinguishable the two categories, they did not have equivalent weight within medieval culture. Demonic possession was an ancient category attested in scripture, whereas claims to divine possession were novel, appearing for the first time in a widespread way in the late twelfth century. This chronological disjunction rendered demonic possession the more "reliable" category, making it the more likely explanation for unusual or extreme behaviors in the minds of many contemporary observers.

Chapter 2, "Ciphers," turns to individual discernment disputes, presenting a series of three case studies of possessed women. This chapter focuses on how spirit possession and the testing of spirits acted as complex processes of identity formation. The individual possessed by a supernatural spirit was a cipher, an unclear sign in need of interpretation by observers. A process of analyzing the observable surface of the body for clues to the spirit within enabled the community to categorize these women as either divinely or demonically possessed. The discernment of spirits conducted informally by local communities who lived with the possessed individual was emergent and negotiable. Gossip tended to dissect closely the meanings of particular trance states, gestures, or facial expressions as clues to the divine or demonic influences exerted upon the individual. Community tensions or alliances, prestige factors, and social needs all inflected this process of local discernment as well, which proceeded on a case-by-case basis rather than according to invariant rules or expectations. In some cases, large-scale political scandals and priorities influenced the evaluation of women who claimed to receive visions or to prophesy. The chapter highlights the degree to which discernment was an ongoing, multilateral process that involved both micro- and macropolitical factors.

Part II of Discerning Spirits is called "Spiritual Physiologies." This section takes a step back from specific discernment disputes to engage with broader epistemological issues concerning the body and spirits. Chapter 3, "Fallen Women and Fallen Angels," delves into the question of why women were believed to be more vulnerable to spirit possession than men. A presentation of medieval gender roles begins with an analysis of medieval etymologies for sex-linked words, showing how female nature was understood as more malleable and impressionable than male. This notion led to the perception that women were inherently susceptible to subtle outside influences, and thus to the loss of individual identity implied in spirit possession states. After the twelfth century, the ever widening scope of medical theories about the four humors and their role in regulating the human organism led to learned explorations of how different kinds of bodies might be more or less vulnerable to spiritual invasion. The female humoral balance, it was said, was characterized by a greater physical "openness" or "porosity," which permitted freer entrance to possessing spirits. In short, the female body was easier for spirits to enter and control than the male. The chapter closes with a discussion of images of fallen angels, or demons, demonstrating their physical similitude to women's bodies. The symbolic alignment of women and the demonic was a growing trend in the later Middle Ages.

Chapter 4, "Breath, Heart, Bowels," shows how intellectuals attempted to naturalize the testing of spirits. Twelfth- and thirteenth-century theologians made creative use of contemporary medical knowledge in elaborating a paradigm of discernment entrenched within the interior physiological systems of the body. These thinkers set forth a physiological model for the differences between divine and demonic possession, theorizing that the Holy Spirit might influence the mortal individual from a different place within the body than that occupied by possessing unclean spirits. The influx of Arabic medical texts in the late twelfth century revolutionized Western conceptions of human anatomy and opened the way for this kind of examination. An elaborate medico-theological literature subsequently developed that discussed the interactions of foreign, possessing spirits with the indigenous human spirit of the individual, and explained how possessing spirits influenced the senses and perceptions. Although these thinkers set forth a theoretical basis for the interior discernment of spirits, they failed to adduce a pragmatic system of discernment from the vantage point of the exterior observer. In order to discern spirits effectively, the observer needed to understand the connections between the interior of the body and its exterior, between depth and surface. The physiological model of discernment theorized about the internal anatomy of the possessed individual, but did nothing to tie these ideas to the observable level of the body.

In Part III, "Discernment and Discipline," I argue that by the turn of the fifteenth century possessed behaviors indicating the incorporation of a foreign spirit were being viewed exclusively as signs of demonic possession rather than as possibly divine in origin. This change is viewed from both sides of the discernment question and within two different textual genres. Chapter 5, "Exorcizing Demonic Disorder," investigates the history of exorcism manuals, a new type of text in the fifteenth century. These manuals were carefully scripted as "self-interpreting" rituals that authorize a narrow spectrum of interpretation to viewers and to the demoniac herself. The ideology of the manuals orchestrates a dramatic confrontation between God and the devil, between a clerical exorcist and a lay victim, and between a male and a female. Ultimately, the former terms in each pair are elided with one another, as are the latter terms: the male cleric is divine, while the lay, female victim is entirely conflated with the demon. In addition, the history of these exorcisms displays a growing emphasis upon purifying each individual body part, as demons are cast out from each limb of the demoniac. The later the exorcistic text, the more elaborate and repetitive the conjurations of body parts, demonstrating an ever stronger emphasis upon the physically incorporative character of demonic possession.

At the same time, however, treatises on the discernment of spirits were being produced: these form the subject of chapter 6, "Testing Spirits in the Effeminate Age." The chapter shows how apprehension about individual revelations, prophecies, and wonders was forced to a passionate climax by a specific set of circumstances. The Great Schism, which between 1378 and 1417 led to a doubling of claims to the papal tiara and its prerogatives, urgently foregrounded the question of how to define legitimate authority within the Church. Such an agenda inevitably turned to questions of individual, as well as institutional, religious leadership. Indeed, the most significant and weighty treatises on the testing of spirits to be produced in the Middle Ages all were penned by leading ecclesiological thinkers like Pierre d'Ailly, Henry of Langenstein, and Jean Gerson. These discernment treatises accomplished three goals. First, they singled out the laity and women as especially unlikely candidates for divine inspiration. Indeed, these thinkers all directly blamed the prophecies of laywomen (notably Brigit of Sweden and Catherine of Siena) for the outbreak of the schism itself. Second, they elaborated a paradigm of sanctity that was nonmaterialist and purely metaphysical. Thus the earlier emphasis upon the ambivalent character of possessed behaviors shifted toward a unilateral interpretation of such conduct as demonically motivated. Third, the discourse of discernment set the stage for the elaboration of the witch stereotype by the succeeding generation of thinkers. Thus did a feminization of religious life in the twelfth century lead to a feminization of the demonic at the end of the Middle Ages.

PART I

"A Protracted Disputation"

CHAPTER ONE
POSSESSED BEHAVIORS

A man's thoughts can be known to another man through certain bodily
signs. . . . But if they do not observe the thoughts directly, but only
through bodily signs, then they cannot know them at all, for the same
bodily sign can indicate many things.
— THOMAS AQUINAS

I n the late thirteenth century, Ida of Louvain scandalized her
community. The daughter of a prosperous wine merchant,
Ida already had refused marriage and become a recluse in a
small cell within her parents' home. One day, however, it
seemed that she went mad. Casting aside even the simple clothes she now
wore, Ida wrapped herself in a dirty rag and draped a mat over her shoulders
for warmth. Aggressively seeking out the most crowded plazas and market-
places, she preened and "strutted about if mad or a fool, offering a monstrous
spectacle of herself to the people."[1] Townspeople murmured that Ida was in
a frenzy, out of her mind; eventually she was tied up to prevent her from
harming herself or others.

What compelled Ida to act in this way? If we believe her hagiographer's
testimony, it was a divine revelation. According to Ida's vita, her radical behavior was traceable to a vision she had just received, the first of many to
come. In Ida's vision, a pauper approached her recluse's cell and stood before
her. He then reached out his hands and peeled back the skin of her chest, revealing her heart. The pauper climbed inside Ida's heart and took up residence there, enjoying her "hospitality." This is why Ida suddenly conceived
a frenzy for such an abject—and visible—kind of poverty: she was divinely
possessed, inhabited by the poor Christ.

---

[1] *Vita Venerabilis Idae Virginis, AASS*, April 2: 163. Parts of this opening discussion are
drawn from Nancy Caciola, "Mystics, Demoniacs, and the Physiology of Spirit Possession
in Medieval Europe." *Comparative Studies in Society and History* 42, 2 (2000): 268–306.

The tale unveils a profound tension in the history of religious mentalities in the later Middle Ages. Whereas Ida and her hagiographer considered her state to be one of internal possession by the divine spirit, outside observers considered her "insane and frenetic," a malady that frequently was attributed to demonic possession.[2] Indeed, her behaviors—dementia, frenzy, trances, convulsions, and episodes of strange bleeding—precisely mirrored those characteristically reported of demoniacs at this time. Nor was Ida alone in being the object of confusion for observers, for accusations of demonic possession were quite a common response to women claiming divine inspiration in the later Middle Ages. Medieval communities struggled mightily over how to understand women who, surrounded by a tumultuous aura of the supernatural, appeared to be possessed by a spirit. Was the Ancient Enemy inside? Or the spirit of the Divine? Although Ida's vision of the pauper entering her heart might have suggested a beneficent interpretation of her behaviors to a medieval audience,[3] ultimately this vision was a purely internal experience. Hence it remained unverifiable. As Pope Innocent III wrote in a letter of 1199, "it is not enough for someone flatly to assert that they have been sent by God, when that commission is internal and private, for any heretic can say as much."[4] From the external vantage point of the observer, Ida's behavior appeared pointless and disordered. Parading through the plazas while proudly modeling rags was taken as an "in your face" gesture by Ida's contemporaries, an indication that something was deeply wrong with her, rather than a sign of divine illumination.

When medieval people attempted to decide whether an individual was divinely or demonically possessed, they were responding to a congeries of ambiguous behaviors that could signify either state. That is to say, the cultural categories of the divinely and the demonically possessed were constructed in similar ways as regards exterior behaviors, even though in terms of interior status the two categories were dichotomous: one involved the penetration of the Holy Spirit, and the other, an evil spirit. It is easy to find expressions of

---

[2] On mental illness and demonic possession, see Barbara Newman, "Possessed by the Spirit: Devout Women, Demoniacs, and the Apostolic Life in the Thirteenth Century," *Speculum* 73, 3 (1998): 733–70; Muriel Laharie, *La folie au Moyen Age, XIe–XIIIe siècles* (Paris, 1991); Erik Midelfort, "Madness and the Problems of Psychological History in the Sixteenth Century," *Sixteenth Century Journal* 12, 1 (1981): 5–12; idem, *A History of Madness in Sixteenth-Century Germany* (Palo Alto, 1999). On madness and divine possession, see Michel de Certeau, *The Mystic Fable*, vol. 1, *The Sixteenth and Seventeenth Centuries*, trans. M. Smith (Chicago, 1992).

[3] See chapter 4.

[4] Innocent III, letter 46, in *PL*, 214:697.

this idea emanating from thinkers of a variety of backgrounds and degrees of sophistication. Thomas Aquinas wrote of trance states, for example,

> Abstraction . . . can occur from three causes. First, from a bodily cause, as is clear from those who through some infirmity are out of their minds. Second, through the power of demons, as is seen in those who are possessed. Third, from the divine power. It is in this sense that we speak of ecstasy, when one is elevated to a supernatural level by the divine spirit, with abstraction from the senses.[5]

This type of comment could be—and was—applied to a host of other ambiguous "bodily signs" or possessed behaviors. Indeed, it is no exaggeration to state that there were two kinds of spirit possession in the Middle Ages, one malign and one benign, that were outwardly indistinguishable from one another. Both were attended by spectacular abilities: "Though miraculous abilities can be gifts that God bestows upon the faithful for the confirmation of the faith—the revelation of the future, or gift of prophecy; the understanding of supernatural things, or gift of wisdom; and the understanding of human things, or gift of knowledge—nevertheless, similar things also can be, and are, accomplished by evil spirits."[6]

This juxtaposition led to an epistemological conundrum for the medieval Church on both the local community level and the translocal, institutional level.[7] How could one tell the difference between divine and demonic possession? The Adversary could so easily deceive the unwary. The demonic character delighted in deception: leading human beings into falsehood was understood to be a basic goal of the demonic hosts. Thus fears about hypocrisy and false sanctity were important currents in later medieval thought, and the ecclesiastical leadership of the time sought to disseminate these concerns among the broader population. One should not reflexively venerate anyone who appears to be saintly, but exercise caution.

The early thirteenth-century theologian and bishop of Paris William of

---

[5] Thomas Aquinas, *Summa theologiae*, 2a 2ae, quaest. 175, reply art. 1, in R. Potter, ed., *St. Thomas Aquinas Summa Theologiae*, vol. 45, *Prophecy and Other Charisms* (Manchester, 1970), 96.

[6] Augustinus de Ancona, *Tractatus contra sompniatores et divinatores*, ed. P. Giglioni, "Il 'Tractatus contra divinatores e sompniatores' di Agostino d'Ancona Introduzione e edizione del testo," *Analecta Augustiniana* 48 (1985): 61.

[7] A corrective to reified views is Gary Macy, "Was There a 'The Church' in the Middle Ages?" in R. Swanson, ed., *Unity and Diversity in the Church* (Cambridge, 1996), 107–16.

Auvergne wrote of "the falsely righteous, whom we call 'hypocrites' in Greek, who seek glory with so many fasts and severe afflictions in the name of a vainglorious sanctity."[8] These hypocrites, William explained, were like human reflections of demons: the deceptive essence of their character was a lower-level representation of the demonic character. The asceticism of such persons was, in itself, no proof of sanctity; it may even be a form of hypocritical pride. Thus one must be careful and constantly look for diabolic deceptions among the apparently saintly. Indeed, William contends that the demonic hosts, in imitation of the Almighty and His Church, have an infernal hierarchy of false saints that is directly modeled after the celestial hierarchy of true saints. "They parallel and assimilate [infernal] orders to [celestial] orders. For instance, false apostles to God's holy apostles, and also false martyrs to God's holy martyrs, and in the same way with confessors and virgins." Such simulated saints are "in thrall to demons,"[9] that is, under the control of unclean spirits.

The tinsel glamour of false sainthood was understood to be particularly attractive to women, however, for the fragile sex gave in to the blandishments of the devil more readily. Thus Pope Innocent IV in 1250 censured "silly women internally loaded down with sins who make an external show of sanctity, though virtue is utterly foreign to them."[10] The notion of the vainglorious woman prophetess deceived by an angel of darkness disguised as a angel of light was something of a late medieval commonplace. It regularly occurs in preaching exempla, for example. Étienne de Bourbon mentions the case of an abbess who respectfully used to consult "a certain woman recluse, whom she believed to have a spirit of prophecy, but this witch (*malefica*) and faker was speaking with the devil."[11] Caesarius of Heisterbach mentions a similar case of a woman recluse-prophetess deceived by the devil transfigured into an angel of light: "There lived a recluse named Bertradis, a holy and religious woman famous for the divine revelations with which she was illuminated. This woman for a long time mistook an angel of darkness for an angel of light, because she was less than cautious. The devil used to enter her little cell through the window, with a fantastic penumbra of light, in order to

---

[8] William of Auvergne, *De universo*, in *Guilielmi Alverni Opera Omnia* (Paris, 1674), 1:1024.

[9] Ibid., 1035.

[10] The Latin of the bull is excerpted in Luigi Pellegrini, "Female Religious Experience and Society in Thirteenth-Century Italy," in S. Farmer and B. Rosenwein, eds., *Monks, Nuns, Saints, and Outcasts: Religion in Medieval Society* (Ithaca, N.Y., 2000), 120 n. 80.

[11] E de B, 113.

prophesy the future to her and to instruct her about the things she asked him."[12] This was not simply a literary and religious topos, however, but an idea with broad currency in daily life. The teachings of bishops, popes, and preachers about how demonic possession could appear to be divine possession had demonstrable effects upon the laity and lower clergy. Thus, laywomen who felt invaded by a foreign spirit often feared that they were demonically possessed and deceived:

> I saw myself as the house of the devil, and as an instrument and an adherent of demons. . . . I turned to those friars . . . and said to them, "I don't want you to believe in me any more. Don't you see that I am a demoniac? . . . Don't you see that everything I have told you is false? And don't you see that, if there were no evil in the whole world, I would fill up the whole world with the abundance of my evil? Do not believe me any more. Do not adore this idol any longer, for the devil is hiding in this idol, and everything I have said to you is false, simulated, diabolic speech."[13]

Conversely, confessors to possessed women dreaded lest their charges were false saints colluding with the Ancient Enemy: "If, in detriment to the truth, she lied repeatedly when speaking about God, about the saints, and about herself, then it necessarily follows that she cannot be a member of Christ, who is Truth, but a member of the devil, who is a Lie and the father thereof."[14]

Thus the later medieval context was marked by a quite successful campaign, on the part of the ecclesiastical intelligentsia, to teach the laity and lower clergy to watch out for demonic deceptions—particularly among women. Not surprisingly, laywomen who claimed visionary experiences were scrutinized harshly under the rubric of discernment, sometimes for years on end. Becoming the target of divisive debates about inspiration counts as one of the most predictable elements in the lives of laywomen visionaries in this period.[15]

This chapter investigates the categories that medieval people were negotiating with when they engaged in the testing of spirits. It thus explores notions of divine and demonic possession in the abstract, without becoming

[12] *DM*, 1:332. Also see Joseph Klapper, ed., *Erzalungen des Mittelalters: In deutscher Ubersetzung und lateinischen Urtext* (Hildesheim, 1978), 348–49.
[13] *Vita B. Angelae de Fulgino*, *AASS*, January 1:188–91.
[14] *Vita Benevenutae de Bojanis*, *AASS*, July 4:185.
[15] Caciola, "Mystics, Demoniacs," 273–79.

engaged with specific case histories. What was a demoniac, or energumen, supposed to look like? How were the divinely possessed expected to behave? By building up a detailed description of these two cultural categories, this chapter establishes the conceptual underpinnings of the testing of spirits.

DEMONIC POSSESSION

Scriptural and Patristic Bases

The Western notion of demonic possession was as ancient as the gospels. Indeed, the plethora of demonic possessions recounted in the New Testament testifies to a new concern that was shared by many Jewish sects of the intertestamental period, among them the Jesus Movement.[16] There is only one case of involuntary spirit possession described in the Hebrew Bible, that of King Saul. Exorcism is, strikingly, among Jesus' favorite miracles in the synoptic accounts of Mark, Matthew, and Luke.[17] These gospels present Jesus as a warrior against the personalized forces of darkness and chaos, forces that both recognize and fear him. In Mark, an exorcism forms Jesus' first public demonstration of supernatural power, and also provides the first occasion on which Jesus' divine identity is recognized by another creature. "There was in their synagogue a man with an unclean spirit and he cried out, 'What have you to do with us, Jesus of Nazareth? Have you come to destroy us? I know who you are, the Holy One of God'" (Mark 1:23–24; see Luke 4:33–35, Matt. 8:29). The demons acknowledge Jesus' divinity long before his disciples: they know reality.

Most accounts of demonic possession in the gospels focus on Jesus' role as a charismatic healer rather than on the state of the afflicted. One exception is the case of the Gerasene demoniac, which contains a fairly dense description of the demoniac's habits and comportment. "When [Jesus] had come out of the boat, there met him out of the tombs a man with an unclean spirit, who lived among the tombs, and no one could bind him any more, even with a chain. For he had often been bound with fetters and chains, but

---

[16] Geza Vermes, *Jesus the Jew: An Historian's Reading of the Gospels* (Philadelphia, 1973).

[17] Traugott Oesterreich, *Possession, Demoniacal and Other, Among Primitive Races, in Antiquity, the Middle Ages, and in Modern Times* (New York, 1930); Jeffrey Russell, *The Devil: Perceptions of Evil from Antiquity to Primitive Christianity* (Ithaca, N.Y., 1977); Henry Kelly, *The Devil, Demonology and Witchcraft: The Development of Christian Beliefs in Evil Spirits* (New York, 1974); Edward Langton, *Essentials of Demonology: A Study of Jewish and Christian Doctrine, Its Origin and Development* (London, 1949).

the chains he wrenched apart and the fetters he broke in pieces, and no one had the strength to subdue him. Night and day among the tombs and on the mountains he was always crying out and bruising himself with stones" (Mark 5:1–5).[18] The incident continues with the demoniac's identification of his horde of possessing spirits as "Legion," and it peaks with the dramatic scene of the spirits being driven into a herd of swine, which immediately stampedes into the sea. An epilogue to the incident tells that the herdsmen ran back to the town and told of Jesus' actions, and that the people came out, "and saw the demoniac sitting there, clothed and in his right mind, the man who had had the legion, and they were afraid. . . . And they began to beg Jesus to depart from their neighborhood" (Mark 5:15, 17).

Several aspects of this tale deserve further comment. Of first importance is the sense that the spirits have taken over the body of their victim, speaking through his mouth in the first person, giving their own collective name, "Legion," and suppressing the man's own personality. The violence of the possession—a supernatural force invading fragile human flesh—is evident in the man's mental and physical alterations. The demoniac possesses superhuman strength that enables him to break all bonds and fetters: no one can subdue him. He also is in a state of acute mental disturbance as a result of the wrenching experience of possession. At war within himself, he attacks his own body with stones, and he shouts uncontrollably. By implication, he goes about naked, that is, in a bestial or uncivilized state, for when he is healed he puts on clothing. Lastly, the demoniac is an outcast who lives among the tombs of the dead—an area associated with evil spirits in the ancient world— and who can be reintegrated into human society only after he has been reintegrated within himself.

Incorporation

The possessed behaviors of the Gerasene demoniac are echoed in medieval depictions of demonic affliction. Physical frenzies, shouting, nudity, subordination of the personality to the invading demon, and superhuman strength often are found in medieval miracle accounts and images of the demonically possessed. Similarly, the responses of the community to the demoniac—avoidance and attempts to bind or physically constrain the victim—recur in the medieval evidence as well. These parallelisms are clear, for instance, in an anonymous mid-thirteenth-century altarpiece, now in the

---

[18] The tale also appears in Matt. 8:28–34 and Luke 8:26–39. The Gospel of John contains no exorcisms.

Figure 1. Exorcism of a half-nude demoniac. The wriggling demoniac woman has regressed to a bestial state, as shown by her disheveled hair and torn clothing. Her tense, twisting figure is barely held in check by a large man as she vomits up a demon. Detail of a panel painting attributed to the "Master of Pisa," thirteenth century. Assisi: San Francesco, lower church. Photo courtesy of Alinari/Art Resource.

Church of Saint Francis in Assisi, which can serve as an apt introduction to specifically medieval representations of demonic possession (fig. 1).[19] One episode depicted in this cycle of the life of Saint Francis shows the exorcism of a disheveled young woman, who is barely restrained by a man behind her who grasps her waist as she squirms and twists, arms flailing wildly. Her dress

[19] For discussion of early Francis cycles, see Eamon Duffy, "Finding St. Francis: Early Images, Early Lives," in P. Biller and A. Minnis, eds., *Medieval Theology and the Natural Body* (York, 1997), 193–236.

Figure 2. Exorcism of a bound demoniac. The woman vomits up three small imps, who are exorcized by the powerful presence of Francis's relics. One demon is just climbing out of the victim's mouth, another runs away across the heads of bystanders, while a third flies off at a low altitude. Detail of a panel painting of the Florentine School, mid-thirteenth century. Florence: Basilica of Santa Croce, Bardi Chapel. Photo by Richard S. Cohen.

is in immodest disarray, echoing the nudity of the Gerasene example, and her regression to a bestial state is evident: her long, loose hair tumbles down and she tilts her head back, as if in a frenzy. A rather large winged demon flies away above her head. Another contemporary illustration of the same miracle envisions the scene slightly differently, demonstrating how various aspects of the stereotype of divine possession could be recombined (fig. 2). In this case, the woman is restrained both by a young man and also by having her arms tied behind her back. The three winged demons that leap from her mouth are notable for their materiality, especially their liability to gravitational pull. In the unknown artist's depiction, one imp flies away at low altitude while the other two scamper across people's heads: the imp at the left has one foot on the victim's head and another on that of an onlooker behind her, while the demon in the center is shown just climbing out of the woman's mouth, one foot poised on her lower jaw, the other stepping up to her forehead. Their arms, raised in dismay, ironically echo the prayerful attitude of the two friars at the extreme right.

These images thus follow scriptural precedent rather closely in depicting the demoniac as invaded by a foreign presence that both lends superhuman strength and provokes subhuman, uncivilized behavior. The sex of the victim, however, is a noteworthy point of divergence from the Gerasene example. In the medieval context diabolic possession primarily was thought to afflict females. Thus one commentator, speaking of the multitude of women vexed or possessed by demons, confessed: "We believe in fact that, by the hidden and just judgment of God, women are brought to this sorry state by an excess of illicit temptation. How it could be otherwise, we do not see."[20] Similarly, Johannes Nider in his influential tract *Formicarius*, includes a bit of dialogue between the "Theologian" and "Mr. Lazy" discussing why women are more prone to demonic molestation than men. The theologian's rather confused answer to this question is that since spirits do not have flesh or bones, they do not have fleshly sexual desires. If they did feel such drives, they would be more attracted to the male body and vex men more than women, but luckily this is not the case. "Blessed be the Most High, who has preserved the male of the species from their disgraceful passion up to the present day!"[21] Nider goes on to speculate that demons are particularly attracted to women with long and lustrous hair, for the care and ornamentation of such locks inevitably involves excessive vainglory.

While it is not difficult to find tales of demonic possession involving males—often children before the age of reason—women dominate the category in every body of sources.[22] Exempla, healings from saints' vitae, and miracle stories demonstrate a marked predilection for female victims, as do iconographic scenes like the ones discussed above. Some texts, not content simply with stating the sex of the victim, ostentatiously draw attention to it by sexualizing the processes of possession and exorcism. Thus the demoniac may display the signs of pregnancy, as in the case of an energumen whose "womb swelled and she began to spin about, and she was so seriously infested by the demon that she could scarcely be held back by two or three men."[23] In an extended case recounted in the hagiography of Hildegard of Bingen,

[20] *Vita S. Lutgartis Virginis, AASS*, June 4:198.

[21] *F* 5.10, 84v–85r.

[22] At least one medieval source contended, further, that demoniacs were more abundant in Italy than elsewhere. Giraldus Cambrensis, *Gemma ecclesiastica*, ed. J. S. Brewer, in *Rerum Britannicarum Medii Aevi scriptores*, vol. 21: *Giraldi Cambrensis opera* (New York: Kraus Reprint, 1964) 2, 54.

[23] Leonardus Lemmens, ed., *Fragmenta Minora: Catalogus Sanctorum Fratrum Minorum* (Rome, 1903), 96.

an exorcized demon exits through his female victim's "shameful parts."[24] Indeed, the identification of demonic possession with women was so strong that when exorcists' manuals first appeared in the late fourteenth century, the very grammar of the texts assumed that the demoniac would be female. Whereas a few manuals used feminine-specific terms such as *daemoniaca, vexata, obsessa, energumena,* and *famula Dei* alongside the expected masculine endings—itself an unusual manifestation of gender inclusiveness—it is not uncommon to find the *exclusive* use of feminine endings as standard terms of reference for the object of the exorcism.[25]

The central element in accounts of demonic possession is the sense that the afflicted individual has incorporated a foreign being within herself. This point was important to the artists discussed above, for they devoted careful attention to illustrating the precise physical relationship between demon and demoniac. The imps were painted as coming out of the woman's body, an event evidently involving a fair degree of violence. Their exit point is the victim's mouth, a detail that suggests the need for a specific bodily opening. In this regard, the artistic evidence was well in accord with broader cultural trends in the conceptualization of demonic possession. Seldom were unclean spirits envisaged as numinous forms wafting out of the victim. Rather, they crawled out from an orifice: usually, though not universally, the mouth. This was the case in numerous miracle stories, where the spirit was said to be vomited forth variously as a toad, blood, frozen coal, black smoke, a hairy worm, unspecified "terrible things," or a red rock together with a leaf.[26] The possessed body was viewed literally as having incorporated a foreign spirit inside itself: the surface appearance of the individual belies the demon in its depths.

Concern with how demons get into and out from their victims was recurrent and symmetrical. Thus the entrance of the unclean spirit often was presented as an ingestion through the mouth. In a tale taken from the Dialogues of Gregory the Great, and repeated endlessly in collections of exempla for centuries thereafter, "A certain nun . . . ate a cabbage without making the sign of the cross and a devil entered into her. When it was driven out by a certain

---

[24] *Vita Hildegardis, AASS,* September 5:695. For discussion of the sexualized aspects of possession in an Early Modern context, see Moshe Sluhovsky, "A Divine Apparition or Demonic Possession? Female Agency and Church Authority in Sixteenth-Century France." *Sixteenth-Century Journal* 27, 4 (1995): 1036–52.

[25] For further discussion, see chapter 5.

[26] For reference to a toad: *Miracula B. Idesbaldi Abbatis, AASS,* April 2:587. Blood: *Vita S. Gualfardi Solatarii, AASS,* April 3:839. Frozen coal: *Vita S. Bernardini Senensis, AASS,* May 5:106. Black smoke: *Processus de B. Petro de Luxemburgo, AASS,* July 1:506. A hairy worm: *De. Ap.* 2.36.4, 386–87. "Terrible things": *Miracula B. Angeli Clareni, AASS,* June 3:575. A red rock and a leaf: *Vita B. Placidi Eremitae, AASS,* June 3:110.

holy man, it asked, 'Why is it my fault? What have I done? Why are you blaming me? I was sitting on the cabbage and she didn't cross herself, therefore she was the one who ate me, along with the cabbage!'"[27]

Gregory's amusing tale was the *locus classicus* for a recurrent topos about possession through the consumption of food. Such themes frequently appear both in exempla collections, and in tales told from an eyewitness standpoint. The latter accounts generally give detailed circumstantial descriptions about the possessions they describe. "One day a certain girl named Pasqua, daughter of Noce, was drinking milk that a neighbor woman gave her. Suddenly the milk in the bottle turned black. Stunned, she flung it away and, looking around the house with wide eyes, she saw a being of the darkest black, with big hair but small stature. He said to her, 'You are dead: I only need to throw you into the well.' Suddenly she went out from the house and emitted horrible voices."[28]

Medieval etymologies, following the authority of Isidore of Seville, derived the Latin word *os* (mouth) from *ostium* (door) and emphasized the mouth as a primary aperture of exchange between the inside and the outside of the body.[29] A generalized fear of the devil entering the body is expressed in a variety of anecdotal evidence, including the Ménagier de Paris's advice to his young wife to "guard the castle door, so that the devil cannot enter . . . into the body."[30] This metaphor of the body as a fortification under siege is made more forceful by the fact that the term *obsessio* was used to refer both to demonic possession and to military sieges.

Often the demon appears to his victim just before entering her body. This was the case when the demon who possessed Pasqua, discussed above, first showed himself to her as a short, black being with big hair, who threatened her with death. Another vivid description of this kind occurs in the vita of Rainerius of Umbria:

Concerning the means of invasion or of besieging of the girl mentioned above, this [is known]: One morning when she had risen before dawn, and her father was just entering the house, it seemed to her that five [demons] in human form, but frightening and black, came in the house also. One of them put his hand on the girl's head and asked his friends, "How many of us are there?" "There are six of us," they answered. But

[27] This retelling is from J de V, 59. The original passage in Gregory is in the *Dialogues* 1.4.7.

[28] Lemmens, *Fragmenta Minora*, 96.

[29] Isidorus Hispalensis, *Differentiarum* 2.17, in *PL*, 83:79.

[30] Quoted in M.-C. Pouchelle, *The Body and Surgery in the Middle Ages*, trans. R. Morris (New Brunswick, N.J., 1990), 148.

the main one said, "That doesn't matter, because this one can only endure three." . . . The fantastic monsters disappeared, but she was struck
with incredible horror and fear. . . . Then for five years she remained
without memory or discernment, although she occasionally had lucid
intervals.[31]

The consultation of the demons about how to deal with this particular victim is intriguing. When the head demon announces, "this one can only endure three," is he speaking of the amount of available space inside her? Or is
the comment meant to indicate her psychological tolerance, that she can only
endure possession by three demons before going insane (which occurs any-
way) or perhaps being killed? The statement remains puzzling.

While demons seem to enter and exit through the mouth more often than
through any other particular orifice, there are examples of possessing spirits
entering the body through other "gates," as the senses sometimes were
called. Caesarius of Heisterbach, for example, gives an instance in which a
woman is possessed by a demon who enters through her ear.[32] The Miracles
of Ambrose Sansedonius of Siena, a prolific thirteenth-century Italian exorcist, yields an instance in which a girl has demons expelled from her eye and
tongue by a vision of the saint,[33] while the canonization process of Clare of
Montefalco mentions a demon who enters his victim "through her fingernail
and flesh."[34] According to the vita of Columba of Rieti, a six-year-old boy
was possessed through his eyes, after gazing into the eyes of a dead cat that
he found in the street.[35] Some examples do not mention a specific point of
entrance or exit but nevertheless focus upon the material and spatial aspects
of the operation. Thus in one woman's possession the demon "invaded the
wretched woman, pushed out her good spirit, and prepared a space for himself inside her."[36] Similarly, an exorcism describes how "a demon in the form
of a kind of monster, in the nature of a black, four-legged beast, came out of
her body and, falling to the ground, ran away."[37]

The experience of possession, for the victim, often was described as un-
ceasing demonic attack and torment. Thus in a tale about a nun named

[31] *Miracula B. Raineri, AASS*, November 1:399. The numeric inconsistency is part of
the text.
[32] *DM*, 1:291.
[33] *Miracula B. Ambrosii Sansedonii, AASS*, March 3:235.
[34] *Antico processo della beata Chiara da Montefalco*, Vatican City: ASV Riti. 2929, f. 1003v.
[35] *Vita B. Columbae Reatinae, AASS*, May 5:190.
[36] *Vita et Miracula Venerabilis Idae Virginis, AASS*, April 2:145.
[37] *De Sancta Rosa Vergine Tertii Ordinis S. Franciscii Viterbii in Italia, AASS*, September
2:449.

Aleida, the victim sees herself as alternately tempted and tormented by a demon, but her sisters consider her to be possessed: they sprinkle her with holy water and fumigate her with incense.[38] Another account describes demonic possession as accomplished through demonic torment, when a group of unclean spirits threatens a woman: "we will make sure that . . . by harassing you we will make you a demoniac."[39] Similarly, an exorcists' manual advises that a demoniac who "sees many diabolic visions and is wholly terrified" should be kept in the church for two days, surrounded with relics and fortified by the Host.[40] Thus individuals who reported an exponential increase in demonic assaults were likely to be viewed either as a full demoniac or as someone whom the devil was attempting to enter and possess.

Possession thus subsists on an elemental tension between the exterior and the interior of the body, as spirits enter into the person's physical territory and assume control. By implication, avoidance of demonic possession involves vigilance over the surface of the body and its interactions with the outside environment. The physical self contains the individual's identity; possession involves both transgression of the boundaries of selfhood and a destabilization of the victim's identity. A fascinating evocation of this notion occurs in the hagiography of Mary of Oignies. Here, Jacques de Vitry recounts how the visionary Mary, after forty days of prayer and fasting, succeeded in exorcising a demon from the body of a young nun. The demon appears before Mary, "as if with his bowels vomited out" and carrying "all his interior parts" on his shoulders as punishment.[41] The apparition is explicitly interpreted by Jacques as the visible "sign" of an invisible, spiritual operation—that is, the exorcism itself. As the exorcism pulls out unclean things from the interior of the body, so too, the demon is shown as having his unclean bowels and interior pulled outside his body. The demon, turned inside out, is an image of the identity disorder of the demoniac.

Interior and Exterior

The delicate mesh between the external and the internal levels of the body echoes throughout descriptions of demonic possession in medieval texts. The physical incorporation of a foreign spirit was understood to be an interior vi-

---

[38] *DM*, 1:125–27. See also *Vita Mariae Oignacensis, AASS*, June 5:553–54, for a similar case of an external obsession transforming into internal possession.

[39] *VCS*, 918.

[40] Exorcists' manual from Schlägl Praemonstratensian Institute, Plaga, Austria, ms. lat. 194, 73r; cited in Adolph Franz, *Die kirchlichen Benediktionen im Mittelalter*, 2 vols. (Freiburg-im-Breisgau, 1909; reprint, Graz, 1960), 1:574 n. 1.

[41] *Vita Mariae Oignacensis*, 554.

olation manifested in the body through extreme exterior signs: thus was spirit possession inscribed on the body's surface. This inscription or remolding of the body was constructed as an external signifier of the victim's internal, spiritual violation.

For this reason, demoniacs sometimes were said to enter a physically depressed state of trance involving removal from the senses. As Aquinas noted, "abstraction . . . can occur . . . through the power of demons, as is seen in those who are possessed."[42] This state sometimes was accompanied by an intense bodily rigidity maintained with supernatural strength: "Without delay, the hand and limbs of the nun were contracted with the most extreme rigidity, and her mouth closed so tightly that a knife could not open it even a little bit."[43] Another describes the victim as so fully entranced, and her body so distorted, that "she presented the appearance of a dead woman rather than a living one."[44] Demoniacs sometimes were struck mute when possessed, and failed to respond to the concerned inquiries of observers, remaining in a silent daze.[45] Yet equally characteristic of demonic possession was a remarkably heightened level of activity. Thus some demonically possessed victims raved or seemed insane, like the woman whose demon "used to plunge her into fire and water. . . . and sometimes, when she was not confined by her relatives, she would seek out the forests and plains and used to howl like a dog."[46] Or the "insane woman who had a demon. She gnashed her teeth, spit out rivers of saliva, and her spirit was completely raging and disordered within, for the evil spirit was afflicting her wretchedly."[47] Such behaviors rendered the possessed individual unfit for human society, much like the Gerasene example. In severe cases of demonic infestation, family members were made wretched as well as the victim: "The miserable husband didn't know what to do or where to turn. To cohabit with a demoniac seemed a harsh thing, but to relinquish her seemed impious."[48] Another husband managed to persevere only by tying up his wife, possessed of seven demons: "For four years she had to be tied up in order to lessen [the demons'] vexation. Whenever her husband attempted, out of compassion, to tie her up, the woman hit him repeatedly, pulled his hair, and hurled many insults at him."[49]

[42] Thomas Aquinas, *Summa theologiae*, 2a 2ae, quaest. 175, reply art. 1, p. 96.
[43] *Vita Lutgartis*, 198.
[44] Lemmens, *Fragmenta Minora*, 96.
[45] *De Sancta Rosa Virgine*, 449.
[46] *Vita Roberti Salentini*, *AASS*, July 4:77.
[47] *De B. Alpaide Virgine*, *AASS*, November 1, part 1: 196; see also 195.
[48] The tale is in Bernard of Clairvaux's *Vita*, *AASS*, August 4:104–6.
[49] R. Stachnik, A. Triller, and H. Westpfahl, eds., *Die Akten des Kanonisations-prozess Dorotheas von Montau* (Cologne, 1978), 47.

An even more extreme case concerns a woman energumen who terrorized the city of Ferrara:

> So harshly was she tormented by the demon, she filled the whole city with terror. She gave terrible bites with her teeth to the hands and feet of anyone who was able to catch her. She hurled insults and curses at everyone, mixing in terrible slanders. She threw her body about in almost unspeakable and foul ways. She even tried to burn down her house. . . . [Her family] became impatient and fed up with this, and since they could find no other solution, they tied her up with a strong chain like a dog, and concealed her in a corner of a certain house, so that she could not harm anyone.[50]

These descriptions of the demoniac as an emblem of misrule could be a textual companion to figures 1 and 2, in which the demoniac woman writhes and gnashes her teeth. The profoundly antisocial character of demonic possession divides the victim from her own senses and from her community. Indeed, any person displaying immoderate physical behaviors was at risk of being considered demonically possessed. As Jean-Claude Schmitt has shown, a clear moral hierarchy was attached to different kinds of bodily movement, yielding an "ethics of gesture." Whereas a *gestus* was a dignified sign of moral composure, a *gesticulatio* of the kind common to demoniacs indicated a fundamental disordering of the self and a moral disintegration.[51] William of Auvergne, for example, assured readers of his tract *On the Universe* that there would be no dancing, leaping, capering, singing, or other histrionic gesticulations in Heaven, while Vincent of Beauvais offered his audience a chapter or two on "discipline in gesture."[52] Not surprisingly, the dance manias that periodically swept through parts of Germany and the Low Countries in the thirteenth and fourteenth centuries were characterized as mass outbreaks of possession, an interpretation apparently based on the convulsive movements of the dancers.[53]

Aside from either depressed or heightened sensory states, demoniacs also were thought to be prone to physical alterations that included acquisition of

---

[50] *Analecta S. Antonii Paduae, AASS*, June 3:759.

[51] Jean-Claude Schmitt, "The Ethics of Gesture," in M. Feher et al., *Fragments for a History of the Human Body*, 3 vols. (New York, 1989), 2:128–47; expanded in idem, *La raison des gestes dans l'Occident médiévale* (Paris, 1990).

[52] William of Auvergne, *De universo*, 746; *Spec. Hist.* 26.57, 1073–74.

[53] Madeleine Braekman, "La dansomanie de 1374: Hérésie ou maladie?" *Revue du Nord* 66 (1981): 339–54; Ernesto De Martino, *La terra di rimorso* (Milan, 1961); Midelfort, *History of Madness*, 32–49.

unusual marks on the surface of the skin, bloating, or levitation. These themes represent the eruption onto the surface of the body of its unruly interior state. Thus an exemplary anecdote tells of a girl who refused to stop dancing in deference to the arrival of a preacher, and who therefore was possessed by a demon and struck with a case of boils. Another demoniac, in a detail reminiscent of the stigmata, was said to be marked with a demonic seal on the palm of his hand.[54] The motif of bodily bloating or swelling was common as well. An example of a possession-pregnancy has been noted above, and more attenuated forms of this phenomenon were widely reported. For example, *Jewel of the Church*, by Gerald of Wales, and the anonymous *Book of Exempla* both tell of a demoniac whose possessing demon was apparent as a large bump under the skin that flees from saints' relics and gospel books placed on the victim's body.[55] An even more extended and dramatic version of this motif appears in Thomas of Cantimpré's *On Bees:*

> A certain girl danced with other young people on the Lord's day, and finally, after a long time, returned home exhausted. As soon as she got home, she was filled with a demon. . . . In the morning she was brought to the oratory of the Blessed Virgin, outside the city. . . . This is a place where boys listen to scholars: they all ran to where the girl was being possessed, into the oratory. One of them, a boy scarcely twelve years old, but bolder and brighter than the rest, began to constrain the demon, and to adjure it to leave the body it possessed and to come out. Immediately, the demon showed where it was by a swelling around the navel, and the boy transfixed it by making the cross with his thumb against it. Thus little by little, by making the cross, he compelled it to ascend toward the mouth. Finally, everyone could see it sticking in the back of her mouth, in the form of a hairy worm. Once it was seen, it began trying to go down again—everyone screamed!—but the boy instantly opposed it with the sign of salvation and forced the demon to come out very violently.[56]

This bizarre game of somatic tag along the possessed girl's torso and limbs, combined with the violent exit through the mouth, highlights again the materiality of spirit possession for medieval observers. Thomas's tale also is notable for its highly gendered juxtaposition of purity and impurity: the sinful demoniac girl contrasts sharply with the innocent boy exorcist.

[54] E de B, 161, 158.
[55] Giraldus Cambrensis, *Gemma ecclesiastica*, 53–54. A. Little, ed., *Liber exemplorum ad usum praedicantium* (Aberdeen, 1907), 9.
[56] De. Ap. 2.36.4, 386–87.

Although many reports of demonic possession employ cautionary rhetorical strategies designed to elicit horror and revulsion in the audience, this was not universally the case. Some accounts of the physical changes undergone by demoniacs indicate a spiritualizing, lightening, or cleansing of the body. Thus, a group of possessed nuns reportedly were levitated into the air by the unclean spirits possessing them, a miracle that may be read as a kind of remaking of the possessed body into a more spiritual form.[57] A similar transformation of the body into a magical object, outside the normal bounds of nature, is represented in the common theme of demoniacs who were able to live in a state of extended fasting.[58] In a similar vein, the ability of demons to manipulate the bodies of those whom they possessed in ways that impersonated the saints is seen in certain energumens whose bodies smelled sweet and fragrant with a flowery "odor of sanctity."[59]

Intellectual Gifts

Intellectual, as well as physical, effects frequently were reported of demoniacs. As Jan van Ruusbroec states in his *Adornment of Spiritual Marriage,* "Some persons can be deprived of their external senses by means of a kind of light which is produced by the Devil and which surrounds and envelops them. They sometimes have various kinds of images shown to them, both false ones and true ones, or they hear different kinds of locutions."[60] In other words, the devil can induce a state of trance, in which the victim might receive visions and hear revelations that mingle truth and falsehood. Ruusbroec's description accords well with the kinds of supernatural intellectual endowments routinely reported of demoniacs. Visions, prophetic or occult knowledge, xenoglossia, and otherworldly revelations are the most common motifs. Medieval texts tell of demoniacs who suddenly knew foreign tongues or could resolve difficult conundrums: "The demon spoke elegant Latin through her mouth, even though the girl was entirely ignorant of all Latin. It responded to extremely deep and difficult questions [and] uncovered a great many sins and secrets."[61] Similarly, in a case that concerned an entire monastery of possessed nuns, an inquisitor consulting on the case recounted

---

[57] *Vita Columbae,* 180.
[58] E de B, 165; 189. See also the accusations in *De B. Alpaide Virgine,* 180; *De S. Lidwina Virgine, AASS,* April 2:334; *VCS,* 904.
[59] *Vita S. Dominici, AASS,* August 1:553; *De Ap.* 2.57.47, 574–75.
[60] John Ruusbroec, *The Spiritual Espousals and Other Works,* trans. J. Wiseman (New York, 1985), 89.
[61] *VCS,* 928–29.

that many of them spoke in tongues and predicted the future.[62] In yet another example, a demoniac recites the same text in three different languages, word for word.[63] Two variants of a story told by Jacques de Vitry recount how a demoniac made a career of passionate religious preaching and exhortations to accept the truth of divine scripture.[64]

Indeed, the demonically possessed could come to be socially valued for their special mental powers: not only did they sometimes preach the truth of scripture, they even castigated others for sin. A tale from Caesarius of Heisterbach describes a demoniac who became famous in his village and abroad for his special ability to divulge his interlocutors' hidden sins, for which he would bitterly upbraid them.[65] A sort of inverse pilgrimage flow began; with visitors coming from afar to visit the demoniac prophet, who apparently was regarded as constrained by God to tell the truth. A variant use of this motif illustrates the effectiveness of confession, by having a demoniac proclaim the unconfessed sins of certain bystanders, only to forget each infraction after it is confessed.[66] The skill of demoniacs in divining occult knowledge also could be exploited to humorous effect in collections of preachers' exempla, as in a case from Jacques de Vitry. A demon named Guinehochet gained fame for the occult knowledge he revealed through the mouth of his possessed victim. One day a man, wishing to test Guinehochet's prowess, asked if he knew how many sons he had. When the demon replied, "One," the man triumphantly responded that he in fact had two sons. Smirking, the spirit defended himself, "I have told you the truth. You have only one son: the other one belongs to the priest."[67] Since the demon refused to reveal which son was the bastard, the man was forced to continue rearing both.

Folk Demons

Finally, a few words about the differences between learned ecclesiastical, and popular or folkloric conceptions of demonic possession. The scholarly category of "popular culture" is a complex and highly contentious one. With-

---

[62] *Vita Columbae*, 180. The motif of group possession in a nunnery was more popular in the early modern than the medieval period. For further discussion see Michel de Certeau, *The Possession at Loudun*, trans. M. Smith (Chicago, 2000); and Moshe Sluhovsky, "The Devil in the Convent," *American Historical Review* 107 (2002) 1379–411.

[63] *Vita Norberti Archepiscopi Magdeburgensis*, *AASS*, June 1:821.

[64] J de V, 67; Jacques de Vitry, *The Historia Occidentalis of Jacques de Vitry*, ed. J. Hinnebusch, *Spicilegium Friburgense* 17 (Fribourg, 1972), 86–87.

[65] *DM*, 1:113.

[66] Giraldus Cambrensis, *Gemma ecclesiastica*, 53.

[67] J de V, 97.

out wishing to advance a reductionist vision of medieval culture as a "two-tiered" system,[68] I find it useful to observe certain contrastive distinctions between "popular" and "elite" cultures as expressing ideological tensions between models of cultural interpretation, rather than as static strata or levels of culture in opposition.[69] Popular tales about demonic possession differ from elite theological understandings in two important ways: the moral status of the victim and the precise character of the possessing spirit.

Whereas ecclesiastical discussions of demonic possession often focus upon the sinfulness of the possessed victim, popular conceptions seem to operate according to a "bad luck" theory: an innocent happens to come near a demon and is possessed. Thus a group of popular possession tales involve chthonic, arboreal, aquatic, or otherwise nature-linked spirits who attack their victims without the provocation of sin. These tales include several stories of individuals spontaneously possessed while drawing water, chopping wood, or otherwise entering into wild and uncultivated portions of the landscape.[70] Forests, for example, presented a danger of possession, though watery places were even more risky as places of encounter with supernatural spirits. Thomas of Cantimpré tells the story of children who were playing by a river-bank when suddenly "a sort of man, terrifying and hairy, came forth from the water and attacked the playing children, saying, 'Why are you bothering me, brats?'"[71] The twelfth-century vita of William the Abbot tells of a girl who is sent by her "spiritual mother" to wash in the river and is possessed while doing so.[72] Similar tales are found in the thirteenth-century vitae of Aegidus of Assisi and Ambrose Sansedonius.[73] The latter vita also includes a tale of a girl who is spontaneously possessed while gathering wood in the forest: she tries to throw herself into a gurgling stream nearby.[74] This detail, of immersion in running water, makes an interesting juxtaposition with a tale in the *Dialogue* of Caesarius of Heisterbach, in which the crossing of a river provides a cure for demonic ailments.

[68] Peter Brown, *The Cult of the Saints* (Chicago, 1981).

[69] See Nancy Caciola, "Wraiths, Revenants and Ritual in Medieval Culture," *Past and Present* 152 (1996): 6. This article contains further citations concerning popular culture and a fuller statement of my own position.

[70] Peter Dinzelbacher, "Il ponte come luogo sacro nella realtà e nell'immaginario," in S. Boesch-Gajano and L. Scaraffia, eds., *Luoghi sacri e spazi della santità* (Turin, 1991).

[71] *De Ap.* 2.57.11, 544.

[72] *De S. Gulielmo Abbate, AASS,* June 7:133–34.

[73] *De B. Aegidio Assisinate, AASS,* April 3:244; *De B. Ambrosii Sansedonio, AASS,* March 3:199; *Miracula B. Ambrosii Sansedonii,* 236.

[74] *Miracula B. Ambrosii,* 236.

She was made so demented and was so out of her senses, as much from grief as from diabolic influence, that she used to put little worms . . . into her mouth and eat them. The father was saddened, and he sent her across the Rhine, hoping that the change of air would do her good, and that she might be liberated from the incubus demon through the interposition of the river. After the girl was sent across, the demon appeared to the priest and said in shouting words (*apertis vocibus*), "Wicked priest, why have you stolen my wife from me?"[75]

Thus the Rhine formed some sort of boundary that the demon could not cross. Perhaps it was the territory of some other spiritual entity, on which he hesitated to infringe. Alternatively, perhaps immersion in water somehow "returned" the possessing spirit to its natural sphere: if one can be possessed by entering a stream, perhaps one can undo the possession in the same way. The stress on the active quality of the water—it must be moving—may also be related to these concerns: its mobile quality may have been seen as an indication of an inhabiting spirit that gave it life. Exorcists' manuals advise against immersion as a curative procedure: "Put aside the superstition that the ignorant hold, to send [possessed persons] to running rivers."[76]

Indeed, the intimate cosmology of local belief is better described as animist than as demonic or eschatological. This is seen, as well, in the character of possessing spirits described in these tales. The spirits that inhabit rivers and forests do not appear to be understood as fallen angels, but rather as nature elementals. In addition, possessing spirits sometimes were associated with the lingering ghosts of those who died a "bad" death through violence or crime.[77] At times these possessing spirits confessed their names, former trades, and the circumstances of their deaths through the mouths of their victims, lending verisimilitude to their identity claims. In at least one instance, such a confession led to a public disputation between a priest, who insisted that possessing spirits were demonic fallen angels, and a crowd of layfolk, who believed the spirit to be that of a recently murdered gambler named Mazzanto.[78] In sum, within the popular universe, supernatural spirits were

---

[75] *DM*, 1:121.

[76] Buonaventura Farinerio, *Exorcismo mirabile da disfare ogni sorte de malefici et da cacciare i demoni* (Venice, 1567), 361r.

[77] Nancy Caciola, "Spirits Seeking Bodies: Death, Possession, and Communal Memory in the Middle Ages," in B. Gordon and P. Marshall, eds., *The Place of the Dead: Death and Remembrance in Late Medieval and Early Modern Europe* (Cambridge, 2000), 66–86; idem, "Wraiths, Revenants and Ritual."

[78] Caciola, "Spirits Seeking Bodies" 79.

actually natural. They were associated with human beings, with forests, streams, or particular locales. Seldom were they abstract embodiments of malice, as Catholic doctrine would have it.

Yet elite and popular cultural forms often existed as contiguous interpretations along a continuum of belief. As such, the popular and the elite often shade into, rather than oppose, one another. Such is the case in an unusual tale from the canonization process of Dorothy of Montau, which may be read from dual cultural perspectives. As the victim himself testified,

> It happened one time that during Lent he disguised his face with a mask (*larva*), which he testifies that he made, and that thus disguised he went out of his house in Gdansk, saying, "I'm going to go commit some sin!" As he was leaving his house, he met someone else disguised with a mask. He didn't know who it was, and he didn't care, so he left and went to a certain brotherhood or party.... When he got there, he joined the dance, whereupon all the dancing girls and women rushed away from the dance, terrified on account of the witness being masked/enchanted (*larvatus*) that way.... When the witness took off the mask, his face was turned around backward. Taking his head in his hands, he began to twist his face around to its accustomed place, but as he was unable to do so he fell down on the ground like a dead man, destitute of reason or understanding.... His friends and everyone else standing around while he was on the ground told him that his face was amazingly similar to that of the mask he had been wearing.... The witness adds that he firmly believes that the masked man, who associated himself with him when he left his house, was an evil spirit who left him while he was at the party.[79]

This story is complex. For the ecclesiastical envoys conducting the canonization proceeding for Dorothy, the tale functions as an exemplum underlining the importance of maintaining the Lenten fast. The victim of demonic possession enthusiastically sins by breaking Lenten taboos, by attending a mixed-sex party, and by dancing, an activity that moralists' tales frequently presented as a prelude to demonic possession. This wicked series of actions apparently delivered him into the power of a demon. On the other hand, the evocative language and temporal setting of this tale, during the ember days of Lent, also gives precious clues as to how this possession case might have been read within a popular framework of interpretation.

The key to this alternate reading lies in the story's temporal setting dur-

---

[79] Stachnik, Triller, and Westpfahl, *Kanonisations-prozess Dorotheas von Montau*, 367.

ing the ember days, when processions of the dead were believed to be abroad. This was a particularly important week for the procession of the dead known as the wild horde, which made its most important yearly appearance at precisely this time.[80] The carnival masks and costumes traditionally worn during this period may have been intended as an apotropaic "disguise" to ward off the dead by pretending to be one of them;[81] while the carnival tradition of loud clashings of cymbals, drums, and bells may have served protective or exorcistic functions against possession by ghosts of the wandering dead.[82] The possibility that the possessing spirit may have been drawn from among the dead, rather than from among the fallen angels, is emphasized by the repetition of the word *larva* and its variants. The word means either ghost or mask, while the variant *larvatus* may mean either masked or enchanted (literally, "ghosted," possessed by a ghost). The snarled web of symbolic linkages within medieval folklore among demons, masks, possession, and the dead is rich indeed. To put on a mask (*larva*) is to commune with the spirits of the dead, to adopt the identity of a ghost (*larva*), and thus to risk becoming possessed by a ghost (*larvatus*). From this perspective, the man's misfortune was actually to encounter one of these wandering trickster spirits, who enacted a typically playful, though frightening, practical joke on him. What is fascinating is how well the tale functions within both semantic fields.

To sum up, demonic possession was a labile cultural category. The most stable element of the conception was the predominance of female victims: though males could be possessed, women were more common as energumens. Aside from the sex of the possessed, however, demoniacs are described in varied ways. They may be rigidly entranced or thrashing about in a frenzy, struck mute or endowed with prophetic gifts, extremely passive or preternaturally strong and aggressive. At the heart of all these symptoms, however, lies an understanding of demonic possession as an intimate—and violent—invasion of the body. This invasive entity makes its presence known through the victim's adoption of an extreme behavioral and gestural code. Thus fren-

[80] See Karl Meisen, *Die Sagen vom wütenden Heer und wilder Jäger* (Münster, 1938), 39, under "Chronicon Saxonicum." See also Claude Gaignebet and Marie-Claude Florentin, *Le carnival: Essai de mythologie populaire* (Paris, 1979).

[81] Richard Bernheimer, *Wild Men in the Middle Ages* (Cambridge, 1952), 78; Carlo Ginzburg, "Charivari, associations juvéniles, chasse sauvage," in J. LeGoff and J.-C. Schmitt, eds., *Le charivari* (Paris, 1981), 131–40, for discussion of links between the wild horde and other masked processions; on masks, Jean-Claude Schmitt, "Les masques, le diable, les morts," in *Le corps, les rites, les rêves, le temps: Essais d'anthropologie médiévale* (Paris, 2001), 211–37.

[82] Nicole Belmont, "Fonction de la dérision et symbolisme du bruit dans le charivari," in Le Goff and Schmitt, *Le charivari*, 15–21.

zies and trances both were viewed as the eruption, onto the surface of the body, of an otherwise hidden interior state of disorder. These immoderate actions rendered the demoniac an antisocial being on the fringes of civilization, as she adopted violent, bestial or immodest behaviors. As a result, demoniacs frequently were tied up to prevent them from harming themselves or others. Yet, demoniacs could exhibit socially beneficial traits. Prophecies, xenoglossy, inspired preaching, and occult knowledge sometimes turned energumens into public spectacles who attracted crowds of the curious. Such possessed behaviors also testified to the subordination of the victim's own personality to that of the possessing spirit who spoke through her mouth, exhibited its own supernatural powers, and recounted its own demonic history. Lastly, the emphasis in both texts and images upon the use of a particular orifice as an entry or exit point reinforces the literal sense of the demoniac's physical incorporation of the spirit. Possession thus is sustained by a tension between the interior and the exterior of the human body, as spirits move into the body, replace its human identity, and transform its exterior comportment. The integrity of the possessed victim is disrupted as the body is invaded and remolded, and the identity of the possessing spirit becomes dominant.

DIVINE POSSESSION

A New Cultural Idiom

Let us now turn to divine spirit possession. As in the case of the demonically possessed, the observations to follow will not add up to a single, unitary definition, for perceptions of what it meant to be divinely possessed varied across time and between different social groups. Thus the following pages focus on the broad contours of how the category of divine possession was constructed within medieval culture, collating various texts that employ common topoi or themes in order to build up a detailed description of the concept. What attributes were singled out for attention when medieval people described someone whom they believed to be possessed by the spirit of God?

Two aspects of the category deserve immediate prominence. First, the divinely possessed were a new conceptual category. Unlike the category of demonic possession, which had an unbroken history since the time of Jesus, serious, plural claims to possession by the Holy Spirit had not been advanced in the Latin West since the demise of Montanism. Second, the divinely possessed, like the demonically possessed, were mostly women. These two aspects of the category were linked in the minds of many medieval contemporaries, who commented upon them together. Hildegard of Bingen dated the beginning of a *muliebre tempus*—an "effeminate age"—to around 1100, close to her own date of birth.[83] Subsequent writers also explicitly commented on the diffusion of a new and uniquely female strain of religiosity that flourished between the late twelfth and the fifteenth centuries, thus ratifying Hildegard's perception. Jacques de Vitry wrote at length concerning the devotional conduct of the new Beguine movement in the Low Countries, and in his letters he noted the high number of female tertiaries in Italy.[84] Lamprecht of Regensburg in the thirteenth century spoke of how a new "art" of feminine piety was being pioneered in Brabant and Bavaria.[85] These sentiments were echoed in Italy by Raymond of Capua, who commented, "What is even more to be marveled at, and in my opinion to be taken notice of, is that these days an abundance of grace seems to be operating particularly in the weaker (that is, the female) sex."[86] And Raymond's brother-Dominican Franciscus Silvestris, in the late fifteenth century, noted that "there are a great number of women who . . . exceed men in sanctity and charity."[87] Thus several highly placed late medieval men were struck by what they perceived as a new phenomenon of holy laywomen adopting leadership roles alongside—or even above—men.

However, these statements were not entirely unambiguous. Their marveling tone belies the essentially controversial character of this new movement. Medievalists have long become used to reading the phrase "new and unheard-of" as strongly derogatory. Novelty was dangerous in the eyes of medieval contemporaries, and comments about religious innovation have a more intimate association with the history of heresy than with that of sanctity. In this context, the idea of a new effeminate age appears fraught with ambivalences. In fact, Hildegard's statement was not sounded on a celebratory note. The necessity for women to take on positions of leadership, far from being liberating, was for the "Sibyl of the Rhine" a sign of the world's senescence. Men, having become weak, had ceded their natural preeminence to women, who are not suited to lead. This inversion of gender roles was distinctly detrimental to civilization. Indeed, the concept of the effeminate age

---

[83] Barbara Newman, *Sister of Wisdom: St. Hildegard's Theology of the Feminine* (Berkeley, 1987), 239.

[84] Jacques de Vitry's comments are in *Vita Mariae*, 847–49.

[85] Lamprecht von Regensburg, *Sankt Francisken Leben und Tochter Syon*, ed. K. Weinhold (Paderborn, 1880), 430.

[86] *VCS*, 863.

[87] *Vita B. Osannae Mantuanae, AASS*, June 4:577–78.

had strong eschatological valences; it was a corrosive image evoking the descent into sin and immorality that was thought to herald the approach of the End Times. Hildegard's comments became widely known after the 1220s, when many of her prophetic writings were gathered together by the monk Gebeno of Eberbach in a compilation titled the *Mirror of Future Times*.[88] As we will see, the ambiguous associations of the effeminate age encapsulate many of the contradictions of the history of discerning spirits.

Similar misgivings were present in other writers. Raymond of Capua's remark (quoted above) ends with the words "perhaps [this is] in order to confound the pride of men." On the one hand, these writers viewed the achievements of individual holy women as remarkable; on the other hand, they found the idea of female leadership anathema, a rebuke to male undiscipline. Moreover, since medieval religious women were deeply attracted to "the magic of extremes," they could become sources of contentious debate among observers.[89] Thus Lamprecht of Regensburg went on, in his poem "Tochter Syon," to warn against women visionaries' lack of moderation (*Mâze*) and their attraction to exaggerated behaviors and lifestyles.[90] It was this very extremism that was to be the propulsive force behind the revival of the discernment of spirits debate.

The new notion of the divinely possessed laywoman became a familiar idiom by the mid-thirteenth century. Thus in 1240 a chronicler described how one aspiring visionary "saw many silly women (*mulierculae*) flourish under the appearance of religion . . . , who are called Beguines, and she wanted to imitate them in words and deeds."[91] Similarly, another thirteenth-century laywoman aspiring to holiness declared to friends at the outset of her career, "The time will come when you will call me saint, for saint shall I be."[92] Both women went on to display quite similar behaviors: rejection of social life and individual reclusion, frequent fasting, and reports of raptures and revelations as well as of demonic torments. In short, they engaged in a form of public self-fashioning aimed at presenting themselves to an audience as divinely inspired visionaries. Medieval observers, for their part, realized that these women exhibited a particular set of behaviors that constituted a distinct re-

---

[88] André Vauchez, "Le prophétisme médiéval d'Hildegarde de Bingen à Savanarole," in *Saints, prophètes et visionnaires: Le pouvoir surnaturel au Moyen Age* (Paris, 1999), 114–33; *Speculum futurorum temporum*, ed. J.-B. Pitra, in idem *Analecta sacra spicilegio Solesmensi parata* (Paris, 1876–91), vol. 8.

[89] André Vauchez, *Sainthood in the Middle Ages*, trans. J. Birrell (Cambridge, 1997), 354.

[90] Lamprecht von Regensburg, *Tochter Syon*, 436–37.

[91] Richer of Sens, *Gesta Senonensis ecclesiae* 4.18, in L. d'Achery, ed., *Spicilegium sive collectio veterum aliquot scriptorum qui in Galliae bibliothecis delituerunt* (Paris, 1723), 634.

[92] *VMC*, 184.

ligious profile, understood that this was a new ideal of religious devotion, and labored to understand the broader social and spiritual implications of these patterns.

Incorporation Again

The Latin vocabulary for demonic possession and its victims is quite rich— *possessio, obsessio, arreptitio, daemoniaci, energumeni, indaemoniati, vexati*—but there are no equivalent words for divine possession. Rather, the language used to describe the latter state often was vague and circumlocutory. Yet divine possession was recognized by medieval theorists and seen as a direct parallel to demonic possession, despite this slippage between words and ideas. Medieval writers, such as those quoted in the introductory section to this chapter, discussed the two states together and stressed their similarities.

We may begin with the essentially incorporative character of this religious idiom.[93] The indwelling, penetrative, and unitive character of medieval women's relationship to Christ or the Holy Spirit is explicit in the texts:

Christ is joined to [her] and she is made one spirit with him. . . . Who can imagine a sweeter inhabitant than God Himself?[94]

It is I, the Holy Spirit, who enters you.[95]

I [Christ] shall place my words in your mouth. Through your speech you will penetrate the hearts of your listeners, and they will recognize beyond any doubt that I speak through you.[96]

She had [the gift of] reading minds, and of knowing the intent of the heart, through the Holy Spirit which lived inside her.[97]

One woman actually was called "Holy Spirit" by her devotees,[98] and there may also have existed paintings of women in this role. A sinopia from the apse of the Abbey of Viboldone near Milan, originally a Humiliati foundation, de-

---

[93] J. Deploige, "Intériorisation religieuse et propagande hagiographique dans les Pays-Bas méridionaux du 11e au 13e siècle," *Revue d'histoire ecclésiastique* 94, 3–4 (1999): 808–31.

[94] Peter of Dacia, *Vita Christinae Stumblensis,* ed. Johannes Paulson (Göteborg, 1896; reprint, Frankfurt am Main, 1985), 77–78.

[95] *Vita Angelae de Fulgino,* 194.

[96] *Vita B. Margaritae Faventinae, AASS,* August 5:850.

[97] *De B. Juetta sive Jutta, vidua reclusa Hui in Belgio, AASS,* January 2:161.

[98] F. Tocco, "Il processo dei Guglielmiti," *Rendiconti della reale accademia dei lincei, classe di scienze morali, storiche, e filologiche,* ser. 4, 7 (1899): 309–84, 407–69.

Figure 3. An unusual representation of the Trinity. This fourteenth-century sinopia shows the underlying sketch for a fresco that either was never completed or was destroyed. The sketch represents the Trinity, as shown by its location in the apse, over the main altar of the church, and the cruciform haloes of the figures, an iconography reserved for images of the divine. Sinopia for a fresco by an unknown artist, fourteenth century. Milan: Abbey of Viboldone, church apse. Photo by Richard S. Cohen.

picts a Trinitarian group holding eucharistic chalices (figs. 3 and 4). The personage on the left, with a beardless face and a curvy physique, appears to be female. The triune composition of the group, their cruciform haloes, the eucharistic reference, and the gestural parallelisms among the three figures strongly suggests a Trinitarian reading.[99] In fact, we know that a prominent cult for a woman as Holy Spirit existed in this area: the devotees of Guglielma.[100] The logical extension of the idiom of divine possession is self-

[99] *Un monastero alle porte della città: Atti del convegno per i 650 anni dell'Abbazia di Viboldone* (Milan, 1999); Mari Moro, *L'Abbazia di Viboldone: Storia, arte, vita religiosa* (Milan, 1995). For discussion of cross-gendered typologies of Christ in images, see Susan Smith, "The Bride Stripped Bare: A Rare Type of the Disrobing of Christ," *Gesta* 34, 2 (1995): 126–46; and on images of female dominance, idem, *The Power of Women: A Topos in Medieval Art and Literature* (Philadelphia 1995).

[100] Tocco, "Processo dei Guglielmiti," is the main primary source. While the Abbey of Viboldone does not appear in the process, the nearby Abbey of Chiaravalle does so prominently. Since Guglielma's most prominent woman follower, Mayfreda de Pirovano,

Figure 4. Guglielma, the female Holy Spirit? This detail of figure 3 shows the person on the left in the group. The physique is clearly that of a woman, with the unmistakable curve of her right breast visible under her gown. This area of Milan was the setting for a contemporary cult of veneration for the so-called female Holy Spirit, a woman named Guglielma. Photo by Richard S. Cohen.

identity with the spirit of God, as the woman speaks divine prophecies, reads the minds of others, and in a sense becomes part of the Godhead. In some cases, divinely possessed women's faces even were said to be temporarily transfigured into the likeness of Christ, with bearded melancholy features. Thus was the visionary re-sexed and remolded into the physical image of the indwelling divine spirit.[101] Similarly, many divinely possessed women were reputed to bear stigmata, which sometimes remained open and bleeding.[102] This last miracle, while self-evidently a signifier of spiritual union with Christ, also had a complex theological background that can briefly be sketched. Since reception of the stigmata often followed upon a vision of mystical marriage, the wounds seem to have been regarded as a literalizing of the canon law principle that through marriage the two spouses are made one flesh. Thus in marrying Jesus, the woman subsequently took on the most distinctive marks of the bridegroom's incarnate flesh: the signs of the passion. Variants on this motif involved diverse forms of miraculous bleeding from the eyes, nose, or mouth.[103] Thus beyond claims to privileged speech and knowledge through possession by the divine lay a variety of incorporative motifs and behaviors that were both highly materialist and richly symbolic.

Just as descriptions of demonic possession focused upon the mouth as the most important point of access into and out from the body, so too descriptions of divine possession had their own anatomical preoccupations. The Holy Spirit frequently is described as entering into, and then remaining

---

was a Humiliata who spent time at the Abbey of Chiaravalle, it seems possible that she had links to the nearby Humiliati foundation at Viboldone. For treatments, see Marina Benedetti, *Io non sono Dio: Guglielma di Milano e i figli dello Spirito Santo* (Milan, 1998); Luisa Muraro, *Guglielma e Maifreda: Storia di un'eresia femminista* (Milan, 1985); Stephen Wessley, "The Thirteenth-Century Guglielmites: Salvation through Women," in D. Baker, ed. *Medieval Women* (Oxford, 1978), 289–304; Barbara Newman "WomanSpirit, Woman Pope," in *From Virile Woman to WomanChrist: Studies in Medieval Religion and Literature* (Philadelphia, 1995), 182–223; Alain Boureau, *The Myth of Pope Joan*, trans. L. Cochraine (Chicago, 2001), 171–78.

[101] *VCS*, 884; Peter of Dacia, *Vita Christinae*, 244.

[102] For literature, see Herbert Thurston, *The Physical Phenomena of Mysticism* (Chicago, 1952); Pierre Debognie, "Essai critique sur l'histoire des stigmatisations au Moyen Age," *Études Carmelitaines* 21, 2 (1936): 22–59; Caroline Bynum, *Holy Feast and Holy Fast: The Religious Significance of Food to Medieval Women* (Berkeley, 1987). The early symbolic history of stigmatization as a form of tattooing is discussed in Susanna Elm, "'Pierced by Bronze Needles?' Anti-Montanist Charges of Ritual Stigmatization in their Fourth-Century Context," *Journal of Early Christian Studies* 4 (1996): 409–39.

[103] *Vita Idae Virginis*, 163, 164, 174; Peter of Dacia, *Vita Christinae*, 237; *De Lidwina Virgine*, 293; 304–5. See Caroline Bynum, "' . . . and Woman His Humanity': Female Imagery in the Religious Writing of the Later Middle Ages" and "The Female Body and Religious Practice in the Later Middle Ages," both in *Fragmentation and Redemption: Essays on Gender and the Human Body in Medieval Religion* (New York, 1991), 151–79, 181–238.

within, the possessed woman's heart. One example of this motif is Ida of Louvain, with whom this chapter began: her divine possession and pursuit of poverty resulted from her belief that she had incorporated the poor Christ into her heart. Others claimed to bear Christ crucified in their hearts, to have exchanged hearts with Jesus, or to have supernaturally expanded hearts from the infusion of the Holy Spirit.[104] Nor were these simply metaphorical understandings. Rather, they were quite literal and material expressions of incorporation, into the human body, of the divine. Finally, some religious laywomen were reported to manifest a severe bloating that they explained as being made "pregnant" with Christ, in yet another image of literal incorporation.[105] One woman claimed that Christ had first purified her heart, explaining that it is "in order that it might be a fit living space (*habitaculum*) for me to inhabit frequently"; and then "the individual things that are inside you, that is, skin, veins, blood, and bones."[106] Yet when Christ actually took up residence inside her, he entered her womb:

Her bridegroom . . . made her uterus as large as if she had within it a remarkably large living fetus already close to parturition, and the character of it was such that she weighed more from the bearing of it and the pressure, than if she were bearing in her uterus a huge natural fetus. For on account of the inconvenience and the constriction of the pressure she was undecided where and how she should turn herself, or in what way to sit down, lie down, stand, or walk. . . . To this the Lord responded, "I have generously come to you with a violent affection, desiring to do you a great violence in your body. I desire that it should give birth to me into your soul. But how would my bride be able to know that she had conceived me or that she was bearing me if I did not grow or increase within her?"[107]

Another laywoman likewise claimed to be pregnant—possessed—with a baby Jesus who leapt and moved within her; her spiritual director claimed to have observed these spunky fetal movements through her skin.[108] Indeed, it may be that the association of women with pregnancy contributed to the

---

[104] For further discussion see chapter 4.

[105] Hillary Graham, "The Social Image of Pregnancy: Pregnancy as Spirit Possession," *Sociological Review* 24, 2 (1976): 291–308.

[106] Stachnik, Triller, and Westpfahl, *Kanonisations-prozess Dorotheas von Montau*, 163.

[107] Ibid., 319–20.

[108] Arne Jönsson, ed., *Alfonso of Jaén: His Life and Works with Critical Editions of the* Epistola solitarii, *the* Informaciones *and the* Epistola servi Christi (Lund, 1989), 137.

Figure 5. Transparent visitation scene, allowing the viewer to peer inside the female body and see other bodies inside. Sculptured visitation group from Katharinenthal, thirteenth century. New York: The Metropolitan Museum of Art. Photo by Richard S. Cohen.

broad sense that they were particularly apt at incorporating other bodies within their own. A thirteenth-century sculpture of the Visitation sums up this series of associations nicely (fig. 5). Mary and Elizabeth embrace while turning slightly outward to show their torsos, covered with transparent crystals that extend from their hearts to their wombs. Painted inside would have been the images of Christ and the Baptist. The piece viscerally represents the sense of the female body as incorporative, as formed with a transparent integument that links exterior and interior, and here unveils the interior incorporation of the divine body.

The set of somatic miracles associated with religious women—stigmata, other bleedings, bloating, facial transfigurations—not only was a broad manifestation of the essential "corporeity" of feminine devotion, but also an expression of something narrower and more precise: the literal interior incorporation of the divine. The observable physical transformations that were so distinctive to religious laywomen were viewed by sympathetic devotees as an outburst, to the surface of the body, of characteristics derived from their interior union with the Holy Spirit. Thus cases of levitation frequently were attributed to a divine spiritualizing of the physical body that rendered it lighter than air.[109] Fasting, too, was described as the result of a spiritualizing process that freed the body from its mundane needs.[110] In sum, the external body was regarded as a fluid representation of the individual's internal state, a highly expressive material aggregate of her spiritual transformation. From the medieval perspective, the somatic miracles so frequently reported of such women merely made visible a hidden truth: the Holy Spirit dwelt within that body.

Interior and Exterior

Although the divinely possessed were described by their admirers as being in constant contact with God, and as being physically and intellectually transformed by this union, there were moments when their state of possession was particularly overwhelming and intense. It was during these times that the individual entered into trances, witnessed visions, and gained access to prophetic revelations. Indeed, women's claims to be divinely inspired seers were predicated largely on the visions and revelations they reported having

---

[109] Lucetta Scaraffia (*La santa degli impossibili: Vicende e significati della devozione a Santa Rita* [Turin, 1990], 71–87) discusses the ambiguities of flight and levitation. See also Pierre Debognie, "Les lévitations de saint Brigitte de Suède," *Revue d'histoire ecclésiastique* 34, 1 (1938): 70–83.

[110] *Vita Lutgartis*, 192; for fasting, see Bynum, *Holy Feast and Holy Fast.*

received during trances, which represented the apotheosis of their possession. These trances are described as states that transcended bodily boundaries and individual self-consciousness. Either the woman's spirit would leave her body entirely and visit supernatural realms, or it would recede into her deepest depths, relying only on her "interior senses." There were four of the latter: common sense, fantasy or imagination, estimation, and memory.[111] Retraction to these interior senses was understood to be a means of communing with the more imaginative and visionary possibilities of the human intellect. Aquinas explained that the soul was more sensitive to spiritual impressions (both divine and demonic), when in a state of rapture, absent the distractions of external sensory stimuli.[112]

Since the visions themselves could not be authenticated or corroborated by others, medieval observers scrutinized what they could: the physical condition of the seer's body and her comportment, especially during the trance state and its immediate aftermath. There existed a strong consensus that a true state of trance would render the individual rigid, immobile, and insensible.[113] This complete insensibility commonly was described as miraculously resistant to all stimuli, no matter how intense: rough handling, pinpricks, even dental surgery.[114] Indeed, so completely immobilizing was the trance state thought to be, it often was likened to a temporary death:

> I approached her bed and . . . placed my hand before her mouth, and absolutely no, or very faint, breath or respiration was coming from her mouth and nostrils. And so a certain monk who was with me said she was in trance, and that her spirit was not inside her vitals. . . . With her eyes closed, lying supine on the bed, she gave no sign of life, no breath or respiration of the living; yet she gave no sound or noise of the sleep-

---

[111] Aquinas was the origin of this idea in the West, following Avicenna and Aristotle. See Thomas Aquinas, *Summa theologica*, pars prima, quaest. 78, art. 4; Ruth Harvey, *The Inward Wits* (London, 1975). See also Deploige, "Intériorisation religieuse"; on rapture, see Richard Kieckhefer, *Unquiet Souls: Fourteenth-Century Saints and their Religious Milieu* (Chicago, 1984), 150–79; Dyan Elliott, "The Physiology of Rapture and Female Spirituality," in Biller and Minnis, *Medieval Theology*, 141–74.

[112] Thomas Aquinas, *Summa theologiae*, 2a 2ae, quaest. 172, reply art. 1, p. 32.

[113] See Donald Weinstein and Rudolph Bell, *Saints and Society: Christendom, 1000–1700* (Chicago, 1982), 229; CPCS, 263; *Vita Osannae*, 571; *Acta S. Francescae Romanae, AASS*, March 2:105; *Vita Columbae*, 163; *Vita Lukardis*, 317–18.

[114] Daniel Bornstein, "Violenza al corpo di una santa: fra agiografia e pornografia: a proposito di Douceline di Digne," *Quaderni Medievali* 39 (1995): 31–46. Also see *VCS*, 962 (rough handling and a sunburn); *Vita Humilianae de' Cerchi, AASS*, May 3:394 (dental surgery).

ing; so that she looked like nothing so much as a dead woman, except for the flush on her face.[115]

During such [trances] you might see flies . . . gather on her eyes, which she always held partly open at such times. [Her eyelids] would not move about or flutter up and down, and so they seemed to be the eyes, not of a living person, but of someone already dead.[116]

This last, unattractive detail seems to have been selected precisely in order to confirm the idea of trance as a temporary death, both in terms of the subject's insensibility and in presenting her as a sort of carrion. Not surprisingly, we know of some cases in which family members called in a doctor to see whether or not an entranced woman was still alive.[117]

Some descriptions of trance emphasize in clinical detail the progressive rigidity that sweeps over the body of the divinely possessed woman as she enters into the state:

The extremities of her body, that is her hands and feet, used to contract. It would begin in the fingers, actually, but at last reach the [hands and feet] themselves. In the places where they were touching, they were joined together so rigidly that they would be crushed or broken before they could be moved in any way from their place. Her eyes used to close entirely, and her neck would dissolve with rigidity, such that it was no small danger to her body to touch her neck at that time.[118]

The rigidity of the body that is so emphasized by this author found counterparts among others' observations.[119] Aquinas, for example, treated the question of ecstasy at length in his *Summa theologica*, while noting that seemingly identical trances could occur from natural, demonic, and divine causes. In addition, however, Aquinas made a distinction between ecstasy and the even more intense experience of rapture: "Rapture adds something to ecstasy. For ecstasy means simply 'to be outside oneself.' . . . But rapture adds a certain violence to this."[120] The distinction between ecstasy and the violent "taking" of rapture was not widespread outside Aquinas's highly intellectual

[115] *De B. Alpaide Virgine*, 183–84.
[116] E. Paoli and L. Ricci, eds., *La Legenda di Vanna da Orvieto* (Spoleto, 1996), 145.
[117] *Vita Columbae*, 163.
[118] *VCS*, 893.
[119] See Peter of Dacia, *Vita Christinae Stumblensis*, 34, where an observer considers a trance to be inauthentic because the body is not rigid.
[120] Thomas Aquinas, *Summa theologiae*, 2a 2ae, quaest. 175, reply art. 2, p. 100.

milieu, for non-elite writers tended to use the two words interchangeably. Yet the expectation that a trance involved insensibility was broadly shared by less learned or sophisticated people. Indeed, the notion formed part of the broader common sense of medieval culture.[121] Thus a female witness at a canonization proceeding defined rapture thus: "Asked, 'What is rapture?' she said that she believed that rapture is an intense and powerful elevation of the mind into God. She said that when someone is in rapture, they feel nothing, nor perceive external stimuli with their corporeal senses."[122] The reason for this complete insensibility was that the spirit was literally absent from the body. A common metaphor was that the body "clothed" the spirit like a garment or cloak that could temporarily be cast off and put on again. Jacques de Vitry described the relationship between the human spirit and human body thus: "The spirit existed inside the body as if laying inside a clay jar; the body surrounded and clothed the spirit like a clay vestment. Hence she was removed from her senses, and taken above herself into a certain abstracted trance."[123]

Yet not all trance states were passive. Occasionally, a divinely possessed woman in a state of trance was described as producing sound, apparently involuntarily. Thomas of Cantimpré gives at least two instances of this phenomenon, one in a hagiographical text and another in *On Bees*, in which a woman produces an inchoate sound between her chest and her throat.[124] Others, while remaining insensible, did *not* remain immobile. Indeed, insensible trance states sometimes were paired with extreme physical and emotional outbursts, and these unpredictable oscillations left observers puzzled and embarrassed. "[Sometimes] suddenly and unexpectedly she would be rapt in spirit and her body would twist around into a whirling circle, like the rattles children play with. She whirled around with such extreme violence that one could not make out the shape of the individual limbs of her body."[125] Another putatively divinely-possessed woman broke out in boils, and banged her head about wildly.[126] The convulsions and contortions described in passages such as these were perhaps more dramatic than the immobilizing form of trance, but either could elicit confused or negative reactions from observers.

[121] In the sense meant by Clifford Geertz, "Common Sense as a Cultural System," *Antioch Review* 33 (1975): 5–26.
[122] *Antico processo della beata Chiara da Montefalco*, Vatican City: ASV Riti. 2929, f. 45v.
[123] *Vita Mariae*, 552.
[124] *De Christina Mirabilis*, AASS, July 5:656; *De Ap.* 2.41.3, 411. The reference in *De Apibus* could perhaps be to Christina.
[125] Ibid.
[126] Peter of Dacia, *Vita Christinae Stumblensis*, 43, 3–4, respectively.

Intellectual Gifts

The incorporative character of the category of divine possession was manifested not just through physical alterations and eruptions but also through supernaturally heightened intellectual capacities. The idea that Christ possessed, or inhabited, the individual and spoke through her mouth was one that many aspiring holy women and their supporters wished to promote. Implicit in this notion was the expectation that the possessed woman would receive knowledge and intellectual gifts beyond her natural capacities. Thus prophetic powers or occult knowledge were commonly ascribed to individuals who were thought to have special contact with the Holy Spirit. One was said to be able to tell when alms given to her were wrongly acquired, and also was credited with the ability to foresee events occurring at a far distance, including the outcome of military campaigns in the Holy Land.[127] There are tales of divinely possessed women speaking previously unknown foreign tongues—the gift of xenoglossy—when a need for such skills arose.[128] Thomas of Cantimpré relates the case of a woman who saw, in trance, the visages of all those to be saved and whether they would be virgins, widows, or married at the time of their death. Verification of her powers was provided to Thomas, "as clear as day," by the fact that she also had gained occult knowledge of his hidden thoughts, which he had revealed only to his confessor.[129] Many a divinely possessed woman was said to fall into a visionary trance state in which she witnessed the events of the Apocalypse unfold, from the advent of the Antichrist to the Resurrection and Last Judgment; others reported detailed tours of Hell and Purgatory.[130]

These supernatural prerogatives were viewed as a logical side effect of divine possession. The notion that these women had received supernatural intellectual gifts effectively highlights the disruption of individual identity inherent in the phenomenon of spirit possession. Thus in the same way that certain demoniacs were said to relay the indwelling demon's memories of the angelic Fall, so too the holy woman possessed by the Holy Spirit could speak in God's voice and see into others' hearts and minds. Possession is characterized by an unstable sense of deixis, a conception that more than one spirit or "self" coexisted within a single body and competed for preeminence.

---

[127] *De Christina Mirabilis,* 655.
[128] *Vita Lutgartis,* 203; *VCS,* 890.
[129] *De Ap.* 2.50.6, 461.
[130] *De B. Alpaide Virgine,* 184–95.

An Antisocial Immoderation

The most controversial aspect of the category of divine possession, as described in the texts, was the disregard of social convention that frequently was displayed by holy women. As Richard Kieckhefer has termed it, such individuals had "unquiet souls."[131] Many texts purporting to describe the divinely possessed, for example, note that these women were thought to be insane on account of their antisocial behavior, while others were described as acting drunk.[132] One was examined by doctors who checked for a physiological basis for her peculiarities;[133] another was accused of being brain damaged.[134] Yet another recounted her memory of a very public seizure or frenzy to her cousin thus:

> I began to shriek in a loud voice, and to scream, and to shout, and I was shrieking without any shame. . . . I wanted to form [words] and to speak, but I could not form [words] . . . and so my speech wasn't understood by anyone who heard it. This shriek and this clamor happened to me in the entrance hall of the church of Saint Francis. . . . I was sitting there languishing and shrieking and shouting in front of everyone, so much so that the people who had come with me and who were known to me stood apart at a distance, embarrassed, thinking that [this had happened] from another cause.[135]

This so-called "gift of tears," a supernatural capacity for penitential remorse, was reported of many lay religious women, and was expressed as frenetic shouting, sobbing, and convulsions when overcome with religious impulses.[136]

Another extreme example of a holy woman's disregard for social convention—indeed, a profoundly antisocial avoidance of human contact—is as follows:

---

[131] Kieckhefer, *Unquiet Souls*, esp. 180–202.

[132] *Vita Idae Virginis*, 164, 172; *Vita S. Julianae Corneliensis, AASS*, April 1:448.

[133] *Vita Columbae*, 187.

[134] Isak Collijn, ed., *Acta et Processus Canonizationis Beate Birgitte: Samlingar utgivna av Svenska Fornskriftsällskapet*, ser. 2, Latinska Skrifter (Upsalla, 1924–31), 1:488.

[135] *Vita Angelae de Fulgino*, 194.

[136] *Vita Idae Virginis*, 164, 172; *VMC*, 320; *De Christina Mirabilis*, 656; Peter of Dacia, *Vita Christinae Stumblensis;* Margery Kempe, *The Book of Margery Kempe*, ed. B. Windeatt (New York, 2000). For an extended treatment of the motif, see Piroska Nagy, *Le don de larmes au Moyen Age* (Paris, 2000).

[She] fled from the presence of men with incredible horror, going to deserted places, up trees, to the tops of towers or churches or any high place. . . . She used to go into furnaces vomiting fire. . . . She would often enter the graves of the dead. . . . On another occasion she got up in the middle of the night and, provoking all the dogs . . . to bark, ran before them like a fleeing beast. . . . Like a sparrow, she hung from the smallest branches of the trees.[137]

Not surprisingly, observers regarded this woman with hostility mingled with pity, and she often was bound with ropes and chains. In another extreme case, a possessed woman fell into the town water supply (prompting fears of contamination), and wandered through both city and countryside stark naked.[138] Indeed, in her nude peregrinations she made a point of visiting every religious foundation she knew. Most controversially, she was infamous for strange episodes in which invisible demons covered her body with supernaturally produced shit.[139] Deprived of human comfort, she turned for companionship to the fish and the animals, whose language she believed she understood.[140]

Such transgressions of social convention—of the principle of ordered bodily comportment, and of the modesty and mildness that was expected of women in particular—were challenging to observers. Could there be a divine disorder? Not according to Aquinas, who noted that "alienation from the senses does not occur in [true] prophets with any disordering of nature, as it does in the possessed or the insane, but through some ordered cause."[141] In this sentiment, Aquinas was not far removed from the sensibilities of local communities. Even close neighbors or kin to such women perceived their distortions of nature as profoundly antisocial and troubling. Several women described as divinely possessed by admirers nonetheless were tied up or chained by family who found them unbearable to live with. Regarded with a mixture of shame and fear, the extremism of many divinely-possessed women repelled those who had to coexist with them. The angry husband of one such

---

[137] An encapsulation of *De Christina Mirabilis*, 652–53.

[138] Neither of these incidents from the vita of Christina of Stommeln appear in the edition by Paulson, which in fact leaves out some fifty pages present in the *Acta Sanctorum* version. Paulson apparently found these elements too objectionable to include. This section is from *Acta B. Christinae Stumblensis, AASS*, June 5:302; 295. Henceforth cited as *Acta B. Christinae Stumblensis (AASS* ed).

[139] Peter of Dacia, *Vita Christinae*, 43.

[140] *Acta B. Christinae Stumblensis (AASS* ed.), 296.

[141] Thomas Aquinas, *Summa theologiae*, 2a 2ae, quaest. 173, reply art. 4, p. 62.

woman "bound [her] at home for three days with a chain."[142] This kind of example could readily be multiplied. Reactions of this sort demonstrate the degree to which such women were considered incapable of regulating themselves or of living freely within human society. Binding and chaining are treatments for those who, like animals or demoniacs, are bereft of human reason or sense.

Some such behaviors were attributed to the belief that those in close contact with God become targets of demonic persecution. According to the data given in Donald Weinstein and Rudolph Bell's *Saints and Society*, the vitae of females were far more likely than those of males to emphasize struggles with demons as a major component of their supernatural power.[143] And the most intense exemplars of this phenomenon were the divinely possessed, such as the Beguine who reported a series of humiliating and creative demonic attacks: visions of her food being infested with toads and snakes, being befouled with various unclean substances, and images of her own dismemberment and vivisection.[144] Other visionaries fell prey to demons who tormented them with sexual visions: rehearsing memories of youthful erotic enjoyments, forcing the visionary to lay with a male corpse, and even prompting libidinous thoughts about a particularly well-formed crucifix.[145] This predilection of demons for women recluses, Beguines, and tertiaries stems from three sources. First, women, as the "weaker sex" were viewed as the natural target of demonic seductions and temptations. All daughters of Eve were suspect, for the inheritance of their sex was a special culpability for the female role in the Fall. Second, demonic torment was considered to be a particular career risk for penitents in general.[146] As Étienne de Bourbon wrote in his treatise on the seven gifts of the Holy Spirit, "We must conduct penitence because it greatly displeases the devil. . . . It is clear from this that he attacks penitents more than others."[147] Thus the very form of religious life that was most intimately associated with women visionaries and divine possession also was linked to demonic interference.[148] Lastly, demonic attack of-

[142] Stachnik, Triller, and Westpfahl, *Kanonisations-prozess Dorotheas von Montau*, 107. See also *De Christina Mirabilis*, 652, 653.
[143] Weinstein and Bell, *Saints and Society*, 228–29.
[144] Peter of Dacia, *Vita Christinae; Acta B. Christinae Stumblensis* (*AASS* ed.).
[145] *VMC; Acta S. Francescae Romanae*. See also P. Lugano, ed. *I processi inediti per Francesca Bussa dei Ponziani (Santa Francesca Romana)* (Vatican City, 1945). On the crucifix, *Vita Clarae de Cruce Virginis, AASS*, August 3:680.
[146] Bynum, *Holy Feast and Holy Fast*; Kieckhefer, *Unquiet Souls*, 122–49.
[147] E de B, 143. The ellipses reproduce those in Lecoy de la Marche's edition.
[148] Significantly, the most common form of male penitential existence—eremeticism— also was closely associated with demonic attack.

ten was represented by penitents themselves as a direct result of their closeness to God. The devil, in his capacities as Ancient Enemy of the human race and as primal rival of God, made particular efforts to assault the special friends of God, either in the hope of making them backslide or simply out of hatred. Yet laying claim to such afflictions, while it could help undergird a reputation for divine possession, also placed the subject within a liminal and antisocial position. Those who are repeatedly attacked by demons do not make easy friends and neighbors.

Even without spectacularly antisocial behaviors, those who lay claim to divine possession frequently were regarded as flouting social conventions in smaller ways. Many of the bold ascetic demonstrations that were so characteristic of the penitential lifestyles adopted by these women—starvation-level fasting, self-flagellation, bodily mutilation, repetitive prostrations, and constant bemoaning of sin—were viewed by neighbors and kin not as an *imitatio Christi*, but as a belligerent rejection of the basic social niceties that were expected of someone who remained within the lay world. Spurning all food meant spurning the fellowship of the table; refusing marriage meant refusing to enter into social networks. Severe forms of bodily punishment certainly did not make one good company, and constant complaints about sin simply were tiresome. The contrast between the warm fellowship of the family and the cool independence of the divinely possessed religious woman is clearly evoked in descriptions such as this:

> She fled the public companionship of girls and of other people, remaining always at home and especially in her secret little room for prayer. And so when her father, during the wintertime, used to joke around at night with the family next to the fire, as is the custom of secular people, she refused to be present at such entertainments, but gave herself over to prayer and contemplation, alone in her little room.[149]

However admirable such behaviors might appear to many ecclesiastics and hagiographers, they were antithetical to the sensibilities of the laity. Medieval people assumed that an unmarried laywoman would spend time joking with her family and girlish peers: this was an interdependent society that valued easy sociability around the fire. In refusing such pleasantries, the woman risked achieving a reputation, not as a holy woman, but as an antisocial termagant or worse.

In sum, the cultural category of divine spirit possession was constructed

---

[149] *Vita Benevenutae*, 153.

as a state of interior union with God, publicly manifested through a series of exterior, physical transformations and particular possessed behaviors. The latter included frequent susceptibility to trance states, which most often would be immobile and insensible, and a disregard of lay social conventions ranging from an ascetic rejection of sociability to more extreme behaviors like convulsions, shouting, self-mutilation and self-humiliation. Not surprisingly, several texts purporting to describe the divinely-possessed noted that their protagonists were tied up or chained by unsympathetic observers, who feared they might commit some bodily harm against themselves or others. Indeed, the divinely possessed were at risk of becoming outcasts if their possessed behaviors became too extreme, and even their most fervent admirers sometimes noted their lack of moderation. Yet, the divinely possessed also could function as oracles and prophets for their communities, relaying information about deceased loved ones in the afterlife, reading minds, and foretelling events to come. For observers of the divinely possessed, the balance between these impressive intellectual feats and the antisocial immoderation of their physical comportment was a difficult one to judge.

Folk Trances

Finally, a few words about beneficent possession states within the realm of popular culture. Medieval folklore throughout Europe recognized a specifically female trance state closely analogous to divine possession. In popular culture, too, we find groups of laywomen entering into immobile and insensible trance states, during which they reportedly visited the realms of the dead and consorted with supernatural figures. Efforts to rouse such women when in this state proved fruitless: the trance was like a temporary death in which the spirit was wholly absent. These women often were credited with healing powers and oracular abilities, and sometimes they attained positions of local prestige—or marginalization—as a result of their activities. Known variously as the "good things," the "good ladies," or the "nighttime ladies," these women believed themselves to be destined, by an accident of birth, occasionally to leave their bodies in order to follow, in spirit, in the train of a mysterious female supernatural being. Germanic folklore calls this figure Perchtha or Holda, but learned discourse usually endowed her with more classical appellations, such as Diana or Herodias, or with names evocative of fertility, such as Abundia or Satia.[150] In Italy she sometimes was known

---

[150] Investigation of these ideas has been more vigorous in Continental than in Anglo-American scholarship. See Carlo Ginzburg, *The Night Battles: Witchcraft and Agrarian Cults in the Sixteenth and Seventeenth Centuries*, trans. J. Tedeschi (New York, 1983); idem, *Ec-*

as Madonna Oriente.[151] However she is designated, this mysterious being was said to hold in thrall a group of both dead and living spirits, occasionally in mixed sex companies,[152] but more frequently in exclusively female groups.

All the sources we possess about the good things are hostile, penned by churchmen who regarded these beliefs either as foolish superstitions with no basis in reality or as vivid fantasies conjured through the illusions of demons. Yet the lineaments of the belief are not difficult to discern. The good things widely were credited with a power of blessing: if they visited a household and found it well-kept, their appreciation would guarantee an increase in good fortune. Thus devotees who were not themselves called to the service of the goddess strove to please her followers by leaving out gifts of food on nights when the cavalcade of spirits was expected to be abroad.[153] William of Auvergne complained that belief in these beneficent female spirits was passed down through female generations, from old women to young: "In regard to the nighttime ladies, old women chiefly persuade [other] women that they are good ladies, and that they bestow great good things on the households that they visit."[154] Exempla writers caustically commented on this aspect of the belief by recounting the tale of a foolish peasant who allowed some male neighbors dressed in women's clothing to convince him that they were the good things, and that a gift to them would be recompensed one hundredfold. Carrying little torches and conducting a "neat little dance," the impostors sang what may have been a popular sort of "hymn" to the spirits of abundance: "Take one, return one hundred; take one, return one hundred!"[155]

The good things further were valued for their ability to converse with the

---

stasies: Deciphering the Witches' Sabbath, trans. R. Rosenthal (New York, 1991); Giuseppe Bonomo, Caccia alle streghe: La credenza nelle streghe dal secolo XIII al XIX con particolare riferimento all'Italia (Palermo, 1959); Luisa Muraro, La Signora del gioco: Episodi della caccia alle streghe (Milan, 1976); Martine Ostorero, "Folâtrer avec les demons": Sabbat et chasse aux sorciers à Vevey (1448) (Lausanne, 1995); Martine Ostorero, Agostino Paravicini Bagliani, and Kathrin Utz Tremp, L'Imaginaire du sabbat: Edition critique des textes les plus anciens (1430 c.–1440 c.) (Lausanne, 1999); Franco Cardini, Radici della stregoneria: Dalla protostoria alla cristianizzazione dell'Europa (Rimini, 2000); Jean-Claude Schmitt, Ghosts in the Middle Ages: The Living and the Dead in Medieval Society, trans. T. Fagan (Chicago, 1998); Maurizio Bertolotti, "The Ox's Bones and the Ox's Hide: A Popular Myth, Part Hagiography and Part Witchcraft," trans. E. Branch, in E. Muir and G. Ruggiero, eds., Microhistory and the Lost Peoples of Europe (Baltimore, 1991), 42–70.

[151] Bertolloti, "Ox's Bones"; Muraro, Signora del Gioco, 240–45; Bonomo, Caccia, 15–17.

[152] E de B, 88–89, is a good example of a man riding with the bonae res, who even invites a priest to accompany him, mounted on a beam.

[153] Jacobus de Voragine, Legenda aurea, ed. T. Graesse (Osnabruck, 1965), 449.

[154] William of Auvergne, De universo, 1066.

[155] E de B, 324–25.

dead. Indeed, some such women made a vocation of their abilities, as in the case of a woman named Anna la Rossa, who collected small tokens of appreciation from the living who wished to know of the fate of their dead loved ones, whom she saw in trance.[156] Some, like a woman named Sibillia, claimed that the leader of the women—the "Mistress of the Game"—revealed the future to her followers and explained other secrets and occult knowledge. To Sibillia's companion Pierina de' Bugatis, the Mistress taught knowledge of herbs and healing arts, as well as how to recover thefts and lift maleficent spells inflicted upon the innocent.[157] Clearly, the good things functioned as beneficent cunning folk within their communities, valued for their abilities as healers and ecstatic seers.

The classic description of the cult is the *Canon episcopi*, a text dating from the early tenth century. Medieval people mistakenly attributed the text to the fourth century, thus adding to its prestige. As a result, it was frequently recopied and incorporated into later compilations. The canon in its earliest form runs as follows:

> Certain wicked women, turned after Satan and seduced by the fantasies and illusions of demons, believe and assert that they ride on certain beasts at night with Diana, the Pagan Goddess, and an innumerable multitude of women, and that in the silence of the dead of night they traverse great distances over the earth. They say they must obey her as their mistress, and that they are called to serve her on certain nights. . . . [But] such fantasies enter the minds of the faithless from an evil spirit, not a divine one. For Satan transfigures himself into an angel of light; and when he has taken over the mind of some silly woman and subjugated her with faithlessness and unbelief, then he transforms himself into the appearances and simulacra of various people, and deludes her mind, which he holds captive, in dreams. . . . Although all this happens only in the spirit, the faithless mind believes that it occurs in the body, not the mind.[158]

Consideration of the good things or nighttime ladies adds to our understanding of the highly gendered character of possession states in the Middle Ages at all cultural levels. The ecstatic technique of the good things was de-

[156] Ginzburg, *Night Battles*, 33–37.

[157] The sentence pronounced against Sibillia and Pierina appears in Muraro, *Signora del Gioco*, 240–45.

[158] Joseph Hansen, *Quellen und Untersuchungen zur Geschichte des Hexenwahns und der Hexenverfolgung im Mittelalter* (Hildescheim, 1962), 38–39.

scribed in identical terms to that of the divinely possessed. In each case, the boundaries of the body were said to be transgressed by the spirit, leaving the physical shell empty and immobile; meantime, the possessed individual visits the dead, associates with divinity, and gains prophetic and healing abilities. Indeed, some contemporary authors, such as William of Auvergne, argued that precisely the same qualities that predisposed women to Dianic visions also rendered them peculiarly sensitive to divine revelations.[159] And the good things sometimes were used in discussions of discernment as a preeminent example of delusive, demonic visions targeting ignorant women. We shall return to them in later chapters.

In conclusion, I would like to propose a brief thought experiment. If, into a thirteenth-century town square, there arrived a ragged, shrieking, crying woman, how might she be categorized? Suppose she read the minds of others or prophesied some event? If she fell into a rigid trance or foaming frenzy, how might these behaviors be interpreted? To take this imaginative scenario one step further: Can we look at the women depicted in figures 1 and 2 and see holy women? For these writhing, screaming, nude, and disheveled women could well fit the descriptions that medieval texts provide of the divinely possessed.

Although the two categories of divine and demonic possession were diametrically opposed in abstract moral terms, in regard to observable behaviors the two categories were largely identical. An ambiguous set of possessed behaviors characterized both forms of possession, the divine and the demonic, equally. Both categories involved incorporating a puissant foreign spirit into the body, which resulted in a physical and intellectual remolding of the individual into a partial image of her indwelling, supernatural possessor. Hence at the root of the debate over the discernment of spirits was a congeries of ambiguous physical and intellectual signs that rendered it difficult for observers to categorize a possessed individual as either a visionary prophet sent by God or an energumen in thrall to the devil. These individuals were ciphers to be interpreted, rather than transparent exemplars. The reported similarities in their behaviors grays the chiaroscuro of good and evil. A community with a self-proclaimed ecstatic seer in its midst, possibly performing miracles, reporting interior union with a spirit, as well as the constant presence of demons, would have good reason to be suspicious. Until the process of discerning spirits was complete, the identity of the possessing

[159] William of Auvergne, *De universo*, 1066. See chapter 4 for commentary on the passage.

spirit would remain in doubt, leaving observers to wonder, *Which spirit is in there?*

Furthermore, the fact that notions of demonic possession had long pre-existed the "new and unheard-of" category of divine possession is a point of some importance. It was only in the thirteenth century that the idea of divine possession first came to be broadly disseminated as a recognizable religious idiom within the Church, one acknowledged by contemporaries and imitated by aspiring saints. As more and more women visionaries attempted to forge a new idiom of pious devotion predicated on the idea of incorporating the divine spirit, they adopted an expressive language and gestural code that foregrounded connections between interior spiritual penetration and exterior bodily transformation. Trance, levitation, frenzy, uncontrollable tears, bloating, rigidity, prophecy, rejection of society: all were representations of an eruption to the surface of the body of powerful spiritual changes within. Yet however apt this language and this gestural code, these possessed behaviors already held a preexisting set of significances: demonic possession had long been diagnosed from the very same bodily signs. Indeed, the connection between such behaviors and possession by unclean spirits had a greater pedigree and a longer tradition. And since medieval society was quite conservative in its cultural traditions, medieval people were predisposed to be suspicious of these new forms of religious life, which appeared so similar to demonic possession.

Indeed, it is striking that diagnoses of demonic possession increased dramatically after the turn of the thirteenth century. One study of miracles at saints' shrines indicates that the number of exorcisms performed at these sites more than doubled in the thirteenth century and remained relatively high in the fourteenth century before declining sharply in the fifteenth century.[160] Thus reports of demonic possession began to proliferate at precisely the same moment that reports of women claiming divine possession first appeared. This temporal convergence provokes questions: Are these two historical developments correlated? Is the sudden inflation of the first category (demonic possession) related to the contemporary emergence of the second (divine possession)? While it is impossible to draw firm conclusions, the evidence categorically indicates a swift rise, beginning in late twelfth century, in the total number of individuals displaying possessed behaviors. We may

[160] André Goddu, "The Failure of Exorcism in the Middle Ages," in A. Zimmermann, ed., *Soziale Ordnungen im Selbstverstandnis des Mittelalters* (Berlin, 1980), 540–57. For reasons behind the fifteenth-century decline, see chapter 5.

speculate, then, that this group, which was loosely unified in terms of external comportment, ultimately was split between the two conceptual categories of divine and demonic possession.

Matters of gender constructions and social stratification inflected the discernment of spirits in myriad ways. Since sainthood overwhelmingly was associated with the masculine sex, with noble blood, and with clerical or monastic status, poor laywomen's claims to divine possession were inherently controversial.[161] Inversely, since demonic possession also was a sex-related, if not entirely sex-specific, phenomenon that primarily was held to afflict women, a negative interpretation of unusual or extreme behaviors among women must have seemed natural to many observers.[162] The doxic predicates that women were the weaker sex and more prone to succumb to demonic wiles, and that poor laity were too ignorant to be bearers of divine truth, exacerbated this perception: "The things that little old women, or silly pauper women and lowly little persons (*vetulae aut mulierculae pauperes, vilesque personulae*) declare to be visions of God are just dreams or deceits. . . . For a wretched bestial person does not perceive things which are of the Spirit of God."[163]

The naturalization of these categories as gendered and socially situated— saintliness as essentially masculine, clerical, and noble; demonic possession or delusion as essentially feminine, lay, and lowly—fostered resistance to interpretations of laywomen's spirit possession as divine, rather than demonic, in character. Few women claiming to be divinely possessed were accepted as such without contentious struggles. Although much recent work has emphasized the potentially empowering aspects of feminine religiosity in the "effeminate age" of the later Middle Ages, in fact few of these women achieved purely positive reputations as a result of their claims. In sum, we

[161] Vauchez, *Sainthood*, documents the masculine (85.7 percent), noble (63.7 percent), and clerical (74.3 percent) aspects of sainthood. See table 22, p. 268; table 6, p. 184; and table 10, p. 256. In order to extract the percentage of noble saints overall from table 6, I added together the total number of saints whose social origins are known; then I calculated the percentage of nobility among them, including both "Reigning families and high nobility" and "Middle and lesser aristocracy." It is noteworthy that, if these statistics were based upon actual canonized sainthood, as opposed to the opening of a canonization inquiry, they would be significantly higher. See also Michael Goodich, "The Politics of Canonization in the Thirteenth Century: Lay and Mendicant Saints," in S. Wilson, ed., *Saints and their Cults: Studies in Religious Sociology, Folklore, and History* (Cambridge, 1983), 169–87.

[162] The terms are taken from Christina Larner, *Enemies of God: The Witch-Hunt in Scotland* (London, 1981).

[163] *De Juetta vidua reclusa*, 165.

must adjust our view of the "typical" inspired woman of the later Middle Ages. She may be described as an urban laywoman, socially isolated by her own choice and pursuing a life of harsh asceticism, subject to trance states in which she receives prophetic visions and occult knowledge . . . and considered highly suspect by her community precisely because of these characteristics.

CHAPTER TWO
CIPHERS

All the farts that the Beguines make cannot be weighed in scales.
— MEDIEVAL DUTCH PROVERB

The possessed were ciphers: figures imbued with an electric aura of significance that could not readily be grasped, signs requiring interpretation. Far from being transparently holy or demonic, they presented an opaque and impenetrable public deportment that invited—indeed, demanded—engagement from observers. They claimed divine visions and revelations, but they behaved like demoniacs. And as the Dutch proverb observes, the immaterial the evanescent cannot, finally, be judged: visions, like farts, cannot be weighed in scales.

This chapter is about the social construction of religious identities. In particular, it treats the negotiations and accommodations that went into decisions about the social and acceptability of laywomen who appeared to be possessed by a foreign spirit. How and why were individual possessed women placed into categories? How did these ambivalent ciphers acquire a specific social meaning and an identity?

Although contestation over the identities of possessed laywomen was widespread in medieval culture, this chapter concentrates on three individual case studies. This close focus on particular examples permits a more nuanced and closely contextualized unraveling of the process of discernment "on the ground." What behaviors attracted particular attention? Who adopted which interpretation and why? How did interpretations evolve over time and through debate? Was consensus ever reached regarding discernment of the person's spirit? If not, what doubts lingered? A micro-reading of these individual case histories helps expose how the testing of spirits was negotiated in local communities, as well as how discernment was related to broader forms of power relations in medieval society.

Before moving on to the case studies, however, I would like to pause briefly in order to interrogate some of the unspoken social dynamics underlying the processes of possession and discernment. For spirit possession, first and foremost, must be understood as the process of constructing an identity; and discernment, as the attempt to define and situate that identity vis-a-vis the broader group and its social and religious values. In the next few pages I discuss two classic approaches to the study of spirit possession. I then attempt to synthesize their insights in my own theory of spirit possession as a performative process of identity formation. This material lends analytic depth to the discussion of specific cases of discernment debate that follow.

A THEORETICAL EXCURSUS: SPIRIT POSSESSION AS IDENTITY FORMATION

Students of spirit possession have long been aware of the predominance of women among the possessed: the gender imbalance is cross-cultural as well as transhistorical. There are two principal schools of thought as to why this should be the case.[1] The first, represented in divergent ways by the anthropologist I. M. Lewis and the historian Michel de Certeau, views the phenomenon as a subtle form of transgression or resistance by subordinate (specifically female) sectors of society.[2] Women, lacking access to culturally sanctioned avenues of expression, gravitate toward accepted paradigms of alienation, such as possession, that allow them covertly to articulate their desire for increased attention, respect, or social prerogatives. This license is

---

[1] A third school of thought, which relies upon the diagnosis of psychological disorders as underlying possession, has produced work of varying quality. See William James, *The Varieties of Religious Experience* (New York, 1958), esp. 267–71; 314–17; Sudhir Kakar, *Shamans, Mystics, and Doctors* (Delhi, 1990); Jeffrey Chajes, "Judgements Sweetened: Possession and Exorcism in Early Modern Jewish Culture," *Journal of Early Modern History* 1 (1997): 124–69. An incisive critique of psychological approaches is in Erik Midelfort, *A History of Madness in Sixteenth-Century Germany* (Stanford, 1999), 10–11.

[2] I. M. Lewis, *Ecstatic Religion: An Anthropological Study of Spirit Possession and Shamanism* (New York, 1971); idem, "A Structural Approach to Witchcraft and Possession," in M. Douglas, ed., *Witchcraft Confessions and Accusations* (London, 1970); Michel de Certeau, "La parole de la possedée," unaccountably translated by T. Conley as "Discourse Disturbed: The Sorcerer's Speech," in *The Writing of History* (New York, 1988). Such a translation obscures the gender implications of the original title. Michel de Certeau, *The Possession at Loudun*, trans. M. Smith (Chicago, 1996).

made possible by the adoption of a new identity: that of the possessing spirit, which is supernaturally powerful and thus commands far greater respect than that due a mere woman. Beyond this point, however, the interpretations of these two authors diverge significantly. Whereas Lewis stresses the possessed woman's enhanced prestige, seen as a desired, functionalist outcome of the possession, de Certeau notes the dramatic displacement of self that occurs in the European model of spirit possession. For de Certeau, the essential Otherness of women in male-dominated early modern Europe is both exaggerated and inverted by possession. Exaggerated, because her alterity is magnified from a human to a cosmic scale; and inverted, because her marginality is subsumed by her physical incarnation of a puissant supernatural being that speaks through her. As de Certeau notes in his challenging essay, the speech of the possessed woman is always Other: it exists outside normative fields of discourse, because the speaking subject is unrepresentable, displaced from speech. Indeed, the originary enactment of possession is manifested as an inchoate "disturbance of discourse." This disrupted speech can only be represented once it has been reclassified and named by the exorcist as the discourse of a specific, indwelling demon. Thus, to the degree that the speech of the possessed woman appears in texts, it does so as a demonological replacement authorized by her ecclesiastical interlocutors. Yet despite the dramatic differences between these two scholars, both Lewis and de Certeau present the possessed woman's "experience" as an irreducible category dictated by transgressive desires.

An alternate approach is provided by Mary Douglas, who follows Durkheim in regarding society as the ultimate source of religious phenomena and their categorization.[3] For Douglas, the key factor in explaining attitudes to-

[3] Mary Douglas, *Natural Symbols* (London, 1970); Émile Durkheim, *The Elementary Forms of the Religious Life*, trans. J. Swain (London, 1915). Janice Boddy, "Spirit Possession Revisited: Beyond Instrumentality," *Annual Review of Anthropology* 23 (1994): 407–34, is an excellent review of the literature on this topic. See also Erika Bourguignon, *Religion, Altered States of Consciousness, and Social Change* (Columbus, 1973); idem, "The Self, the Behavioral Environment, and the Theory of Spirit Possession," in M. Spiro, ed., *Context and Meaning in Cultural Anthropology* (New York, 1965); Raymond Jamous, "Le saint et le possédé," *Gradhiva* 17 (1995): 63–83. For cultural histories of possession, illness, and madness, see Jean-Claude Schmitt, "Corps malade, corps possédé," in *Le corps, les rites, les rêves, le temps: Essais d'anthropologie médiévale* (Paris, 2001), 319–43; Anita Walker and Edmund Dickerman, "'A Woman under the Influence': A Case of Alleged Possession in Sixteenth-Century France," *Sixteenth Century Journal* 22, 3 (1991): 535–54; Midelfort, *History of Madness*; Michel Rouche, "Miracles, maladies et psychologie de la foi à l'époque carolingienne en France," in *Hagiographie, cultures et sociétés, IVe–XIIe siècles* (Paris, 1981), 319–37; Lyndal Roper, "Exorcism and the Theology of the Body," in *Oedipus and the Devil: Witchcraft, Sexuality, and Religion in Early Modern Europe* (New York, 1994), 171–98.

ward spirit possession is the issue of bodily control, seen as a function of so-cial control. In a wide-ranging and cohesive theory of culture and its self-re-production through the imposition of symbolic codes of order, Douglas argues that there is a direct correlation between the degree of social control of a given group and the valuation of bodily control within that group. Groups that are unstructured and informal tend to regard spirit possession and trance as beneficent states, while those that are more rigid and formal in their social structures find the dissociative elements of spirit possession to be disturbing and dangerous. Both types of social values can coexist within a sin-gle society, distributed among different social groups. Thus the predomi-nance of women among the possessed, argues Douglas, is not necessarily due to an internal desire to acquire prestige; it reflects an external, social factor: the lower cultural significance of women's activities. Since women's duties tend to be both devalued and confined to domestic spaces, they are less sub-ject to rigorous control and structure imposed from without. Rather, they are effectively left to their own devices within their own sphere. The relative ab-sence of a constant external, disciplining social force enables a lack of bodily control, expressed as trance or other immoderate physical displays tradi-tionally associated with spirit possession. Thus possession is only possible in the absence of restrictive social norms that are enacted, in part, as a high level of control over the body and its gestural code.

These are valuable insights. As Lewis and de Certeau point out, women's subordinate social status surely is linked with their predominance among the spirit-possessed. And Douglas's notion of bodily control and comportment as a basic cultural ground that influences perceptions of spirit possession is gracefully formulated and accords rather well with the medieval evidence. However, each theory also has distinct disadvantages, in that neither fully in-tegrates both external-social and internal-individual factors into the analysis of how possessed identities are constructed. On the one hand, Lewis and de Certeau both focus on the possessed woman's experience—though this ex-perience is seen as transparent and functional by Lewis, and as opaque and unutterable by de Certeau. Yet the use of "experience" as an irreducible cat-egory has been carefully critiqued as overly reliant upon a self-contained reading of the individual, with little attention given to the collective cultural constructions of particular social roles.[4] Douglas, on the other hand, would appear to be a cultural determinist, giving little consideration to the self-rep-resentations of individual actors within their particular contexts of social con-trol, or lack thereof. Furthermore, the medieval situation is somewhat more

[4] See introduction, note 56.

complex than those discussed by any of these authors, in that we are dealing here with not one, but two indistinguishable forms of spirit possession: one "good," one "bad."[5]

I would suggest that this particular evidence requires a more dynamic view of possession, one that takes account of both internal-individual and external-communal factors in the formation of a particular possessed identity. Thus theorizing medieval spirit possession requires an integration of Lewis's and de Certeau's experiential individualism with Douglas's sensitivity to cultural attitudes toward the body and its comportment. The performative view of spirit possession that follows borrows from theories of ritual in religious studies and anthropology, from recent feminist critiques of conventional identity politics, and from gossip theory.[6] Briefly put, a performative view of spirit possession sees the phenomenon as a particular cultural process of identity formation that subsists upon three interdependent factors: first, the cultural constructions of particular identity "roles"; second, the self-representations of the individual as she "performs" such roles; and third, the collective evaluation of the individual's actions on the part of observers, or the "audience." This triad of factors is drawn together by a fourth element: the surface of the body itself, which both contains individual identity and mediates its relationships with outside observers.

The study of identity formation begins with the embeddedness of the individual within her culture and community. It is the collective culture that constructs individual experience, lending significance to particular memo-

---

[5] De Certeau, however, notes the "structural homology between problems raised by sorcery, possession, and mysticism." Unfortunately, this point remains tantalizingly brief ("Discourse Disturbed," 249–50).

[6] The literature on performance theory is extensive. A helpful, though older overview is Lawrence Sullivan, "Sound and Senses: Toward a Hermeneutics of Performance," *History of Religions* 26, 1 (August 1986): 1–33; Catherine Bell, *Ritual Theory, Ritual Practice* (New York, 1992); Stanley Tambiah, *Culture, Thought, and Social Action* (Cambridge, Mass., 1985); Roy Rappaport, "The Obvious Aspects of Ritual," in *Ecology, Meaning, and Religion* (Berkeley, 1979), 173–222; Edward Schieffelin, "Performance and the Cultural Construction of Reality," *American Ethnologist* (1985): 707–24; Jonathan Z. Smith, *To Take Place: Toward Theory in Ritual* (Chicago, 1987). A collection of classic articles is Ronald Grimes, *Readings in Ritual Studies* (Upper Saddle River, N.J., 1996). A medievalist's use of performance theory is Kathleen Biddick, "Genders, Bodies, Borders: Technologies of the Visible" *Speculum* 68, 2 (1993): 389–418. For application of performance theory to the realm of gender formation, see Judith Butler, *Gender Trouble: Feminism and the Subversion of Identity* (New York, 1990). I have gone over some of this ground before in Nancy Caciola, "Through a Glass, Darkly: Recent Works on Sanctity and Society," *Comparative Studies in Society and History* 38, 2 (1996): 301–9, and "Mystics, Demoniacs, and the Physiology of Spirit Possession in Medieval Europe," *Comparative Studies in Society and History* 42, 2 (2000): 268–306.

ries, actions, conversations and emotions above others. In performance theory, this principle may be understood as the availability of particular identity roles, such as "visionary woman" or "demoniac," transmitted through texts, legends, conversation, images, and sermons. These cultural roles serve the epistemological function of mediating bare experience: they represent the cultural idioms through which an inherently chaotic individual level of experience is endowed with broader social meanings. Individuals come to regard certain of their own (and others') actions as conforming to a pattern, one that is recognizable through association with one of these roles. These privileged experiences are then incorporated into a personal narrative that constitutes, for the individual, the basis of identity, memory, and self-understanding.[7]

This leads me to the second factor of the triad. Presumably, the women whom I discuss throughout this book were aspiring to the role of a divinely possessed woman, or even to the role of a demoniac, and were structuring their lives through traditional cultural ideals of these roles.[8] Thus the self-representations of an individual, as she engages in various actions associated with a particular role, constitute a "performance" of an identity, a stylization of the visible self (i.e., the body and its gestures, clothing, conversation, daily habits, and living spaces) into a recognizable pattern. It is well known that hagiographies, for example, are a highly conventional genre, and I would suggest that this is only partly a reflection of the authors' biases. Hagiographical subjects, too, attempted to fashion themselves as saints by conforming to conventional religious idioms, such as that of the divinely possessed visionary.[9]

Finally, there is the reception of the performance on the part of an audience, which participates by scrutinizing and evaluating the performer's actions. Ultimately a "saint" (and, mutatis mutandis, a "demoniac") is always a saint *for* others.[10] Only the surrounding society can confer these labels upon the individual. Thus the construction of an identity is an emergent process, one that is negotiated between the cultural idioms of a given society, the self-representations of an individual performer, and the scrutiny of her society or

[7] Stephen Crites, "The Narrative Quality of Experience," *Journal of the American Academy of Religion* 39, 3 (September 1971): 291–311.

[8] See the comments of Barbara Newman about the attractions of the demoniac role in "Possessed by the Spirit: Devout Women, Demoniacs, and the Apostolic Life in the Thirteenth Century," *Speculum* 73, 3 (1998): 733–70. Also on this point, Clive Holmes, "Women: Witnesses and Witches," *Past and Present* 140 (1993): 45–78.

[9] Gábor Klaniczay, "Legends as Life-Strategies for Aspirant Saints in the Later Middle Ages," in *The Uses of Supernatural Power* (Princeton, N.J., 1990), 95–110.

[10] Pierre Delooz, *Sociologie et canonisations* (Liège, 1969).

audience. In essence, "discernment of spirits" is simply a technical name for these processes of representation and evaluation. Yet the fact that possessed women elicited skepticism as well as veneration, insults as well as prayers, alerts us to the fact that the interpretation of these individuals was both multilateral and evolutionary. Disputes over inspiration were an ongoing series of complex social mediations over the meanings of ambivalent behaviors, with different groups advancing competing or contradictory claims. Confessors, ecclesiastics, other religious, neighbors, family members, rivals, all had different stakes in the discernment of spirits. Each group hewed to its own individual or collective ideologies, which inflected their interpretations. Questions of social stratification and association were vitally important in discernment disputes: those in leadership positions helped mold the consensus of others, while affiliations with broader religious orders or groups often dictated the responses of particular observers. Thus the forging of a local consensus (or at least of a dominant opinion) frequently occurred through informal social processes of gossip, debate, and argumentation among these different interpreters. These individual "gossip cells" functioned to structure responses to the performer in multilateral debate with one another, and evolutionarily in response to the individual's continued public performance.[11] To quote the anthropologist Edward Schieffelin, performative processes are "socially emergent . . . constructed through the interaction of the performers and participants but not reducible to them."[12] Or, as Kathleen Erndl writes of possession in India, "the theological, cultural, and individual dimensions are mutually dependent and must be considered together."[13]

A performative theory of identity formation discloses the complex dynamic at work both in the claims of women to be inspired by God and in the evaluations of these claims by others. For example, we can see the appeal that a role of authority—the "divinely possessed visionary" or the alienated yet

[11] Max Gluckman, "Gossip and Scandal," *Current Anthropology* 4, 3 (1963): 308; Robert Paine, "What Is Gossip About? An Alternative Hypothesis," *Man*, n.s., 2, 2 (1967): 278–86; Sally Merry, "Rethinking Gossip and Scandal," in D. Black, ed., *Toward a General Theory of Social Control*, vol. 1, *Fundamentals* (Orlando, 1984), 271–302; Jorg Bergmann, *Discreet Indiscretions: The Social Organization of Gossip* (New York, 1993); Patricia Spacks, *Gossip* (New York, 1985). Works that discuss gossip in a medieval context are Chris Wickham, "Gossip and Resistance among the Medieval Peasantry," *Past and Present* 160 (1998): 3–24; and Karma Lochrie, *Covert Operations: The Medieval Uses of Secrecy* (Philadelphia, 1999), 56–92. I also found helpful Miri Rubin, "Small Groups: Identity and Solidarity in the Late Middle Ages," in J. Kermode, ed., *Enterprise and Individuals in Fifteenth-Century England* (Stroud, 1991), 132–50.
[12] Schieffelin, "Performance and Construction," 722.
[13] Kathleen Erndl, *Victory to the Mother: The Hindu Goddess of Northwest India in Myth, Ritual, and Symbol* (Oxford, 1993), 134.

powerful role of "demoniac"—held for women: this corresponds to the first factor of the theory, the availability of particular cultural roles that mediate experience. In the second factor of the performative triad, we can identify the stylization of the self—particularly the body and its gestures—in ways that are characteristic not only of the "divinely possessed" but also of the "demonically possessed." The performance of divine possession was conducted in much the same way as a performance of demonic possession, for both displayed the same set of behaviors. This is what made the possessed woman a cipher, an ambiguous sign requiring interpretation. Finally, in the third factor, the evaluations of the audience, we see the discernment of spirits.

Yet only the final strand in this model can spin together these gossamer threads of interpretation. This element is the surface of the body itself, that which contains a given spirit or identity, or else permits the entrance/construction of a new one. The surface of the body is a site of particular significance, for it represents the locus of mediation between the internal-individual and the external-communal. Possession subsists on a dialectic between the interior and the exterior levels of the body, as spirits/identities move through the integument that separates outside from inside. Control of the body's surface and its public representation is thus a means of controlling identity itself. If identity is, as Judith Butler asserts, "fabricated as an interior essence," then "that very interiority is an effect and function of a decidedly public regulation of fantasy through the surface politics of the body . . . [the] border control that differentiates inner from outer and so constitutes the 'integrity' of the subject."[14] The quotation is uncannily appropriate to a discussion of spirit possession: within the terms of performance theory, discernment becomes a collective process of reifying, and then projecting into the body, a particular identity betokened by the word "spirit," whether unclean, holy, or simply human. Thus social identity was socially negotiated, then reified into an interior essence that was labeled as this or that spirit: human, demonic, divine. Identity was essentialized into the body from without by the collective judgments of the local community. These judgments—never free from questions of ideology and power—authorized a particular interpretation of the possessed body, assigning meaning to the cipher.

Focus on the surface of the body as a mediating element also serves to remind us that the discernment of spirits was always really a discernment of bodies. There simply was no way to prove that the visions and revelations to which many of these women lay claim even had occurred, much less that they were divine in origin. To be sure, the content of these reported visions was

[14] Butler, *Gender Trouble*, 136.

important to observers; it was neither disregarded nor free from scrutiny. Descriptions of revelations, for example, had to be doctrinally correct, and the seer had to avoid any hint of hubris in recounting visions of heaven and the saints. Private experiences of demonic torment, similarly, could become an influential part of the public gossip and fame about a particular individual. Yet ultimately these interior experiences were not enough to guarantee a positive outcome of the discernment of spirits, for anyone could "disguise themselves as servants of righteousness" by feigning celestial revelations. Thus witnesses looked to exterior comportment and behaviors as the only tangible test and proof of the interior experiences these possessed women claimed. The body was the mediating frontier between unverifiable private experiences and the public social context, and as such became the locus upon which the discernment of spirits was worked out.

Let us now see how these ideas operated in practice through a close reading of three case studies. The first example, from a border region of the Empire, focuses on the question of audience, discussing the multiplicity of different "gossip cells" spiraling outward from a woman in a small village. The second case study, drawn from Italy, highlights the issue of self-fashioning, focusing on the saintly performances of the woman involved and the serious challenges to this self-representation that emanated from individual observers as well as ecclesiastical institutions. A third and final section is more international in scope. This section examines a Beguine from the Low Countries known both for her stigmata and for her prophetic gifts. Her divisive reputation for possessed behaviors eventually reached the court of the French king Philip III. This discussion, which unlike the other two is drawn from a relatively rich documentary base of five different texts, focuses on how the reputation of a single individual may be appropriated for several competing—and contradictory—ideological agendas.

SIBYLLA, THE BISHOP, AND THE DEMON

In 1240, a woman named Sibylla began to attract attention in the village of Marsal, which lies near Metz in the Upper Lorraine, at the western border of the German Empire.[15] Sibylla was one of a number of Beguines liv-

---

[15] The tale is in Richer of Sens, *Gesta Senonensis ecclesiae* 4.18, in L. d'Achery, ed., *Spicilegium sive collectio veterum aliquot scriptorum qui in Galliae bibliothecis delituerunt* (Paris, 1723), 634–36. A French version of the tale is reprinted in *Monumenta Germaniae histo-*

ing in the area, who were under the loose direction of the local Order of Preachers. Sibylla stood out from this group, however, for the intensity of her commitment: she arrived at church early every morning and returned for each mass throughout the day. Soon Sibylla began to gain a reputation for exceptional piety among the villagers of Marsal, extending even to the parish priest, a man named Louis. A local matron convinced her husband to take the Beguine into their home, and they took great care thereafter to provide for all of Sibylla's material needs. Thus freed from the burden of worldly cares, the Beguine's spiritual life truly began to flourish. Sibylla confided to her patroness that she had begun to receive celestial visions, and the housewife arranged for her to have a private chamber in which to devote herself to prayers and vigils. As Sibylla's devotions mounted, she reported that she was rapt in ecstasy to Heaven. At this, her hostess became even more devoted to Sibylla's visionary career, jealously guarding her privacy from the curious and hastening to bring her refreshments between trances. Eventually Sibylla began to refuse all food and drink, claiming that she no longer required earthly nourishment, but was fed on celestial delicacies during her trance states. She also began to recount instances of demonic attack, advising her patroness not to become concerned if she heard a tumult at night.

As Sibylla's reputation spread, groups of Dominican and Franciscan friars arrived and began observing her, skeptically. However, being unable to find any traces of deceit in her, they duly began praising Sibylla in their sermons as a living saint. As a result, pilgrims converged on Marsal from neighboring villages, including Bishop Jacques of Metz (1239–60) and a crowd of "counts and knights, clerics, monks, and all people of both sexes."[16] All apparently arrived around the same time, indicating a coordinated effort on the part of the mendicants to induce a pilgrimage flow. Few were able to see Sibylla, however, for she entered into a three-day trance and asked not to be disturbed. The inhabitants of Marsal, however, eagerly recounted tales of their local visionary, with the result that the lay pilgrims returned satisfied and spread Sibylla's reputation among their own neighbors.

The higher ecclesiastical authorities, however, were not so easily satisfied. Bishop Jacques, "a truly good man, of sound judgment,"[17] was suspicious of the reports he heard of Sibylla, particularly her trances and purported ability to live in a state of total fast. The bishop, along with his personal retinue

---

rica, Scriptorum (Hannover, 1880), 25:308 n. 1. The latter will hereafter be referred to as MGH version, with all citations from page 308.

[16] Richer of Sens, *Gesta*, 635.
[17] MGH version.

of clerics and Dominicans from out of town, decided to test her spirits, ordering that Sibylla be transferred to a different house where they could observe her behaviors and where no one could bring her food secretly. In these controlled circumstances, Sibylla continued to fast entirely and to fall into trance states; she also began to complain of exponentially increasing demonic torments. After three days and three nights, she asked to return to the home of her patroness, predicting that if she were to remain in this place of greater demonic power, the devil surely would destroy her body entirely in his frustration. Jacques acquiesced: Sibylla had passed this test of her fasting and trances, and the bishop was ready to allow her to resume her previous life.

Even after Sibylla's return to the home of her patroness, however, her demonic afflictions continued to multiply. A demon was spied lurking about the house, and many were struck with fright to hear it snarl in a horrible, guttural voice. Later the demon was seen scurrying through the streets and squares of Marsal at night. Whenever this monster encountered local inhabitants, it would introduce itself as a devil and complain loudly about the attacks it endured from "that nasty, impious virgin Sibylla!"[18] On another occasion the demon appeared to a group, including the bishop, in order to complain that Sibylla's prayerful intercession with God had deprived it of the soul of a recently deceased local sinner. Her intervention, the demon continued, would cost him dearly when his master Satan learned of it. The unclean spirit went on to lament its inability to harm Sibylla, because of the angels who watched over her. The bishop was highly impressed, so on the following day, accompanied by some Preachers, he went to see Sibylla again and found her in an immobile and insensible trance state: "she was laying on the bed with a flushed face, as if sleeping ... with such shallow breath that one could scarcely perceive whether she was breathing at all."[19] She wore sweetly scented garments of dazzling white, and a head covering so subtly worked, it seemed impossible that it could have been made from human hands.[20] No one dared touch her. Sibylla's hostess explained that she had received all these things, along with a quantity of holy water in an elaborate vial, as gifts from her familiar angels. It was the water that kept her safe from demonic attack, the matron elaborated, so everyone present indulged in a sip and a sprinkle themselves. The bishop, now wholly convinced of the Beguine's sanctity and miraculous means of existence, began considering building a church especially for Sibylla, in which he could display her as an object of pilgrimage.

[18] Richer of Sens, *Gesta*, 635.

[19] Ibid.

[20] It is unclear precisely what this covering was. It may have been a metal ornament or fillet; more likely a cloth veil with refined embroidery or woven patterns.

There, he mused, she could be installed as a recluse and her superhuman way of life could edify those who came to see her. "There was no one in the village," observed one source, "who believed more in her sanctity than this bishop."[21]

By this time, the household that hosted Sibylla had become the epicenter of a group of her local devotees. The core of the group apparently was composed of Sibylla's hostess, along with some of the local friars and many of the other Beguines from the area. In any event, this was the group that was present for Sibylla's next ecstatic trance. Sibylla remained locked in her room, but those present could hear the harsh, throaty voice of a demon arguing against the sweet and mellifluous speech of an angel. It seemed that the two kinds of spirit were contending over Sibylla. A Dominican Preacher, wishing to steal a glimpse of the unseen action, went close to the wall and searched for a crack. Finding a slender fissure where the wall met the ceiling, he peeked through to spy on the hidden supernatural spirits he heard locked inside the closed room. To his amazement, all he saw was Sibylla making her bed.

The bishop was summoned forthwith, and the whole group burst in and accused Sibylla of fraud. The main chronicler of these events states that a search revealed damning evidence of her deception, including a demon costume complete with an ugly mask. The bishop and Preachers were stunned to have been led astray by a "silly woman," and they eventually uncovered an accomplice, a young priest who had supplied her with food during her supposed fasts. Veneration swiftly turned to cries for vengeance, as various groups in the community cried out for Sibylla to be burned, to be drowned, or to be buried alive. The local Beguines went into a state of shocked mourning, covering their faces and wailing. The bishop of Metz initially wished to kill her but eventually only incarcerated her in a cell with a little window through which she might receive bread and water. Sibylla soon died but remained the subject of local gossip for some time to come.

Sibylla's story is untidy, but the challenges it presents to the historian are well worth pondering. Should she count as evidence for feminine piety or women's religiosity? Should the debates about her count as evidence for cultural and social attitudes toward lay religious women? Or is this *garce [qui] fit de la sainte*[22] chiefly of interest to the historian of lies, fraud, and deceit?

I would argue that the tale of Sibylla is provocative and revelatory precisely because it is so untidy. The oscillating course of Sibylla's career pro-

---

[21] MGH version.
[22] Ibid.

vides an uncommonly rich example of tested and contested inspiration. Sibylla's behaviors engendered a peculiar dynamic of public display and community scrutiny, of conflictual interpretations and shifting reinterpretations, of hopes for a celestial civic patron coupled with fears of fraud and diabolic deception. Richer of Sens included this tale in his *Chronicle of the Church of Sens* as a cautionary exemplum against facile belief in visionaries, especially when they were lay and female. Yet Richer's discussion may be mined for a wealth of competing alternative interpretations of Sibylla and her behavior, interpretations that belie his own viewpoint.

The retelling of Sibylla's story above edits out Richer's frequent judgments from hindsight and presents a more neutral account of the Beguine's career. Like most medieval chronicles, however, Richer's text adopts an omniscient narrator's perspective, presenting what was logically unseen along with what was seen. Thus Richer introduces Sibylla as a liar and a sham from the outset: the first line of the entry reads, "we undertake to speak of a certain young woman who deceived many people through her subtlety."[23] Thus when Richer goes on to tell how Sibylla gained a reputation as an ecstatic seer and a living saint, the reader knows that she is not a "real" visionary at all but merely aping the exterior comportment of one. The casual reader hence is unable to evaluate the unfolding of Sibylla's public career and the development of her reputation over time, for Richer has already introduced her as a fraud, and he consistently refers to her unseen motivations and stratagems of deception.

Like nearly all ecclesiastical redactors, Richer attempted to be "the creator of a universality *a posteriori*,"[24] employing a strategy that camouflages a single interpretation as immutable fact. Yet it is evident that the interpretation of Sibylla as a fraud was only the last in an extended series of shifting interpretations attached to Sibylla's behaviors by those around her. Ironically, it is possible to see in Richer's text an extremely complex evolution in the interpretation of Sibylla of Marsal, involving a multiplicity of actors evaluating her behavior in different ways over the course of several months.[25] There were at least seven individual gossip cells involved in the story, each of which had a slightly different perspective on, and interest in, these events: the local Beguines, Sibylla's unnamed hostess, the wider community of Marsal (including the parish priest), the mendicant groups of Franciscans and Do-

[23] Richer of Sens, *Gesta*, 634.
[24] Hughes Neveux, "Les lendemains de la mort dans les croyances occidentales (vers 1250–vers 1300)," *Annales E.S.C.* 34 (1979): 249.
[25] It is unclear how long Sibylla's career lasted. The chronicle entry is dated 1240, but this could well indicate only the date of her death.

minicans based in and around Marsal, the pilgrims from outlying areas, and Bishop Jacques of Metz along with his retinue of clerics and out-of-town Dominicans. Lastly, there is Sibylla herself.

All the local groups shared an interest in Sibylla's success. Hers was a sympathetic audience, anxious to collaborate with Sibylla in constructing her reputation as a divinely inspired visionary. Marsal was an ancient village of Roman provenance, connected to Metz by one of the Roman roads that continued to serve trade, pilgrimage, and migration needs throughout the medieval period.[26] However, the town never had attained a broader prominence, a situation that Sibylla's fame promised to rectify. Various lay religious movements had been gaining visibility in this area over the past half century, particularly the Waldensians and Beguines. The Waldensians, or Poor Men of Lyons, had been a presence since the turn of the thirteenth century; and it had been less than a decade since the inquisitor Conrad of Marburg had been active in the archdiocese, hunting them.[27] Conrad's travels between Mainz and Trier in the late 1220s to early 1230s had been authorized directly by Pope Gregory IX. Moreover, rumors about the spectacular supernatural feats of visionary laywomen in the territory of Lorraine surely had reached Marsal by 1240. Lorraine was divided into the archdioceses of Trier and Cologne, and the latter already was becoming famous for its concentration of visionary Beguines and recluses in and around Liège.[28] Sibylla could provide a local exemplar of this phenomenon for the villagers of Marsal.

The Beguines appear only twice in the story—once as Sibylla is introduced and once as she is, literally, unmasked—but they frame her entire career, providing the initial context for her public displays of devotion and later responding with the greatest distress when Sibylla is arrested. Their reputation as a group would have been well served by nurturing a genuine visionary, especially given the polemical literature against Beguines that was proliferating at this very time. Indeed, the word *béguine* was fast becoming a synonym, in Old French, for hypocrite.[29] Popular ditties such as the French poet Rutebeuf's satirical *Diz de Béguines* were not uncommon:

---

[26] François-Yves Le Moigne, *Histoire de Metz* (Toulouse, 1986), 25.

[27] A. Mackay with D. Ditchburn, *Atlas of Medieval Europe* (New York, 1997), 122–24; Charles McCurry, *Urban Society and the Church: Medieval Metz, ca. 1200–1378*, ed. Thomas Bisson (Berkeley, 1985), 218–20. The latter work is an incomplete, posthumous Ph.D. dissertation that was lightly edited and published in typescript by T. Bisson.

[28] Walter Simons, *Cities of Ladies: Beguine Communities in the Medieval Low Countries, 1200–1565* (Philadelphia, 2001).

[29] Alan Hindley et. al., *Old French-English Dictionary* (Cambridge, 2000), 73.

Anything a Beguine says
you must take in a good light.
For it is all about religion,
everything in her life:
Her utterances are prophecy.
If she laughs, it is her good fellowship;
If she weeps, it is devotion.
If she sleeps, she is in a trance;
If she dreams, it is a vision.
If she lies, don't worry about it.[30]

Sibylla's unmasking, in short, had fulfilled the worst cultural stereotypes of Beguines. Their desolation at Sibylla's eventual disgrace testifies to dashed hopes and perhaps fears of a backlash.

Yet if the Beguines wished for the prestige that came with fostering a saint from among their ranks, so, too, did the broader inhabitants of Marsal hope for a reflected glow of celebrity from Sibylla. The parish priest Louis, along with his parishioners, "regarded her as most graced."[31] Breathless gossip about Sibylla, her trances, and her demonic torments evidently was widespread in Marsal. The local laity were instrumental in transmitting the particulars of her behavior to pilgrims from out of town, convincing them that Marsal was indeed blessed by God with a divinely possessed visionary. Sibylla's trances likely were among the more exciting events in Marsal in generations, bringing important visitors, an economic boost, a sense of civic pride, and endless fodder for chatter in the lanes and markets. In particular, encounters with the demon must have kept the local gossip lively, lending a thrilling sense of importance to those who could regale the crowds with tales of having met the devil and hearing it complain of Sibylla. Merchants and taverners, meanwhile, benefited from the nascent pilgrimage trade. Similarly, the woman who gave Sibylla shelter, and who jealously guarded her privacy, must have been gratified to see her pious charity produce such dramatic

[30] Alfons Hilka, "Altfranzösische Mystik und Beginentum," *Zeitschrift für Romanische Philologie* 47 (1927): 167. See also Herbert Grundmann, *Religious Movements in the Middle Ages*, trans. S. Rowan (Notre Dame, Ind., 1995); Ernst McDonnell, *The Beguines and Beghards in Medieval Culture, with Special Emphasis on the Belgian Scene* (New York, 1969); Jean-Claude Schmitt, *Mort d'une hérésie: L'Église et les clercs face aux béguines et aux béghards du Rhin supérieur du XIVe au XVe siècle* (Paris, 1978); Gordon Leff, *Heresy in the Later Middle Ages* (Manchester, 1967); Robert Lerner, *The Heresy of the Free Spirit in the Later Middle Ages* (Notre Dame, Ind., 1972). Lerner's book includes a persuasive critique of Leff's work.
[31] Richer of Sens, *Gesta*, 634.

results. Under her very roof, Sibylla's graces mounted from frequent prayers and vigils to ecstatic trances, to complete fasting, to demonic afflictions and angelic protectors. This matron was particularly impressed with Sibylla's abstinence and trance behavior: "She spent the whole day laying on the bed as if sleeping, neither eating nor drinking. . . . and then at some hour of the night, in order that it might be believed that her spirit had returned, she let out a moan in a soft voice."[32] When Sibylla's hostess cared for her so diligently, surely she hoped not only to exchange earthly for heavenly patronage, but also to gain a position of respect and honor in Marsal. As the Beguine's career reached its apex, Sibylla acquired the habit of prophesying her trances in advance: at such times, the matron's household would be filled with Sibylla's devotees. At other times pilgrims, some of noble birth, visited from out of town, perhaps leaving alms; and important people like the bishop of Metz with his extensive retinue came to visit the matron's home and spoke with her respectfully. In sum, the local Marsal gossip cells each sincerely wanted to believe in Sibylla's holiness for the greater glory of their religious group, their town, or their household. Her behavior was consistent with the cultural idiom of a divinely possessed lay visionary, and was read as such by those who had a stake in her success as divinely inspired. The trajectory of their attitude toward Sibylla was one of escalating excitement and conviction.

Some locals had hesitations regarding Sibylla, however: namely, the Franciscans and Dominicans. As inhabitants of the general area, but with ties to a translocal organization and a fair degree of mobility, their allegiances were somewhat more complex than those of the strictly Marsal groups. The Dominicans had the additional local bond of being spiritual directors to the Marsal Beguines. The Order of Preachers seems to have been particularly prominent in this role in the diocese of Metz, fulfilling the same oversight function vis-à-vis the Beguines in the episcopal seat itself.[33] When Richer introduces the mendicants into his story, however, he notes that "they came and observed her, and never were able to perceive any . . . fraud." The sentence suggests that the friars did not simply accept the reports they had heard about Sibylla, but were concerned about the possibility of deception and wished to verify for themselves what her behavior was like. The mendicants, more than most other inhabitants of Marsal, may have hesitated out of a concern for heresy, remembering the recent trips of Conrad of Marburg. Yet despite these initial apprehensions, the mendicants soon were preaching "both

---

[32] Ibid.
[33] McCurry, *Urban Society and Church*, 217–27; Le Moigne, *Metz*.

about her sanctity and about her actions. What next?"[34] This boost to Sibylla's reputation spurred a wave of pilgrimage activity, attracting individuals of many different social statuses to Marsal and provoking even more rumors and storytelling. Thus we can trace the chain of gossip cells that spread outward from Sibylla: admiring gossip about trances and devils circulated among the Beguines, the matron, the priest, and then the general community. Eventually this gossip overcame the hesitations of the mendicant friars and thence, through their preaching, Sibylla's fame was passed to other laity farther afield. Within these segments of the community, Sibylla's fasts, prayers, vigils, and meditations, not to mention her ecstatic trances and the later demonic apparitions in town, signified that a divinely possessed saint was living in their midst.

This interpretation of Sibylla, however, did not go uncontested. If the local Dominican and Franciscan friars alike gave in to her charms and her charisma, the higher ecclesiastical authorities were not as easily satisfied. Jacques, bishop of Metz, and his retinue ("his clerics and the Preachers that were with him")[35] were more cautious in regard to Sibylla, and they went farther in scrutinizing her possessed behaviors. Jacques had only just been elevated to a troubled see the previous year, one of three episcopal seats subject to the metropolitan archdiocese of Trier. Though Metz was in the thirteenth century a prosperous center of trade and the banking capital of Lorraine, the episcopal coffers in 1240 were bare.[36] Jacques's immediate predecessors had left him a see burdened with debts and recently alienated properties. Furthermore, the see of Metz also was experiencing a distinct decline in prestige and power, as the commune had waged a successful campaign over the past four decades to arrogate an increased number of privileges to the city at the direct expense of the bishop. In view of Jacques's difficulties, he must stringently have wished to avoid the additional humiliation of having a false saint proclaimed as authentic within his diocese.

Perhaps Jacques even had seen, in the episcopal archives, a letter that Innocent III had directed to the church at Metz in 1199. Innocent's missive complained about the religious devotions of "a multitude of women and of laity" and cautioned against easy acceptance of visionary claims made by members of these lowly groups. Sibylla may well have reminded Jacques of Innocent's warning that "when vices sneak in secretly under the guise of

---

[34] Richer of Sens, *Gesta*, 635.
[35] Ibid.
[36] For the economic context and Jacques of Metz, see Le Moigne, *Metz*, 140–43, 146; McCurry, *Urban Society and Church*, 67–72.

virtues, and an angel of Satan transforms himself into an angel of Light, then greater discernment is required."[37] Such a letter almost seemed like a direct injunction to investigate Sibylla. Lastly, Jacques recognized that the Beguine represented a competitive source of religious authority within the area of Marsal, and potentially beyond. As a member of the "weaker sex" and of secular status, the acceptance of Sibylla as divinely inspired held the risk of undercutting the prestige and authority enjoyed by the male clerical elite. Given the recent degradation in status of the see of Metz, it was understandable that this new competitor was greeted with intense suspicion by Jacques and his Dominican entourage. Accordingly, they placed Sibylla in isolation so that they might study her fasts, vigils, and trance states. Yet since Sibylla managed to continue her possessed behaviors, the bishop and his clerics had no choice but to allow her to return to her former life. At this point they seem neither to have suppressed nor to have endorsed her claims to divine illumination, but simply to have tolerated or ignored her.

However, the clerical elite was to alter its interpretation of Sibylla yet again. After the bishop personally witnessed two supernatural events—the complaints of the demon about Sibylla and, the next day, the opportunity to view her entranced and vested with celestial garments—he, too, became convinced of her holiness. Gossip relayed by Sibylla's hostess about her vial of holy water, about the angel who guarded her from demons, and about the glittering garments she wore persuaded him that his misgivings had been unfounded. A later, anonymous Old French account of the incident (said to be based on the notes of Jacques's contemporary Erhard of Regensburg) emphasizes that Jacques became one of Sibylla's most ardent supporters, so impressed was he with her fasts and the rumors that she "had extended debates and fights with Lord Lucifer."[38] Thus was a new consensus reached in the ongoing debate over the meaning to be attached to Sibylla's behaviors. Significantly, once the bishop accepted Sibylla as a legitimate source of divine supernatural power, his immediate concern was how to subordinate her raw power to his authority. The plan to place Sibylla on public display and to encourage pilgrimage traffic might have offered the means for Bishop Jacques to cleanse the spotted prestige of his see by channeling Sibylla's ecstatic abilities and supernatural power to his own advantage. Building Sibylla a church would have been a costly investment, but one that could have brought both

[37] Innocent III, letter 141, in *PL*, 214:695. The original context of the letter was a response to the presence of Waldensians in Metz.

[38] MGH version. If it is true that this account derives from Regensburg, nearly five hundred kilometers away from Metz, then the story of Sibylla must have achieved a fair degree of circulation.

spiritual and financial rewards: the laity would thank him for patronizing one of their own; pilgrims might provide some additional religious income to alleviate debts; and the see of Metz would gain a newly positive reputation. At this point, to judge from Richer's text, the bishop, his clergy, the friars, the Beguines, and the laity were all in harmony concerning the interpretation of Sibylla.

Of course, this consensus, too, was to break down after Sibylla was seen making her bed while she was supposed to be in a state of trance. The gaze of the Preacher, penetrating into Sibylla's private chamber, finally made manifest to the community of Marsal what has been the privileged information of the chronicle reader all along: despite Sibylla's exterior comportment as divinely possessed, privately she was a hypocrite, a demonic false saint. The moment gives vivid physical expression to the inchoate tensions between seen and unseen, surface and depth, interior and exterior, that are central to the discernment of spirits. Peering through a crack in the wall at the "real" Sibylla substitutes for gazing past the surface of her body and identifying the nature of the spirit dwelling within her.

What of Sibylla's perspective? In Richer's tale, she and her shadowy priest accomplice (who appears only once, as the secret bearer of food) seem to have concocted the fraud mainly for the sake of prestige. Sibylla not only achieved a more comfortable living situation than before, but might have attained a position of considerable local influence in advising, and prophesying for, her devotees. Surprisingly, Richer's text does not hint at a sexual dalliance between the girl and the priest, who is merely described as her "friend" (*familiaris*). The anonymous Old French account, however, is more damning. According to this version, Sibylla and the young priest were lovers who contrived to conceal their illicit attachment by establishing her as a saint, and thus as above sexual reproach. After Sibylla's detection and imprisonment, her "galant" disappeared, never to be heard from again.

Sibylla's unmasking, however, did not prevent her from remaining a topic of gossip and conversation for some time thereafter. Richer writes, "although the whole region knew about her rather bold actions, it does not tire of speaking about her."[39] Might we discern in this elliptical statement the possibility of continued support for Sibylla, a debate about the meanings of her behaviors even beyond her death? The concessive clause at the beginning of the sentence seems to hint at this: amazingly, everyone continued to speak of her *even though they knew* about her unmasking as fraud.[40] Such gossip would in-

[39] Richer of Sens, *Gesta*, 634.
[40] A parallel case is provided in Judith Brown, *Immodest Acts: The Life of a Lesbian Nun in Renaissance Italy* (New York, 1986).

deed be surprising to Richer of Sens if it were positive or admiring in tone. The passage is reminiscent of another in Johannes Nider's *Formicarius*, concerning the persistent local veneration of a woman who prophesied her own public death but then failed to expire on cue: "[These people] gave many belabored twistings of the facts. Indeed, this confusion gave rise to a spectacle of such baseness, that for a time [she] still gave herself out as a prophetess, though not as before."[41] Lacking further evidence, this remains a tantalizing speculation about Sibylla that cannot be verified.

In sum, the interpretation of Sibylla's behaviors as a nefarious hoax was merely one in an extended series of interpretations of specific behaviors and events—prayer, fasting, trances, demons—given by different segments of the population. Significantly, it is always a question of behavior and deportment that is under debate, not the content of her private visions. Even the demonic episodes were tangible encounters for residents of Marsal, not private experiences for Sibylla alone. In fact, we know nothing of the content of Sibylla's supposed visions and celestial revelations: none are described in Richer's text. Observers of her career, however, from the Beguines to the matron to the bishop, were perpetually evaluating her behaviors and external appearance: her attendance at mass (frequent), her vigils and prayers (constant), her trances (immobile and insensible), her fasting (total), her clothing (beyond human capacity to fashion), her skin (flushed), even her smell (sweet). As Jean-Claude Schmitt has noted in a different context, "External appearances, individual comportments, and gestures situated people within the urban landscape of the Middle Ages, classifying them into social or moral categories, authorizing judgments about them."[42] The discernment of spirits in this case has little to do with the spiritual content of Sibylla's internal life, and everything to do with the interpretation of her external behaviors and comportment, as she performed the role of divine possession.

FROM PARAMOUR TO PARAGON

Let us now turn our attention south to Italy. Margaret of Cortona entered adulthood as a highly unlikely candidate for veneration as a divinely possessed visionary. Her adolescence had been characterized by vanity and by

[41] *F* 3.8, 48v.
[42] Schmitt, *Mort d'une hérésie*, 97.

sexual trespasses, unwed motherhood and luxurious self-indulgence.[43] Although Margaret embarked upon an ambitious remaking of herself, her conversion to the penitential life did not entirely mend her public reputation. Observers continued to be divided as to her merits throughout her life and beyond her death. After her passing in 1297, Margaret was appropriated by one faction within the Franciscan order to serve its own needs: this group envisioned her as a perfect penitential founding figure for the newly established Franciscan third order. Other interests within the Order of Friars Minor, however, provided unremitting resistance to any association with this sinner turned self-proclaimed saint. Margaret's adopted home of Cortona, similarly, was split in opinion about her. While some reviled her as insane or demonically possessed, the leading men of the commune—in particular the Casali family, gaining in civic prominence in the late thirteenth and fourteenth centuries[44]—made efforts to have her recognized as a saint soon after her passing. To this end, Margaret's postmortem miracles were carefully recorded and a sumptuous new church was erected on the site of her reclusion cell (originally attached to the ancient Church of Saint Basil) to display her relics. By the late 1330s the new building was adorned with an extensive series of frescoes illustrating Margaret's life, which recently have been attributed to Pietro and Ambrogio Lorenzetti.[45]

Of paramount interest in the present context, however, is the question of Margaret's self-fashioning as a "saintly performer"; and the collaborative remolding of her as an exemplary Franciscan saint on the part of her hagiographer, Giunta Bevegnate. The latter phenomenon is all the more interesting in that Margaret's relationship with the Franciscans was deeply vexed during her lifetime, with many friars expressing grave doubts about her. A recurring, contrapuntal pattern of rejection and embrace of Margaret culminated, after her death, in Giunta's hagiography, which thoroughly appropriated her for the order. Giunta composed the vita within a decade of Margaret's passing,

[43] Fortunato Iozzelli, "Introduzione," in *VMC*, Joanna Cannon and André Vauchez, *Margherita of Cortona and the Lorenzetti: Sienese Art and the Cult of a Holy Woman in Medieval Tuscany* (University Park, Pa., 1999); Anna Benvenuti Papi, *In castro poenitentiae: Santità e società femminile nell' Italia medievale* (Rome, 1990): 141–68, 376–402; Daniel Bornstein, "The Uses of the Body: The Church and the Cult of Santa Margherita da Cortona" *Church History* 62 (1993): 163–77; David Burr, *The Spiritual Franciscans: From Protest to Persecution in the Century after Saint Francis* (University Park, Pa., 2001), 325–34. Background on Margaret's adopted home may be found in Girolamo Mancini, *Cortona nel Medio Evo* (Rome, 1969).

[44] Benvenuti Papi, *In castro poenitentiae*, 142; Bornstein, "Uses of the Body," 172; Cannon and Vauchez, *Margherita of Cortona*, 15.

[45] Cannon and Vauchez, *Margherita of Cortona*.

basing it on his notes and memories of conversations with Margaret, to whom he had acted as primary confessor and spiritual director for the brief span of a year or so in the late 1280s.[46]

An outline of Margaret's unlikely career can swiftly be sketched. Born in 1247 to a peasant family in the village of Laviano, Margaret was orphaned of her mother at the age of eight. Her father subsequently remarried, but he chose a woman with whom Margaret did not get along. After this, Margaret was anxious for an opportunity to leave the parental home. Having reached her teens, an opportunity for flight presented itself when a young nobleman took a fancy to her and proposed that she steal away from home by night and come to live with him as his paramour. Of Margaret's lover we know only that he was wealthy, noble, and lived in Montepulciano. Local tradition records his given name as Arsenio, and historians have tentatively associated him with the del Monte family, the only prominent noble line in the area of Laviano in the thirteenth century.[47] For the ensuing nine years, Margaret lived in contented luxury with her illicit lover in his palazzo, "adorned with many different kinds of clothing . . . with gold nestled in her hair . . . and her face painted, so as to show off the wealth of her lover" (204).[48] She eventually bore him a son. However, when Margaret's protector died an untimely death, according to legend as a victim of the violent code of honor among the nobility, she was expelled from his home by his family and heirs. Having nowhere to go for sustenance for herself and her young son, Margaret returned to her father and stepmother, but was cast out by them as well. It was then that Margaret decided to devote herself to poverty and the religious life.

Making her way to Cortona in about 1272, Margaret and her illegitimate child were taken in by two charitable noblewomen named Marinaria and Raniera. These two also apparently were single, and it seems likely that they were widows who had adopted the quasi-religious life expected of "good" women who survived their husbands in this time period. Margaret's patronesses probably belonged to the lay Order of Penitence, an informal association of laypeople that was loosely under the aegis of the Franciscan order in the town of Cortona. Members conceived of themselves as an independent confraternity devoted to works of charity, and they themselves chose the lay and clerical officials who acted as their directors. Margaret soon exceeded Marinaria and Raniera in religious devotion. She began to pursue extravagant austerities and penances, while managing to support herself and

[46] The chronology is difficult to clarify. See Cannon and Vauchez, *Margherita of Cortona*, 24–25.

[47] Mancini, *Cortona*, 38; Cannon and Vauchez, *Margherita of Cortona*, 23.

[48] Page numbers in the text refer to *VMC*.

her son by serving as a midwife to noble ladies. Margaret was well-regarded by many families in Cortona, who frequently asked her to become god-mother to the children she helped into the world (207). After a probationary period, the former concubine joined the Order of Penitence in the mid-1270's and moved to a small cell of reclusion that was close to the Franciscan convent. She was formally received into the order by Ranaldo da Castiglione, then Franciscan custos of the diocese of Arezzo. Her primary supervisor and confessor over the next several years, however, was Friar Giovanni da Castiglione, the local Franciscan inquisitor. Margaret likely was given over to Giovanni's care precisely because he held this position, one that traditionally was associated with oversight of lay penitents and scrutiny of them for any signs of heresy.[49] Giovanni was assisted in his supervision over Margaret by a number of other friars, including Ranaldo da Castiglione, Ubaldo da Colle, and Giunta Bevegnate. These latter figures constituted Margaret's most en-thusiastic supporters, even as Giovanni maintained a more skeptical attitude. He was not alone. The acceptance of Margaret into the Order of Penitence was controversial, prompting continual murmurs and disapproval among certain Cortona friars whose names are delicately left unrecorded in Mar-garet's hagiography. These tensions reached a climax in about 1288, after which Margaret relocated to a more remote reclusorium situated near the Church of Saint Basil, in the upper part of town and near the perimeter. She chose a new spiritual director from among the secular clergy, Ser Badia, the rector of Saint Basil. She remained there until her death in 1297.

It is hardly surprising that these external facts, particularly those relating to Margaret's early career as an unmarried lover and mother, are de-empha-sized in her hagiography. The work is more literary than historical, and Giunta is skilled in his emplotment of scenes and in the development of the text. The hagiography opens with a dramatic scene of Margaret entering the Order of Penitents, followed by a meditative flashback that describes her early life. Indeed, much of the factual information just related derives from the brief, four-page introductory chapter of what is nearly a three-hundred-page text in its most recent edition. Even after Margaret's conversion, how-ever, Giunta Bevegnate's vita is stingy in dispensing details related to Margaret's exterior life. The thematic arc of the ten-chapter work (an eleventh chapter of miracles was added later) stretches from the initial vesti-tion scene, culminates with a dramatic "mental crucifixion" in chapter 5, and

<hr>

[49] Mariano d'Alatri, "Genesi della regola di Niccoló IV: Aspetti storici," in R. Pazzelli and L. Temperini, eds., *La "Supra montem" di Niccoló IV (1289): Genesi e diffusione di una regola* (Rome, 1988), 93–107; *VMC*, 477.

ends with Margaret's triumphal death scene. Throughout, the text consists largely of recitations of Margaret's visions of, and conversations with, Christ, in which he repeatedly praises both her and the Order of Friars Minor. These expressions often are laced with grand hyperbole: "the Holy Spirit dwells among the brothers of your order more than any other order under the sky" (241); "from the depths of time up until the present day, there has never existed any other woman to whom such exalted things were shown" (268). Thus if Margaret herself engaged in a process of penitential reformation of herself into a saint, Giunta was a shrewd hagiographer who took the step of remolding her further into an exemplary *Franciscan* saint. Strategically, Giunta adopted an omniscient narrator's voice that recounts Margaret's trance-visions as objective fact, rather than as subjective experiences he received secondhand from Margaret herself. The friar thereby crafted an artful presentation of Margaret as a Magdalene-like paragon, a foundress for the third order of secular penitents parallel to the figures of Francis and Clare for the first and second orders.[50] Giunta indirectly refers to his own role as hagiographer when he has Christ tell Margaret, "The Lord said: I will give to you my apostles the Friars Minor, and they will preach about the things that have been accomplished in you, just as the apostles preached my gospel among the peoples" (224).

Yet Margaret's vita was not cut from whole cloth. When we unstitch a few seams in the narrative, we find some interesting alternative viewpoints about her. In order to begin unraveling Giunta's Margaret, let us look at an early instance of Margaret's direct speech. After Margaret is bereft of her lover and patron, some female acquaintances ask cattily, "What will become of you, Margaret fancypants (*vanissima*)?" And she said, "The time will soon come when you will call me saint, for saint shall I be. And you will visit me with a pilgrim's staff and with purses hanging from your shoulders" (184). It is one of those startling moments when the language of a medieval source suddenly seems to vault to a different level. This speech is clean, fresh and direct, free of the fuss and ornamentation that is so common in medieval Latin texts. What is important, however, is not whether Margaret really spoke these words—we cannot know, in any case—but the awareness they display about Margaret's conscious self-fashioning as a saint. They hint at a fascinating choice on Margaret's part. Cast out by her dead lover's family, and by her father and his new wife; burdened with the care of a young son who also would

---

[50] Cannon and Vauchez, *Margherita of Cortona*, 25–29. On the medieval cult for the Magdalene, see Kate Jansen, *The Making of the Magdalen: Preaching and Popular Devotion in the Later Middle Ages* (Princeton, N.J., 2000).

be a liability in finding a new male patron, Margaret committed herself to performing a new role: the divinely possessed, penitential saint. She must have possessed a flair for the dramatic if she was able to envision this future for herself, given her past as a kept woman and unwed mother.

Margaret embraced the new role fully. She moved to Cortona, began a program of good works and assiduous prayer, and acquired a Franciscan confessor and friends. In a typically Franciscan pattern of charitable outreach, Margaret made health care a priority, attending women in childbirth and caring for the ill and neglected urban poor. Her piety made such a positive impression on one of the noble ladies whom she attended as a midwife, a woman we know only by the name Diabella, that she was moved to donate a house to Margaret. This building Margaret converted into a charity house for the poor, which later came under the direction of the Confraternity of Santa Maria della Misericordia.[51] Yet when Margaret first applied to the Franciscans for direction as a member of the Order of Penitence, she was denied. Looking back on this refusal, Giunta comments, "Why, O reader, did the friars hesitate to give her the habit? Certainly, at that time it was because they doubted the constancy of her mind" (184).[52] Yet even after Margaret was accepted as a penitent, gaining the simple plaid robe that was the public indicator of penitent status, there continued to be those among the friars and laity alike who doubted her truthfulness and commitment. Despite Giunta's presentation of Margaret as the "third light" of the Franciscan order, in point of fact her relations with the Minors were vexed and strident. Giunta's hagiography rapidly pulses between the poles of praise and revilement: the author frequently mentions gossip and murmurs against his heroine, criticizing everything from her trance states to her level of humility.[53]

Christ himself, in one of Margaret's visions, referred to the relentless debate among the Friars Minor about her. As described by Giunta, in the vision Christ consoled Margaret, telling her that she should not be surprised "if the friars hold various opinions about you and are disputing" (249–50). The controversy had begun the moment Margaret sought direction from the order, and it escalated from there. At the time she arrived in Cortona with her illegitimate son, seeking legitimacy as a lay penitent, Margaret was still young and attractive, a fact that fostered fears that this former concubine

---

[51] VMC, 187; Iozzelli, "Introduzione," 75; Mancini, Cortona, 103–4.

[52] Although the vita dates her acceptance of the habit to 1277 (VMC, 181), Cannon and Vauchez place it at 1274. She probably arrived in Cortona between 1272 and 1274, so the length of time she remained outside the order is unclear. See Cannon and Vauchez, Margherita of Cortona, 3, 23.

[53] VMC, 218, 250, 260–61, 271, 324, 328–29, 335, 395, among others.

might easily stray from the path of virtue. In response to these hesitations, Margaret attempted violently to reject all vestiges of her former life. She forbade her son even to mention his father in her presence, and found it difficult to care for the child at all. "She was so shorn of maternal affections that it was as if she had never existed in the secular world, which she abhorred, and had never borne a child" (196). Furthermore, Margaret asked Giunta for permission to revisit Montepulciano, the site of her earlier pride and luxury, in order to indulge in an exquisitely detailed scenario of self-humiliation: another woman would lead her, blindfolded, by a rope around her neck and proclaim to everyone that this was the vainglorious woman who had endangered all their souls through her evil example. Later, Margaret begged Giunta for permission to disfigure her face, proposing to cut off her nose and upper lip so that her beauty might no longer present an impediment to her, or a temptation to others (205–6). Yet these tactics were too extreme to be positively received. Giunta summarily refused to allow either Margaret's trip to Montepulciano or the proposed attack on her face, explaining that such expressions of "indiscreet fervor" should be reigned in lest they become a source of arrogance. As for Margaret's son, her neglectful treatment of him only sowed scandal. At one point, gossip spread around Cortona that the poor child, in suicidal despair from want of motherly love and attention, had drowned himself in a well in Arezzo, where he had been sent to be educated (196). Though found alive and unharmed, the son's absence must have fostered opportunities for rumors such as this, suggesting that Margaret was a cruel and unnatural mother. Ultimately, Margaret's son joined the Order of Friars Minor, a fact that may be read either as a measure of her influence upon him or as a reflection of the limited social options for the illegitimate child of an impoverished single parent.

Despite the controversy that perpetually swirled around Margaret, she persisted in her austerities and devotions. The years 1288–90, however, marked a sharp turning point in Margaret's relationship with the Order of Friars Minor. A series of performative actions and reactions galvanized debate about Margaret locally, with the result that she came to the attention of the translocal level of the Franciscan order at a provincial chapter. Around the same time Margaret was, through various circumstances, deprived of the company of her closest supporters. Lastly, the Order of Penitents was transformed by the papal bull *Supra montem* in 1289, a piece of legislation that had direct repercussions on Margaret's status. The confluence of all these events in a brief span of two to three years resulted in Margaret's partial estrangement from the Franciscan order—though the order did not entirely let go of Margaret, as we shall see.

The precise sequence of some events is unclear, but it must have been in the later 1280s that Margaret first began performing the role of the divinely possessed saint in a particularly vivid and public manner, in a series of trances in the Church of Saint Francis that lasted for several days.[54] The description of these trances constitutes the apex of Giunta's hagiography, occurring at the beginning of the fifth chapter of the ten-chapter work. Whereas her earlier trances had been private affairs, Margaret now moved to a higher performative level, publicly enacting Christ's Passion with frenzied vehemence. Indeed, Margaret was anxious to have witnesses to the event, for Giunta tells us that she made him promise in advance to stay in the Franciscan compound on the first day of the planned extravaganza (242–43). This display attracted more public attention and gossip than any previous actions undertaken by Margaret. Indeed, the event undoubtedly was publicized in advance by the friars, acting upon a tip from Giunta. As a result, a substantial audience assembled for the performance: "This spectacle, so new and so filled with compassion, moved all Cortonese. Men and women put aside work and tools, and along with children in cradles and the feeble confined to beds, many times they filled with wails and tears the oratorium of our place, which is dedicated to the honor of our and their father, blessed Francis. For it was as if they saw Margaret placed, not beside the cross, but on the cross" (244).

Giunta presents the audience as both edified and moved to tears by Margaret's extreme behavior. There are no hints in this description of Margaret's crucifixion trance of any dissent or division in the opinion of "all Cortonese." Yet the details of Margaret's behavior during these ecstasies were extremely unsettling. Within a social context that valued bodily calm and control, and modesty in women, actions such as Margaret's were inherently controversial: "She was gnashing her teeth, twisting about like a worm or like a ring. She was discolored until ashen, lost her pulse and the power of speech, and became completely ice-cold" (244). These behaviors could—indeed, did—sustain more than one interpretation. In fact, Giunta's initial conceit that there existed unanimous, pious approval of Margaret's actions as an expression of her divine possession was soon abandoned. A scant few paragraphs after describing the spectacular trances, Giunta disclosed that certain friars in Cortona suspected that they were accomplished through demonic illusion or deception (249). Margaret, it was said, had been led astray by the evil one into seeking local fame and tawdry celebrity. Rather than ratifying her divine

---

[54] The dating of these trances to this time period emerges from the fact that Giunta mentions responses to them immediately afterward, at the Franciscan provincial chapter, which took place in 1288.

possession, the trances prompted rumors that Margaret was a demoniac. The evaluations of Margaret's audience were entering into a phase of intense negotiation, as some argued for her astonishing conformity to Christ, while others became firmly convinced that she was a liar and a fraud led astray by diabolic powers. While it seems likely that the majority of Cortonese either were supportive of Margaret or indifferent, her detractors were an influential group that succeeded in bringing their concerns to the highest level of the Franciscan hierarchy.

The "zealots" (*emuli*) who believed that Margaret's trances were sinister relayed negative gossip about her to the administrative level of the Franciscan order. In 1288 the provincial chapter met in Siena, and Margaret's strange new possessed behavior was placed on the agenda for discussion. The inquisitor Giovanni da Castiglione, Margaret's main supervisor, was in attendance,[55] and undoubtedly he expressed his personal concerns about Margaret. We may assume his opinions were well regarded, since he was promoted to custos for the diocese of Arezzo at this meeting. The chapter ended by concluding that Margaret was likely a false saint deluded by the devil. In a typically canny rhetorical move, Giunta introduces the debates at the provincial chapter by offering Margaret's account of a prophetic revelation she received about the meeting, then gives his own explanation:

> My Father, Brother Giunta, I have learned that . . . on account of . . . the multiform illusions that are found in many people, certain people have doubts about my status. . . . And when our Ancient Enemy saw that certain brothers doubted about her steadfastness, lest those consolations were brought about either by illusion or by deception for the sake of gaining fame in the talk of the people, he began to say in her cell that the friars, Brothers taught by experience, illuminated by the wisdom of the scriptures, and fully enlightened by the grace of the Holy Spirit, had begun to doubt her in this regard, because they recognized truly that her whole life, revelation, and consolations, which seemed divine, were nothing other than a deception. (249)

The spectacle of a former concubine claiming divine prerogatives apparently struck the high-status friars in attendance at the chapter as a scandal rather than a wonder. Fallen women simply were not to be found in the corteges of the saints, whose female members traditionally were defined as virgins, wives, or widows.

[55] Cannon and Vauchez, *Margherita of Cortona*, 23; Iozzelli, "Introduzione," 66.

This interpretation of Margaret's role, further propelled by the explosive matter of her sexual history, elicited a harsh disciplinary response from the Franciscan leadership. Immediately after the chapter broke up, Giunta was instructed strictly to limit his contacts with the controversial woman: "When the chapter was over . . . the new custos [Giovanni da Castiglione] for the friars arrived in Cortona. On behalf of the chapter, he laid down the law for me as her confessor: I should not abandon her, but should visit her only once every eight days" (249). Giunta presents the injunction as a stringent ultimatum, conveying the distinct impression that the provincial chapter feared Margaret as a potential source of corruption, both supernatural and sexual. Charity dictated that she could not be abandoned outright, but she was to be kept at arm's length. Margaret's complaints to Christ about this treatment are recorded by Giunta thus:

> Lord, the Friars Minor, to whom you commended me, seem to have doubts about the swift change of grace which you have brought about in me, without any prior merits of my own. Because of this, they restrict themselves to visiting me in turns and they harbor doubts, fearing lest they are being deceived by me. Therefore, holy father, master and Lord, who has already revealed the names of these doubters to me, I pray you . . . expel the obstacle of all doubt from their hearts. (376)

Margaret was resentful at being treated as a pariah upon the orders of the provincial chapter.

Giovanni da Castiglione's role in the debates about Margaret is complex. On the one hand, as her first confessor he was her "spiritual father" (477); yet evidently he had terrible doubts about her from early in her career. As an inquisitor, Giovanni had known, from the beginning of his association with Margaret, that he had to proceed with the utmost caution in cases of "indiscreet fervor" like hers, which could potentially bring scandal and disrepute upon the Order of Friars Minor. Giovanni was a careful skeptic, however, and he dealt with his deep ambivalence by asking Giunta to keep detailed records about her visions and behaviors (477). These notes could help Giovanni in the project of discerning Margaret's status. Meanwhile, he exerted a strict control over her and her supporters alike. When Margaret became too extreme in her trance behavior, Giovanni raised the issue at the provincial chapter; when Giunta became too close to Margaret, Giovanni enforced some salutary distance between them by circumscribing his visits. Yet Giunta, of course, was able to have the last word.

On May 1, 1288, Margaret moved her cell far away from the Franciscan convent, relocating to a remote area above the town of Cortona next to the Church of Saint Basil. While it is unclear whether Margaret's move preceded or followed the fallout from the provincial chapter, it seems likely that she elected to move her habitation as a result of these doubts and criticisms, which Giunta describes as "terrifying" to her (249). In any event, the move certainly must be read as a bid for more independence from the friars, whose debates about her continued to be heated.[56] Giovanni was opposed, presumably because this would make her more difficult to control. The supportive faction of the Cortona friars also was dismayed: "the friars did not want to consent to this change, in part because the location was very far from the convent of the friars, and in part because they feared lest she be buried elsewhere, as turned out be the case" (199). Indeed, according to Giunta, Margaret had promised her body to the Franciscans, placing her hands between those of Brother Ranaldo and loudly swearing into the public record that her body would forever belong to the order (200). This concern over proprietary rights to Margaret's body indicates an incipient veneration for her even before her death.

Yet Margaret's supporters were rapidly dwindling. Her firm insistence upon relocating despite the friars' objections created resentment among some erstwhile supporters, many of whom who began to fall away from Margaret after the move. Giunta has Christ refer to this defection process when he tells Margaret, "The time is coming when few Friars Minors will remain on your side, and many of the people will persecute you with murmuring" (433). Here, gossip about Margaret acted as a structuring mechanism, helping both to facilitate consensus about her nature and to give a more precise form to that consensus. As one classic view of gossip has noted, "gossip is a catalyst of social process . . . [that] serves to pattern issues which were but vaguely or confusedly perceived by a local population."[57] Beyond serving this epistemological function, however, gossip also can have a disciplining function. That is, negative gossip—the kind that "persecuted with murmuring"—is a means of asserting social control of transgressive behaviors and of attempting to bring the gossiped-about individual back in line with dominant social values and expectations.[58]

Margaret already had lost the confidence of Giovanni da Castiglione.

---

[56] Bornstein, "Margherita da Cortona," 166–67. David Burr suggests that at this time Margaret may have been moving closer to the spiritual wing of the order and distancing herself from the growing worldliness of the mainstream Franciscans. Burr, *Spiritual Franciscans*, 333–34.

[57] Paine, "What Is Gossip About?" 283.

[58] As noted by Merry, "Rethinking Gossip."

More losses occurred through the debt of the flesh. Ranaldo da Castiglione, who had received Margaret into the Order of Penitents, died in about 1288; the following year saw the death of Ubaldo da Colle, another friend. Of Margaret's original inner circle of Franciscan devotees, only Giunta Bevegnate remained to her, though he was forced to limit his time with her. In 1289 or early 1290, however, Giunta suddenly was reassigned to the Franciscan convent in Siena, undoubtedly as a means of forcing an even greater distance between the friar and the penitent.[59] Now bereft of friends and increasingly isolated, Margaret was swiftly becoming more dissatisfied with the order that, fifteen years after her vestition as a penitent, continued to doubt her. Without Ranaldo, Ubaldo, and Giunta, with the "zealots" making trouble, and the provincial chapter expressing doubts, Margaret's ties to the Franciscan order were rapidly attenuating.

In 1289, Margaret was faced with a formal choice regarding her relationship with the Friars Minor. In this year, Pope Nicholas IV issued the bull *Supra montem*, a document that formalized the Order of Penitents and transformed it into the Third Order of Saint Francis.[60] Issued largely in response to growing concerns about the informal character of the penitential movement, *Supra montem* recognized these fraternities for the first time and also provided for their oversight and control. Indeed, whereas earlier penitents had been allowed to select their own religious directors, that function now was assigned to officials chosen by the order. One of the foremost duties of these directors was to be vigilant against all suspicion of heresy: "One must carefully guard against admitting to this observance any heretic or anyone suspected of heresy, or even anyone rumored to be a heretic. And if any such person is found to have been admitted, he shall immediately be given over to the Inquisitor of Heretical Depravity for punishment."[61]

The bull thus formalized the kind of inquisitorial scrutiny Margaret had long been receiving from Giovanni. Nevertheless, Margaret resisted adopting the new vision of the Franciscan third order proposed by *Supra montem*; instead, Margaret's rift with the Minors opened further. Rather than becoming a Franciscan tertiary in the newly organized Third Order, she chose to remain an independent penitent. This fact is clearly signaled by Margaret's clothing, which by the late thirteenth century was used to communicate a rather complex set of visual cues about religious and social affiliations. Rather

---

[59] Cannon and Vauchez, *Margherita of Cortona*, 25.

[60] Edith Pasztor, "La '*Supra montem*' e la cancellaria pontificia," in Pazzelli and Temperini, *Supra montem*, 65–90. The text of the bull is on pages 84–90, edited as an appendix.

[61] Pasztor, "Supra montem," 85.

Figure 6. The relics of Margaret of Cortona, clothed in the plaid dress that in the thirteenth century simply designated penitent status, rather than in the official dress of the Third Order of Saint Francis, formalized in 1289. Her relics are on display under the altar of the Church of Santa Margherita in Cortona. The glass-fronted coffin is a later, baroque design. Photo by author.

than adopting the undyed, brownish robe of a Franciscan tertiary, Margaret retained the plaid dress she always had worn. Art historians have pointed out that this robe, which Margaret wears in the fresco cycles and in a late-thirteenth- or early-fourteenth-century panel painting, and which her corpse still bears, is not that of a Franciscan tertiary (fig. 6). Rather, plaid garments of this type were the common garb of independent lay penitents, without specific associations with any one order.[62] Margaret's choice to preserve this mode of dress is highly significant within a culture of complex sumptuary codes such as late-thirteenth-century central Italy. Changes in social status customarily were rendered final and public through the adoption of new dress—what one scholar has referred to as a "rite of clothing"—in this time

[62] Cannon and Vauchez, *Margherita of Cortona*, 165 nn. 34, 35; Alessandra Gianni, "Iconografia delle sante e beate umbre tra il XIII e gli inizi del XIV secolo," in *Sante e beate umbre tra il XIII e il XIV secolo: Mostra iconografia* (Foligno, 1986), 108–9; Servus Gieben, "L'Iconografia dei penitenti e Niccolò IV," in Pazzelli and Temperini, *Supra montem*, 289–304.

and place.[63] The mendicant orders in particular were becoming increasingly insistent about regularizing the dress of their members, both in life and in artistic representations. If Margaret had become a formal Franciscan tertiary after *Supra montem*, surely she would have signaled this fact through adoption of the appropriate dress in the last eight years of her life. In short, it seems that faced with continual doubts on the one hand and new restrictions on the other, Margaret elected not to enter the newly formalized third order, but to maintain the general penitential habit that she long had borne.

Although Margaret retained some ties to the order after these events, she also began transferring her allegiance to the secular clergy attached to the church of Saint Basil, whose rector now acted as her confessor. In 1290 Margaret obtained an indulgence from the new bishop of Arezzo for those helping to rebuild the church of Saint Basil. She also arranged for the appointment of a rector: Ser Badia, who became her new confessor. Though the rector cooperated with the Franciscans in overseeing Margaret—by corresponding with Giunta in Siena, for example, to keep him apprized of Margaret's progress—the ultimate responsibility for Margaret's career had shifted from the Friars Minor to the city itself. At her death, the church of Saint Basil retained Margaret's body on behalf of the commune of Cortona. It was the commune, too, that sponsored the construction of a new church to house her relics and later commissioned frescoes to adorn it. Finally, it was the commune that set aside funds in 1325 for the rector of Saint Basil to travel to the papal curia in Avignon and seek Margaret's canonization, at considerable expense, though in vain.[64] The children to whom Margaret had acted as midwife and godmother remained more faithful to her than the order that had fostered her vocation—and which now housed her own son.

Thus did the Friars Minor of Cortona lose control of the relics of a potential saint, forcing them to fight for proprietary rights to her. Needless to say Giunta's text, composed sometime between 1297 and 1308, was on the front line of this battle. With the order having lost her relics, Giunta was determined to prove Margaret's Franciscan bona fides by composing a hagiog-

[63] Christiane Klapisch-Zuber, "The Griselda Complex: Dowry and Marriage Gifts in the Quattrocento," in *Women, Family, and Ritual in Renaissance Italy*, trans. L. Cochraine (Chicago, 1985), 213–46; Diane Owen Hughes, "Distinguishing Signs: Ear-Rings, Jews, and Franciscan Rhetoric in the Italian Renaissance City," *Past and Present* 112 (1986): 3–69.

[64] Cannon and Vauchez, *Margherita of Cortona*, 30–31; Bornstein, "Margherita da Cortona," 171. André Vauchez (*Sainthood in the Middle Ages*, trans. J. Birrell [Cambridge, 1997], 66, 72) gives the date as 1318, presumably an error, corrected in Cannon and Vauchez, *Margherita of Cortona*. Margaret was sainted in 1728 (Cannon and Vauchez, *Margherita of Cortona*, 36).

raphy that bound her firmly to the Minors. Factions within the order had contested Margaret's sanctity throughout her life; now that she was safely dead and unable to backslide or sow scandal, Giunta was free to appropriate her as a good Franciscan penitent.

But if, for Giunta, the founding figure of the third order was Margaret, then her image existed in perpetual tension with the foundational document of Nicholas IV, which irrevocably tied the third order to inquisitorial scrutiny. By making the hagiography a glorification of the Franciscan order as well as of Margaret, Giunta staved off potential criticism. Even so, the finished work was offered to various ecclesiastical authorities for approval, testifying to a continuing perception that Margaret's unconventional path to sanctity required extra caution and certification. The work was not suppressed, but neither was it broadly disseminated. Only three manuscript copies of the text survive, all in Cortona, an indication that her cult was scarcely diffused outside the town in which she lived.[65] Other Franciscan convents or locales were not interested in acquiring copies of this life of an unmarried mother dedicated to Christ.[66] In the 1330s, as the commune was paying for the Church of Saint Basil—now expanded and known locally as Santa Margherita—to be painted with frescoes to honor Margaret, a general "Catalogue of Franciscan Saints" was produced in central Italy, organized by country and region: Margaret's name does not appear.[67] This is all the more striking in that the mendicant orders were widely known to be tireless, competitive promoters of their own saints: "the friars, especially the mendicants, are overcome by a certain self-interest in the praise of their saints. They are accustomed to depart from the path of reason, covering over their rabble and human defects with the veil of a woman saint or a man saint."[68] The fact that Margaret was denied this support testifies to the depth of the Franciscan concern about her.

Margaret's declaration that "the day will come when you will call me saint, for saint shall I be," must be read as nothing less than a challenge. Yet the multiple audiences that evaluated her performance did not always, as predicted, call her saint. Her story is ultimately a tale of two processes of reconstruction: Margaret's and Giunta's. If Margaret needed to refashion

---

[65] Cannon and Vauchez, *Margherita of Cortona*, 22.

[66] The phrase is Benvenuti Papi's.

[67] Leonard Lemmens, ed., *Fragmenta Minora: Catalogus Sanctorum Fratrum Minorum* (Rome, 1903). The volume includes several Franciscan texts, each separately paginated; the "Catalogue" is the first.

[68] Maria Lungarotti, ed. *Le Legendae di Margherita da Città di Castello* (Spoleto, 1994), 66.

herself as a saint, after her sexual past, so too did Giunta need to refashion her posthumously as an exemplary Franciscan, after decades of rejection by the broader order. Margaret remade herself from paramour to penitent; but it was Giunta who transformed her from penitent to saintly paragon.

TWO MOMENTS IN THE LIFE OF A BEGUINE

Elizabeth of Spalbeek exists for historians only in two moments, ten years apart.[69] She first surfaced from a murky obscurity in 1267. A detailed report composed in that year described the vivid pantomimes of Christ's Passion that Elizabeth, then a teenage Beguine still living in the small village of her birth, was accustomed to act out each day. She keyed the main events of her divine impersonation to the liturgical hours, breaking out in stigmata at the climax of her performance. This text circulated throughout the Low Countries, galvanizing debate in subsequent years. But Elizabeth herself vanished: there is no more direct evidence of her existence until a decade later.

Then, Elizabeth was living in Nivelles. Descriptions of her from 1277 make no mention of the Passion trances and stigmata that dominate the earlier portrayal. Rather, Elizabeth now was supporting herself through a reputation for prophecy. A cluster of documents from this period mention Elizabeth's prophetic gift in connection with a scandal that was then unfolding at the court of the French king Philip III. Elizabeth's reputation for occult knowledge prompted the French royals to seek her advice in sorting out accusations of murder, simony, and secret sins against nature that were swirling about the court in the aftermath of the young dauphin Louis's untimely death. The twin chronicles and various legal depositions that record the details of this scandal also preserve a highly pragmatic view of Elizabeth, one shorn of the hagiographical conventions that dominate the report of a decade earlier.

We thus possess an exceptionally rich dossier of documents about this Be-

[69] For studies, see Walter Simons, "Reading a Saint's Body: Rapture and Bodily Movement in the *Vitae* of Thirteenth-Century Beguines," in S. Kay and M. Rubin, *Framing Medieval Bodies* (Manchester, 1994), 10–23; Walter Simons and Joanna Ziegler, "Phenomenal Religion in the Thirteenth Century and Its Image: Elisabeth of Spalbeek and the Passion Cult," in W. Sheils and D. Wood, eds., *Women in the Church* (Oxford, 1990), 117–26; Joanna Zeigler and Susan Rodgers, "Elisabeth of Spalbeek's Trance Dance of Faith: A Performance Theory Interpretation from Anthropological and Art Historical Perspectives," in M. Suydam and J. Zeigler eds., *Performance and Transformation: New Approaches to Late Medieval Spirituality* (New York, 1999), 299–355.

guine, written from several different viewpoints but centering on two limited moments in time. All the documents that discuss Elizabeth begin with gossip and rumor. The Beguine appears in texts only secondarily to her reputation: the authors hear of her, then decide to meet her and investigate further. Gossip about her supernatural gifts piqued the interest of observers, each with their own ideological agendas. Clerics used her variously as an illustration of divine illumination—and of hypocritical histrionics. Courtiers used her reputation as an imprimatur to further their own political causes. Chroniclers called her a holy woman and a demoniac. In short, Elizabeth, more so than the other cases examined here, remains a cipher to the end, for no consensus on her character ever was achieved.

All current studies of Elizabeth begin and end with the hagiographical material about her, dating from 1267. In that year Philip, abbot of Clairvaux, was conducting a visitation to Cistercian foundations in the area around Liège. Arriving at the nunnery of Herkenrode, Philip heard talk of the trances and possessed behaviors of a young Beguine named Elizabeth, who lived in the nearby village of Spalbeek. The rumors suggested, as Philip writes in his characteristically ornate style, that "within her virginal purity, our merciful and magnanimous Lord, magnifying his mercies, miraculously and munificently brought forth the clearest proofs of our faith and of His Passion."[70] Philip was intrigued but hesitant. He thus decided to visit the virgin himself in order to examine her behaviors firsthand. Arriving at the village of Spalbeek, he was astounded by what he saw. "When I, brother Philip of Clairvaux . . . heard about these marvelous works of the Lord, I did not believe the people who were telling me about it. Not until I myself went and saw with my own eyes did I realize that I had not heard the half of it."[71]

What did Philip witness to inspire his purple prose? Elizabeth's stigmata, viewed by Philip as the ultimate ratification of her inhabitation by Christ. The transformed surface of her body announced the inner reality of her holy spirit possession. The Cistercian abbot was at pains to assure his readers that he examined the marks closely and found them to be "recent wounds that were exposed very clearly, without any doubt of pretense or suspicion of fraud."[72] The wounds on her limbs were round, and that on her side, oblong. All the marks frequently flowed with streams of blood, particularly on Saturdays. Having viewed the wounds, Philip decided to compose a report about them. Though this document clearly intended to present Elizabeth as a saint,

[70] Philip of Clairvaux, *Vita Elizabeth sanctimonialis in Erkenrode*, in *Catalogus codicum hagiographicorum bibliothecae Regiae Bruxellensis* (Brussels 1886), 1:363.
[71] Ibid.
[72] Ibid.

it departs from formal hagiographical conventions: it does not consist of a vita so much as a detailed description of Elizabeth's participatory meditations on the Passion.

Philip was aware that this report on Elizabeth's stigmata would be troubling to some, and he consistently anticipates criticism and argues against possible doubts. For example, the text directly confronts the issue of whether stigmata are suitable for the female body: "what if perchance someone should . . . protest that the infirmity of the female sex abhors the representation or demonstration of such a glorious victory?"[73] Philip has a justification of Elizabeth's wounds ready to hand. After sketching out the various roles of women in biblical history, Philip turns to the role that Elizabeth and her stigmata may play for her thirteenth-century contemporaries. Arguing that Christ's salvific insignia were made manifest in a woman in order to achieve sexual symmetry for pious observers, Philip presents Elizabeth as a female Saint Francis.

[Christ] recently revealed the same miracle in the virile sex, in the person of blessed Francis. Thus, each sex may discover that which it honors, venerates, reveres, imitates, and loves not only in the testimony of scripture, but also in living exemplars of the human condition on the cross of Christ; and thus no one, however illiterate or simple, can put forth an excuse . . . saying, "I cannot read and understand such deep mysteries, because I am unlettered" or "because the book is closed [to me]." For an unlearned person may "read" just like a literate person, not on parchments or papers, but in the girl's limbs and body . . . a vivid image of salvation and a living history of redemption, a living, open Veronica.[74]

The notion that Elizabeth's body could be read like a text is among the more intriguing aspects of Philip's presentation. Indeed, Philip consistently presents Elizabeth as a transparent window onto the divine—in particular, onto the character and significance of the Passion narrative. The body of Philip's account is taken up with a detailed description of Elizabeth's custom of acting out the events of Jesus' Passion seven times each day, at the hours of matins, prime, terce, sext, nones, vespers, and complines. This cycle followed a repetitive and predictable form over the course of the day, with each hour devoted to a different aspect of the Passion story.

[73] Ibid.

[74] Ibid. On Veronicas, see Jeffrey Hamburger, "Vision and the Veronica," in *The Visual and the Visionary: Art and Female Spirituality in Late Medieval Germany* (New York, 1998), 317–82.

Elizabeth herself surely was not responsible for designing this pious pantomime. As we have seen, other women such as Margaret of Cortona enacted such performances publicly as well. Moreover, the thirteenth century saw the broad diffusion of devotional works that offered guided meditations on the Passion narrative, sometimes even tied to the liturgical hours of the day. Such texts counsel deep engagement with and mimicry of the Passion narrative as a means both to arouse salvific compassion and to spur greater asceticism. Thus Pseudo-Bede's *Little Book of Meditation on the Passion of Christ through the Seven Hours of the Day*[75] provides a step-by-step, hour-by-hour meditative guide through the arrest, trial, death, and burial of Jesus for the delectation of the devout. The most recent dating of the text ascribes it to the mid-twelfth century and speculates that it derives from a specifically Cistercian milieu.[76] If so, it is not unlikely that the text could have been known to Elizabeth, through sermons and other informal means of oral transmission, since she moved in Cistercian circles. This manual is particularly intriguing for its insistence that the user should precisely mimic each gesture that Christ is envisioned making. Thus at compline—the hour devoted to Jesus' prayers in the Garden of Gethsemane—the pious Christian should pray along with Jesus to the Father: "Therefore, pay attention to all these words and their aspect, for you should do the same. That is, fall on your face; do not look back, but keep that which you seek before you. . . . Do not pray tepidly, but with great effort and pain, just as the Lord did; and not just a little, but at great length."[77] Similarly, at terce, as the devotee envisions the journey to Calvary, she should insert herself into the scene, offering to bear the cross for Christ: "Then they place the cross on his shoulders for him to carry. Certainly, dearest, you will do well if you help your Lord, and say, 'I beg you, my Lord, give the cross to me and I will carry it.'"[78]

The meditative exercise of imagining a New Testament scene, and then inserting oneself into it, seems to have been a well-known devotional practice among the laity. Margery Kempe, for example, enjoyed contemplating the Nativity, imagining how she sought shelter for the Holy Family and later swaddled the infant Christ.[79] Thus Elizabeth's activities were a highly accomplished public performance of a fairly common type of devotional prayer.

[75] Auctor Incertus (Beda?), *De meditatione passionis Christi per septem diei horas libellum,* in *PL,* 94:561–68.
[76] Flavio Di Bernardo, "Passion, mystique de la," in *Dictionnaire de la Spiritualité,* vol. 12, part 1 (Paris, 1984), 330.
[77] Pseudo-Bede, *Libellum,* 563.
[78] Ibid., 565–66.
[79] Margery Kempe, *The Book of Margery Kempe,* ed. B. Windeatt (Harlow, 2000), 76–78.

Her enactments of these meditations were particularly noteworthy, however, for three reasons. One was undoubtedly their public character, for Elizabeth, like Margaret after her, performed her participatory meditations in the local church rather than in the more common setting for such exercises, the home. In addition, she repeated this performance on a daily basis, rather than as a unique event. Finally, and most crucially, Elizabeth's body underwent a physical transformation as a result of these devotions; as stigmata erupted on her hands, feet, and side, she became the image of Christ crucified.

Each portion of the performance began when Elizabeth entered into a trance state, in which she "remained completely rigid, like an image of wood or stone, without sense or movement or breath."[80] Then she would rise and pace her room, going round and round while beating her breast with each open-palmed hand in turn. This activity would gradually crescendo into a full-scale pounding and beating, in which she threw herself against walls and floors; pulled her own hair, gouged her eyes, and seemed to drag herself about by force, while somehow resisting at the same time. Indeed, Elizabeth's pantomimes included both Christomimetic and prosecutorial roles: she embodied both victim and tormentor, presenting the Passion narrative from dual perspectives at once. At terce she demonstrated, in a display that Philip found admirably contortionist, how Christ had his arms bound behind his back and was tied to a column and whipped. At sext, nones, and vespers, the play reached its climax with Elizabeth's remembrance of Christ's crucifixion, death, and burial. When Elizabeth demonstrated her participation in the crucifixion, Philip marveled at her ability to remain balanced in an appropriately evocative position, with arms extended, one foot placed upon the other, and standing on tiptoe. This element invariably was followed by her miming of burial. So forceful were these pantomimes, Philip noted admiringly, Elizabeth sometimes bled from her eyes.[81]

While Philip began from a position of skepticism, he not only gave in to his desire to believe in Elizabeth, he constructed a rather ornate theological edifice of interpretation around her. "She figured and exhibited not only Christ—and Him crucified—in her body, but also the mystical body of Christ, that is the Church."[82] Philip used Elizabeth as an image of integration and unity: the divine disorder evident in her pantomimes was for him a harmonious and wonderful figuration of both Christ and His Bride, the Church. Elizabeth thus became for Philip a living exemplar of divine pos-

---

[80] Philip of Clairvaux, *Vita Elizabeth*, 364.
[81] Ibid., 368–69, 371.
[82] Ibid., 378.

session on both a literal and a figurative scale. On a more worldly level, Elizabeth could bring credit to the Cistercian order, since she was loosely associated with them, and perhaps even provide the white monks with their own stigmatic to rival that of the Franciscans.

If no other documents about Elizabeth existed, then Philip's text would be our only window onto this peculiar Beguine. However, Philip's 1267 report had a contested afterlife. Philip's claim that Elizabeth had miraculously been marked with the five stigmatic wounds was probably the first widespread rumor concerning a woman in this role, and it shocked contemporaries. Not surprisingly, those who were critical of the Beguine movement in general, and of women who exhibited extreme behaviors in particular, responded negatively. One such commentator was Gilbert of Tournai, author of a 1274 treatise titled *Scandals of the Church*. "There are among us some women," he noted, "who we do not know whether to call laity or monastics. They partake of some secular, and some monastic, usages."[83] Thus does Gilbert introduce the Beguines as a hybrid novelty of the times. He went on to censure the miraculous claims of Beguines, their arrogation of religious authority, and the dangerous innovations of their lifestyles. "[They] thrive on subtleties and rejoice in novelties. They have interpreted the mysteries of the scriptures, and Gallicized them into the common tongue. . . . These they read together, irreverently, boldly; in meetings, in prisons, in the streets! . . . If this disease spreads, there will be as many scandals surging up as there are listeners; as many blasphemies as there are streets."[84] The case of Elizabeth, however, perturbed Gilbert most of all: "Among this type of silly women was one who achieved a semipublic reputation for being marked with Christ's stigmata. If this is true, it should not be rumored in secret, but let it be known openly. If, however, it is not true, let this hypocrisy and simulation be thwarted."[85]

Gilbert was eager to contest Philip's account of Elizabeth. It seemed to him absurd that women should debate points of scripture and claim religious authority while remaining of lay status, and even more bizarre that they should bear the wounds of Christ. Rather than viewing Elizabeth as Philip did—as a possessed woman whose skin betrayed the divine identity of her possessing spirit within—Gilbert regarded her as a hypocrite and an impostor.

In addition to these general objections, however, Gilbert certainly was

[83] Gilbert of Tournai, *De scandalis ecclesiae*, ed. A Stroick, *Archivum Franciscanum Historicum* 24 (1931): 58.
[84] Ibid., 61–62. See Stroick's editorial note 3.
[85] Ibid.

motivated to attack Elizabeth's stigmata for another reason, namely, partisanship for his own religious order. As a Franciscan, Gilbert must have been particularly struck by Philip's attempt to create a parallelism between Elizabeth and Francis. While Philip argued that Elizabeth's stigmata were complementary to Francis's, in order that each sex might see an image of the divine imprinted upon itself, Gilbert regarded the stigmata not only as a uniquely male, but also a uniquely Franciscan, miracle. Indeed, the Order of Friars Minor consistently acted as jealous guardians of Francis's stigmatic status, attempting to squelch competitive claims to this miracle whenever and wherever they arose. In this, they were aided by the highest levels of the ecclesiastical hierarchy, which prescribed veneration of Francis's wounds while tacitly ignoring other claimants to the miracle.[86] The result was that, though stigmatic wounding became a characteristically female saintly claim over the next century, no female stigmatic was canonized during the Middle Ages except Catherine of Siena—whose "wounds," significantly, were invisible. Gilbert's hostile dismissal of Elizabeth, her stigmata, and the Beguines in general highlights the ideological dimensions of discernment disputes, in which hagiographical outlooks contended with other, more belligerent views.

This was not the end of Elizabeth's story, however. We are fortunate to possess a particularly rich dossier about her, expressing a range of different viewpoints. A later set of documents reveals how her reputation continued to be appropriated by others for their own ends.

A decade after Philip encountered the strange girl in Spalbeek, Elizabeth had changed her surroundings and her habits. In 1277 Elizabeth was known neither for stigmata nor Passion enactments. Had Gilbert of Tournai's harsh response prompted Elizabeth to relinquish these behaviors? It is impossible to know. What is clear is that Elizabeth had not abandoned her claim to supernatural prerogatives, for she was now widely known as a prophetess. Elizabeth emerges from the juxtaposition of these two years as something of an opportunist, willing to try various different possessed behaviors in order to sustain a reputation as an inspired figure.

Before we turn to the Elizabeth of 1277, some background is in order. In the same year that Gilbert of Tournai was writing *Scandals of the Church*, a scandal of the court was erupting in France. In 1274 King Philip III (the Bold) married Marie of Brabant, his second wife. The new teenage queen had

[86] See André Vauchez, "La stimmatizzazione di san Francesco d'Assisi: Significato e portata storica" and "Le stimmate di san Francesco e i loro detrattori negli ultimi secoli del Medioevo," both in *Ordini mendicanti e società italiana, XIII–XV secolo* (Milan, 1990), 54–64, 65–91.

scarcely settled into court when she found herself surrounded by intrigues and enemies. Prominent among the latter was the king's chamberlain, Pierre de la Broce, whose broad influence Marie threatened to displace.[87] The chamberlain sensed an opportunity when the dauphin Louis, son of the king's first wife, Isabelle of Aragon, died suddenly and mysteriously: he covertly sponsored a rumor that Marie had caused the death of the young prince. Pierre de la Broce's relative by marriage, Pierre de Benais, bishop of Bayeux, spread gossip that Queen Marie had poisoned the dauphin in order to clear a path to the throne for her own progeny. However, a competing rumor of uncertain origin blamed the sexual sins of Philip for the dauphin's death.

Precisely how Elizabeth came to be involved in these events is unclear. There exist two chronicle versions of the scandal: the Latin text of Guillaume de Nangis's *Deeds of Philip the Third, King of France* and an Old French translation of Guillaume's work.[88] A legal deposition concerning the scandal, taken in 1278 from the papal legate to France Simon de Brion, and a letter to Philip from various religious officials in the Diocese of Liège, also have been preserved. I shall begin with the legal document, which gives the fullest account of these events.

Simon de Brion's legal deposition begins by recalling that in 1276 Pierre de Benais told him that rumors of the queen's murder of the dauphin were all over Paris. Simon undertook to verify whether this was the case, but in fact found no one else gossiping in this way.[89] He had, however, heard different rumors about the dauphin's death: an unidentified *sant home* had told him that the king was addicted to unnatural sexual practices—a phrase that usually means homosexuality—which would result in the deaths of all his children if he did not soon repent. This gossip apparently *did* have enough currency eventually to reach the ears of the king, for two months later Philip took Simon aside during a visit to Tours and asked him about it. Philip explained that a *vidame* of Laon (a kind of secular representative of the bishop) had "defamed him most criminally and outrageously with the sin against nature. The *vidame* said that two holy women from the diocese of Liège, one named Alice, who was a leper, and the other named [Elizabeth] of Sparbeek, had told him that the king was involved in this vice. . . . [and that] if the king

[87] Little has been written on this episode other than Richard Kay, "Martin IV and the Fugitive Bishop of Bayeux," *Speculum* 40, 3 (1965): 460–83.

[88] Both the *Gesta Philippi tertii Francorum regis* and *Vie de Philippe III par Guillaume de Nangis* are in M. Bouquet, ed., *Recueil des historiens des Gaules et de la France*, vol. 20 (Paris, 1840), on alternate pages. The incident is described on pages 502 (Latin) and 503 (Old French); all de Nangis quotations to follow are drawn from these pages.

[89] J. de Gaulle, ed., "Documents historiques," in *Bulletin de la société de l'histoire de France* (1844): 87–100; this discussion at 88–89.

did not soon repent of this sin, one of his children would die within half a year."[90]

Thus in 1277 Elizabeth was suddenly, again, the subject of rumors requiring investigation, though this time she was playing a different role: the prophetess who could uncover the secret shame of a king that drew the wrath of God.

Simon continued his account. Since Elizabeth and Alice had been identified as the source of the rumor about Philip's sexual proclivities, the king decided to send an envoy to the women in order to find out more about their prophecies and what light they might throw on the death of the dauphin. Pierre de la Broce succeeded in having Pierre de Benais—his proxy in the gossip about the queen—nominated for this visit. Pierre de Benais sent back the following report. During the first interview with the women, which took place before various local officials, Elizabeth and Alice denied having said anything about the king's sexual behavior. The dauphin had not died as a result of God's wrath for Philip's sodomy; indeed, the king was good and loyal and honest. However, Pierre continued, Elizabeth subsequently had taken him aside and confided privately that the dauphin's death was indeed a murder. According to Pierre's rather suspect account of this private conversation, Elizabeth revealed, through her prophetic inspiration, that the royal child had been poisoned by someone in the household of the queen. When pressed as to the precise identity of the poisoner, however, Pierre de Benais demurred, claiming that Elizabeth had constrained him not to divulge the name of the criminal. This strategic silence allowed Pierre de Benais to continue fostering rumors of royal poisonings: in effect, Pierre was using Elizabeth's prophetic reputation to further his own political ends against the young queen.

Efforts to obtain further information met with mixed results. At first, Elizabeth refused to meet with a new envoy, saying that she already had told all to Pierre. Later, when the bishop of Liège and other local officials intervened, Elizabeth categorically denied ever having breathed a word about poison, affirming that the queen was above all suspicion. She claimed that in her private conversation with Pierre, he simply had asked her to remain silent about the situation. A letter to Philip III from the bishop of Liège and other local clerics corroborates Simon's account of this aspect of the case.[91]

The portrait of Elizabeth that emerges from the legal depositions shows

[90] Ibid., 89. Simon de Brion actually calls the second woman "Ysabel," a gallicization of her name. Other documents in the dossier name her as "Lizebeth." For commentary on this point, see Kay, "Martin IV," 468 n. 32.
[91] Printed in de Gaulle, "Documents Historiques."

a weak, vain, and manipulable woman. First the *vidame* of Lyon (source of the homosexuality rumor in her name) and then Pierre de Benais (source of the poisoning rumors, now authorized with her imprimatur) used her reputation to advance their own favored gossip—and in each case she did nothing to disavow these reports until explicitly pressed to do so. Indeed, her vaunted oracular gifts appear to have been seriously undermined by this affair, in which she twice was credited with explosive statements about sex and murder that she later denied. Furthermore, her agreement to Pierre's request that she remain silent suggests that she was ready to collude with scandalous gossip when it suited her—that is, when it favored the advancement of her prophetic reputation. Her performances were so transparently adapted to the exactions of her changing interlocutors that ruptures and contradictions in her self-representation were inevitable. Although the depositions indict Pierre de Benais above all, Elizabeth emerges as an opportunist: different agents attributed various positions to her, and she did nothing to disavow these positions until they became inconvenient. Her only interest was to extend her reputation as an inspired prophetess.

Turning now to the chronicle versions of the scandal, we may note some interesting divergences. First, Guillaume de Nangis omits all mention of Philip's alleged homosexuality and concentrates on the rumors that Marie de Brabant was the murderess. This was an intelligent choice for a chronicler acting under royal patronage. However, altering the chain of events in this fashion required that Elizabeth appear on the scene in a slightly different manner. Elizabeth could no longer be introduced as the source of the homosexuality rumor, and instead is presented simply as one of three famous prophets. She acts as a professional consultant to the court, who is asked to illuminate the truth or falsity of the rumors about the queen.

The tale of the interviews with Elizabeth roughly accords with the legal documents just examined. Both the Latin and the Old French versions of Guillaume's chronicle tell us that two legates initially were sent to interview Elizabeth: Matthew, abbot of Saint-Denis, and Pierre de Benais. In their reports to the king, the abbot complained that Elizabeth had refused to speak with him; and Pierre de Benais indicated that he had received damning words from her about the queen under seal of confession. A second deputation made by others ended in Elizabeth's vindication of the queen.

Where the chronicles do provide significant new information, however, is in their interpretation of the character of Elizabeth's prophetic inspiration. Interestingly, although the Old French is purportedly a translation of the Latin, the two versions present diametrically opposed categorizations of Elizabeth in this regard. In the original Latin version, she is one of three religious specialists consulted about the death of the dauphin. "The third, a pseudo-prophetess, was a certain Beguine from Nivelles. [All three] lived without the approval of any religion: they lied to God through the conduct of the life they displayed outwardly. They were said to have the spirit of prophecy, but in fact it was a spirit of deceit in their mouths." Thus according to this text, Elizabeth and the others were possessed by lying spirits and lived as demonic hypocrites and frauds. There is no question that her prophecies might be divine in character: indeed, she is introduced as a deceitful pseudo-prophetess from the outset.

The Old French version, however, adapts its interpretation of Elizabeth even as it adapts the language from Latin to Old French. This version of the chronicle rehabilitates Elizabeth completely: "It was said and told that there was a prophetess at Nivelles who revealed marvelous things about past and future events. She wore the habit of a Beguine and conducted herself like a holy woman of good life." Indeed, the Old French not only insists that the Beguine was truthful, and therefore by implication divinely inspired, but claims that she was the most famous and credible prophet of the age. The three prophets involved are first collectively described as "the three considered the most wise," and Elizabeth is then identified as "more renowned than the others." This *sainte fame et de bonne vie* is here represented as a direct conduit to the divine, one blessed with occult knowledge and the ability to discern hidden mysteries and crimes.

Here, then, is the puzzling phenomenon of two quite different interpretations of a possessed woman, given in what is putatively the same text in different languages. The slippage between the two versions hints, tantalizingly, at a possible divergence of interpretation according to audience. The Latin version, aimed at a clerical audience, defines her as possessed by a lying spirit, while the vernacular version endorses her gifts as divinely inspired and revels in her fame. This juxtaposition is all the more striking in that the remainder of the episode is rendered from Latin into Old French rather faithfully.

The scandal ended in 1278, with the execution of Pierre de la Broce for treason and libel. Elizabeth disappeared thereafter from the evidentiary record, and we know nothing further of her. Yet our knowledge of these two moments in her life suggests a significant challenge to hagiographical texts as privileged sources for the history of responses to possessed women. If our evidence about Elizabeth were limited only to the laudatory work produced by Philip of Clairvaux, in fact we would know very little about her—and about what observers thought of her. Philip's narration was intended to propagate her reputation as a living saint inspired by Cistercian spirituality: a woman interiorly possessed by the divine and displaying this status in "readable" form on the exterior of her body. The other texts, however, tell different stories, for they arise from within different power structures and subordinate Elizabeth to their individual ideological viewpoints. In view of the wide range of these interpretations of Elizabeth, we must wonder whether hagiographical texts about other individuals mask a similar diversity of opinion, now lost to us.

Philip's presentation of Elizabeth was but a single, early testimony concerning a woman whose reputation persisted, for good *and* ill, much longer. If, for Philip, Elizabeth's Passion enactments proved that she was divinely possessed, for Gilbert of Tournai, Elizabeth was the crowning "scandal of the church," a lying fraud who appropriated to the weaker sex the peculiarly Franciscan and male prerogative of stigmata. From the chronicle of Guillaume de Nangis, we glean that Elizabeth either was a demoniac pseudo-prophetess possessed by a lying demon, or else a *sante fame*. Yet it is Simon de Brion's legal deposition that finally provides the most insight into the phenomenon of the discernment of spirits in Elizabeth's case. Simon's testimony exposes most clearly how Elizabeth's reputation as an inspired prophetess could be exploited by others for their own ideological ends. Her performance, intended as a representation of divine possession, was dependent upon the participation of an audience for its final meaning. The construction of her identity as either divinely possessed, demonically possessed, or fraudulent depended not just on her behaviors, but also on the interpretation of observers. Yet since reports of supernatural behaviors like trances and prophecy were inherently subjective and difficult to verify, they could easily be molded to the different agendas of various observers. The fact that Elizabeth always appears first as the subject of gossip and rumor, and only secondarily as a particular individual, highlights how her reputation was used by others to mold consensus and influence public opinion. Elizabeth's self-representations ultimately were subordinate to the representations of her crafted by others, either through rumor mongering or through the production of a written text. Just as the *vidame* and Pierre de Benais used Elizabeth to further their own political agendas, so too did Philip of Clairvaux, Gilbert of Tournai, Guillaume de Nangis, and the Old French translator of Guillaume. We are fortunate to possess such a diverse group of documents about this one individual, in which two moments of life yield the manifold perspectives of a diverse, highly politicized audience.[92]

[92] There is an ironic epilogue to the tale of Elizabeth and Philip. A generation later, Philip's son and heir Philip IV (the Fair) also was inclined to listen to Beguine prophet-

Although this chapter has focused only on three possessed women, explorations of this kind could be conducted for nearly all lay religious women living in the later Middle Ages.[93] However, the narrow focus of this chapter permits greater insight into the process of discerning spirits "on the ground," exposing the multiple axes of interpretation that influenced the social construction of identity. Surrounding each inspired woman was a series of competing and overlapping communities, from family to neighborhood to town to diocese to religious order. It was characteristic of the careers of laywomen exhibiting possessed behaviors that each of these surrounding communities would discern spirits according to a different scale of values. Each inspired woman was a cipher to be interpreted as demonically possessed, divinely inspired, ill, insane, or faking; sometimes all these judgments were rendered upon the same individual at the same time. Moreover different groups or gossip cells interacted and debated with one another over time, sometimes changing one another's evaluations, sometimes becoming more intractable. Indeed, what becomes clear through these case studies is that the discernment of spirits was not a neutral decision. Attaching a category to a particular woman was more than a measure of social interpretation, it was an epistemological statement about good and evil, the boundaries between them, and their immanence in the bodies of human beings. Above all, however, discernment was an ideological act, an interpretation inflected by local mentalities, the observers' self-interest, and the exigencies of power.

---

esses. The *Chronicle* of Girard de Frachet relates that in 1304 "A certain counterfeit woman (*pseudo-mulier*) from Metz used to simulate sanctity under the habit of a Beguine, while living in Flanders with the Beguines. Pretending to receive certain fabricated and deceptive revelations . . . she deluded the king as well as the queen and the foremost men [of court] with her lying words on many occasions." Upon the instigation of the king's brother, Charles of Valois, this Beguine was arrested and tortured through the application of flames to the soles of her feet, "until she was said to have confessed the aforementioned sorcery." Imprisoned for a short while, the nameless woman eventually was released and allowed to go her own way. Girard de Frachet, *Chronicon*, in Bouquet, *Recueil*, vol. 21 (Paris, 1855), 23. It was also during the reign of Philip the Fair that Marguerite Porete was executed for heresy. Clearly the relationship between the Valois dynasty and prophetic Beguines was a mutually vexed and dangerous one, risking the dignity and the souls of the former, the reputations and bodies of the latter.

[93] Caciola, "Mystics, Demoniacs," 273–79.

PART II

Spiritual Physiologies

CHAPTER THREE
FALLEN WOMEN
AND FALLEN ANGELS

In brief, a woman is nothing other than a devil in the likeness
of a human form.
— ALBERTUS MAGNUS

The body of a possessed person was thought to be inhabited by more than one identity, or spirit. Though her human spirit or personality still remained within her physical shell, it was subordinated by this more powerful, invading supernatural spirit. The possessed called themselves by new names: Mazzanto, Pen-in-ink,[1] or Holy Spirit. Their very aspect and appearance might be transformed: a bearded man, a grimacing mask. They uttered speech in the voice of their possessing spirit, adopting the personality of the indwelling entity.

As Michel de Certeau has pointed out, the speech of the possessed woman is not hers but is deferred to another entity. The lips and tongue that utter prophecies are physically that of the possessed woman, yet they are controlled, as in a marionette, by a spirit other than her own.[2] Thus spirit possession is most fundamentally and originally a disruption of identity: the possessed lack deictic integrity or stability. The term "deixis," which I have adopted from the vocabulary of rhetoric, refers to the proper use of demonstrative words and pronouns. Hence deixis targets the individual's ability to adopt a consistent point of view or subject position within language or, by extension, social and physical interaction. It is precisely this function that is

---

[1] J de V, 97; *Miraculi S. Joannis Gualberti Abbatis, AASS,* July 2:417; and Jacques de Vitry, *Historia occidentalis,* ed. J. Hinnebusch (Fribourg, 1972), 86–87, respectively.

[2] I am playing on the French title of Michel de Certeau's article "La Parole de la Possedée," translated as "Discourse Disturbed: The Sorceror's Speech," in *The Writing of History,* trans. T. Conley (New York, 1988), 244–68.

disabled by spirit possession: the possessed cannot maintain her accustomed identity but is instead subdued by a foreign, invasive identity or spirit that controls her body and actions. She may switch identities, alternating between self and other and uttering words of her own and those of her possessing spirit in turn. Or her own identity may be entirely subverted and over-whelmed, as she wholly adopts the new personality and expressions of the in-dwelling spirit that controls her body. In either case, the state of spirit possession is most startlingly manifested to observers through a primal dis-ruption of personal identity.

In this chapter I ask why women were held to be more vulnerable than men to this particular disruption of identity. The answer, I argue, is that me-dieval conceptions of the differences between male and female physiology constructed the female body—and with it, the female character—as funda-mentally more changeable, more highly impressionable, and thus as more re-ceptive to outside spiritual influences than the male. Women, in short, were considered to have a weaker claim to deictic integrity than men, a less sharply bounded self. This debility, in turn, rendered them more prone to spiritual influences and invasions. If, as I suggested in chapter 2, avoidance of spirit possession requires a vigilant "border control"—an ability to control the sur-face of the body and keep foreign spirits out—then vulnerability to spirit pos-session suggests that the victim's surface boundaries are especially permeable, frangible, or breachable in some way. This chapter investigates the issue of male and female bodily boundaries and their respective vulnerability to spir-itual transgressions.

This set of ideas will be pursued through four different discursive realms that echo and reinforce one another. The following pages thus present a se-ries of loosely interlinked analyses that build upon one another, even as they work through slightly different sets of problems. The intended effect should be like piecing together a mosaic, tile by tile, until a larger picture is built up from small fragments. The discussion begins with a brief overview of the et-ymologies that medieval writers offered for sex-specific words. This study re-veals that women were associated with the qualities of softness, changeability, and malleability; men with strength, force, and virtue. Second, an examina-tion of texts about the differences between male and female physiologies shows that women's bodies were regarded as more vulnerable to external in-fluences than men's. The humoral composition of the female body con-structed women both as more apt to enter dissociative states and as more receptive to outside impressions from foreign spirits. The third section of the chapter investigates a different coding of the same concept. By closely inter-rogating the medieval trope of the "open/porous" versus the "sealed/dense" body, I explore how ideas about gender intersected with ideas about sinfulness and vulnerability to possession by various kinds of spirits. The final piece in the mosaic inverts the terms of inquiry, looking for images of the feminized demonic rather than of the demonized feminine. These diverse realms of discourse each in their own way established the feminine as inherently unstable, prone to dissociative or anomic states, and especially vulnerable to the depredations of exterior spirits.

GENDERED ETYMOLOGIES

Medieval etymologies offer a convenient point of entry into how medieval intellectuals understood the categories of male and female. Historians often employ a strategy of triangulation, in which a comparison between the symbolic associations of the same words, ideas, or gestures within different contexts lends nuance to their meanings overall. It is to our great advantage that in studying etymologies, the medieval sources have themselves already engaged in triangulation for us, demonstrating the assumptions that medieval intellectuals made about gender roles when explaining words for "woman" and for "man." Although no modern philologist would agree with the word derivations presented in these texts, such associations are deeply revelatory of fundamental medieval attitudes. Indeed, etymologies may be seen as a window onto a vista of cultural common sense, as defined by Clifford Geertz: "what the mind filled with presuppositions . . . concludes."[3]

The derivations of words and names was an area of knowledge that medieval people themselves found fascinating. The book of *Etymologies* of the seventh-century bishop Isidore of Seville was a wildly popular text, one frequently recopied and referenced throughout the subsequent medieval centuries. Encyclopedias, bestiaries, and books of natural history often initiated discussions of new topics with short etymologies. By the thirteenth century, even compilations of saints' lives such as the *Golden Legend* began to include etymological meditations upon the names of the saints. In this culture that worshiped the divine word, a highly essentialist conception of the relationship between words and derivations, sign and significance, held sway. Etymologies were regarded as unveiling the central truth of a thing's character.

In proposing etymologies for sex-specific Latin words, medieval thinkers

[3] Clifford Geertz, "Common Sense as Cultural System," *Antioch Review* 33 (1975): 16–17.

associated positive and vigorous qualities with words for male, and they aligned negative, malleable qualities with words for female. The most commonly repeated discussion, found in many thirteenth-century encyclopedias and natural histories, runs thus:

> Man (*vir*) is so called because there is greater strength/virtue (*virtus*) in him than in women. It is for that reason that he takes the name, or because he acts with strength/virtue in his relationship with woman. Woman (*mulier*) however, gets her name from her weakness (*mollicia*), for she is "weaker" (*mollier*) with the letter "l" removed or changed, giving "woman."[4]

The phrase "weaker sex" derived from this etymology for the word *mulier* from *mollier*, an idea transmitted to medieval thinkers by Isidore and endlessly repeated for generations thereafter. Isidore probably took the idea from the fourth-century theologian Lactantius, who in turn ascribes it to Varro; but it is Isidore's name that is invoked continually by later medieval authors. While woman was associated with weakness and softness, *vir*, by contrast, was associated with *virtus*. This adjective has an exceptionally broad range of exalted connotations including strength, vital force, power, virtue, and righteousness. Indeed, this sense of physical power combined with moral virtue and physical vitality is one reason why *virtus* was a particular characteristic of the saints, aptly demonstrating the emphatically positive connotations of the word.[5]

Women's malleability, weakness, and softness made them easily fall under the sway of external persuasions and spiritual influences. These adjectives construct a gender role for women that centers on the idea of personal instability: the soft, weak, and malleable woman receives an imprint more easily, and is quickly remolded to new habits and ends, whether for good or ill. These qualities were further exaggerated, and viewed in more exclusively negative terms, when the diminutive suffix -*cula* was added, to the word *mulier*, producing *muliercula*. This term was the overwhelmingly preferred form employed in discussions of laywomen visionaries: it carries the additional negative valences of foolishness and lack of discretion. I translate it as "silly woman," and the reader will see this phrase often. Significantly, a cor-

---

[4] The Aberdeen Bestiary. http://www.clues.abdn.ac.uk:8080/besttest/alt/translat/trans92r.html. See also *RP* 6.12, 145. The medieval *fons et origo* is Isidorus Hispalensis, *Etymologiarum libri XX* 11.2.18, in *PL*, 82:417. Compound translations are meant to convey the full range of associations of the words.

[5] Peter Brown, *The Cult of the Saints* (Chicago, 1981); André Vauchez, *Sainthood in the Middle Ages*, trans. J. Birrell (Cambridge, 1997), 427–44.

responding diminutive form of *vir* does not exist. The common medieval Latin words for aged persons display a similar disparity: while the word for old man, *vetus*, is simply a masculine substantive adjective, the word for old woman adds a diminutive ending, forming the inherently derogatory *vetula*. This term, in the course of the later Middle Ages, acquired increasingly sinister and superstitious connotations, culminating in an intimate association with witchcraft at the end of the period. As Jole Agrimi and Chiara Crisciani have noted, the *vetula* "is placed at the intersection of femininity, advanced age, and simplicity; she extends these three qualities of the human condition to their point of incandescence, or rather the incandescence of their negativity."[6] In sum, the etymologies for words associated with men defined them as essentially moral and honorable, suited both for rule and for saintly virtue. Women, by comparison, were defined as lacking a strong sense of self and of right and wrong, a fact that made them more easily manipulable by either beneficent or maleficent forces.

Women also were thought to be the more carnal sex in the Middle Ages.[7] Debilitated by sexual urges, women's limited moral judgment and rational capabilities were easily overwhelmed by desire. The suggested derivations for another Latin word for woman, *femina*, underscore this point. According to the same text quoted above, "We get the word *femina* . . . from those parts of the thighs (*femorum*) by which this sex is distinguished from the man. Others think that *femina* derives by Greek etymology, from the phrase 'fiery force,' because a woman lusts fiercely; for females are more lustful than males, among women as among animals."[8] Given these associations between women and the sin of lust, it is hardly surprising that later the *Malleus maleficarum* would derive *femina* from a compound of *fe* (faith) and *minus* (lesser), "since she is ever weaker to hold and preserve the faith."[9] Although this particular etymology does not appear until the fifteenth century, the sentiment it expresses about female weakness and lack of moral sense is fully in accord with the content of the late medieval tradition.

[6] Jole Agrimi and Chiara Crisciani, "Savoir médical et anthropologie religieuse: Les représentations et les fonctions de la *vetula* (XIIIe–XVe siècle)," *Annales E.S.C.* 48, 5 (1993): 1281–308.

[7] For a theological history, see Peter Brown, *The Body and Society: Men, Women, and Sexual Renunciation in Early Christianity* (New York, 1988). For a psychohistorical approach, Dyan Elliott, *Fallen Bodies: Pollution, Sexuality, and Demonology in the Middle Ages* (Philadelphia, 1999).

[8] Aberdeen Bestiary. See Isidorus, *Etymologiarum libri* 11.2.24, in *PL*, 82:417.

[9] Henry Kramer and Jacob Sprenger, *Malleus maleficarum* (Lyons, 1669), 43. Modern scholarship ascribes the entire work to Kramer alone, but in citations I list both names in accordance with bibliographical convention.

The thirteenth-century Franciscan Bartholomew the Englishman, in his wildly popular natural encyclopedia *On the Properties of Things*, offers an etymology for the word *puella* (girl), that likewise emphasizes female susceptibility to exterior influences. This vulnerability is not without some positive effects, though ultimately it renders women the less capable sex. Bartholomew oscillates ambivalently between positive and negative traits:

> "Girl" (*puella*) is from "pure" (*pura*) and "minor" (*pupilla*), as Isidore says, because of all the things that are valued in a girl, modesty is valued most. . . . Because a woman is of greater piety than a man, she more quickly gives forth tears. She is greater in hatred and she loves more. Wickedness of the soul is greater in woman than in man, and she is weaker in hope and better at lies and immodesty. She is more sluggish and slower of movement.[10]

Thus the female nature is inherently more labile and impressionable. Her greater piety moves her to quicker identification with suffering, causing her to "more quickly give forth tears"—one of the classic possessed behaviors. Yet despite this inherent religiosity, the female also is more susceptible to evil influences and spiteful behavior as well. Bartholomew constructs the feminine as caught between competing poles of piety and wickedness, love and hate, tears and lies. These contrary impulses effectively portray her as more strongly moved by external influences than the masculine. The girl Bartholomew describes is fundamentally impulsive, quickly breaking into tears, emotionally passionate, and abandoned to the influences of the moment. Whether good or bad, the female is excessive in her responses to things, for she is led by a sensual nature.

Again, there is a striking contrast between this etymology and those designating males. "Male" terms tended to be associated with rationality, with intellect, and with spirit, as opposed to the more material and carnal nature associated with women. When, a few pages later, Bartholomew turns to the word *masculus*, the contrast with *puella* is marked. Invoking Isidore along with a host of other pedigreed authorities, Bartholomew expands on his view of sex differences:

> Man (*masculus*) is said to be a diminutive of male (*mas*), which (as Isidore says) occupies preeminence in terms of the worthiness of the sexes in all kinds of animals. The male is superior to the female in terms of com-

[10] *RP* 6.7, 141. See Isidorus, *Etymologiarum libri* 11.2.12, 416.

plexion, in terms of work, in terms of common sense (*sensus discre-tionum*), and in terms of power and dominance.... In every species of animal, the male has a more careful and adept mind than the female for guarding against insidious snares and in avoiding harmful things (as Aristotle says in book five). For this reason the man excels the woman in rationality and in the sharpness of his intellect (as Augustine says). The man is above the woman (according to the Apostle) because of his honor and his figuration of the divine image, and on account of this honor the man is exalted in authority and power.[11]

Bartholomew adds another layer to the series of gender associations I have been tracing. Joined to his enumeration of the now familiar litany of positive, male-oriented adjectives (including, here, "preeminent," "worthy," "power[ful]," "dominan[t]," "honor[ed]," and "exalted") is the idea that male prudence and rationality render him naturally more adept at avoiding evil than the female. He is better able to avoid "insidious snares" (*insidiis*), a word with strong demonic overtones, and "harmful things" such as moral and physical dangers. He is above the woman both socially and morally by virtue of his physical sex alone; even male animals possess this preeminence, which is simply the natural order of all existence. The diminutive suffix of *masculus* does not add negative valences to the word, as it does in the case of the feminine terms *muliercula* and *vetula*. The female physical constitution, by contrast, is more susceptible to evil temptations precisely because of her motility. She is easily manipulated by others because she lacks a firm rational identity.

The most instructive medieval debate about word meanings, however, concerns the more neutral term *homo*, best translated either as "human being" or as "person." *Homo*, of course, is the term used in the Latin vulgate for that which is *imago Dei*, the image of God. A series of vigorous medieval debates centered on whether the term *homo* referred to men alone or to the whole of humanity. If women were included in *homo* then they, as well as men, must be considered in God's image; if the term was exclusive of women, then they did not share an image with the divine. As early as 585, Gregory of Tours reports that a council of bishops assembled in Macon considered the issue after one of their number raised the question and argued for a definition of *homo* limited to men.[12] Although the Council ultimately decided that *homo*

[11] *RP* 6.12, 144. Isidorus, *Etymologiarum libri* 9.7.2, 363; he links *mas* to *maritus* and *masculus*.

[12] Gregory of Tours, *History of the Franks* 8.20, trans. L. Thorpe (New York, 1974), 452. It should be noted, however, that Gregory may have been trying to impugn the character of the bishop concerned.

included both sexes, echoes of this debate persisted, with respected authorities arguing both sides of the issue throughout the Middle Ages.[13] The famed twelfth-century canonist Gratian, for example, wrote that a woman ought to keep her head covered in Church (1 Cor. 11:7) precisely because she was *not* in the image of God.[14] The veiling of the female head was a symbol of her subordination before God and His image and representatives, men. The bared male head, by contrast, demonstrated his dignity and physical perfection as the divine image. Thirteenth-century theologians continued to struggle with the *imago Dei* problem, mainly because being in the image of God was held to be a prerequisite for the priesthood.

On one end of the spectrum are writers like Bartholomew the Englishman who, in the final sentence of the passage quoted above, uses the male figuration of God to legitimate his social and political preeminence. The thirteenth-century Dominican Vincent of Beauvais, another quite popular and influential encyclopedist, went even further in categorically denying that women could be in the image of God. Woman was "said to be the glory of man, not the image of God."[15] Vincent goes on to present a startlingly circular argument: women are subjected to men because of their lack of divine image; yet women cannot bear the divine image because they are subject: "She is not Lady of all" as God is Lord of all, and as man holds dominion over creatures. She is, then, naturally ruled by the man. Furthermore, another result of her lack of the divine image is that "she, not the man, was seduced by the devil." This detail is significant: to be in the image of God is to enjoy a special kind of protection against demonic aggression, as we shall see.

Writers like Aquinas, Bonaventure, and Alexander of Hales, by contrast, hesitated to exclude women altogether from the divine image. Yet this created a conflict, for they wished to preserve the priesthood as an exclusively masculine prerogative, and in their writings they linked the *imago Dei* problem to clerical prerogatives. This group of writers thus made a distinction between body and soul that helped them both to assert male and female similarities in terms of being in God's image and to preserve enough differences to reserve the priesthood for men alone. Arguing that the *soul* is sexless, they concluded that both men and women were in the image of God as regards

[13] For a later sequel to this debate, Manfred Fleischer, "Are Women Human? The Debate of 1595 between Valens Acidalius and Simon Gedicus," *Sixteenth-Century Journal* 12, 2 (1981): 107–21.

[14] Gratian, *Decretum* 33.8.19, cited in A. Minnis, "*De impedimento sexus:* Women's Bodies and Medieval Impediments to Female Ordination," in P. Biller and A. Minnis, eds., *Medieval Theology and the Natural Body* (Suffolk, 1997), 116.

[15] This and the following quotations in this paragraph are from *Spec. Nat.*, 1654.

their souls. In particular, the capacity to reason—however weak in women—was held to be the signifying factor in the soul's similitude to God. However, as regards the *body*, only adult males were in the image of God, because they were reflections of the male Christ and able to reenact His originary priesthood at mass. The female body, as well as an immature male body, could not constitute an appropriate *signum* for Christ.[16] Indeed, Leo Steinberg has remarked upon the increasing emphasis placed on Christ's penis in the art of the late Middle Ages, as a means of demonstrating his fully human—and, not coincidentally, his definitively male—nature.[17] If to be in Christ's physical image required male anatomy, then one side effect of this trend, of course, was to emphasize female difference from the body of Christ. Women were included in the word *homo*, but nevertheless were only halfway, so to speak, *in imagine Dei*. And to the degree that female anatomy was distanced from the image of God, it could become—in an oppositional universe of good and evil—an image of the demonic.

This idea is neatly encapsulated in a fourteenth-century fresco inside the Church of San Petronius in Bologna (fig. 7). The painting presents a dense set of figural relationships: between the Fall and the Redemption, between the Tree of Knowledge and the "Tree" of the cross, and between Old Testament patriarchs and New Testament figures. Most interesting for our purposes, however, are the parallelisms that are established between Adam and Eve and other figures. Adam is closely aligned with Jesus: indeed, this was a traditional association first made by Paul, who refers to this pair as the "first man Adam," and the "last man Adam" (1 Cor. 15:45–49), in order to emphasize Christ's re-creation of human nature through his redemptive sacri-

---

[16] Minnis, "*De impedimento sexus*"; Prudence Allen, *The Concept of Woman: The Aristotelian Revolution, 750 B.C.–A.D. 1250* (Grand Rapids, 1985), 388–89; Alexander of Hales, *Summa theologica*, inq. 4, tract 1, sec. 1, quaest. 3, tit. 1, 340, ed. P. Bonaventura Marrani (Florence, 1928), 412–13.

[17] Leo Steinberg, *The Sexuality of Christ in Renaissance Art and in Modern Oblivion* (New York, 1983). It is true, as Caroline Bynum has argued, that certain symbolic chains of association could lead to a reading of Christ's *substance* as feminine. Medieval reproductive theory after the thirteenth century held that the mother of a child provided the matter or raw material for the new life, while the father provided the generative force or active "seed." Given this distinction between the respective contributions of each parent, one could view Christ's matter—derived from his mother Mary—as fundamentally "female" in some way. However, since all fleshly matter was viewed as transmitted to children from mothers, Christ would be no different from any other human being, male or female, in this respect. One could, then, argue that *all* males were somehow composed of "female" flesh inherited from their mothers. Yet it is questionable whether medieval theorists viewed flesh as fundamentally gendered on this "molecular" level, so to speak. Taking precedence over such a conception, I would suggest, would be the fact that Christ's actual form—the way his flesh was organized—was male.

Figure 7. The images of God and of the devil. This fresco establishes a dense set of connections between Adam and Eve's fall from grace after eating of the forbidden tree, and Christ's redemptive death on the "tree" of the cross. Note that the head of the serpent is that of a human woman quite similar in appearance to Eve. Fresco by Giovanni da Modena, c. 1420. Bologna: Church of San Petronius. Photo by Richard S. Cohen.

fice. Adam thus both historically prefigures, and is created in the image of, the God-Christ. The two nude males at the central axis of the painting thus are perfect, recursive images of one another: Adam is in Christ's image, and He in turn is in Adam's image. Eve, however, resembles no one in the picture so much as the devil: she gazes into the smiling face of the serpent to whom she succumbs as if into a mirror. They are twinned: both have lush, wavy blond hair, smooth foreheads, and delicate features. However, beneath the tempter's skillfully made-up face lie the green, scaly coils of a snake. Theologically, of course, the painting also juxtaposes Eve with the figure of Mary, who is standing on the other side of the tree and who often was regarded as the woman who brought salvation to the postlapsarian world engendered by Eve's trespass. Insofar as Eve's physical form exists in the image of something else, however, it is an *imago diaboli*, of the devil whose visage lies so near to hers. The iconography of the female-headed serpent had become increasingly popular since the thirteenth century: such a motif also is found, for example, in the portals of Notre Dame cathedral in Paris.[18]

Anything that existed in the image of God had resistance to demons. Thus medieval theologians and preachers regularly asserted that the human soul, of either sex, was off-limits to demonic invasion: "when it is said that a devil is inside a person, we must not understand this to mean the soul."[19] This invulnerability of the soul to demonic infiltration is, of course, intimately related to its sacrosanct status as an image of God: demons would not dare to try to enter that which bears the imprint and likeness of the Omnipotent. Thus anything *in imagine Dei* possesses the apotropaic quality of warding off demonic attack. The implications of this position are clear: if, as Aquinas and others argued, the souls of men and women were equally images of God, then the souls of both sexes were equally resistant to demons. In the case of the body, however, there was a distinction between the two sexes. A man's physical participation in the image of God constructed his body as more fully resistant to the physical invasions of unclean spirits than the female body. Vincent of Beauvais, as noted above, directly attributed the Fall to Eve's lack of the divine image and her consequent vulnerability to demonic persuasion; Bartholomew the Englishman advanced much the same idea in his *On the Properties of Things*. Lacking the physical image of God, the female body lay open and defenseless against demonic invasion. Though it certainly is true that adult men sometimes were believed to be physically possessed by demons, their relative scarcity among demoniacs may be attributable, in part, to the prevalence of broad symbolic associations such as these, which were transmitted throughout all levels of culture through popular media such as natural encyclopedias and preaching. Since women's bodies did not possess the imprint and image of the divine, demons had little to fear from entering them. Unclean spirits could transgress, boldly, into female bodily space, possessing their physical territory and stopping short only at the borders of the soul.

[18] See Michael Camille, *The Gothic Idol. Ideology and Image-Making in Medieval Art* (Cambridge, 1989).
[19] *DM*, 1:293.

The discussion of etymologies already has begun to shade into a discussion of male and female bodies.[20] If the female body was not in the image of God, then the physical differences between men and women were of paramount importance for understanding the ordering of Creation. The notion that the word *homo* did not include women in their physical existence raised questions about where to place women's bodies in the scheme of nature. The fact that women's bodies were not in the image of God subtly suggested that women were not as fully human as men. Yet women could not be considered nonhuman—or could they?

In the thirteenth century, theologians and natural philosophers did question whether women were part of the human species, or whether they belonged to some other taxonomic group. The question, while linked to the issues surrounding the word *homo*, arose more directly from a passage in Aristotle's *Metaphysics*, which had recently been made available to the West in Latin translation.[21] The Philosopher wondered how man and woman can form a single species, given the vast differences between them. The logic of the inquiry ran as follows: If contrariety establishes taxonomic classifications of species, and if woman is the opposite of man, then is not woman a separate species?

Medieval thinkers, following Aristotle himself, answered in the negative:

[20] The following discussion draws upon Joan Cadden, *Meanings of Sex Differences in the Middle Ages: Medicine, Science, and Culture* (Cambridge, 1993); Prudence Allen, *Concept of Woman*; Nancy Siraisi, *Taddeo Alderotti and his Pupils* (Princeton, N.J., 1981); idem, *Medieval and Renaissance Medicine: An Introduction to Theory and Practice* (Chicago, 1990); John Baldwin, *The Language of Sex: Five Voices from Northern France around 1200* (Chicago, 1994); Luis García-Ballester et al., eds., *Practical Medicine from Salerno to the Black Death* (Cambridge, 1994); Marie-Christine Pouchelle, *The Body and Surgery in the Middle Ages*, trans. R. Morris (New Brunswick, N.J., 1990); Jole Agrimi and Chiara Crisciani, *Les consilia médicaux* (Louvain, 1994); Danielle Jacquart and Claude Thomasset, *Sexuality and Medicine in the Middle Ages*, trans. M. Anderson (Princeton, N.J., 1988); M. Hewson, *Giles of Rome and the Medieval Theory of Conception* (London, 1975); Jean-Claude Schmitt, "Le corps en Chrétienté," in *Le corps, les rites, les rêves, le temps: Essais d'anthropologie médiévale* (Paris, 2001), 344–59; Michel Tarayre, "Le sang dans le *Speculum Majus* de Vincent de Beauvais: De la science aux *miracula*," in M. Faure, ed., *Le sang au Moyen Âge: Actes du quatrième colloque international de Montpellier, Université Paul-Valéry (27–29 novembre 1997)* (Montpellier, 1999), 343–59. While not of direct relevance, I also have benefited from the works of David Gentilcore, particularly *From Bishop to Witch: The System of the Sacred in Early Modern Terra d'Otranto* (Manchester, 1992) and "Contesting Illness in Early Modern Naples: Miracolati, Physicians, and the Congregation of Rites," *Past and Present* 148 (1995): 117–48.

[21] Allen, *Concept of Woman*, 361.

woman is *not* a distinct species, despite her distance from the male paradigm of fully realized humanity.[22] Even though women are the opposite of men, they both still belong to a single species. The broader significance of posing such a question, however, lies in the assumption that the fundamental differences between the sexes very nearly override their natural similarities. The thirteenth century, in fact, saw the gradual substitution of a highly polarized (Aristotelian) model of sex differences in place of the more complementary (Galenic) model that had prevailed in earlier centuries. I shall not rehearse this change in depth here, as it already has received excellent treatment from the pen of Joan Cadden.[23] It is worth noting, however, that this new emphasis on sex differences was viewed from within a hierarchical framework, which perceived woman's differences from man as inferiority. In turn, this widening gulf between men and women also implied a wider distance between women and God, in whose image man alone existed.

Female physiology was said to be inferior to the male in several important ways: in terms of reproduction, in terms of form or shape, and in terms of humoral balance or "complexion." The latter issue is of considerable complexity and importance for our investigation into why women were more vulnerable to spirit possession, but a brief sketch of the first two issues will help to clarify the broader context of gender imbalance in thirteenth-century medical thought. According to newly influential, Aristotelian ideas about conception circulating at this time, the female provided the raw matter for the generation of the fetus and the male, the active seed or form. Thus the woman's role was to be a passive receptacle and nourisher of the male seed, which provided all the vital force required for reproduction. These notions harmonized well with the ancient opposition between female "softness" and male "vital strength." Yet a problem arose in this system: the prevailing Aristotelian logic held that like reproduces like. Since it was the male who provided the active principle of generation, his active form should only reproduce something like itself: a male. Why, then, did the male seed sometimes produce a female infant? The resolution of this conundrum was dictated by the original, teleological terms of inquiry: males will reproduce males *if* the seed develops perfectly. This logic demanded, then, that female births be placed in the same category as deformities: the female infant is a male manqué who failed to develop in the expected way. In an immortal phrase derived from Aristotle and repeated by thinkers such as Albertus, his

[22] See ibid., 362–64; 389–90. Albertus Magnus, *Questiones super de animalibus* 15.3, ed. Ephrem Filthaut, in *Alberti Magni Ordinis Fratrum Praedicatorum Episcopi Opera Omnia*, vol. 12 (Aschendorff, 1955), 261.
[23] Cadden, *Sex Differences*; Allen, *Concept of Woman*.

student Aquinas, and Bonaventure, woman is a *mas occasionatus:* a "misbegotten" or "deformed" male.

The phrase strikes many modern readers as excessive, and it should be noted that medieval thinkers placed limits upon its implications. Aquinas and others advanced a double viewpoint: though the generation of female offspring was in individual instances a failure of the male seed to reproduce itself perfectly, from the broader viewpoint of nature itself the generation of females as well as males was a more perfect ordering. Indeed, the creation account in the book of Genesis would definitively preclude considering all females as a defect of nature *strictu sensu*, since God Himself brought them into being. The highly formalistic mode of scholastic argumentation permitted the presentation of this dual viewpoint, effectively undercutting any absolutist definition of females as unnatural or monstrous. Yet as one scholar has noted, delicately, the idea of the female as a defective male, "when entertained in less formal contexts, projected a derogatory notion of the feminine."[24]

If the "misbegotten" woman lacked the appropriate corporeal form to act as a sign of Christ and image of God, so, too, was her physiology distinct from the male on what we might call the molecular, and medieval people the elemental, level. The elaborate medieval theories of elements, humors, complexion, and temperament have significant implications for the question of why women were viewed as more vulnerable to spirit possession than men.[25] In order to arrive at the point where these implications become clear, however, some background information on the components of this all-encompassing macro- and microcosmic system is required.

According to medieval theories of materialism, all of creation was formed from the four universal elements of fire, air, water, and earth. These were arranged in a hierarchy of descending nobility, with the more immaterial elements (first fire and then air) taking priority over those of grosser substance (water and, lastly, earth). Regardless of sex, all four elements were present in the composition of the human body, though in varying proportions. In medical terms, the four universal elements were said to be carried by the four humors, or physiological fluids: yellow bile (in which the element fire was dominant), blood (dominated by air), phlegm (primarily water), and black bile (mostly earth). The balance of the four humors within the body was determined partly by sex, with males usually being dominated by yellow bile and blood, and a little phlegm and black bile; and women characterized by a

---

[24] Cadden, *Sex Differences*, 195.
[25] *RP* 4.6–11, 99–114, gives an exemplary exposition of the humors and temperaments.

high admixture of phlegm and black bile, and secondarily blood and yellow bile. This understanding of physiological sex differences was augmented by various bits of close observation and argument. Menstruation, for example, was advanced as proof that the female body was unable to absorb or process as much blood as the male body; and the thick quality of menstruum was attributed to its debasement through admixture of women's overabundant phlegm.[26]

To translate the language of humors back to the hierarchically ranked language of the elements, this system aligned women with the "grosser" elements of water and secondarily earth; and men with the "nobler" elements of fire and secondarily air. Such facts alone are not surprising. Discussion of the elements and humors becomes more intriguing, however, when another layer of the fourfold system is added: the medieval concept of complexion. Each bodily humor or fluid was aligned, not only with a particular element in the chain of universal matter, but also with a set of four physical qualities: hot, cold, moist, and dry. Thus yellow bile, containing fire, was primarily hot and secondarily dry. Blood, dominated by air, was primarily moist and secondarily hot. Phlegm, which was mostly water, was primarily cold and secondarily moist. Lastly, black bile, containing earth, was primarily dry and secondarily cold. The balance of the four humors resulted in a particular combination of the four qualities, and the resulting admixture was known as the individual's complexion. Thus the masculine complexion was primarily hot and dry, while the feminine complexion was primarily cold and moist: they are opposites. The quality of temperature was of singular importance, for the masculine complexion was dominated by two "hot" humors, while the feminine complexion was dominated by the two "cold" humors, a point to which I shall return below.

Finally, individual complexions corresponded to differing personality types, or "temperaments." The typical female temperament types were the "phlegmatic" and the "melancholic," as opposed to the typical male personality types, which were the "choleric" and the "sanguine." The phlegmatic personality was essentially sleepy, sluggish, and dull, while melancholics were described as self-centered and prone to hysterical delusions. (The latter personality type, interestingly, was held to be particularly characteristic not only of women but of Jews, who also were physiologically parallel to women through the medieval belief that Jewish men were subject to various bloody fluxes assimilated to menstruation.)[27] As for the male personality types, cho-

[26] Albertus Magnus, *Quaestiones de animalibus* 3.22, 135–36.
[27] Pseudo-Albertus Magnus, *De secretis mulierum*, in H. Lemay, *Women's Secrets: A*

lerics were highly energetic and volatile, while the sanguine type was described as cheerful and generous. In sum, the chain of reasoning from elements to humors to complexions to temperaments was one of increasing gender imbalance. Moreover, this imbalance was conceived in ways that directly echo the associations of the words *vir* and *mulier:* the male types are vital, forceful, and strong; the female types are soft, foolish, and dull.

The concept of masculine and feminine complexions was used to instantiate three ideas about women that are of relevance for an understanding of women's perceived vulnerability to spiritual influences. First, feminine coldness was associated with a lack of moral constancy. Second, cool and moist humors occasioned a melancholy temperament, which was held to be highly impressionable. Third, coolness was associated with a greater need for physical purgation, and this in turn engendered an association between cool bodies and the surface quality of "openness" or "porosity." I shall briefly discuss the first two points here and devote a new chapter section to unpacking the third.

To begin, then, coolness was a predictive sign for moral instability. For it was heat that gave rise to masculine *virtus:* heat was the very basis of the vigor, force, and virtue that characterized the virile sex. Indeed, contemporary theories of sex determination held that the warmer the uterine environment, the more likely the gestation of a male child. A variant held that the degree of heat of the male "seed" in conception determined sex, again with more heat being conducive to a male child.[28] The minimal amount of humoral heat present in the typical female complexion emphasized her distance from the exuberant vitality and natural morality of the warmer male. Indeed, the warmest female was said to still be cooler than the coolest male.[29]

Thus Albertus Magnus, having discussed the elements and humors in his *Questions on Animals*, asks whether men are better able to learn moral behavior than women. The answer: yes, "because the coldness of complexion in the woman diminishes her perceptive abilities . . . and in consequence she is of weaker intellect." In the next paragraph, responding to an objection that some might consider women to be more prudent than men, he peevishly explains,

> The woman is not more *prudent* than the man, properly speaking, but more *cunning*. For prudence tends toward the good, and cunning toward

---

Translation of Pseudo-Albertus Magnus' De Secretis Mulierum *with Commentaries* (Albany, 1992), 74. See Willis Johnson, "The Myth of Jewish Male Menstruation," *Journal of Medieval History* 24 (1998): 273–95.

[28] Cadden, *Sex Differences*, 117–34.

[29] Albertus Magnus, *Quaestiones de animalibus* 15.6, 262–63.

evil. For the woman is more "prudent"—that is, more cunning—in evil and perverse deeds than the man, since to the degree that her nature is deficient toward one thing, so much is it directed toward another. And so since the woman is deficient in intellectual operations, which consist in the understanding of good, and the grasp of truth, and fleeing from evil, she therefore is more directed toward the sensual appetites, which tend toward evil. . . . Hence the senses move woman to every evil, just as the intellect moves man to every good.[30]

Thus coldness renders women intellectually weak, and this leads to a correspondingly greater strength in her sensory attachments. The result of this situation is a mental inability to grasp truth and goodness, combined with a proclivity for sensory indulgences—that is, sin. In man the situation is, of course, reversed. His vital heat begets virile *virtus* and righteousness. Thus women, being fundamentally the weaker, and hence the more sensual sex, also present an easier target for demonic illusion and attack.

If feminine coolness begets irrationality and therefore sensual perversity, feminine moistness engenders other ruinous qualities. Moistness begets a changeable, inconstant, and highly impressionable nature, like mud retaining a footprint. (Women were, after all, composed primarily of the elements earth and water.) Albertus states:

The complexion of the woman is more moist than the man's, and moistness receives an impression easily, but retains it poorly. A moist thing is easily influenced, and therefore women are inconstant and are always looking for novelties. . . . Hence there is no faith in a woman.
  Believe me! If you believe her, she will deceive you;
  Believe an experienced master.[31]

Indeed, women are so itching for novelty, according to Albertus, they will not hesitate to gain their desires "through lies and diabolic deceptions" if necessary.[32] Their cool and moist complexions make them more susceptible to sinful external influences and impressions than men, and thus lead them to seek new stimuli at any cost.

These flighty fancies may well take the form of excessive religious devotions and self-deceptions, Albertus warned. The teacher of Aquinas derided

[30] Ibid. 15.11: 266.
[31] Ibid., 265.
[32] Ibid., 266.

women's delusive pursuit of supernatural gifts. In his sermons, he denigrated the religious aspirations of contemporary laywomen, comparing them unfavorably to the Magdalene: "She did not do as many women do, who always want to be exalted on high and amidst supernatural occurrences (*in mirabilibus*) that are above them. They want to be surrounded by visions and by things of a sort that they cannot possibly attain."[33] When Albertus heard of a woman who claimed to have nursed the infant Jesus in a visionary trance, he termed it an "idiocy."[34]

My point is not simply that these complexion types served to legitimize female inferiority by providing a naturalized explanation for already existing gender roles, however. It is, rather, to observe the precise form this inequality takes, and the relationship it bears to spirit possession and the discernment of spirits. It is noteworthy, for example, that the description of women as cold and moist constructs them not only as dull-witted and changeable but also—and here I reach my second point—as quick to receive an imprint, easily influenced and persuaded. There is a sense in these passages that women do not have a stable identity in the same way that men do: they have no strong convictions, opinions, or preferences, but are easily impelled in any direction by outside forces. They are fundamentally malleable—*mollier*, after all. Women lack a strong inner core of unchanging identity or a stable positioning deixis, a presupposition that goes to the heart of the perception that women were more readily subdued by foreign spiritual entities.

Indeed, the notion that "moistness receives an impression easily" explicitly was extended to the depredations of spirits, both good and bad, into women's moist bodies. Women's diminished strength of self or subjectivity vis-à-vis men led to a conception of the female constitution as more open to exterior spiritual influences of all kinds. This is true both because of their impressionable nature and because of their characteristic temperament. Thus although Albertus Magnus used the principle of feminine impressionability to advance a case for feminine sinfulness, other authors were more measured. For example William of Auvergne, bishop of Paris in the early thirteenth century, notes:

> Many visions and phantastic apparitions are produced in many people from a melancholy disposition, but primarily in women, as you can see even in the case of true visions and revelations. And the doctors say that

[33] J. Schneyer, "Predigten Alberts des Grossen in der HS. Leipzig, Univ. Bibl. 683," *Archivum Fratrum Praedicatorum* 34 (1964): 45–68.

[34] Caroline Bynum, *Holy Feast, Holy Fast: The Religious Significance of Food to Medieval Women* (Berkeley, 1987), 337 n. 87.

this is due in particular to the nature of feminine souls, for they are easier to make an impression on than masculine souls, even at a distance.[35]

William suggests that women's impressionable nature can lead them to either of two extremes. On the one hand, their melancholy temperaments, arising from the dominance of black bile in their humoral makeup, made them prone to phantasies and illusions. The larger context of William's remark is a discussion of popular beliefs and errors, such as those of old women who report their own entranced, shamanistic flights with the nighttime ladies or "good things."[36] William regarded such beliefs as fundamentally diabolic impressions, misguided and delusory. Indeed, William already had explained the effects of demonic possession as derived from various kinds of spiritual impressions made on the soul or the "perceptive faculties."[37] On the other hand, the special receptivity of women to spiritual impressions also could work to their advantage, since it rendered them generally more receptive to good spiritual influences, "as we see even in the case of true visions and revelations." Thus women could also receive divine or angelic impressions more readily than men. This notion persisted two centuries later, when Johannes Nider quoted this passage of William's, word for word, in his *Formicarius*.[38] The same notion appears in the *Malleus maleficarum*, which notes that women, "because of the motility of their complexions, are easier to impress with revelations brought to bear by the impressions of disembodied (*separatorum*) spirits. Indeed, because of women's complexion, when they are used well, many good things result; but when used for evil, they are the worst."[39]

Phrased differently, we might say that the more imperfect female complexion meant that women could easily be dominated by invading, foreign spirits. They could be used by spirits as tools and vessels. Male vitality, by contrast, made them more resistant to spiritual encroachment. The male

[35] William of Auvergne, *De universo*, in *Guillelmi Alverni Opera Omnia*, 2 vols. (Paris, 1674; reprint, Frankfurt-am-Main, 1963), 1:1066.

[36] Carlo Ginzburg, *The Night Battles: Witchcraft and Agrarian Cults in the Sixteenth and Seventeenth Centuries*, trans. J. Tedeschi and A. Tedeschi (New York, 1986); idem, *Ecstacies: Deciphering the Witches' Sabbath*, trans. R. Rosenthal (New York, 1991), 89–121; Jean-Claude Schmitt, *Les revenants: Les vivants et les morts dans la société médiévale* (Paris, 1994), 115–46; Richard Bernheimer, *Wild Men in the Middle Ages* (Cambridge, Mass., 1952), 23–24, 78–81; W. Peuckert, *Deutscher Volksglaube des Spätmittelalters* (Stuttgart, 1942), 86–96; Walter Liungmann, *Traditionswanderungen Euphrat–Rhein: Studien zur Geschichte der Volksbräuche* (Helsinki, 1938); Karl Meisen, *Die Sagen vom wütenden Heer und wilder Jäger* (Munster, 1938). See also the works cited in note 61.

[37] William of Auvergne, *De universo*, 1040–41.

[38] *F* 5.10, 85v.

[39] Kramer and Sprenger, *Malleus maleficarum*, 42.

body was more difficult for any foreign spirit—even a good spirit—to over-power and control. Whereas the male in the image of God retains his deic-tic integrity, the unstable female is continually vulnerable to the suasions of other, invading spirits or identities.

As a corollary to this principle, we might note the degree to which female physiology was believed to predispose women to fantasy states and self-delu-sion. Vincent of Beauvais, for example, wrote that cold-complected individ-uals—who were, of course, most likely to be female—were prone to trances and fantasies that temporarily deprived them of thought and memory. "This habit is called 'alienation of the mind,' and it certainly either enfeebles them or brings about harm."[40] Thus the predominance of women among ecstatic seers could be interpreted, in Vincent's terms, as a harmful, fantasy-laden alienation of the mind. Similarly, Bartholomew the Englishman describes melancholics (again, read "women") as prone to devastating fantasies and il-lusions, and gives examples ranging from irrational fears and suicidal thoughts, to the delusion that they hold the world in their hands and must not drop it, to paranoid beliefs that their friends are really persecutors.[41] The focus here is upon the melancholics' lack of a firm grasp on reality: they are likely to have an exceedingly active fantasy life in which they perpetually ex-ist at the center of great, unfolding dramas. Antoninus of Florence attributed a melancholic condition to a "commotion" of the humors, and he went on to explain that severe cases of melancholy can cause a permanent alteration of the senses leading to mania and insanity. In particularly severe cases, some melancholics "lament, others jump, others believe that the stupidest things are absolutely true . . . [such as] that they bear frogs in their womb, or that they see or are possessed by demons." For Antoninus, significantly, extreme melancholy of this kind may be caused "by inordinate vigils, fasts, zeal, scrupulosity, or deep thinking."[42] Presumably women, already predisposed to a melancholic temperament, also should avoid excessive asceticism and in-tellectual challenges, lest they suffer from mania or the perception of de-monic possession.

An anonymous commentator on the late-thirteenth-century treatise *On the Secrets of Women* (a text attributed to Albertus Magnus in the Middle Ages and thus granted an added luster) added a new detail to the understanding of female physiology by asserting that women can sometimes fall into a fictive ecstasy or trance. This was the result of noxious vapors ascending to the head

[40] *Spec. Doc.* 13.121, 1248.
[41] *RP* 4.11, 113.
[42] Antoninus of Florence, *Summa theologica* 1.2.6 (Verona, 1740), 92. I am much in-debted to the anonymous reader for Cornell University Press who directed me to this text.

from the mixture of menstrual blood and putrefying humors that gathered in women's wombs. The disease was related to the disorder known as "suffocation of the womb," but was formally distinguished from it and known as "vertigo." The coolness of the female body was unable to process or utilize foods and fluids as fully as the warm male. As a result, humoral wastes gathered together in the womb until being purged on a monthly basis. Although men could suffer a similar infirmity from digestive vapors, females were thought to be more susceptible to this affliction, which sent them into a deathlike trance state. The commentator continues,

> Old women who have recovered from it say that it was caused by an ecstasy during which they were snatched from their bodies and borne to heaven or to hell, but this is ridiculous. The illness happens from natural causes; however, they think that they have been snatched from their bodies because vapors rise to the brain. If these vapors are very thick and cloudy, it appears to them that they are in hell and that they see black demons; if the vapors are light, it seems to them that they are in heaven and that they see God and his angels shining brightly.[43]

Thus the otherworldly visions of women were inherently subject to debate and criticism. Female visionaries relaying information about the regions of the afterlife may well be suffering simply from an excess of rotten humors. Vincent of Beauvais referred to the same illness in his *Mirror of Doctrine*, noting that menstrual retention generates morbid vapors which, if they ascend to the head, can cause headaches and migraines, darkened vision, vertigo, and trance states.[44] Bartholomew the Englishman added frenzy to the maleficent symptoms of the syndrome.[45]

The distinction between the vertigo syndrome and divine or demonic spirit possession was entirely eroded by William of Auvergne. William explicitly described how demons may mimic the symptoms and etiology of vertigo through a manipulation of their victim's internal physiology. He first explains the natural illness, which occurs, "through a corruption of the humors or of the limbs, either from exterior things or from vapors released interiorly from the body and ascending to the brain, which then fix certain passions and impressions onto the perceptive organs in the brain. However,

[43] Pseudo-Albertus Magnus, *De secretis mulierum*, ed. Lemay, 134. Unfortunately, this particular commentary is not reproduced in any of the printed copies of *De secretis mulierum* available to me. I have therefore quoted Lemay's translation.

[44] *Spec. Doc.* 13.96, 1232.

[45] *RP* 4.8, 105.

these kinds of impressions are produced in a such way that it is easy for evil spirits to approach these organs and to imprint similar passions upon them through their own effort."[46] These demonically induced, vaporous impressions can become so persuasive and overwhelming that one victim known to William believed himself to be, by turns, the son of God, the Holy Spirit, the son of the devil, and the Antichrist. A woman victim believed herself to be possessed by the devil and made many other tiresome claims that William declined to elaborate. William ascribed this condition to an unusual degree of impressionability, which he describes as having a "porous spirit, which received imaginary appearances and forms of this kind easily, and conducted them intimately inward."[47] Thus vertigo and an inherent susceptibility to invasions of demonic influence were linked in William's mind.

This complex of ideas about female physiology constructed female trance states as manifold in origin. Though there was some acknowledgment that women could truly be divinely inspired, there also was an increasing tendency to multiply alternative explanations for female reports of trances and visions. And of course, the more explanations that were advanced for specifically female trance states, the more difficult it became for observers to interpret altered states of consciousness in women as indicators of divine inspiration. The coexistence of several heuristic frameworks for women's possessed behaviors rendered the percentage of "authentic" cases of women's divine inspiration correspondingly smaller, as this was only one of several possible explanations.

Thus natural—and highly gender-specific—explanations were advanced for an understanding of trance as pathology. Yet even if natural causes were ruled out, the presumption of moral frailty in women made it seem likely to many medieval intellectuals that they would be more readily influenced by evil spirits than by good. Nor were these ideas simply isolated in medical texts. If we look forward for a moment to the late fourteenth and early fifteenth century, when the earliest discernment of spirits treatises were composed, we see the direct effects of these ideas in the evaluation of female spirit possession. Writers like Jean Gerson listed women's essential inconstancy, desire for novelty, mendaciousness, and melancholy temperament as reasons why female claims to divine inspiration should be regarded with skepticism: "How, then, could it be suitable for [the female] sex to walk in greatness, surrounded with miracles? To receive visions added to more visions daily? To

[46] William of Auvergne, *De universo*, 1041.
[47] Ibid.

consider injuries to the brain, like epilepsy or catatonia (*congelatio*), or else the appearance of melancholy, to be a miracle?"[48]

In pathologizing women's trances and visions, and attributing them to female complexional qualities, these thinkers implicitly were naturalizing possessed behaviors. While the issue of testing spirits had long been associated with the careers of laywomen, this set of medical ideas provided the imprimatur of a scientific and rationalistic explanation for why women were more vulnerable to demons and delusions alike. The significations of these behaviors thus were extended into new realms: trances were not only possible indicators of divine or demonic possession but also highly charged signifiers of a primal feminine weakness and instability. In sum, this recursive movement back to the body simultaneously engendered and legitimated the predominance of women among the possessed.

OPEN/SEALED — POROUS/DENSE

Women were the weaker sex, the softer sex, the less rational sex. Women's bodies were the glory of man, not the image of God. Women were moist; they were cool; they received impressions readily. The female temperament was sluggish, but paradoxically women also were hysterical, prone to fantasies and frenzies. Women's wombs filled up with corrupting humors that clouded their minds and their vision.

Women's bodies also were *open*. This is not my adjective, but a medieval word choice: the descriptive pairings open/sealed and porous/dense frequently were applied to female and male physiology. In a sense, these words are simply a recoding of the idea that women are more prone to receive spiritual impressions: the porous, open body is an impressionable body. However, these pairs of words also were overlaid with other dichotomies, such as sin and righteousness, body and soul, and divine and demonic possession. The richness of this particular semantic field thus presents a choice opportunity to explore how gender notions overlapped with other categories of analysis.

The conception of the female body as singularly porous and open may be viewed as a pneumatic version of Mikhail Bakhtin's notion of the grotesque body, which is open in terms of the physical ways it interacts with—even in-

[48] *ED*, 456.

terpenetrates—its environment.[49] Forever oozing, excreting, and devouring, the grotesque body is, for Bakhtin, bound to its surroundings in a relationship of continual exchange. By perpetually taking in and expelling pieces of its environment, the grotesque body continually processes, contains, and encapsulates that environment. There is an interpenetration of the interior and exterior conditions of the body, an intermingling of self and context. The grotesque body is elementally unbounded, ever-changing, and fluid. Bakhtin's description echoes medieval constructions of the female body, though he refocuses the body's openness from a highly refined spiritual plane to a grossly physical one.

The opinion that female bodies were more porous or open than male bodies may be found in a number of different medieval discursive traditions, including medical works (where it was adopted from Aristotle),[50] hagiographies, and exempla compilations. For example, these associations are laid forth in fascinating detail by Vincent of Beauvais in book 13 of the *Mirror of Doctrine*, which is devoted to theoretical medicine. After discussing the various humors and complexion types, Vincent inserts a short chapter on sex differences, in which he links women's cooler complexions directly to a physiological characteristic best translated as "porosity":

> Women have colder complexions than men, and therefore among creatures they are smaller than the males, and moister. Also, because of the coldness of their complexions, and lack of exercise, they have many superfluities. And so, the substance of their flesh is more porous (*rarior*). However, a man's flesh may become more porous as concerns the local complexion that mingles with her, for when he is in a dense state he is unable to penetrate her.[51]

Vincent is referring, in the euphemisms of his last sentence, to the need for an erection of the penis before intercourse can take place. His understanding of this process is that penile erection involves a process of inflation, an idea that relates to the medieval commonplace of the testicles as a pair of bellows. The latter would inflate the penis with air, rendering it more expansive and porous, and thus more compatible for mixing with the female body that it is about to penetrate. The man's genitals in their more usual "dense" state are incompatible with female porosity. An intriguing modern reiteration of

[49] Mikhail Bakhtin, *Rabelais and His World* (Bloomington, 1984).
[50] Cited in Ruth Padel, "Women: Model for Possession by Greek Daemons," in A. Cameron and A. Kuhrt, eds., *Images of Women in Antiquity* (Detroit, 1983), 3–19.
[51] *Spec. Doc.* 13.16, 1178.

this idea has been recorded by the anthropologist Giovanni Pizza in oral interviews in twentieth-century Campania. An informant named Amelia explains: "A woman has all her pores open, all of them, her entire person, not like a man, a man is closed, he *sbuccia* (opens) only when he's making love and that's the end of it . . . she's open, while a man, no, he doesn't get stung and serious things don't enter."[52]

Vincent of Beauvais later returned to the relative merits of porous versus dense bodies. According to the hierarchy he proposed, the best type of body is midway between porous and dense. At either extreme, porous and dense bodies each have their drawbacks. The denser kind of body Vincent describes as fat, easily tired, and prone to frequent urination and evacuation. In sum, the dense body is physically similar to Bakhtin's grotesque body, in constant physical exchange with its environment. The highly porous body, on the other hand, is a pneumatic counterpart, open to winds and more subtle environmental exchanges. This build therefore is more prone to various indispositions that arise from subtle environmental penetration. Vincent draws the contrast vividly:

> [Dense-bodied people] are not easily made ill by exterior things, like cold air, the sun, et cetera. The stings (*ictus*) of these things cannot pierce through to their interiors, on account of the density of their bodies. However, porous-bodied people are long-limbed and lean due to the excessive looseness [of their flesh]. External forces can quickly pierce into them because they are porous. . . . They suffer many infirmities from external forces.[53]

The conception Vincent seems to be advancing here is that porous-bodied and dense-bodied people both have roughly the same amount of matter or substance, but this matter may be either densely or loosely packed. The example of the penis, employed earlier, may have provided a comparison point for Vincent's thinking in this regard: the same amount of matter may be densely or loosely arranged, shorter or longer, compact or dilated. The effect of loose, expansive flesh is a greater amount of air incorporated into the body and, correspondingly, a more penetrable, larger-pored skin surface that readily admits exterior forces or influences. Indeed, female flesh often was described as "loose" in medieval medical texts, a quality that was linked to fe-

[52] Giovanni Pizza, "The Virgin and the Spider: Revisiting Spirit Possession in Southern Europe," in Cristina Papa et al., eds., *Incontri di etnologia europea. European ethnology meeting* (Naples, 1998): 66.

[53] *Spec. Doc.* 13.52, 1204.

male softness. And as we shall see, the subtle "stings" that pierce porous bodies from outside include aggressive spirits seeking to possess a human—or again, more likely a female—body.[54]

The association of males with densely packed, and women with open or expansive arrangements of material substance, is one that recurs in other descriptions of sex differences as well. Albertus Magnus stated it as a given principle that "the body of a woman is more porous and the body of a man is more dense."[55] He argued that the greater porosity of the female body was due to the greater need of the female body type for exchange with her outside environment. "The porosity (*raritas*) of a woman's body is . . . from the abundance of undigested humors. By contrast, the density (*compactio*) of a man's body derives from . . . the strength of his heat."[56] The special purgative requirements of the female body were seen as a by-product of her diminished heat. Her cool body lacks sufficient warmth to digest and process all the humors it produces; thus, cool bodies have an excess of unprocessed humoral material requiring purgation in some way. This occurs most notably in women's menstrual flow. However, extra humors also were thought to dissipate or otherwise be cleansed from the system through more refined openings in the body, porous gaps between material substance, which were especially abundant in women's cooler physiologies and uncompacted flesh. Conversely, however, male bodies possessed clearer internal passageways. Albertus elsewhere notes that the coolness of the female body often led to a blockage or narrowing of these internal channels, which resulted in their inability to emit seed during intercourse.[57]

Ideas regarding female porosity already were current in the twelfth century, though the earlier thinkers do not elaborate them as fully as the thirteenth-century writers just cited. Hildegard of Bingen, for example, wrote of women's bodies as punctuated by "windows, openings, and wind-passages."[58] Her phrasing, though laconic, would seem to refer to the same conception of porous female bodies shot through with air passages. Similarly Heloise, in a letter to Abelard, quoted Macrobius Theodosius to the effect that women's bodies are pierced with more "holes," "channels," and "outlets" than the

---

[54] Males, however, were supplied with special, large pores for the ejection of superfluities in the form of body hair and beard growth. Cadden, *Meanings of Sex*, 182–83.

[55] Albertus Magnus, *Quaestiones de animalibus* 15.6, 262. In my edition this segment was omitted from the page, but included in a sheet of errata.

[56] Ibid., 263.

[57] Albertus Magnus, *De animalibus libri XXVI* 9.1, ed. H. Stadler, 2 vols (Münster, 1916), 1:676. Here as elsewhere I have rendered *rarus* as "porous" and *porus* as "internal channel" or "internal passageway."

[58] Quoted in Pouchelle, *Body and Surgery*, 148.

male. She ascribes this—as would Albertus—to women's need for more frequent purgation of humors. Heloise goes on to argue that women can tolerate the effects of wine better than men because alcoholic vapors can more easily be dispersed through the pores in a woman's skin.[59]

The notion that women's bodies were more open to exchanges with their environments provides a fascinating counterpoint to the conception of spirit possession as involving a literal entrance into the body. For porous bodies were especially open to spiritual penetration and exchanges. The openings inherent in the porous body type provided spiritual pathways that spirits could exploit. Thus Albertus argued that spirits exist as very fine bodies and that they therefore require physical passages to move through when entering or existing inside a human body. Speaking of the human spirit, he writes, "A spirit is a subtle body that is very penetrative. . . . Parts of the animal body are porous and have passageways . . . thus when the spirit moves around inside a body, it goes through the channels of the body."[60] There must be open, unoccupied space for the spirits to move through, special interior channels. Yet the corollary to Albertus's statement is that a porous bodily surface may more easily permit the entrance into the body of a "penetrative" foreign spirit. As Vincent of Beauvais phrased it, the subtle "stings" of external forces can get inside a porous body more readily than a dense one. William of Auvergne, as we have seen, linked the false ecstasy of the vertigo syndrome (whether natural or created through demonic manipulation of humors and internal vapors) to a special porosity of spirit, by which he meant the apprehensive facilities of the mind. This displacement is much in accord with William's approach to spiritual interference, for he consistently tends to regard the impressions of spirits as attacks on the perceptual and cognitive facilities, rather than as attacks on the flesh and limbs of the body.

The linguistic trope of porosity may be read against the perception that women were more vulnerable to spiritual invasion than men—though my intention is to probe the strains and linkages among different realms of discourse, rather than to establish a causal priority. This interrogative procedure necessarily involves a careful layering, as in a series of transparencies, of evidence about the understanding of spirit possession as a literal entrance in to the body; with evidence about the marked gendering of states of possession and ecstasy; with evidence about women's greater impressionability; with evidence about the greater porosity or penetrability of the female body, and so on. Through this process of layering and juxtaposition, we can arrive at a

---

[59] Betty Radice, trans., *The Letters of Abelard and Heloise* (London, 1974), 166.
[60] Albertus Magnus, *Quaestiones de animalibus* 16.8, 279.

more textured understanding of spirit possession as a phenomenon that de-rives complex meanings from broader cultural assumptions and mentalities.

From this perspective, the assumption of an elemental porosity or open-ness to the female body may be seen as a translation, into medical terms, of an inchoate idea that propels the logic of women's relationships with the spir-itual realm in medieval texts. The dichotomy between inner and outer, and questions of controlling the body's surface vulnerability to spirits, typically frame discussions of both divine and demonic possession in many sources. The twin emphases of transgressive ecstasy and internal union found in women's vitae, for example, center precisely on the issue of the spirit's access to and egress from the body. Descriptions of ecstacy and inspiration, of spir-itual dislocation and penetration, portray the surface of the visionary's body as frangible, breachable, open. Nor were hagiographic exemplars and their imitators the only medieval women to lay claim to the experience of spiritual transgressions of physical boundaries. Indeed, the medieval popular folklore of the good things, good ladies, nighttime ladies, or followers of Lady Abun-dance provides an intriguing comparison to the careers of inspired women as described in hagiographies.[61] Like the predominantly female ranks of di-vinely possessed seers, the predominantly female good things claimed to leave their bodies in spirit in order to follow a divine figure. In both cases, the female is associated with the ability to engage in shamanistic spirit flights, leaving the body behind in an immobilized trance state. Upon returning to the body, the spirit reanimates it; sometimes the visionary is then able to make pronouncements about the fate of the dead she has seen, or dispense occult information about secret events that she has witnessed in her invisible spiritual wanderings. Indeed, the trances of the good things and of divinely inspired laywomen seem to draw upon a common set of cultural presuppo-sitions about the ease with which spirits may go into and out from the female body.

The construction of male bodies as dense, compact, and *sealed* rendered males more impervious to spirit possession, for their surfaces could not so

---

[61] I discuss these ideas briefly in Nancy Caciola, "Breath, Heart, Guts: The Body and Spirits in the Middle Ages," in É. Pócs and G. Klaniczay, eds., *Demons, Spirits, Witches: Christian Demonology and Popular Mythology* (Budapest, forthcoming). On the fairy cult, see Gustav Henningsen, "'The Ladies from Outside': An Archaic Pattern of the Witches' Sab-bath," in Bengt Ankarloo and Gustav Henningsen, eds., *Early Modern European Witchcraft: Centres and Peripheries* (Oxford, 1990), 191–215; Éva Pócs, *Between the Living and the Dead: A Perspective on Witches and Seers in the Early Modern Age* (Budapest, 1999); and idem, *Fairies and Witches at the Boundary of South-Eastern and Central Europe*, Folklore Fellows Com-munications 243 (Helsinki, 1989). Also see the works cited in note 36.

easily be breached. This is clear in a particularly provocative exemplum reprinted in more than one compilation. According to this tale, the Pagan emperor Diocletian had a daughter, Arthemia, who was violently possessed by a demon. The unclean spirit revealed that only the saintly deacon Cyriacus could cast him out of the girl. Yet when the demon was conjured by Cyriacus, it complained that it would not leave without another "vessel" to enter into. Cyriacus obligingly responded, "'Here is my body: come in if you can.' The demon answered in turn, 'I cannot enter into your vessel, for it is sealed and closed off on all sides.'"[62] The body of the girl apparently was not so inviolate. Yet even as the exemplum reinforces gender distinctions in regard to the openness or sealed quality of Cyriacus's body, it also unveils another set of associations underlying this physiological opposition. The open/sealed duality is inscribed upon the body not only as a matter of gender but as a result of the individual's moral status. It is significant that the deacon Cyriacus is male and Christian, whereas the demoniac is female and Pagan. Thus the conception of bodies as either porous and open or dense and sealed also alludes to notions of sin and righteousness. Here again, the normatively male body type is aligned with inviolacy and virtue; the normatively female, with transgression and sin. These conceptions mutually sustain one another. The discursive construction of the female as open is yet another variant on the female as easily impressionable, as unstable and frivolous, and as morally inconstant.

Reinforcing this point is the fact that many exemplary tales of demonic possession present the entrance of unclean spirits as the baleful result of sinful behavior, as we have seen in chapter 1. Sin alters the composition of the body, opening up the flesh so as to allow the demon to enter in. This linkage between vulnerability to possession, openness, and sin and is vividly expressed by John of Salisbury, who defined the senses as "seven windows into the soul [that are] in the head. . . . Through them . . . the intelligence (*mens*) goes out from and returns to the mind (*animus*). . . . Therefore if these windows are closed to the devil, and open to God, the soul will go out wisely following the prescribed ways. . . . Confession, and a healthy remorse, are a perfect fortification for the windows against all the treacheries of the Enemy."[63] Similarly, William of Auvergne wrote that possessing demons can interfere with the flow of sensory information to the soul, for "the senses are like gates into the body through which ingressions and egressions of this kind

[62] Jacobus de Voragine, *Legenda aurea*, ed. T. Graesse (1890; reprint, Osnabrück, 1965), 487. The exemplum is also incorporated into Jean de Mailly, *Abrégé des gestes et miracles des saints*, ed. A. Dondaine (Paris, 1947), 316.

[63] John of Salisbury, *De septem septennis*, in *PL*, 199:950–51.

are made."[64] And Vincent of Beauvais warned against demons who subtly joined themselves to sensory stimuli and thereby entered into the body by hitching a ride, so to speak, on an odor or color.[65] Though both men and women were made vulnerable by the seven sensory openings of the body, however, the additional association between women and a more general porosity rendered her especially defenseless.

SAINTLY SEALING TECHNIQUES

Historians have long noted that medieval writers and theologians spoke about the body as a material aggregate of the individual's moral status.[66] Indeed, the idea that one's degree of bodily openness could be a labile element of one's moral status irresistibly raises the question of whether some individuals might manipulate the porosity of the body through either devotional practices or spiritual sloth. There are clear indications in some medieval texts that this was indeed believed to be the case, sometimes mechanically so. Thus, Gerald of Wales tells of a Jew who crossed himself while spending the night in a Pagan temple, even though he had no faith in the gesture. As darkness fell, a terrible horde of wicked spirits filled the room, but they were unable to possess him. "Alas! Alas!" they cried, "An empty vessel, indeed, but a sealed one."[67] The Jew is empty because of his lack of faith, but even so he is physically sealed by virtue of the cross.

Even more striking is an exemplum recounted by the thirteenth-century Cistercian monk Caesarius of Heisterbach. The tale is similar to the one about Arthemia and Cyriacus, but with one significant difference: the body of the exorcist is sealed through contact with the divine. Thus, the demon possessing a woman, when conjured by an abbot to depart, responds,

> "Where will I go?" The abbot said, "Look, I am opening my mouth, enter if you can." It said, "I cannot enter, because today the Most High entered." To which the abbot responded, "Climb up on to these two

---

[64] William of Auvergne, *De universo*, 1042.

[65] *Spec. Hist.* 2.115, 151.

[66] Saul Brody, *The Disease of the Soul: Leprosy in Medieval Literature* (Ithaca, N.Y., 1974).

[67] Giraldus Cambrensis, *Gemma ecclesiastica*, ed. J. S. Brewer, in *Rerum Britannicarum Medii Aevi scriptores*, vol. 21: *Giraldi Cambrensis opera* (New York: Kraus Reprint, 1964) 2, 101–2. There is a pun in the Latin. The demons lament that the Jew's body is *signatum*, meaning both sealed up and "signed" or crossed.

fingers," offering his thumb and index finger. "I cannot," it said, "for to-day you held the Most High." Indeed, the abbot had said mass that morning.[68]

Thus the Eucharist provides a temporary seal for the body, in this case rein-forcing the saintly male qualities of the abbot protagonist. His mouth is open, but his body is sealed by the holy presence of the Eucharist; his fingers are offered as a perch, but they are sealed against demonic touch. As in the pre-vious case, however, the woman victim is markedly vulnerable and open to demonic incursion, a gender distinction rendered all the more visible by the centrality of the performance of the mass to the story.

There are additional valences to this cluster of linkages that are worth ex-ploring, briefly. If, for example, the Eucharist was believed to "seal" the body against demonic influence, then the predilection of lay religious women for frequent communion may have had additional overtones beyond the obvi-ous, and well-documented, aspects of divine union implied in the practice.[69] In addition, one could interpret the incorporation of the Body of Christ as a temporary means of enfolding within oneself the *imago Dei*—Christ himself. Since all that was in God's image was thereby rendered more invulnerable to demonic possession, frequent reception of the Host would indeed have been a sealing technique. Many of the spiritual exercises most intimately associ-ated with inspired women in the later Middle Ages may be read as attempts to "seal" the elementally open and porous body. Caroline Bynum has pointed out the degree to which extended fasting acts to seal the body from inter-change with its environment. Not only does fasting involve refusal to bring food or drink from outside the body in, but there is a corresponding cessa-tion of normal purgative activities, such as menstruation, sweating, urination, and evacuation.[70] Frequent purgation, as we have seen, was held to be a prime characteristic of the porous female body type: indeed, the female body was porous precisely because it required outlets for frequent purgation. Thus by putting a stop to all such purgative processes and exchanges, the ascetic woman may be understood as having de-feminized—that is, sealed—her body. The body that did not need to purge was less female and less open, therefore more masculine and closer to God. Similarly, emphasis on main-

---

[68] *DM*, 1:314.
[69] Caroline Bynum, "Women Mystics and Eucharistic Devotion in the Thirteenth Century," in *Fragmentation and Redemption: Essays on Gender and the Human Body in Me-dieval Religion* (New York, 1991), 119–50; André Vauchez, *Les laics au Moyen Age: Pratiques et expériences religieuses* (Paris, 1987), 259–64.
[70] Bynum, *Holy Feast, Holy Fast.*

taining the intact physical "seal" of virginity may have had the additional symbolic appeal of thereby closing off a potential openness to the surrounding environment. A few medieval tales of possession and exorcism involve demons entering or exiting through the "shameful parts,"[71] and it may well be the case that intact virginity was thought to provide a blockage against this particular kind of demonic access. To say this is not to detract from the complex history and symbolic connotations of these practices as ascetic forms of *imitatio Christi*, it is merely to note that the duality of sealed and open was played out in these behaviors even as they also fulfilled other priorities.

Some hagiographies quite self-consciously deploy the trope of sealing off the female body. Humiltà of Florence, for example, was said to worry about the openness of her senses to sin and demonic temptation, and to have prayed for their sealing:

> You, my strong angels . . . bind up my mouth so well, that it may remain closed off from every vain or careless word. . . . Place two seals of love upon my eyes, so that they may not contemplate anything of this world at the same time as the Beloved; but nevertheless keep them open and alert, so that they will not impede the recitation of the Divine Office through sleepiness. . . . Keep my ears open to the name "Jesus," but let no other word, which could be a mortal poison to the soul, penetrate into them. . . . Guard all my bodily senses, so that my spiritual senses may take delight, and my soul may calmly spend a moment with its Beloved.[72]

Humiltà's prayer vividly exploits the tension between sealed and open physiologies and combines it with a vigilant border control that rejects all that is unclean while admitting divine influences. She prays that evil forces might not be allowed to penetrate inside her body through the gateways of her senses, while simultaneously begging for them to remain open to divine infusions.

The ideas being advanced here restate in different terms the associations we already have seen in etymologies, medical texts, and theological treatises.

---

[71] The phrase is from a tale recounted in the vita of Hildegard of Bingen. See chapter 1 for this and other examples. For an interpretation of the sexual dynamics underlying possession, see Moshe Sluhovsky, "A Divine Apparition or Demonic Possession? Female Agency and Church Authority in Sixteenth-Century France," *Sixteenth Century Journal* 27, 4 (1995): 1036–52; Lyndal Roper, "Exorcism and the Theology of the Body," in *Oedipus and the Devil: Witchcraft, Sexuality, and Religion in Early Modern Europe* (New York, 1994), 171–98.

[72] *Vita S. Humilitatis Abbatissae, AASS,* May 5:215.

Women are "malleable" for Isidore of Seville and his followers; "impressionable" for Albertus Magnus and William of Auvergne; "mobile" for Henry Kramer, author of the *Malleus maleficarum;* "porous" for Vincent of Beauvais; "open" for hagiographers and exempla writers. All these words recursively turn upon one another, configuring the feminine as both pliable and decentered, always in flux and never stable, her boundaries permeable and her identity labile.

Ultimately, however, the requirement for such extreme vigilance over the female body's borders and entryways recognizes that body as a site both dangerous and debased. The weaker sex was fragile because of its porosity, its humoral coolness, and its lack of intellect. These deficiencies dramatized the female body as a conduit for malign forces into the world. As Albertus Magnus summed up, "It is commonly and proverbially and popularly said that women are more deceitful and weak, irresolute, immodest, eloquent in lies: in brief, a woman is nothing other than a devil in the likeness of a human form."[73]

FALLEN ANGELS AND FALLEN WOMEN

Albertus's statement may be inverted. If women really were devils, then devils really were women, at least for some commentators. The final tile in the mosaic I have been piecing together is a mirror, a fragment that reverses the terms of inquiry. Rather than exploring the demonization of the female, this final section is devoted to the feminization of devils. For the bodies of fallen angels had much in common with the bodies of fallen women.

In the 1230s William of Auvergne commented upon reports of hordes of spirits in female form seen flying through the nighttime skies, a collective apparition known to him the "nighttime ladies." William knew that the nighttime ladies were demonic because they presented a female appearance. Their female bodies were, for William, a spontaneous index of their demonic character:

The female sex was created from man for the sake of reproduction and for children. But reproduction is not possible for an abstract spiritual substance. Spirits cannot have children, and so they cannot have a sex, for sex only exists for the reproduction of sexed beings. Therefore this

---

[73] Albertus Magnus, *Quaestiones de animalibus* 15.11, 265.

difference of sex [among spirits], or the appearance of it, is a clear sign: Good angels only appear in the form of men, and never in female form, as do evil spirits.[74]

Among spirits, a female appearance is an exclusive signifier of demonic status. Male appearance, conversely, is angelic, as William makes clear in the continuation of the passage:

> What if someone should say that the virile sex also has no place among exalted and blessed spirits? I answer that though this is true, nevertheless virtue, and strength, and active ability has a place in men, and those things are quite appropriate to spiritual substances. However, the passive ability and infirmity and weakness that are the womanly characteristics are entirely inappropriate for this kind of spirit.[75]

The *virtus* of men—virtue, strength, active ability—enables a discernment of spiritual character via physiological appearance. In point of fact, angels were depicted exclusively in male terms, in medieval theology as in medieval images.[76] This angelic virility echoes the masculinity of Christ, which was receiving increasing artistic focus in the later Middle Ages: the "good" pole of the supernatural is exclusively, insistently male.[77] By contrast, the feminine is associated, again, exclusively with weakness, sexuality, and evil nature.

Investigating the sexes of spirits provides the historian with a peerless opportunity to map out the broader semantic terrain of terms such as masculine and feminine. Medieval demonologists like William insisted that spiritual beings are neither male nor female in their essence: the appearance of a sex is a mask, a performative representation. Yet if spirits do not have sexes (a material notion), they *do* have genders (in this context, a moral notion): femininity was the province of the demonic hosts, as masculinity was the property of the angelic choirs. And William's association of unclean spirits with feminine characteristics was not unique; indeed there is a fascinating body of medieval evidence that ascribes female characteristics to demons. This may be done explicitly, by depicting demonic spirits as female; or implicitly, by depicting them as having porous and open body types.

The Latin words *demon* and *diabolus* both are masculine: thus demons normally were designated with the masculine pronoun. The default position

---

[74] William of Auvergne, *De universo*, 1068.
[75] Ibid.
[76] David Keck, *Angels and Angelology in the Middle Ages* (Oxford, 1998).
[77] Steinberg, *Sexuality of Christ*.

in medieval texts, then, is that the devil and his legions are symbolically male. Above all, however, demonic bodies were hybrid and unstable: "in Hell there exists no order, only eternal horror."[78] Thus the chaotic character of the unclean spiritual physiology allows a demon to take many forms, including (or, according to William of Auvergne, especially) a female form. We already have seen an instance of this motif in a scene described above, the temptation of Eve. A more disturbing example, painted in the Duomo of San Gimignano by Taddeo de Bartolo sometime in the 1390s, depicts a female demon with large, pendulous breasts punishing a woman fornicator (fig. 8).[79] More common is the theme of the beautiful demon courtesan or temptress with refined clothing and coif, whose demonic nature is revealed by some small detail: delicate horns sprouting from her tresses, claws or hooves glimpsed from beneath the hem of her robe, or perhaps the tip of a tail.

The most feminized fallen angel of all, however, was the morning star himself, Lucifer. A dense set of associations between sin, bodily openness or porosity, and female reproductive anatomy may be seen in certain representations of the devil, images that recapitulate in visual form William of Auvergne's musings on the sexes of spirits. These devils are of an unstable status, nominally sexless yet assuming a female appearance—and the female, in turn, cannot escape from being defined by sexual and gestative functions. The figure of the devil took on increasing importance in art in the thirteenth century, especially on the Italian peninsula, with its precocious development of large-scale public art projects.[80] Despite some earlier examples, the devil

[78] Bull of canonization for Catherine of Siena, CPCS, 516.

[79] One could further note that this is an interesting example of demonic hybridity: though the demon's form is female, the act of sexual punishment it performs places it in a masculine role. This activity—a female penetrating another with an instrument—was considered among the gravest sexual sins in medieval penitentials, precisely because it involved a female arrogation of a male prerogative. For discussion of female homoeroticism, Bernadette Brooten, *Love between Women: Early Christian Responses to Female Homoeroticism* (Chicago, 1996); Judith Brown, *Immodest Acts. The Life of a Lesbian Nun in Renaissance Italy* (New York, 1986). The image also brings to mind the twelfth-century *Vision of Tundale*, with its remarkable description of the punishment of fornicators. Tundale sees fornicating sinners raped and impregnated by a giant beast; they then give birth to vipers and beaked serpents that rend their bodies to pieces. But it is not only female sinners who are represented thus; male sinners, too, conceive, gestate, and give birth. These male mothers conceive offspring within their limbs and chests, where they "gestate" until the time arrives for them to give birth. The sinful body, the open body, is presented as fulfilling a female bodily function—even when its explicit sex is male. Eileen Gardiner, *Visions of Heaven and Hell before Dante* (New York, 1989), 149–95; 252–53; Claude Carozzi, "Structure et fonction de la vision de Tnugdal," in A. Vauchez, ed., *Faire croire: Modalités de la diffusion et de la réception des messages religieux du XIIe au XVe siècles* (Rome, 1981), 223–34.

[80] Jérôme Baschet discusses the orality of representations of Hell in *Les justices de l'au-*

Figure 8. An ugly female demon. This detail of a fresco depicting the Inferno occupies a conspicuous location on the lowest reaches of the wall. A female sinner is sexually punished for the sin of fornication by a bestial female demon. Fresco by Taddeo de Bartolo, 1396. San Gimignano: Duomo. Photo by Richard S. Cohen.

had not been a popular subject in medieval art before this time. Between about 1270 and 1340, however, an extraordinary series of mosaics and frescoes were produced in Italy that nurtured a new style of Satanic representation. This series, as it unfolded, progressively developed and accentuated the open qualities of the devil's and demons' bodies, depicting them as covered with extra orifices that continually incorporate and expel sinners. The culmination of this series of images re-sexes Satan as a female, at least from the waist down, for the figure is in the act of giving birth. Although the analysis that follows in the next few pages centers on a specifically Italian iconography, it has echoes and affinities with the broader mental attitudes adduced in previous pages.

A prelude to the iconography of the birthing Satan is the anonymous, c. 1270 mosaic on the ceiling of the baptistery in Florence. The composition centers on the reptilian figure of Satan enthroned on a pair of dragons, and surrounded by various figures of toads, worms, and serpents. This mosaic was influential in its vivid depictions of the torments of Hell, dominated by ingestion and incorporation into the bodies of demons. The dragons of Satan's throne devour sinners, as does Satan himself and the two snakes that spring forth from his ears. Meanwhile, the surrounding reptilian fauna are all busily engaged in biting, chewing, and vomiting various sinners. The souls of humans vomited up by toads are a fascinating reversal of the typical image of the demoniac vomiting up a spirit. And the openness of these demonic bodies, which constantly are absorbing and expelling human spirits, echoes the openness of female physiology, which is so vulnerable to the absorption and expulsion of demonic spirits. Both kinds of bodies are in constant interchange with their environments.

---

delà: Les représentations de l'enfer en France et en Italie (XIIe–XVe siècle) (Rome, 1993), 219–87. This work is the best and most exhaustive starting-place for a study of Hell motifs. See also Baschet, "L'Enfer et son lieu: Rôle fonctionnel des fresques et dynamisation de l'espace cultuel," in S. Boesch-Gajano and L. Scaraffia, eds., Luoghi sacri e spazi della santità (Turin, 1990), 551–64; Yves Christie, Il Giudizio Universale nell'arte del Medioevo (Milan, 2000); Gary Schmidt, The Iconography of the Mouth of Hell: Eighth-Century Britain to the Fifteenth Century (London, 1995); Luther Link, The Devil: The Archfiend in Art from the Sixth to the Sixteenth Century (New York, 1996); Fulvio Ricci, Chiesa di Santa Maria Maggiore, Tuscania (Viterbo, 1996); Samuel Edgerton, "The Last Judgement as Pageant Setting for Communal Law and Order in Late Medieval Italy," in R. Trexler, ed., Persons in Groups: Social Behavior as Identity Formation in Medieval and Renaissance Europe (Binghamton, 1985), 79–100. On the related theme of apocalyptic representations, see Michael Camille, "Visionary Perception and Images of the Apocalypse in the Later Middle Ages," in R. Emmerson and B. McGinn, eds., The Apocalypse in the Middle Ages (Ithaca, N.Y., 1992), 276–89; Peter Klein, "Introduction: The Apocalypse in Medieval Art," in Emmerson and McGinn, Apocalypse, 159–99.

Figure 9. Satan enthroned. Giotto seems to have been the first artist to depict Satan in the act of expelling a sinner from the lower part of his body. The scene suggests both giving birth and defecation. Fresco by Giotto, c. 1303–5. Padua: Scrovegni Chapel. Photo courtesy of Alinari/ Art Resource.

The form of Satan as depicted on the baptistery ceiling was taken up with slight modifications by Giotto in his 1303–5 fresco of the Last Judgment in the Scrovegni Chapel in Padua (fig. 9). The pose of the figure is identical, as are the dragon throne and the serpents emerging from the devil's ears. However, Giotto added an intriguing and unusual detail. Whereas the Florentine mosaic modestly veils the groin of Satan with a cloth, Giotto boldly disrobed the devil to expose, not a set of male genitals, but an orifice expelling a small body between Satan's spread thighs.[81] In so doing, Giotto established a parallelism between the ingestion of a soul through Satan's mouth and the subsequent evacuation of the sinner from the lower bodily region. Thus one reading of this detail is as a shitting scene: the sinner is eaten, digested, and

---

[81] The birthing aspect of Giotto's devil has recently been treated in Anne Derbes and Mark Sandona, "Barren Metal and the Fruitful Womb: The Program of Giotto's Arena Chapel in Padua," *Art Bulletin* 80, 2 (1998): 274–87.

expelled as excrement. However, the placement of the detail on the front of Satan's body also authorizes a reading of the figure as in the act of giving birth. Indeed, anatomically speaking this is the more viable interpretation. However, the two views surely are meant to complement, rather than to exclude, one another. Together they portray the demonic body as porous, as parturient, and as fundamentally unclean, characteristics that move Satan into a decisively feminine semantic field.

The theme was taken up very dramatically in two subsequent portrayals: the fresco by an unknown artist at the church of Santa Maria Maggiore in Tuscania, executed between 1315 and 1320; and the Last Judgment lately attributed to Buffalmacco in the Camposanto (cemetery) of Pisa, datable to the late 1330s.[82] Unfortunately, both frescoes have been damaged and extensively reconstructed. Tuscania suffered from an earthquake in 1971, while the Camposanto fresco was restored and possibly altered in 1523 and then was severely compromised by a 1944 bombing raid.[83] Although in each case the frescoes have been restored, the clarity and completeness of both works is degraded. However, they remain provocative depictions of devils with hybrid sexual characteristics.

The Tuscania fresco is notable in part for its location on the main apsidal wall of the church, an alteration from the more traditional location over the exit door (fig. 10).[84] Thus rather than being a final reminder of hellfire as congregants left the church, it functioned as a constant presence before the eyes of worshipers throughout the service. The artist was clearly influenced by Giotto's work, for the overall composition is identical. The figure of Satan, however, has been significantly increased in size at Tuscania: it is the largest figure in the fresco, dwarfing even Christ. This devil occupies nearly all the wall space to the right of the apsidal arch, which cuts through the composition.[85] Its body is a male-female hybrid, though with stronger emphasis placed upon the female elements. The head and facial features are those of a bearded, horned man with an elaborate helmet and bestial characteristics. These male elements are in sharp contrast, however, with the lower portion

---

[82] Ricci, *Santa Maria Maggiore*, 36; Baschet, *Les justices*, 625.

[83] Ricci, *Santa Maria Maggiore*, 6; Baschet, *Les justices*, 625–27.

[84] Christie, *Giudizio Universale*, 317, 350.

[85] Interestingly, the positioning of this element of the fresco would place it before the male congregants during services, for men normally would be seated on the southern side of the aisle, women on the northern. One cannot read a specifically didactic intention behind this circumstance, however, for it is dictated by the combined demands of the iconography (blessed on the right hand of God, damned on His left) and of segregated-seating traditions of long standing. Margaret Aston, "Segregation in Church," in W. Sheils and D. Wood, eds., *Women in the Church* (Oxford, 1990), 237–94.

Figure 10. Final Judgment of the righteous and the damned. This fresco, in which Christ is dwarfed by the figure of Satan, is located just behind the altar and would have been a focus of attention for the congregation throughout the service. Fresco by an unknown artist, 1315–20. Tuscania: Church of Santa Maria Maggiore. Photo courtesy of Alinari/Art Resource.

of the figure, which has been reconfigured from Giotto's version so as to accentuate the birthing motif more strongly. As before, Satan eats a sinner through a deeply fanged mouth, but the expulsion of sinners below has become a far more visceral and graphic depiction, with stronger sexual overtones (fig. 11). Now bereft of his throne, the devil squats, with knees turned outward and bent, in the standard birthing position of the premodern world. The figure's swollen abdomen, which bulges to both sides and over his upper thighs, suggests a pregnant belly. Even more strikingly, the devil's groin now appears as a broad lateral gash rimmed with blood-red flames. Two heads emerge from this large opening, along with a pair of legs. These emerging souls are about to be engulfed by yet another fanged orifice: a Hell-mouth located at the very bottom of the fresco. This mouth receives into its jaws the sinners just expelled from Satan's body, and re-ingests them. Two blue-gray demons with pitchforks push the sinners down into the Hell-mouth's gullet. Interestingly, all the sinners shown entering the Hell-mouth are female.[86] This redoubling of the feminine in the lowest section of the fresco—the area closest to the observer—presents a strongly gendered monitory message. In any event, the scale and viewing accessibility of this segment strongly stresses the feminized lower portion of the devil's body, while the cycle of devoration/expulsion/re-devoration by the Hell-mouth plays upon the theme of bodily openness as a relentless cycle of exchange.

The most terrifying Satan in medieval art may well be the figure shown in the Camposanto in Pisa (fig. 12). Completely destroyed in World War II, the fresco was painstakingly restored and may now be seen again in something resembling its original state. However, a prewar photograph supplies better clarity than contemporary reproductions.[87] As at Tuscania, this devil is significantly larger than the figures of Christ and Mary in the adjacent Judgment scene. This devil also is more bestial and monstrous than earlier forebears: it has a green-and-yellow, segmented reptilian hide covered with what appear to be round suckers of the kind found on octopi.[88] The head is characterized by a large pair of horns, a snout with flared nostrils, and red-

[86] All are beardless and wimpled. The exclusively female sex of this group was also noticed by Baschet (Les justices, 228).

[87] The website for Pisa's Camposanto, http://www.compart-multimedia.com/virtuale/us/pisa/affreschi.htm, makes available a virtual tour of the room containing the fresco, though the camera is situated so as to render viewing of the Hell scene nearly impossible. The contiguous Judgment scene is clear; Hell is to the viewer's right, around a corner.

[88] Baschet sees this segmentation as a form of armor, and the suckers as rivets, but the reptilian coloration suggests suckers to me. See Baschet, Les justices, 293–350, for a detailed treatment.

Figure 11. Satan giving birth to women sinners, a detail of figure 10. This Satan has a masculine head but appears to be giving birth to three sinners between his spread thighs. The devil's distended belly, squatting posture, and red-rimmed groin reinforce the impression of a birth scene. The exclusively female sinners who are expelled are immediately devoured by a fanged Hell-mouth at the lowest reaches of the fresco. Photo by Richard S. Cohen.

Figure 12. Hell with a gestating/digesting Satan. Aptly located in the cemetery of Pisa, this fresco is wholly dominated by the tricephalous figure of Satan. This devil ingests sinners through all of his mouths, then gives birth to or defecates them below. Two sinners are shown twisting in torment in the devil's womb or belly. Fresco attributed to Buffalmacco, c. 1332–42. Pisa: Camposanto. Photo courtesy of Alinari/Art Resource.

rimmed, staring eyes. The Camposanto Satan also is the first to be portrayed as tricephalous, a detail derived from Dante's description of Satan in the final cantos of the *Inferno*. Each of the figure's three mouths ingests a sinner, and each clawed hand holds a soul ready for eating. The ejection of sinners in the lower portion of the devil's body is evoked, again, as a birth scene with anatomical precision. Satan squats as a demon-midwife eases out a sinner emerging head-first from an opening between his splayed legs. The reddish coloration and raw, swollen appearance of this orifice rather graphically evoke the labors of birth. Meanwhile, the center of Satan's torso is burst open to reveal a sinner twisting inside his guts. This unveiling of the interior digestion/gestation of sinners in the stomach/womb (the Latin word *venter* could mean either, testifying to a preexisting cultural assimilation between these organs and their processes) completes the incorporative portrayal of the devil's body.[89] Throughout, the fresco teems with vignettes that show

[89] Baschet attributes this detail to a 1523 restoration (*Les justices*, 62–67). Even so, the

demons devouring, dismembering, and otherwise transgressing the bodily boundaries of various sinful souls, including a Hell-mouth located at the upper right. All distinction between interior and exterior is collapsed as these open bodies continually fragment, engulf, and expel one another in turn. Again, whether through actual anatomical means or through the more allusive strategy of representing bodily openness, the Hell realms of these frescoes are dominated by bodies with feminine characteristics. The open body and the female body are symbolically elided with the demonic body.

Later artists extended the motif by multiplying the number of orifices ingesting and expelling souls. Satan is shown continually devouring and shitting, bearing and birthing, the souls of the damned (figs. 13 and 14). Ancillary mouths and orifices—in one case, beaks—appear in the figure's ears, at the elbows and knees, stomach, even on the devil's breast in place of nipples.[90] These elaborations raise the motif of the open-bodied Satan to a frenetic level of incorporative and expulsive activity. If demonic possession is characterized by the incorporation of a foreign spirit into the body, then we may say that Satan is "possessed" by the spirits of the sinners inside her body. Satan, like a possession-prone woman, is characterized by a weak and fluid bodily identity: a changeable, hybrid body that receives impressions easily; a porous body that interpenetrates its environment, absorbing and expelling elements of its surroundings.

As William of Auvergne noted, spirits do not really have a sex, they only assume the appearance of one. Angelic and demonic spirits thus function as a control group in this discussion: lacking an actual sex, they merely masquerade in human form. In brief, exploring the parodic sexes of these spirits allows us to interrogate the deeper associations of masculine and feminine within a context that is divorced from biology, and to discuss gender constructions apart from actual biological sex. From this perspective, the feminine becomes a marker not of sex but of demonic uncleanness and sin. The masculine, by contrast, is a marker for the angels, for human fortitude and virtue, and for Christ himself.

---

dating does not seem too late to be of use in exploring long-standing cultural mentalities of the kind I am treating. I am interested less in the intentions of the original artist than in the fresco as a materialization of broader cultural ideas.

[90] Aside from the locales illustrated in this book, this motif also appears in the Church of the Abbey of Viboldone, outside Milan (fourteenth-century, Giusto da Menabuoi); in the Duomo of San Gimignano (1396, Taddeo de Bartolo); in the Church of San Francesco, Paradise Chapel, Terni (1445–51, Bartolomeo di Tommaso da Foligno), and in the Church of San Fermo Maggiore, Verona (1410–11, by Martin of Vernoa).

Figure 13. Satan giving birth to Pride. In this well-preserved work, a face has been added to the devil's belly, and the sinner to whom the devil gives birth has been labeled "Superbıa"—Pride. Fresco by Giovanni da Modena, c. 1410–12. Bologna: Church of San Petronius. Photo by Richard S. Cohen.

Figure 14. Satan punishing the seven deadly sins. This fresco shows the tendency for the number of ancillary faces and mouths on the devil's body to multiply. The sinners in this fresco are labeled with the seven deadly sins all punished directly by the Devil. The figure cradled in the devil's arms is labeled both "Judas" and "Envy." Fresco by an unknown artist, c. 1488. Pereto: Santa Maria dei Bisognosi. Photo by Richard S. Cohen.

The human body appears to be the most comfortable and natural of things, a given that enables communication because it is a shared ground of human experience. Yet the body is also a cultural artifact, laden with symbolic associations both explicit and implicit. On the one hand, the female body sometimes was represented as able to take on a likeness to God: the stigmata, facial transfigurations, and other surface signs of divine possession could indeed transfigure the female visionary's body into a physical *imago Dei* before the eyes of her devotees. Yet the existence of a set of broader norms derogating and demonizing female physicality suggests that a view of the female body as a site for indwelling divinity was a transgressive view, one that flowed counter to the main currents of the culture. Indeed, women more commonly were viewed as an *imago diaboli*. This chapter has explored a portion of the rugged symbolic terrain associated with male and female bodies in the Middle Ages. I have charted a complex topography, in which the female is associated with weakness, irrationality, impressionability, the sinful senses, porosity, and the demonic; and the male with strength, reason, self-independence, moral understanding, impermeability, the angelic, and the image of God. According to these broad patterns of thought, which spanned several cultural areas, the male body was fundamentally more resistant to spirit possession than the female, which lay open to spiritual infiltrations of various kinds.

It now is time to turn from surface to depth, from porosity to interior bodily systems. Where did these possessing spirits go, once inside?

CHAPTER FOUR
BREATH, HEART, BOWELS

A human being is twofold: inner and outer. The inner is the soul;
the outer, the body.
> —ABERDEEN BESTIARY

On a late afternoon during a sweaty August in 1308, a woman named Francesca began to autopsy the freshly dead body of her sister recluse. A number of other sisters of this community of recluses were present to help: Joanna, Marina, Illuminata, Catharine, Elena, and perhaps also Lucia and Margaret.[1] The intrepid Francesca cut open the body with a sharp little knife, approaching from the back even though this made her goal—the heart—that much more difficult to reach. Presumably this decision was made in order to preserve the frontal integrity of the corpse. The deceased woman, Clare, had expired just that morning, and the autopsy was begun in the afternoon, so by the time Francesca finally reached Clare's heart, darkness was

---

[1] The community eventually adopted the Augustinian rule, though the group also had strong links to the Franciscan order. The nucleus of the community was Clare and her sister Joanna, who lived together as recluses in a cell adjacent to a prison. *Vita Clarae de cruce virginis, AASS,* August 3:676. Other women eventually were drawn into their orbit, and a larger foundation was constructed, over the opposition of some in the town who had negative feelings about Clare (*Vita Clarae,* 678). Although the community is frequently referred to as a "convent" or "monastery" in the documentation, the group had strong links to the outside world. Clare was known to visit friends in town, to receive visitors, and to beg publicly. Testimony about the autopsy was given at the canonization inquiry by several witnesses. These are preserved as ASV Arch. Congr. SS. Rituum, lat. ms. 2929, and ASV Arch. Congr. SS. Rituum, lat. ms. 2927. The printed version of the canonization proceedings (Enrico Menestò, ed., *Il processo di canonizzazione di Chiara da Montefalco* [Florence, 1984]) came into my possession rather late, and for this reason I cite directly from my manuscript notes. Menestò's edition attempts to reconstruct a proof-text: thus on page civ, Menestò synthesizes a stemma showing his reconstruction of the manuscript tradition. He does not, however, supply a chart collating his edition with individual manuscripts.

spreading. The assembled women extracted the heart, but could not proceed to a dissection of the organ itself that day. It was early the next morning, therefore, when the heart, having been preserved overnight in a little casket, was opened with a slice of Francesca's blade. There, the recluses found a miniature image of Christ crucified, formed from a miraculous intertwining of the cardiac nerves and muscles inside the organ itself. Legend has it that a schematic diagram, showing the layout of the crucifix and other signs of Christ's Passion that were found in Clare's heart, was made at the autopsy (fig. 15). However, the drawing is likely of later provenance.[2]

The goal of the autopsy was quite specific: Francesca proceeded straight to Clare's heart. Indeed, Francesca's narrow focus and grim determination may appear puzzling. Why were Francesca and the other sisters so eager to open up Clare's body, delaying scarcely a few hours after she was found dead before beginning the procedure? What made them search so avidly for the heart, remove it, and dissect it? How did they know that something significant was to be found there?

Those in charge of Clare's canonization proceeding asked these questions in 1317, too. The summary report of the canonization inquiry later expressed the consensus that the autopsy was motivated "because God inhabited that heart so much, and they believed that some wonders or signs might be found in it."[3] Indeed, Clare had related to anyone who would lend a willing ear that Christ lived inside her heart. One witness recounted her recollection of Clare's vision thus:

> She heard from the aforesaid Saint Clare that Christ appeared to her in the form of a man with a rather large cross on his neck. . . . Christ seemed very tired, and he said to Saint Clare, "I am searching for a strong place to establish this cross in the earth, and here I have found an apt place for it." And the witness said that she believed that Christ left the aforementioned signs of the Passion and sent them into Saint Clare's heart at the time of this vision, just as they were found existing in Saint Clare's heart after her death.[4]

---

[2] The editorial apparatus in Clare's vita refers to the legend that the drawing was made at the autopsy (*Vita Clarae*, 673). However, since the canonization proceeding makes no reference to the drawing, it is likely of later origin.

[3] Quia Deus multum habitaverat in ipso corde, et credebant in eo aliqua mirabilia vel signa inveniri. ASV Arch. Congr. SS. Rituum, lat. ms. 2927, f. 394r.

[4] Audivit a sancta Clara praedicta quod Christus apparuit sibi in specie hominis cum cruce ad collum satis magna, et erat indutus vestibus candidis, sive albis, et ipse Christus videbatur multum fatigatus; et dixit Sanctae Clarae Praedictae: Ego quaero locum fortem pro fundando in terram istam crucem, et hic reperii locum aptum ad hoc. Et dixit ipsa testis

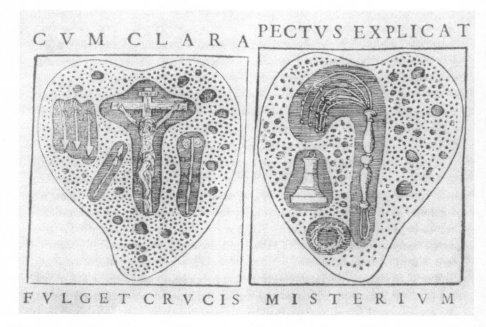

Figure 15. Schematic drawing of the crucifix found inside Clare of Montefalco's heart, depicting the instruments of the Passion found there. The diagram bears the inscription "When Clare's heart is laid open, the mystery of the cross shines forth." Though the drawing was said to have been made at Clare's autopsy, it is likely of somewhat later provenance. Photo by Richard S. Cohen.

Thus the short answer to the question about why the sisters expected to find something special in Clare's heart is: because Clare told them so. Indeed, so often and so vividly did Clare recount this vision, that in 1333 an artist composing frescoes in her honor gave pride of place to a depiction of it. The scene shows a disconsolate Christ thrusting the base of his cross under Clare's robe in the region of her heart.

However, a longer, fuller answer leads us into a new set of cultural problems about the human body and spirit possession. Whereas chapter 3 was devoted to a discussion of the surface border control of the body—its complexional qualities, impressionability, degree of porosity, and sexed external form—this chapter moves inside the body. Here I ask: What did pos-

quod credit, quod Christus tempore visionis praedictae reliquerit et miserit in cor Sanctae Clarae praedictae signa passionis suae, sicut reperta sunt et fuerunt in corde Sanctae Clarae post ejus mortem. ASV Arch. Congr. SS. Rituum, lat. ms. 2929, f. 273v–274v.

sessing spirits do in the body, once inside? Where did they lodge? How did they stimulate, disrupt, or otherwise interact with the interior physiological systems of the body? Was there any difference in the ways that an unclean spirit and the divine spirit were believed to dwell within the body? If so, then why were the surface manifestations of these two kinds of possession so similar?

I begin with an examination of the physiology of the human spirit as it was understood in medieval medical thought, information that provides a groundwork for the rest of the chapter. The next two sections have a chronological focus, exploring how "foreign" supernatural spirits were thought to interact with the "indigenous" human spirit in the late twelfth and thirteenth centuries. These sections investigate the growing symbolic differentiation between two internal bodily zones—the heart and the bowels—as clean and unclean, refined and gross, spiritual and purely physical. The next part shifts focus, to examine how possessing spirits were believed to produce possessed behaviors such as trance, prophecy, and so forth through manipulation of the body's internal physiology. It is possible to correlate descriptions of possession and of possessed behaviors with the understanding of the spiritual system elaborated by twelfth- and thirteenth-century authors. Lastly, in a brief epilogue I discuss some early treatises on the testing of spirits, which utilize notions of the physiology of spirit possession in order to explain how one might discern spirits. These texts were not immediately influential in their own time, but they do begin to knit together some of the strands of interpretation I have been tracing throughout this book.

HEART AND SPIRIT

In order to understand the precise physiological mechanisms of spirit possession in the Middle Ages, we must begin by exploring notions of the human spirit. For in the later Middle Ages the human spirit, far from being conceived as an abstract entity, was seen as having a concrete material existence inside the body. Indeed, there was thought to be an entire physiological system devoted to the production, maintenance, and diffusion of the spirit, or *spiritus*, inside the human body.[5] These ideas were the product of a

[5] The following discussion is indebted to studies of medieval medicine cited in chapter 3, note 20. For discussion of the physiology of the spirit, see James Bono, "Medical Spirits and the Medieval Language of Life," *Traditio* 40 (1984): 91–130; M.-D. Chenu,

synthesis of Galenic notions concerning the rarefied *spiritus* or *pneuma*, found in the brain and nerves, with Aristotelian notions concerning the primacy of the heart as the seat of life and vitality within human anatomy. First worked out in Arabic medical texts, this complex synthetic system was introduced to the West in Latin translation beginning in the twelfth century.

Two Arabic texts were of particular importance in spurring investigation into the physiology of the spirit in the West. Costa ben Luca's (Qustā ibn Lūqā) treatise *The Difference between the Spirit and the Soul*, which appeared in Latin translation sometime between 1135 and 1155, drew a network of connections between various psychic and sensory behaviors, attributed an organic basis to these behaviors in different kinds of corporeal spirits, and located these spirits within the internal human anatomy.[6] This text, together with the works of Avicenna (Husain ibn Abdullāh ibn 'Alī ibn Sīnā), whose medical canon was translated by Gerard of Cremona (d. 1187), sparked an excited response among Latin intellectuals who were exploring connections between macrocosm and microcosm and eager to concretize the operations of the human spirit.[7] Throughout the latter half of the twelfth century there was an efflorescence of works devoted to this subject including Hugh of Saint-Victor's *The Union of Body and Spirit*; Alcher of Clairvaux's highly influential *On Spirit and Soul*; Isaac of Stella's letter to Alcher, known as *The Soul*; and, in a related vein, Richard of Saint Victor's *The Interior State of a Human Being*.[8] By the thirteenth century, the physiology of the spirit was being explored by writers on theoretical medicine like Henry Bate, Alfred of

---

"*Spiritus:* Vocabulaire de l'âme au XIIe siècle," *Revue des sciences philosophiques et theologiques* 41 (1957): 209–32. Idem, "Nature and Man—the Renaissance of the Twelfth Century," in *Nature, Man, and Society in the Twelfth Century*, trans. J. Taylor and L. Little (Toronto, 1997), 1–48. Boyd Hill, "The Grain and the Spirit in Medieval Anatomy," *Speculum* 40, 1 (1965): 63–73; G. Verbeke, *L'Évolution de la doctrine du pneuma du Stoicisme à S. Augustin* (New York, 1987); Marielene Putscher, *Pneuma, Spiritus, Geist: Vorstellungen vom Lebensantreib in ihren geschichtlichen Wandlungen* (Wiesbaden, 1973); Ruth Harvey, *The Inward Wits: Psychological Theory in the Middle Ages and in the Renaissance* (London, 1975); R. B. Onians, *The Origins of European Thought about the Body, the Mind, the Soul, the World, Time, and Fate* (Cambridge, 1951).

[6] Chenu, "*Spiritus,*" 209–19; Bono, "Medical Spirits," 92–96; Harvey, 37–39. Costa ben Luca's treatise was translated by John of Spain. An edition is in Putscher, *Pneuma, Spiritus, Geist*, 145–50, as part of a lovely bibliographic essay placing Greek, Arabic, and Latin treatises on the spirit in chronological order.

[7] For Avicenna, see Harvey, *Inward Wits*, 21–30, 39–53.

[8] Hugh of Saint-Victor, *De unione corporis et spiritus*, in *PL*, 177:285–94; Alcher of Clairvaux, *De spiritu et anima*, in *PL*, 40:779–852. (This text was rather influential because it was attributed to Augustine.) Isaac de Stella, *Epistola ad quemdam familiaren suum de anima*, in *PL*, 194:1875–90; Richard of Saint Victor, *De statu interioris hominis*, in *PL*, 196: 1115–60.

Sareschal, the anonymous compiler of the *Prose Salernitan Questions*, and Giles of Rome.[9] Similarly, theologians like Alexander of Hales, Albertus Magnus, and Thomas Aquinas accepted the broad outlines of this system.[10] Finally, these ideas were widely disseminated to nonspecialists by writers of exempla books and natural histories, such as Caesarius of Heisterbach, Gerald of Wales, Thomas of Cantimpré, Bartholomew the Englishman, and Vincent of Beauvais.

Throughout the development of this discussion in the Latin West, there existed a tension between those thinkers who wished to extend the meanings of the word *spiritus* to embrace a broadly unified system of psychology, physiology, and theology; and those who wished to restrict the word's meaning so as to distinguish it from other, related words such as *anima* or *mens*. Yet the usefulness of this system of thought lay precisely in its fluidity: the term *spiritus* easily absorbed other, contiguous terms and ideas. As James Bono has noted, there were many "Christian Latin authors who wished to create a language embracing both the phenomena of life, and the experience of salvation, within a unified conceptual framework."[11] As a result, notions of spirit and of soul frequently were conflated.[12] An important early statement of what was to become the dominant position derives from Alcher of Clairvaux's treatise *On Spirit and Soul*, composed in the decade of the 1160s: "The soul is called 'anima' because it animates the body for living: that is, it vivifies. The spirit is the same thing as the soul, and is called spirit because of our spiritual [nature], or else because it breathes (*spiret*) into the body."[13] And even more expansively:

> The soul is an intellectual, rational spirit, always living, always in motion, capable of good or evil will. . . . It is known by various names according to its works. It is called soul when it vivifies; spirit, when it

[9] Henry Bate, *Speculum divinorum et quorundam naturalium*, ed. E. Van de Vyver (Louvain, 1960); Alfred of Sareschal, *De motu cordis*, ed. C. Baeumker, *Des Alfred von Sareschal (Alfredus Anglicus) Schrift* De motu cordis (Munich, 1923); Brian Lawn, ed., *The Prose Salernitan Questions* (London, 1979).

[10] Albertus Magnus, *Questiones super de animalibus* (ed. Ephrem Filthaut, in *Alberti Magni Ordinis Fratrum Praedicatorum Episcopi Opera Omnia*, vol. 12 [Aschendorff, 1955]) deals with the heart's physiological centrality and its interactions with the spirit throughout. See also Thomas Aquinas, *In Aristotelis librum de anima commentarium*, ed. P. Angeli Pirotta (Marietti Editori, 1959).

[11] Bono, "Medical Spirits," 99.

[12] Ibid., 98–99. See also Jean-Claude Schmitt, "Le corps en Chrétienté," in *Le corps, les rites, les rêves, le temps: Essais d'anthropologie médiévale* (Paris, 2001), 344–59, esp. 347–51.

[13] Alcher of Clairvaux, *De spiritu*, 784.

contemplates; a sense, when it senses; consciousness (*animus*), when it knows; when it understands, mind; when it discerns, reason; when it remembers, memory; when it consents, will. These are not, however, differences of substance, but of names, for all these things are a single soul: diverse properties, but one essence.[14]

Although Alcher was not a well-known theologian in the Middle Ages, his text was widely cited by later authors because it was erroneously attributed to Augustine, and often copied with the great bishop's works.[15] This borrowed prestige rendered the treatise extremely influential, and it was referred to as an impeccable authority. Thomas of Cantimpré, for example, composed a commentary on the text, believing it to be authentically Augustinian, and he thus endorsed the assertion that the words "spirit" and "soul" can be used indifferently.[16] Similarly, Bartholomew the Englishman included a long chapter in his encyclopedia distilling Alcher's text and attributing it to Augustine; Vincent of Beauvais made the same attribution.[17] Thomas Aquinas refuted its Augustinian credentials, but his critical acumen was rare.[18]

As Alcher's statement demonstrates, the physiology of the spirit was a complex system embracing a multitude of different cognitive and physiological functions. An outline of this labyrinthine set of ideas may briefly be sketched as follows. According to the dominant model of spiritual physiology in place by the late twelfth century, the human body in a healthy state was pervaded by its own spirit or *spiritus*, a refined liquid substance akin to a mist. This spirit was produced in the left ventricle of the heart from inspired air heated by the heart. Some theorists held that there was a "black grain, inside the heart, in which the spirit dwells,"[19] but this detail was not always pre-

[14] Ibid., 788–89.

[15] Chenu dismisses Alcher's text as a "rather banal compilation" (Chenu, "*Spiritus*," 209), but this mitigates its importance for two reasons. First, banal compilations are precisely the sorts of texts that are most useful for the social historian seeking to illuminate general mentalities, as opposed to the intellectual historian seeking the origins of innovative new ideas. Second, the fact that the treatise was attributed to Augustine meant that it was accorded enormous authority in the Middle Ages.

[16] Thomas of Cantimpré, *De anima* 2.6; printed together with Thomas of Cantimpré, *Liber de natura rerum*, ed. H. Boese (Berlin, 1973), 85.

[17] *RP* 3.3, 46–48. *Spec. Nat.* 26.45, 1877, refers to Augustine and cites a line from Alcher.

[18] Thomas Aquinas, *The Soul: A Translation of St. Thomas Aquinas'* De Anima, trans. John Rowan (St. Louis, 1949), 156.

[19] Karl Sudhoff, "Abermals eine neue Handschrift der anatomischen Funfbildserie," in *[Sudhoffs] Archiv fur Geschichte der Medezin und der Naturwissenschaften* 3 (1910): 362–63, quote at lines 32–35. This group of manuscripts is discussed in Hill, "Grain and Spirit."

sent in descriptions of the system. Although the heart was the main seat of the spiritual system, the spirit pervaded the entire body by moving through the arteries, whose throbbing pulse pushed along the spirits inside.[20] The arterial pulse was maintained by the lungs and heart acting in concert as a sort of constant bellows, "which distributes the spirit of life uniformly to the whole body."[21] Medical theorists further subdivided the human spirit into three different categories according to its function and placement within the body: vital spirit, natural spirit, and animal spirit.

Preeminent among the three types of spirit was the "vital spirit," which sometimes was called the "windy spirit." It regulated the vital signs from the heart, maintaining heartbeat, pulse, and respiration. In fact, the vital spirit was the basic principle of life itself, and the heart, therefore, was the physiological seat of life. Thus the heart was thought to be the first part of the fetus to develop, and it was expected to be the first part of the body to resurrect.[22] At death the spirit was exhaled with the last breath, a tradition represented in medieval iconography by showing a small person emanating from the corpse's mouth (fig. 16). The conception of the spirit's egress from the mouth was echoed in various folklore traditions, in which the spirit goes out from the body, via the mouth, in the form of a small animal such as a lizard, a mouse, or a butterfly.[23] The loss of the spirit during these times would result in a temporary death of the body, until the spirit returned and reentered. A rather concise summary of the medical tradition is provided by Alfred of Sareschal, in his 1210 treatise *On the Motion of the Heart:*

> In fact, the motion of the heart, its exhalations and respirations, must be continual, as not only the professional healers of sicknesses know, but even some illiterates who understand correctly. [This motion] is necessary for heat and the spirit of life to perfuse throughout the whole body, animating it. . . . And, when this same spirit exits from a dying person,

[20] Alcher of Clairvaux, *De spiritu,* 795. Albertus Magnus, *Quaestiones de animalibus* 13.12, 244–45. On the micro- and macrocosmic implications of this movement, see Nancy Siraisi, "The Music of Pulse in the Writings of Italian Academic Physicians (Fourteenth and Fifteenth Centuries)," *Speculum* 50, 4 (1975): 689–710.

[21] Alfred of Sareschal, *De motu cordis,* 15.

[22] Albertus Magnus, *Quaestiones de animalibus* 1.55, 107–8; 12.19, 236; 16.15, 285–86. See also *RP* 3.15, 59–61; Thomas of Cantimpré, *De natura rerum* 1.47, 49; and *The Aberdeen Bestiary,* http://www.clues.abdn.ac.uk:8080/besttest/alt/translat/trans90v.html.

[23] See Carlo Ginzburg, *The Night Battles: Witchcraft and Agrarian Cults in the Sixteenth and Seventeenth Centuries* (New York, 1986); idem, *Ecstasies: Deciphering the Witches' Sabbath* (New York, 1991); Claude Lecouteux, *Fantômes et revenants au Moyen Age* (Paris, 1986).

Figure 16. The human spirit exiting the mouth at death. This painting shows the human spirit leaving the body in the form of a naked infant. To the left, the spirit of a man clutching a fat money bag is snatched by a demon; to the right, the spirit of a bishop is taken by an angel. Fresco attributed to Buffalmacco, c. 1332–42. Pisa: Camposanto. Photo by Richard S. Cohen.

it takes out the life along with itself, as is evident from the labored breathing and jerky motions of the spirit, together with a cooling of the extremities, as if the source of heat had been extinguished. There is a continual generation of the spirit in the heart, for the maintenance of constant life.[24]

If the spirit was sometimes envisioned as a tiny figure exiting from the mouth, its existence while inside the body was viewed in more rarefied terms. A 1292 rendering of an "artery man" illustrates the generation and diffusion of the spirit (fig. 17). Filling the figure's trachea are a series of air bubbles which proceed to the heart, where they will be transformed into spirit inside a small black grain shown inside the heart. From there, the arteries transport the spirit throughout the body, including toward the liver (the scalloped item on the figure's proper right side); and to the brain through an organ known as the *retus mirabilis* (indicated by cross-hatching at the top of the figure's head). A slightly different set of emphases is noted in another artery man from about 1420 (fig 18). While this illustration lacks the tracheal tube, it does show a pathway by which the spirit might reach the groin, an important indication of the spirit's instrumentality both in sexual arousal and in the production of new life.[25] Thus Albertus called the heart the "first and truest principle of generation" because the three elements necessary for the formation of a new life—motion, heat, and spirits—all derived from the paternal heart. These elements were used by the "informative power" (*virtus informativa*) of the father's seed in the generation of a fetus, molding the passive matter provided by the mother into a new life.[26]

Since the spirit was understood to be engaged with nearly every aspect of human physiology, it could be used to explain a wide array of physical effects and symptoms. Basic elements of human existence, such as an upright posture or sex, were traced to the vital spirit inside the heart.[27] Sex determination, for instance, was linked to the amount of heat generated in the fetal heart, which then influenced the development of the fetus as either male (hotter) or female (cooler). Moreover, men were said to have larger hearts

[24] Alfred of Sareschal, *De motu cordis*, 13–14.

[25] The *spiritus* was held to be a component of the male seed, and was thought to be important in the production of a new life. See M. Hewson, *Giles of Rome and the Medieval Theory of Conception* (London, 1975).

[26] Albertus Magnus, *Quaestiones de animalibus* 1.55, 107–8; 16.16, 283.

[27] On erect posture, see Aquinas, *The Soul*, 101. On sex determination, Albertus Magnus, *On Animals: A Medieval Summa Zoologica* 18.3, trans. K. Kitchell and I. Resnick, 2 vols. (Baltimore, 1999), 2:1291; and Cadden, *Meanings of Sex.*

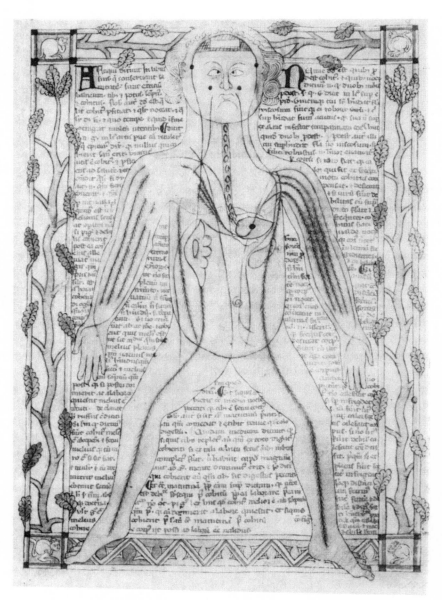

Figure 17. An artery man and the manufacture of the spirit through inspired air. In this illustration from a medical text, the spirit is formed in the heart from inhaled air, shown descending the trachea in the form of air bubbles. Once the air reaches the heart, the spirit is manufactured inside a black grain, then pumped throughout the body via the arteries. Manuscript drawing by an anonymous artist, 1292. Oxford: Bodleian Ashmole ms. 399, f. 19. Photo courtesy of the Bodleian Library.

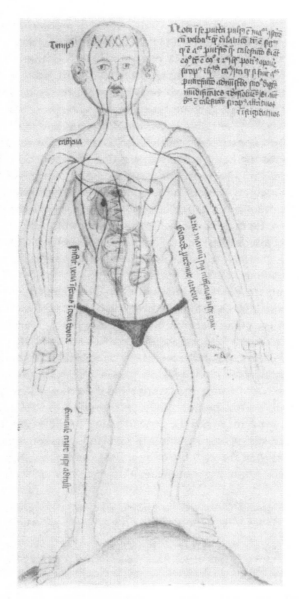

Figure 18. An artery man and the spiritual system. This drawing depicts the spirit's involvement in sexual arousal and reproduction, and in intellectual apprehension. Two arteries lead the spirit to the groin, and two others conduct it to the *retus mirabilis*, an organ that refines the spirit before it enters the brain. The latter feature is indicated by cross-hatching on the artery man's forehead. Manuscript drawing by an anonymous artist, c. 1420. London: Wellcome Historical Medical Library, ms. 49, f. 35v. Photo courtesy of the Wellcome Trust.

than women, hence their greater vitality and complexional heat.[28] In addition to these basic constitutional factors, conditions such as fevers and chills were traced to the operations of the spirit as well. These were said to be caused by a fault in the functioning of the vital spirit, since it was responsible for the maintenance of proper body temperature.[29] The heart and spirit also were involved with the emotional and psychological well-being of the human individual.[30] For example, the physical symptoms of strong emotions were caused by a constriction of the heart, as spirit fled from this central organ and flooded the body; while fear was due to a retraction of spirit from the extremities into the heart alone. According to Richard of Saint-Victor, "just as there are four humors in the body, there are four principal emotions in the heart. . . . Love and hatred, then, and joy and sorrow, are the four principal emotions. From these are derived all desires, wills, resolutions and emotions. . . . And just as with the humors in the body, so it is with the emotions in the heart: they give rise to various infirmities according to how their proper, harmonious order is disturbed."[31]

After leaving the heart, the vital spirit could be transformed into the "natural spirit," which was based in the liver and controlled a variety of involuntary activities, including digestion and sexual response; or it could be purified into the "animal spirit" as it ascended to the head through the *retus mirabilis*. Named for the soul, *anima*, the animal spirit resided in the brain, regulating the nervous system and intellectual responses to sensory stimuli. The animal spirit aided in coordinating the interior and the exterior senses, by carrying external impulses to the brain.[32] Vision, for example, was accomplished when the animal spirit transmitted the appearance of a visible object to the brain along the optic nerve; hearing similarly involved the intermediary of the animal spirit traveling through the cavity of the ear canal.[33] According to one source, various temporary or permanent defects of the spiritual system could

---

[28] Albertus Magnus, *Quaestiones de animalibus* 3.23, 136; 13.7, 241–42.

[29] Peter of Abano, *Conciliator discordantium medecinalium*, BN ms. lat. 6961, 81r–v.

[30] On the heart as the seat of selfhood and subjectivity, see Eric Jager, "The Book of the Heart: Reading and Writing the Medieval Subject," *Speculum* 71, 1 (1996): 1–26; idem, *The Book of the Heart* (Chicago, 2000). Also of interest here is Jeffrey Hamburger, *Nuns as Artists: The Visual Culture of a Medieval Convent* (Berkeley, 1997).

[31] Richard of Saint Victor, *De statu interioris hominis*, in *PL*, 196:1141.

[32] One text attributes the process of gaining knowledge to the movement of the spirits between their point of generation in the heart and the brain: Lawn, *Prose Salernitan Questions*, 138. On the spirit and the senses more generally, see Alcher of Clairvaux, *De spiritu*, 795.

[33] See also A. Crombie, "Theories of Perceiver and Perceived in Hearing," in J. Céard et al., eds., *Le corps à la Renaissance* (Paris, 1988), 379–87; Huldrych Koelbing, "Anatomie de l'oeil et perception visuelle de Vésale à Kepler," in Céard, *Le corps*, 389–97.

affect the ability to vocalize, resulting in a poor singing voice.[34] Touch, taste, and smell each used the animal spirit in particular ways to transmit external environmental information to the brain.[35] Imagination also functioned in ways similar to sensory stimuli: "The imagination is nothing other than an image of a body, conceived exteriorly through the physical senses from contact with the body, introduced inside through the senses, then conducted to the purer part of the body by the spirit and impressed there."[36]

As we have seen, the senses often were regarded as entry points that could be used by outside spirits as pathways to the body's interior: "the senses are like gates into the body through which ingressions and egressions . . . are made."[37] Ideas about the human spirit's role in coordinating the senses explained, in turn, where these pathways led and how they were used. An obvious question is raised by the transposition of these two ideas: How do theories about the invasive quality of spirit possession fit with theories about the physiology of the human spirit? The following two sections discuss how new ideas about the human spirit were correlated with increasingly sophisticated theories about the precise physiological mechanisms of spirit possession.

HUMAN AND SUPERNATURAL SPIRITS IN THE LATE TWELFTH CENTURY

As the human spirit came to be seen as a material entity existing in specific places in the body and moving along certain pathways, the conceptualization of spirit possession underwent a corresponding adjustment. Indeed, this new imagining of the human spirit occurred in tandem with an expansion of interest in, and a multiplication of stories about, the divinely and the demonically possessed. One might say that the turn of the late twelfth into the thirteenth century witnessed a general shift of interest toward investigating the operations of spirits—celestial, infernal, and human alike. Furthermore, there were certain linkages between these discussions, so that as new ideas entered the stream of one discussion about spirits, so did they eventually flow into explorations of other kinds of spirits.

[34] Lawn, *Prose Salernitan Questions*, 270.
[35] For the role of the spirit in the five senses see *RP* 3.17–21, 62–74.
[36] Hugh of Saint-Victor, *De unione corporis et spiritus*, in *PL*, 177:288.
[37] William of Auvergne, *De universo*, in *Guillelmi Alverni Opera Omnia*, 2 vols. (Paris, 1674; reprint, Frankfurt-am-Main, 1963), 1:1042.

Medieval intellectuals wondered: if the physiological operations of the human spirit could be identified and traced inside the body, then should not the movements of foreign spirits be traceable inside the human anatomy as well? As we have seen, dominant opinion in the Middle Ages held that spirit possession, whether by an unclean spirit or the Holy Spirit, involved a literal entry into the body.[38] It might enter through the senses or the pores. Beginning in the late twelfth and continuing into the thirteenth century, medieval theorists began to speculate about precisely how such foreign spirits, once inside, might interact with the body's internal physiology, including the organs, the pathways of sense apprehension, the mind, and the indigenous human spirit of the individual. Although some cultures that have a concept of spirit possession are not particularly concerned to explain how a spirit can enter the human body and assume control over it, medieval Europeans were increasingly interested in this problem. A physiological model for spirit possession, as a counterpart to the physiological model of the human spirit, must have seemed an excellent way to explain the somatic and perceptual changes endemic to both the divinely and the demonically possessed, as well as offering a tangible basis for discerning between them.

How, then, was a foreign possessing spirit believed to interact with the indigenous human spirit of its host body? An apparent clue to the medieval understanding of demonic possession, at least, is provided by portrayals of exorcism, which closely parallel representations of death scenes. Typical of the latter motif is a detail from the Triumph of Death fresco in the Camposanto of Pisa: with their last breaths, dying men expel infantile representations of their spirits from their mouths, which are snatched up by either angels or demons depending on their merits. Structurally, such representations are identical with images of exorcism: here, too, the spirit (usually in the form of a small black imp) leaps out from the mouth of the sufferer as a saint or priest performs the conjuration. Similarly, when exorcisms are described in texts, they often are considered successful only when the victim vomits forth some object from the mouth. Given this parallelism of exit through the mouth, we might formulate the hypothesis that demonic pos-

[38] There were exceptions to this opinion. Certain scientific writers considered forms of mental unbalance and dissociation to be due to natural causes (such as an imbalance of the humors, or an exceptional subtlety of the spirits), rather than possession by demons. Bert Hansen, *Nicole Oresme and the Marvels of Nature: The De Causis Mirabilium* (Toronto, 1985), 287. For discussion of Oresme, see E. Paschetto, ed., *Demoni e prodigi: Note su alcuni scritti di Witelo e di Oresme* (Turin, 1978), 59–60. Lynn Thorndike, *History of Magic and Experimental Science*, 5 vols. (New York, 1934), 3:398–471. I also would like to thank Renata Mikolajczyk for sharing with me a paper on this topic, "*Non sunt nisi phantasie e imaginationes*: A Medieval Attempt at Explaining Demons."

session was seen as the replacement of the human spirit by an invasive unclean spirit, which then controls the behavior and personality of the individual.

Unfortunately, this hypothesis is wrong. The seeming iconographic elision actually masks a complex system of differences. For the mouth was, of course, the entrance to *two* distinct physiological systems: the spiritual system, centered in the heart; and the digestive system, with all its gross impurities. Although the iconographic similarity undoubtedly expressed a basic parallel for the unlettered, the consensus in learned circles was that divine possession by the Holy Spirit and demonic possession by an unclean spirit took place within entirely different parts of the body. To wit, demonic spirits most often entered the bowels or viscera, while only the Holy Spirit could enter the heart, seat of the human spirit and soul. From this perspective, the crucifix and other instruments of the Passion discovered in Clare's heart acquire new resonances.

The origins of this differential physiology of spirit possession are interwoven with concurrent developments in theories of the human spirit. Prior to the late twelfth century, medieval intellectuals had not been particularly concerned to develop a theory of precisely how and why demonic possession occurred. The inheritance of Augustine's writings in this area, as in all others, was formative, though his comments on the topic were not extensive. In his treatise *On the Divination of Demons*, the bishop laid forth the notion that demons can influence people by "using the subtlety of their bodies to penetrate the bodies of men without their feeling it, and intermingling themselves into their thoughts . . . through certain imaginative visions."[39] By the early twelfth century, it was widely held that unclean spirits may possess a person physically but could not affect the soul. Thus the theologian Rupert of Deutz (d. 1129) noted, in highly evocative phrases, that demonic spirits can possess only from inside the "caverns of the body," while "the Holy Spirit can enter the substance of the soul substantially."[40] Rupert's language presumes an interior landscape to the body, one riddled with fleshly grottoes and concavities that may be populated by demons while the soul remains inviolate. Similarly, Hildegard of Bingen (d. 1179) maintained that the soul *strictu sensu* always remained off limits to demons. Unclean spirits might, however, confuse the soul through their infestation of the body and control over it. In a letter discussing the case of a woman possessed by spirits, Hildegard explains, "[The devil] overshadows [the soul] and obscures it with shadows and the

[39] Augustine, *De divinatione demonum* 5.9, in *PL*, 40:586.
[40] Rupert of Deutz, *De Trinitate et operibus ejus*, in *PL*, 167:1597–98.

smoke of his blackness . . . ; meanwhile the soul is as if sleepy and unaware of what the flesh of its body is doing."[41] Aside from a consensus on these basic principles, the deep interior logic of demonic possession was left largely unexplored by twelfth-century thinkers.

Some theorists of the human spirit, however, immediately saw the ramifications of these ideas for an exploration of spirit possession. Indeed, the most influential early theological text about the physiology of the human spirit, Alcher of Clairvaux's pseudo-Augustinian treatise *On Spirit and Soul*, also discussed how various kinds of foreign spirits might enter the human body and interact with its indigenous spiritual system. Alcher's treatment provided an excellent model for later commentators wishing to probe the precise physiological mechanisms of possession, for he turns, in the later pages of the text, to questions of spirit possession and discernment, ecstasies and visions, spiritual seductions and false illusions. Alcher describes the process of divine contemplation, for example, as one of transcending the self and closing off the physical senses, while turning inward to the heart. His language invokes the simultaneously ecstatic and invasive paradox of divine union or possession that is a familiar element in saints' vitae: "The world is exterior, while God is interior. Nothing is more interior than Him, nothing is more present. . . . To ascend to God is to enter into oneself, and not only to enter into oneself, but in some ineffable way to transcend one's innermost self. Whoever goes inside himself and, by penetrating himself interiorly, transcends himself, has truly ascended to God. Therefore, let us bind up our heart from the distractions of this world."[42]

Similarly, a discussion of how the spirit coordinates the senses, imagination, and memories, producing images of things inside the mind, turns into a discussion of how visions and revelations may be produced in the human spirit, through the influence of another, possessing spirit:

> Sometimes while the spirit is entranced, the soul is raised up and it sees, in this way, either good things or bad things. Images of bodily things thus are perceived in spirit, either through intense contemplation or else through some morbid force, as happens with frenzied people through a fever, or through the admixture of some other spirit, either good or evil.[43]

[41] *Vita S. Hildegardis Virgine, AASS*, September 5:693.
[42] Alcher of Clairvaux, *De spiritu*, 791.
[43] Ibid., 796.

Alcher goes on to explain the three different kinds of vision—corporeal, spiritual, and intellectual—first laid forth by Augustine in his literal commentary on Genesis (though without mentioning Augustine by name). The two former kinds of vision both present sensory images to the mind by means of the spirit, and require interpretation, while intellectual vision proceeds through direct illumination. Thus the latter cannot be false, since the individual either understands or does not; but both corporeal and spiritual visions can be deceptive. Alcher warns that corporeal vision sometimes distorts reality, as in the case of looking at a reflection in water that breaks up the image; and spiritual vision, too, can involve deceptive and illusive sensory information that is relayed to the spirit fraudulently. Indeed, demons have long experience and skill in deluding humanity. A preeminent case of a "Satan transforming himself into an Angel of Light," in order to deceive the unwary, is provided by those silly women who believe that they wander at night with "Diana the Pagan Goddess, or with Herodias and Minerva, and a countless multitude of women."[44] Trance-visions of the "good things" as described in the *Canon episcopi*, figure here as an easy discernment case, transparently malign to the learned, though deceptively benign to the silly women who believe in these experiences.

So how can one detect more advanced spiritual deceptions and illusions? According to Alcher, the discernment of spirits is exceedingly difficult because the effects of evil spirits can be identical to the effects of good spirits. Despite the similarities between divine and demonic inspiration, however, there are important differences in the possible physiological locations of good and evil spirits inside the body, as well as in the means each kind of spirit may use to interfere with the human senses, imagination, and memory. Alcher's ideas about divine and demonic possession were to become profoundly important to the developing discourse on discernment, for he molds previous notions about demonic possession to the language of the body in new ways.

However clumsily, Alcher joined to the basic Augustinian understanding of spirit possession a number of innovative new ideas drawn from the emerging science of spiritual physiology. For instance, Alcher invoked Augustine's notion of a secret intermingling of the invading spirit. He also referred to the notion that only the Holy Spirit can enter the soul substantially. But spliced into these traditional concerns was a newly emergent set of ideas about spiritual physiology, including the centrality of the heart as the seat of the hu-

[44] Ibid., 800.

man spirit and soul; the spirit's role as the principle of life; and its coordinating functions on behalf of the senses and cognitive processes. Alcher's thought here is worth quoting in some detail:

> Sometimes a good spirit, and sometimes an evil spirit, assumes control over the human spirit. It is not easy to discern which spirit is assuming control. . . . Thus an evil spirit very often ravishes the human spirit by secretly mixing itself in, so that they appear as if one and the same spirit—both the spirit of the victim and the spirit of the tormentor—as we see in demoniacs. However, no creature can fill up the soul of a man, that is, his mind, according to its substance, except the Trinity alone.
>
> Yet Satan is said to fill the mind of a person, and to become the [vital] principle of the heart, though without entering into it or its senses, but rather by binding it up with fraud and treachery and all evils, and by seducing it through the effect of his evil. . . . When the devil fills a person or inhabits him, it is not through participation in his nature or substance, as some think. However, through fraud, deceit, and malice he is said to inhabit the person he fills up. It is for the Trinity alone to enter into and to fill up the nature or the substance of that which he created.[45]

This passage is the earliest instance known to me of a scholar attempting, in an extended way, to think through the theoretical implications of the notion of a corporeal human spirit for an understanding of spirit possession. Alcher is visibly groping toward a physiological theory of spirit possession. While he does not succeed in terms of either elegance or clarity, he poses an interesting set of new questions about the interaction of demonic spirits with the human spiritual system. Although he concedes that Satan is said to fill the mind or soul of an individual, and even to become the principle of the heart— that is, the animating principle of vitality based in the central organ of the body—he also states that this is not strictly true. Indeed, evil spirits can enter neither into the senses nor enter into the heart in a literal, physiological sense: this is reserved for God alone. Alcher thus initiated a fruitful new perspective on spirit possession by invoking the human spirit, its generation and dwelling place in the heart, its function in human vitality, and its role in relaying the perceptions of the senses and mind.

[45] Ibid., 799. Alcher's language is difficult to render into clear English here. My translation is not perfectly literal.

Alcher's fundamental insight was to coordinate the activities of the human spirit with those of invasive possessing spirits. Thirteenth-century thinkers were to elaborate this idea, far more elegantly than did Alcher, by harmonizing the operations of various kinds of spirits with greater clarity and precision. Nonetheless, throughout the thirteenth century, theologians struggled with a language problem, explaining that even though demonic spirits were *said* to possess individuals, they did not do so at an "essential" or "substantive" level. We can see this, for example, in the *Summa* of Alexander of Hales, one of the most prominent Franciscan theologians of the thirteenth century: "An evil spirit cannot be inside our senses by its essence, nor can it unite to us by its essence, nor fill us essentially. But it can be said to fill us by the effect of its activities, when by a sensory temptation it penetrates to the soul. . . . Satan can be said to fill the heart . . . through his activity . . . while not entering inside."[46]

Alexander's work, begun around 1231 and left unfinished at the time of his death in about 1245, presupposes a grasp of spiritual physiology. By emphasizing that the heart is the seat of the soul, he places strict limits on the interior penetrations of demons: although they can fill us with temptation, they cannot fill us essentially or invade the center of being, the soul. These ideas are intimately related to the question of what it means to be in the image of God. The human soul, since it is an *imago Dei*, is never vulnerable to the predations of the demonic hosts: the imprint of God seals off the soul from such penetration. Similarly, though demons may use, deceive, or tempt the senses, they cannot enter the senses' essence, where the human spirit dwells.

Vincent of Beauvais (d. 1264) went even further in his popular encyclopedia, the *Natural Mirror*, explaining exactly how good or evil spirits engaged with the internal spiritual physiology of the possessed individual. His systematic rendering of the differences between various kinds of spiritual invasions repeats the ideas of Alcher of Clairvaux, but Vincent expresses them in a more systematic and compelling way:

God, angels, and the devil are said to be in the soul, but in different ways. God is there as a [principle of] life, that is, he vivifies the soul. An angel

[46] Alexander of Hales, *Summa theologiae*, 4 vols. (Florence, 1930), 3:175.

is like a comrade, exhorting the soul. An angel, therefore, is in [the soul] such that it does not bring good things inside it, but suggests them. God, however, is inside [the soul], for he is united with it and poured into it. God, therefore, is inside; an angel is outside. However, [an angel] is said to be inside [the soul] to the extent that it performs operations in it, such as counseling it, instructing it, warning it, and so forth. The devil must be understood in the same way: it is not inside the soul substantially, but it can be said to enter into [the soul] on account of the operations it performs within it: that is, seducing it by means of images and suggestions.[47]

This is a rich and fascinating passage. Although all three kinds of spirits are "said to be in the soul," Vincent wishes to clarify this terminology by means of some precise theological hair-splitting. He argues that in the case of angels and the devil, the phrase "inside the soul" is used only loosely. In actuality such spirits always remain strictly outside the soul, but since their effects may penetrate within, through counsel and suggestion, it is customary to refer to them as inside. In reality, only God can fully pour Himself into the soul and unite with it. Moreover, in so doing, God actually replaces the human principle of life, the "vital spirit" of medieval medicine, based in the heart. Through divine possession, God Himself becomes the vivifying principle of the soul and, by extension, the body. The prerogative of actually replacing the human spirit with a supernatural spirit is reserved for God alone.

Albertus Magnus and his pupil Thomas Aquinas, in the avant-garde of thirteenth-century thought, adopted an Aristotelian vocabulary and defined the soul as the form of the body. This principle led to a subordination of the spirit to the soul. For these elite theologians, the spirit was distinct from the soul by virtue of its material nature. Indeed, the spirit acted as the tool of the soul, providing a highly refined intermediary between the grossness of the body and the immateriality of the soul. Moreover, the spirit was mortal and died with the body, while the soul was immortal and lived on.[48] Thus with the ascent of Aristotelian philosophical ideas came a reluctance to view spirit and soul as unified in essence. Given these sophisticated distinctions, Aquinas's view on the physiology of spirit possession is adjusted slightly from the other thinkers quoted above. Rather than focusing exclusively upon the issue of entry to the soul, Aquinas constructed the issue of spirit possession

[47] *Spec. Nat.* 26.69, 1881.
[48] Aquinas, *The Soul*, 112, 122, 132–33, 147. Albertus Magnus, *Quaestiones de animalibus* 13.5, 240.

in more balanced terms. He spoke of both soul and body—which for him translated back to form and matter. This duality constituted, for Aquinas, the basis of a split between the separate spheres permitted to divine and demonic spirits.

> As for the soul, the devil cannot inhabit a human being substantially. . . .
> The Holy Spirit, indeed, can act from inside, but the devil suggests from outside, either to the senses or to the imagination. . . . As for the body, the devil can inhabit a human being substantially, as in possessed people.[49]

The Holy Spirit can enter the soul and possess it substantially; unclean spirits can enter the body and possess it substantially. Demons also may transmit errors and deceptions to the soul by making illicit suggestions to the senses and imagination, while still remaining outside. With this passage, Aquinas was not necessarily presenting a new idea—implicit in all other discussions is the notion that demons can get inside the body—but his rhetorical parallelism clarifies and simplifies the distinction in modes of possession.

If demons could enter the body, but not the heart and the spiritual system, then where did they go once inside? An answer for this question came readily to mind for many medieval authors. We may think of the body in the Middle Ages as divided among two broad conceptual and symbolic zones. The heart was the seat of the immortal soul and the spirit, and thus the purest, warmest, airiest center of the body, appropriate for the indwelling of the divine. This being the case, the principle of contrariety dictated that demons must seek out the most debased and unclean centers, the coolest and moistest portion of the human anatomy. In short, demons must live primarily in the bowels.

Medieval sources occasionally add the prefix *caco-*, derived from *cacus* (shit), to *daemon* (demon) in order to better underline an evil spirit's connection with digestion and the impure regions of the body. As one source rebukes a demon, "You are impure; you speak impurities; you love impurities; you seek impurities. For you were created to live in heaven, and now you seek out toilets and go visiting latrines."[50] Unable to enter the deepest seat of the human essence, where they could do the most damage, demons were assumed to seek out a home for themselves in the digestive tract instead. A

---

[49] Thomas Aquinas, *Quodlibeta.* q. II, art. 8.
[50] *The Chronicle of Salimbene de Adam*, trans. Joseph Baird et al. (Binghamton: 1986), 578.

charming exemplum from an anonymous preaching manual addresses the connection between possessing demons and digestion pointedly, by relating the results of a theological experiment: "The Eucharist was given to a certain woman in whom there was a demon. Then the demon was asked where it was, and whether it was with Christ. It answered, 'No, the Lord is in her soul, and I live in her intestines.'"[51]

This popular tale made its way into more than one preaching compilation. The distinction between the locations of the two spirits is an important one, for with it, the story demonstrates three principles. First, it asserts the inviolability of that which is *imago Dei* to the depredations of demons: the soul that images God remains intact even when the body is possessed. Second, the anecdote locates the unclean spirit within an unclean region of the body. This is a means both of deriding the demon, by aligning it with a scatological reference, and of containing it within the most grossly physical portion of the anatomy, far removed from the heart and spirit. Third, the tale communicates a vitally important principle about the Eucharist and the incorporation of Christ's body. The Host does not undergo a normal digestive process, with all the impurities that this might entail, but instead miraculously enters into the heart, seat of both soul and spirit.

Indeed, this understanding of communion as a form of possession, in which the spirit of Christ enters into the heart and joins with the human spirit, lends depth to the widely noted phenomenon of Eucharistic devotion among religious women.[52] The significance of the act is more than a potent physical ingestion and absorption. It is also a means of voluntary spirit possession, since Christ thereby enters the heart. Or, as Gerald of Wales phrased it, "When we eat other food we take it into ourselves and incorporate it, but this food takes us into itself and incorporates us, making us members of it."[53] A strange and violent exemplum interweaves even more closely these themes of the soul, the heart, and the Eucharist:

Once there was a cleric in the city of Rome who reverently received the body of Christ on Easter. As he left the church he met some Jews with

[51] A. Little, *Liber exemplorum ad usum praedicantium* (Aberdeen, 1907), 9. An earlier version is in Giraldus Cambrensis, *Gemma ecclesiastica*, ed. J. S. Brewer, in *Rerum Britannicarum Medii Aevi scriptores*, vol. 21: *Giraldi Cambrensis opera* (New York: Kraus Reprint, 1964) 2, 54. I have excerpted the *Liber exemplorum* because of its pithier phrasing.

[52] Caroline Bynum, "Women Mystics and Eucharistic Devotion in the Thirteenth Century," in *Fragmentation and Redemption: Essays on Gender and the Human Body in Medieval Religion* (New York, 1991), 119–50; André Vauchez, *Les laics au Moyen Age: Pratiques et expériences religieuses* (Paris, 1987), 259–64.

[53] Giraldus Cambrensis, *Gemma ecclesiastica*, 54.

whom he was acquainted. One of them asked him, "Now where is that body of Christ that you say you have received today?" The cleric responded: "He is in my soul." Then they inquired, "Where is your soul?" The cleric answered, "In my heart, I believe." Then they said, "Let's find out," and with that, they killed him and took out his heart from his body. Immediately after they had sliced open the heart, the most beautiful boy appeared to them. As soon as the Jews saw him, they ran about crazily and shouted so vehemently that all the citizens of the neighborhood came there and saw the miracle. When they were gathered together, then that boy—that is, Jesus Christ—said to the people standing there: "Whoever eats my flesh and drinks my blood remains within me, and I within them. Therefore, I will go back home where I came from." And then, in the sight of everyone, the boy entered into the cleric's heart and suddenly he was living, and immediately stood up unharmed.[54]

The story is meant to be preposterous and entertaining. Nevertheless, below the caustic anti-Semitic humor, linked to the propagation of Eucharistic devotion,[55] lies a substratum of shared cultural assumptions about the heart, the soul, and the possibilities for spiritual possession by Christ. Not only does Christ literally make his "home" in the cleric's heart or soul (by contrast with the Jew's taunting suggestion that Christ had entered the digestive tract), but he provides the vital spirit inside the heart, the principle of life itself. In sum, if demons were unable to enter into the heart and soul, then Christ was, if not actually unable, at least not expected to enter the bowels.

Other authors were to concur in this basic contrast between how a divine spirit and a demon might dwell within a human body. Caesarius of Heisterbach, for example, addressed this question directly in his *Dialogue on Miracles*, one of the earliest exempla compilations. His dialogue on the issue covers a wide range of topics about demonic temptation and divine possession.

How Demons Can Exist inside People:
[Novice:] Some people assert that demons cannot exist inside people but outside, just as a fortification is besieged from outside. . . .
[Monk:] The devil cannot be inside a human soul . . . [for] penetra-

---

[54] From Cambridge, Trinity Coll. Lib. ms. 262 B.11.23, 104; cited in J. T. Welter, *Tabula Exemplorum Secundum Ordinem Alphabeti* (Paris, 1926), n. 102.

[55] On the connection between anti-Semitism and Eucharistic devotion, see Kathleen Biddick, "Genders, Bodies, Borders: Technologies of the Visible," *Speculum* 68 (1993): 389–418; Miri Rubin: *Corpus Christi: The Eucharist in Late Medieval Culture* (Cambridge, 1991).

tion into the mind is possible only for Him who created it. . . . The mind of a man cannot be filled, according to its substance, by anything other than the Creator Trinity.

[Novice:] Why, then, is it said that the devil can enter into, tempt, or be inserted into the heart of a man?

[Monk:] A devil cannot enter into, or fill up, or be inserted into [the heart] except insofar as it drags the soul into a taste for evil by deceiving it. This is the difference between the approach of the Holy Spirit and that of an evil spirit: the former may properly be said to penetrate into it, while the latter is inserted in. . . . When it is said that a devil is inside a person, we must not understand this to mean the soul, but the body, for the devil can live inside the body's open spaces and in the bowels (*visceris*) where the shit (*stercora*) is contained.[56]

Thus demons remain on the loose, as it were, wherever there is open room inside the body. They are likely to be attracted to the digestive tract, but they also possess mobility through a network of open spaces or concavities existing within the body. This latter element is underlined by another exempla tradition that describes the demon as a mobile bump or bulge just under the surface of the skin.[57] Yet the preferred habitation of demons inside the "viscera" was a singularly rich and polyvalent notion, for the word had more than one set of referents. For example, while I translated this term as "bowels," it also could be used to designate sexual organs such as the testicles or uterus. Similarly, the word *venter* can be translated as either womb or bowels, stomach or anus. As we have seen in chapter 1, demonic possession sometimes was described in sexualized terms involving the inflation of the womb into a spiritual pregnancy; and exorcism was sometimes accomplished by an expulsion either through the "shameful parts" or through vomiting from the stomach.[58] Thus a series of associations was established between demons, bowels, and loins, on the one hand, and between the Holy Spirit, the heart, and the soul, on the other.

The contrast between the heart and the lower body as pure and impure zones, each appropriate to a different kind of spiritual indwelling, may be amplified by a number of ancillary traditions. For example, while the spirits of

---

[56] *DM*, 1:293–94.

[57] De Ap. 2.36.4, 386–87. See also Little, *Liber exemplorum*, 9; and Gerald of Wales, *Journey through Wales*, trans. L. Thorpe (New York, 1978), 152, which combines this motif with the experiment involving the Eucharist.

[58] Leonardus Lemmens, ed., *Fragmenta Minora: Catalogus Sanctorum Fratrum Minorum* (Rome, 1903), 96; and *Vita Hildegardis*, 695, for the quote.

most individuals usually were shown as exiting the mortal coil through the mouth with the last breath, the spirits of the most evil of men were represented as leaving their bodies through the stomach or anus. Medieval commentators took delight describing Judas's death as the spirit bursting forth from his belly, rather than exiting his mouth. Two scriptural accounts deal with Judas's demise. Matthew 27:5 simply says that Judas hanged himself, while the author of Luke-Acts gives a more complicated scenario. First, Luke gives the important background detail, in 22:3, that "Satan entered into Judas, named Iscariot," a point reinforced for medieval exegetes by a passage in the Gospel of John (6:71) wherein Jesus notes that one of the twelve is a devil. Thus, Judas was in a state of diabolic possession when he accomplished the betrayal of Jesus to the high priests. Judas's ultimate fate is recounted in the sequel to Luke, the Acts of the Apostles 1:18, composed by the same author as the third gospel. Here, the Vulgate version notes that Judas's middle burst open during his suicide by hanging, and that his bowels gushed out.[59] A complicated tradition of commentary on the death of the traitor identified this grisly moment with the exit of Judas's spirit from his body.[60] As Jacob of Voragine wrote (following a tradition of commentary inaugurated by Bede),

> his middle burst and all his bowels fell out. In this instance, [the spirit] was driven down from the mouth, lest it come out through the mouth, for it was not appropriate that [Judas's] mouth, which had touched the glorious mouth of Christ, should be so vilely defiled. However, it was fitting that the bowels, which had conceived the betrayal, should rupture and fall out.[61]

Thus Judas's mouth had been sealed up by divine contact at the moment of his betrayal of Christ with a kiss: his defiling spirit could not exit from this orifice, and so it exited forcibly through the belly.

The bursting bowels motif was to become a favored means of representing the death of Judas in artistic media.[62] Judas's evil (human) spirit is here elided with evil (demonic) spirits, which live primarily in the bowels (fig. 19).

[59] The Revised Standard Version of Acts renders the passage, "falling headlong, he burst open in the middle and all his bowels gushed out." While this is probably the most accurate translation of the passage from the original, the Vulgate Latin was the version used in the Middle Ages. The latter has "suspensus crepuit medius et diffusa sunt omnia viscera," which would attribute the main cause of death to hanging.

[60] The scatological aspects of the death of Judas are explored by Willis Johnson, "The Myth of Male Jewish Menses," *Journal of Medieval History* 24, 3 (1998): 273–95.

[61] Jacobus de Voragine, *Legenda aurea*, ed. T. Graesse (Osnabrück, 1965), 186.

[62] See W. Porte, *Judas Ischarioth in der bildenen Kunst* (Berlin, 1883).

Figure 19. The death of Judas. Medieval commentators suggested that the reason Judas's middle burst when he hung himself was because his spirit could not exit in the usual way from the mouth, which was sealed because of his kiss of betrayal. However, the motif also acts to align Judas's evil spirit with demonic evil spirits, thought to live primarily in the bowels. Fresco by Pietro Lorenzetti, 1329–31. Assisi: San Francesco, lower church. Photo by Richard S. Cohen.

Thus narratives and portrayals of the death of Judas instantiated a dense set of connections between images of spirits dwelling in the bowels, the physiology of demonic possession, and the righteous punishment of extreme evil. Indeed, Martine Ostorero has seen echoes of Judas's hanging and evisceration in an early description of the diabolic sabbath, an association that further cements the intimate demon-human relationship embodied in this description.[63]

The death of the arch-heretic Arius was understood in similarly scatological terms. Bede compared the two directly: "A most similar death in pain was fitting for the punishment of the heretic Arius. . . . As both had lived void of sense, so each perished through a voiding of the stomach."[64] The death of Arius, however, was envisioned in considerably more humiliating terms: "he endured a miserable death, for he shit out all his bowels and intestines into the toilet," as Jacob of Voragine described it.[65] The inversionary aspects of the motif were highlighted with even more flourishes by Gerald of Wales (died c. 1223) in his *Book on the Education of Princes:*

> While walking in the forum of Constantinople he felt his bowels growling and hurried to a toilet. Not only did he shamefully evacuate himself by the lower orifice, he also poured out all his intestines by his upper mouth . . . his life thus ended before his treacheries. . . . The same thing happened when Judas, Christ's betrayer, hanged himself by his own noose, and his middle burst and all his bowels poured out. In that case, though, it was not by the mouth but by the stomach that the guts were spilled.[66]

Two interesting parallelisms are deployed in this passage. First, there is a substitution of Arius's entrails for his spirit: at the moment of death, these come out of his mouth. Simultaneously, however, he evacuates through the anus: thus the death of Arius is depicted as an effusion or spilling of impurities from both ends of his body at once. The exit of his spirit acts to turn his body inside-out, with his physical uncleanness displayed to the world. Second, a

---

[63] Martine Ostorero, "Commentaire sur anonyme *Errores gazariorum seu illorum qui scopam vel baculum equitare probantur*," in M. Ostorero, Agostino Paravacini Bagliani, and Kathrin Utz Tremp, *L'Imaginaire du sabbat: Edition critique des textes les plus anciens (1430c.–1440c.)* (Lausanne, 1999), 317–19.

[64] Bede, *Expositio super Acta Apostolorum*, in *PL*, 92:944.

[65] Jacobus de Voragine, *Legenda aurea*, 452. See Johnson, "Myth of Male Jewish Menses," for more on this example, including several passages of commentary.

[66] Gerald of Wales, *De principis instructione liber*, in *Giraldi Cambrensis Opera Omnia*, ed. G. Warner, 8 vols. (London, 1891), 8:68.

general parallelism between Arius and Judas is made explicit by Gerald: both these men had betrayed God, the former spiritually through his teaching, and the latter physically, to the temple priests. As a result, the spirits of these two betrayers leave them through impure means—symbolically assimilating their evil human spirits to evil demonic spirits through association of both with the bowels.

The example of Arius's death made its way into monastic maledictory formulae intended to chastise those perceived as preying upon Church prerogatives. A text from Reims, for example, included among its curses the hope that such oppressors would "drain out through their bowels, like the faithless and unhappy Arius."[67] Exempla writers associated miscreants and sinners with death by disemboweling. Caesarius of Heisterbach tells of a knight given over to dice games. "In order that it might be shown to posterity how contrary such games are to God—for in them wrath, envy, quarrels, and curses are nourished, and sinful words are exchanged—it was permitted to the devil to play with him who had outplayed many, and to disembowel him who had emptied (*evacuerat*) many purses."[68] Caesarius indulges in a scatological pun that parallels the coming evisceration of the man's bowels and his habit of emptying—literally, "evacuating"—the bowels of others' purses. Caesarius goes on to tell how, as the evening drew to a close, the devil dragged the knight to his death across the rooftops of the town. All that remained of him were some fragments of his bowels clinging to the roof tiles. These were duly buried in the cemetery; his body, the text solemnly tells us, never was found.

These traditions about the deaths of Judas, Arius, and enthusiastic sinners symbolically align the human spirits of evil men to possessing demonic spirits, with their habitation inside the digestive tract. Johannes Nider tells of how a virtuous man narrowly escaped death because of a scatological joke at a demon's expense.

Nor should anyone make a joke of the solemnity that the holy order of Exorcist requires. For at the Council of Cologne I saw a brother who was fond of wisecracks, but very famous for his grace of expelling demons. This man, at the end of the Council of Cologne, was casting out a demon from a possessed body. The demon asked the brother for a place to withdraw into, to which the brother gaily said in jest, "Go into

[67] Lester K. Little, *Benedictine Maledictions: Liturgical Cursing in Romanesque France* (Ithaca, N.Y., 1993), 36.

[68] *DM*, 1:318. Frederic Tubach, *Index Exemplorum: A Handbook of Medieval Religious Tales* (Helsinki, 1969) gives several other citations: see motif no. 745.

my latrine!" The demon therefore left, and at night, when the brother went to empty his bowels, the demon tormented him so severely in the latrine that he survived only with difficulty.[69]

This material also may be read against a variety of other cultural fragments that gain an extra measure of symbolic interest. For instance, the burial practices of elites often called for the heart and entrails to be interred separately from the remainder of the body. This practice, known as plural burial, was widespread among the nobility of northern Europe, and it distressed Pope Boniface VIII, who forbade the custom. Yet the preference for singling out these particular internal organs for special treatment implies a recognition that they are highly charged bodily zones.[70] Similarly, images in which Satan is depicted excreting or birthing spirits of the dead focus on an association between the demonic and the unclean lower bodily zone. Indeed, the organization of the punishments of Hell in these frescoes suggests that disemboweling was reserved, in the medieval imagination, for the very worst and most demonic of sins. To return in passing to the Camposanto rendering, we see that this torment is shown only as a recompense for pride, the foremost sin, at the summit of the composition. Even more striking is the detail of the burst bowels in the figure of Satan, where we may discern some sinners being digested preparatory to their excretion/birthing below. The demonic, the bowels, the womb, and the theme of war against God were here aligned in graphic and violent ways.

Finally, let us turn our gaze back to Clare of Montefalco for a moment. The tension between two different bodily zones, one pure and one impure, is tantalizingly expressed in a descriptive displacement that occurs between the vita and the canonization inquiry of Clare. The episode concerns a lust-inspiring crucifix. In Clare's vita, we are told how she was tempted by the masculine verisimilitude of a demonic Christ effigy:

That crafty old demon projected onto the wall the effigy of a crucifix of almost unbelievable beauty, with the graceful form of an elegant body, in order to inflame libidinous little sparks that had long been sleeping.[71]

---

[69] F 5.11, 88v. See also Henry Kramer and Jacob Sprenger, *Malleus maleficarum* (Lyons, 1669), 191.

[70] Elizabeth Brown, "The Ceremonial of Royal Succession in Capetian France: The Funeral of Philip V," *Speculum* 55, 2 (1980): 266–93; idem, "Death and the Human Body in the Later Middle Ages: The Legislation of Boniface VIII on the Division of the Corpse," *Viator* 12 (1981).

[71] *Vita Clarae*, 680.

Yet, strikingly, at Clare's canonization proceeding it is not Clare who is singed by those libidinous little sparks but a group of heretics whose defilement is revealed to Clare in a vision:

> In a certain house there seemed to her to be a great multitude of people, [and] a certain demon in the form of a certain crucifix. After viewing it, many of those gathered there strongly conceived a desire for carnal delights and a false love within their minds, and that from this desire and false love they fell into carnal sins. . . . After the revelation of this vision . . . [Clare] said that she feared, but believed, that from this there would appear many evil men and women having an evil and a false spirit.[72]

The hagiography presented a physical temptation of Clare that does not appear in the canonization proceeding. Instead, this canonization witness attributes the demonically libidinous crucifix to another group entirely: heretics who have an evil spirit. Furthermore, even as the temptation of the demonic crucifix is removed from Clare and projected onto another group, the "true" image of the crucified comes to be lodged in Clare's heart. As we have seen, the presence of a crucifix in Clare's heart was a dominant concern of Clare's canonization proceeding.

This process exemplifies the rather common sequence of purgation and reconstruction that customarily accompanied the movement of a saint's cult into a more elite sphere of investigation.[73] It is a fascinating three-way displacement. First, the opposition between the sensual and the spiritual is mapped onto the symbolic geography of Clare's body with a shift of Clare's crucifix from loins to heart, flesh to spirit. By simultaneously displacing the incident of the demonic crucifix onto another group, a fully purified version of Clare is produced. Her spirit possession is pure and divine, for she bears the crucifix in her heart, while the others are possessed of "an evil and a false spirit." In sum, the two opposing forms of spirit possession are split into an

---

[72] [I]n quodam domo ibi videbatur sibi esse magna gentium multitudo, erat quidam diabolus ad modum crucifixi cujusdam, ex cujus inspectione multi ex illis ibi astantibus quamdam dilectiones carnalis affectionem et falsum amorem in animis suis fortiter concipiebant, ex quibus affectione et falso amore in peccatis carnalibus incidebant. . . . Post cujus visionis revelationem . . . Clara dixit quod timebat, seu credebat, quod exinde multi mali homines et mulieres habentes malum et falsum spiritum apparerent. ASV Arch. Congr. SS. Rituum, lat. ms. 2929, 351v–352r.

[73] For investigation of a parallel process, see Sofia Boesch-Gajano and Odile Rédon, "La *Legenda Maior* di Raimondo da Capua: Construzione di una santa," in D. Maffei and P. Nardi, eds., *Atti del simposio internazionale Cateriniano-Bernardiniano* (Siena, 1982).

opposition between Clare and another group, rather than persisting as two competing versions of Clare's *own* inspiration and visionary life.

NATURALIZING THE DISCERNMENT OF SPIRITS

The discussion has moved from the surface of the body to its interior, following the breath of life into the heart and through the arteries, probing the sour depths of the belly, and turning aside briefly to the loins. I have argued that the body was viewed as encompassing two symbolic internal zones: an exalted spiritual system and a debased, unclean system. Further, I have shown that divine and demonic forms of possession were mapped onto these different internal zones by medieval theologians and encyclopedists, who wished both to distinguish between the operations of the Holy Spirit and those of unclean spirits and to reserve a privileged space—the heart and soul—for the creator.

This set of distinctions was elaborated primarily for aesthetic and theological, rather than pragmatic, reasons. Yet, an additional virtue of this physiological understanding of spirit possession was that it could, at least in theory, provide a viable basis for the discernment of spirits. If the spirit was located in the heart, then it was divine; if located in the "caverns" or "open spaces" of the physical body, then it was likely demonic. (According to the terms of the theory elaborated above, a spirit inhabiting the body could also be angelic, but this possibility was not a central focus of discussion.) Thus this set of ideas worked to naturalize the testing of spirits by adducing a set of physiological distinctions between divine and demonic possession. Yet however appealing the tidiness of this theory, it remained only partially successful in explaining the similarities between the divinely and the demonically possessed and in providing pragmatic ways for discerning between them. Short of finding a convenient crucifix inside the heart, there was no way to discern, from the surface of a body, which spirit lay latent within, and where.

One point of particular interest here is the fact that, according to medieval theologians, it was *only* the Holy Spirit that could truly "unite essentially" with the human essence, the soul. Thus, paradoxically, the only complete form of spirit possession recognized by medieval theorists was divine possession. On a linguistic level, however, only demonic possession could formally be designated: there is no divine equivalent to the words *daemoniaca* or *energumena*. This slippage between words and ideas compounded the difficulties medieval writers grappled with when discussing possession and discernment. Although divine possession arguably was construed as more deep and "real" than demonic possession, the language used to describe it was weaker than the language of demonic possession.

However, those who wished to perform the role of a divinely possessed holy woman were well aware of the symbolically charged language of spiritual physiology. A great variety of texts, both hostile and friendly, describe inspired women as strongly attracted to heart themes, a fact that must be read against medieval ideas about spiritual anatomy and understood as an important part of these women's performances of divine possession. Clare of Montefalco's heart is but one example of this phenomenon. More common is the motif of the exchange of hearts between the woman and Jesus, such as Catherine of Siena's vision in which "her heart was made one with the heart of Christ."[74] A painting of this vision shows Catherine kneeling and holding up her arm with a heart in her hand as Christ leans down from a mandorla over an altar, offering his heart in return (fig. 20). It is not difficult to parse this symbolism as expressing the suffusion of the body with the Holy Spirit— indeed, as a direct replacement of the human spirit with a conjoined divine spirit that henceforth acts as the principle of life. A similar motif also may be found in a vision reported by Na Prous Boneta of Marseilles, in which she sees Christ holding up his heart, with rays of light pouring out from it and into her own body.[75]

An even more striking example of the heart as a seat of divine possession is provided by Ida of Louvain, whose vision of a pauper clambering into her heart produced such dramatic results:

> One time a certain pauper, of the most wretched appearance, his form covered with a few tattered clothes, stood before the entrance of the little cell of God's dear virgin, as if he were going to ask for hospitality. . . . Behold, the pauper . . . respectfully approaching his hostess, stood before her face, and with his own hands, it seemed to her, opened her breast. Then, entering right into the opening in her breast, she herself taking him in utterly, he disappeared externally as he entered internally. . . . Suddenly the mind of the venerable Ida began to be inflamed

[74] *VCS*, 908. This theme is also found in the hagiographies of Dorothy of Montau, Osanna Andreasia of Mantua, and Lutgard of Aywières.

[75] William May, "The Confession of Prous Boneta, Heretic and Heresiarch," in *Essays in Medieval Life and Thought, Presented in Honor of Austin Patterson Evans* (New York, 1965), 3–30. See especially the vision on p. 7.

Figure 20. Catharine of Siena exchanging hearts with Jesus. The motif of the exchange of hearts between a woman and Christ takes on added significance once we realize that the heart was the seat of the spirit. Panel painting by Guidoccio Cozarelli, fifteenth century. Siena: National Pinacoteca of Siena. Photo by Richard S. Cohen.

from within with such a desire for poverty and abjection that . . . casting off her own clothing . . . wrapping herself in a certain paltry little rag, and over that a mat in place of a cloak . . . she began to wander through the streets and plazas . . . through the places where great crowds of people were gathered together, so that wherever she formerly used to strut in refined clothing . . . there now she strutted as if mad or a fool, offering a monstrous spectacle of herself to the people.[76]

The entrance of the pauper into Ida's heart is communicated with an apparently intentional lack of economy. Indeed, the high number of verbs used in the description seems to magnify the moment, giving it an expanding sense of time and of importance: "approaching . . . he stood . . . it seemed . . . he opened . . . entering . . . she taking him in . . . he disappeared . . . as he entered." The thick linguistic construction of this scene, with its multiple evocations of bodily openness and transgression of the body's surface integrity, signals that this is a pivotal moment, an important transformation of Ida's identity, as the spirit enters the seat of her soul. If the surface of her body contains the hidden identity of her heart, it also mediates the expression of that identity to the outside world through the performance of new behaviors: possessed by the poor Christ, Ida seeks a spectacular poverty. Soon thereafter, we are told, Ida attended mass, and the emotional effects of the ritual caused Ida's heart to dilate so rapidly, from the exaltation of the Holy Spirit within, that blood suddenly gushed from her nose and mouth.

Two centuries later, we find a counterexample in the hagiography of Osanna Andreasia. Osanna prayed to God to infuse his Holy Spirit directly into the heart of a sinful friend. Christ responded, "I cannot find any place through which I might enter so hard a heart."[77] This sort of example could be multiplied: the heart was the seat of the human spirit, and thus the proper receptacle for the spirit of God. Thus, Brigit of Sweden asserted that she felt the infant Christ move and leap within her heart; her defender Alphonse of Jaén even claimed to see these movements through her skin.[78] Other women, like Lukardis of Oberweimar and Margaret of Cortona, were said to interpret the reception of the Eucharist as initiating a temporary divine possession that took place in the heart,[79] while Ida of Louvain's hagiographer

---

[76] Vita Venerabilis Idae Virginis, AASS, April 2:163.

[77] Vita B. Osannae Mantuanae, AASS, June 4:624.

[78] Arne Jönsson, ed., Alfonso of Jaén: His Life and Works with Critical Editions of the Epistola Solitarii, the Informaciones, and the Epistola Servi Christi (Lund, 1989), 251.

[79] Lukardis communicated another nun by breathing her spirit into the nun's mouth, thus making an equivalence between Lukardis's spirit, joined to God, and the Eucharist;

claimed that the Host so entirely overflowed her heart and soul that her body bloated and swelled into a miraculous corpulence.[80] Hearts also figured prominently in certain traditions of devotional painting that were closely associated with a female milieu. Jeffrey Hamburger has recently described the "visual culture of a medieval convent" in an engrossing study that examines a series of about a dozen drawings made by a nun of the convent of St. Walburg around 1500.[81] Three in the series depict images of union with Christ through the vehicle of a heart. In one, the heart of Christ on the cross is magnified and opened, and inside we see a nun receiving a Eucharist from a child Christ. Another shows an enormous heart enclosing a nun along with the Trinity, as all four share a Eucharistic banquet. In the third, the Trinity embraces the female soul inside a large heart that has been transformed into a house, complete with a door and a set of steps. The images deploy the trope of the heart as a seat of spiritual union to striking effect.

Lastly, one might also note the centrality of breath as a vehicle for the inspiration of the Holy Spirit, a notion that recapitulates the idea that the human spirit is manufactured within the heart through inspired air. A passage from the hagiography of Bona of Pisa aptly illustrates this conception: "Christ placed his most holy hand upon her head and said to her: Open your mouth. When she did so, Christ blew into her mouth three times and said to her: Accept the Holy Spirit. Immediately, [she] was filled up with that spirit, that thereafter the grace of that spirit flowed over into her expression, words, and gestures."[82] This passage identifies the indwelling Holy Spirit with Bona's own breath. A similar incident in the vita of Lukardis of Oberweimar has Christ counsel another nun, who is desirous of the Eucharist, to join her mouth to Lukardis's, "so that you can capture into your mouth the spirit of her mouth."[83] The implication is that Lukardis is in a permanent state of possession by Christ, whom she can communicate through her breath, vehicle of the spirit.

The differential physiology of divine and demonic possession, in turn, can cast significant new light upon the distinct group of possessed behaviors with which this book began. Given medieval ideas about the physiology of the spirit, it is not surprising that an infusion of the Holy Spirit into the fragile human heart might overload all sensory, emotional, and intellectual chan-

---

see *Vita Venerabilis Lukardis, Analecta Bollandia* 18 (1899): 337–38. See also *De B. Alpaide Virgine, AASS*, November 1, part 1:182; *Vita Bonae Virginis, AASS*, May 7:145.

[80] *Vita Venerabilis Idae Virginis,* 186.
[81] Hamburger, *Nuns as Artists.*
[82] *Vita Bonae Virginis,* 145.
[83] *Vita Venerabilis Lukardis,* 337.

nels. In turn, this overload would explain the greater emotionality, visionary focus, prophetic powers, and somatic changes for which divinely possessed women were known. Since the spirit coordinated the emotions, the senses (especially vision), the mind, and the body, the incursion of a divine spirit was thought to jolt all these things to a higher level of intensity and perception. Prophesying, trances, tears, somatic changes—in short, the whole complex of supernatural gifts associated with divine possession—flows from a single source: the claim to have the Holy Spirit, conjoined to the human spirit, acting within the body. Johannes Nider hints at this explanation when discussing the gendering of possessed behaviors in a fascinating bit of dialogue from the *Formicarius*. "Mr. Lazy," the interlocutor, explicitly refers to raptures, and to Christ's inhabitation of the breast or heart; the "Theologian" respondent then goes on to explain the characteristic behaviors of laywomen visionaries as due to an overload of divine love within their "weaker" hearts:

> [Mr. Lazy]: I have sometimes seen, and often heard of women . . . who are rapt . . . from their exterior senses to their interiors, just as they sometimes go into an ecstasy from devotion. Also, I saw a woman who, having heard some pronouncements about Christ's charity during a public sermon, brought forth on high a certain clamor in front of everyone, as if she could not manage to contain the love in her heart for Christ, who had formerly been enclosed there. Nevertheless, such things are taken as fictions by many literate men.
>
> [Theologian]: The general rule is . . . not to believe all spirits, but spirits are to be tested to see whether they are of God. . . . Nevertheless, I do not want you to draw from this a general rule about deception . . . for divine love . . . has not lesser, but greater effects than human love in certain individuals who . . . are rapt to the beloved through meditations. They express this in groaning, sobbing, lamentation, song, and clamors. . . . The fire of devotion is more mobile in the heart of the weaker vessel, and more likely to burst forth in clamors.[84]

The "weaker vessel" of the female body is unable to contain the expansion of the heart when remembering the presence of Christ within. This spiritual overload results, according to Nider, in those possessed behaviors that are typical of women: the "gift of tears," ecstatic trances, or uncontrollable shouting or "clamors." Thus there existed a persuasive series of correlations between the internal physiology of divine possession in the heart and the external behaviors observable by others.

[84] *F* 3.1, 39r.

The possessed behaviors of demoniacs could likewise be understood through the terms of these physiological differentiations. All the theorists of spiritual physiology and spirit possession examined above agreed that, though the internal mechanisms of divine and demonic possession were different, the effects produced were similar. The contortions commonly reported as a possessed behavior, for example, are explicable by the idea that demons move through the viscera, digestive tract, or open spaces in the body. Thus, Gerald of Wales explained how a demon was seen to move throughout the body of a possessed woman in Poitou, and "it was quite clear what parts of her body he was hiding in from the swellings and convulsive movements there."[85] Trances could likewise be explained by the insistence of medieval theorists that demons can "besiege," "confuse," or "deceive" the senses. This dampening of the individual's contact with the outside world would result in a dissociative or trancelike state. Indeed, trance states accompanied by brilliant visions similar to vivid dreams can be provoked by the demonic spirits' interference with the humors and sensory spirits, according to Aquinas:

That which occurs naturally in sleeping persons, apparitions of dreams caused by the local motion of spirits and humors, can also occur through an identical local motion brought about by demons, in either sleeping and waking persons. For demons can move the internal spirits and humors, sometimes even to a point where the use of reason is completely hampered, as is apparent in the possessed . . . but at other times without the fettering of reason, as in waking persons who have the use of reason. . . . Similarly, demons can impress something onto the external senses by manipulating the sensory spirits, which perceive a thing either more acutely or more obtusely according to the diminution or multiplication of the sensory spirits—for one sees or hears acutely when the sensory spirits are more abundant and pure, and more obtusely when the opposite is the case. On this issue, Augustine says that the evil brought into people by demons slithers in through all the senses.[86]

Thus even though demons cannot enter into the heart, they can interfere with the operations of the spirits in other parts of the body, such as the senses. Through a rousing of the senses, they may cause great acuteness of percep-

---

[85] Gerald of Wales, *Journey*, 152.
[86] Thomas Aquinas, *Quaestiones disputatae de malo*, quaest. 3, reply art. 4, in Thomas Aquinas, *Opera Omnia*, Leonine Commission edition (Rome, 1982), 23:76.

tion or, alternatively, depress the individual's sensory abilities. Demons can manipulate humors so as to produce the effects of madness, frenzy, or melancholy.[87] And they can cause visions and hallucinations by stirring up both the humor and the spirits in the blood.

Aquinas's contemporary and fellow Dominican Vincent of Beauvais, too, noted that demons can "insert themselves into the blood, that is, the humors, and imprint images" on the mind of the individual.[88] Indeed, Vincent strained to systematize the vocabulary of demonic interference, linking different demonic operations within human physiology to different words.

> Energumens, properly speaking, are people whom demons harass interiorly, so that they cannot control the operations of their natural powers through the exercise of free will. Such persons are not called obsessed, but are termed energumens, on account of the interior operation of the devil. . . . As for those whose body the devil does not enter, but harasses from the outside, interfering sometimes with their sight and hearing and things of this kind, such persons properly are termed obsessed ["besieged"], like a castle.[89]

Thus even without entering the heart, demons could interfere with the spiritual system of the body and all its operations; and could so interiorly oppress the victim as to deprive her of free will, subordinating her identity to the demon's own. In such a case, the superior knowledge and intuitions of the demon may be pronounced through the mouth of the possessed victim, resulting in prophecies, xenoglossy, and other impressive intellectual feats. In sum, the physiological theory of discernment could explain the external behaviors characteristic of demoniacs as well as of the divinely possessed. The contortions, trances, prophecies, and visions attributed to each could be closely correlated with the disruptions of the spiritual system involved in either kind of possession.

Ultimately, however, the physiological approach to the discernment of spirits was of little pragmatic use in actual case histories. Understanding the physiology of possession was of no help to someone who had to evaluate a woman's claims to divine inspiration or supernatural gifts. How could one verify the internal disposition of a possessing spirit if one's only basis for judgment was a group of external behaviors—behaviors that were equally char-

---

[87] On the thin line between madness, possession, and melancholia, see Erik Midelfort, *A History of Madness in Sixteenth-Century Germany* (Stanford, 1999).

[88] *Spec. Nat.* 2.118, 152.

[89] Ibid. 2.122, 154.

acteristic of both kinds of spirit possession? Short of an autopsy revealing a convenient crucifix in the heart, as in the case of Clare of Montefalco, the elaboration of a differential physiology of possession was of limited use in actual case histories. Although the physiological model of discernment succeeded as an explanatory tool that naturalized different spiritual identities into the body, it could not be applied pragmatically. There was no clear system of correspondences between the different internal mechanisms of divine and demonic possession, on the one hand, and the actual external signs of each possession, on the other. Holy women and demoniacs remained ciphers that looked alike on the surface, even if they were different inside.

Chapter 2 discussed the importance of the "surface politics of the body" as mediating individual-internal and cultural-external factors in the formation of a particular possessed identity. It is precisely a mediating element that was lacking in the physiological theory of discernment. One could observe the external actions of an inspired woman, but one could not interpret them as exclusively divine or demonic. Conversely, these theories set forth a modality for interpreting the inside of a possessed body, but of course one cannot observe an individual's internal physiology while that person remains alive. The theory required a connecting link between inside and outside, a way of reading the surface of the body to search for clues to the possessing spirit within. The physiological model did not help because it remained at a purely internal level of analysis. Two spiritual identities, one demonic and one divine, were manifested identically on the surface level of the body, even if the internal mechanisms of possession, and the spirits involved, were radically different.

A TRANSITIONAL MOMENT:
THE EARLY FOURTEENTH CENTURY

Just as we see that a rose, in the presence of gentle dew and the warmth of the sun, opens itself naturally, and also closes itself in the presence of cold winds, in the same way the human heart expands from the sweetness of calmness and serenity and is rendered more capable of receiving divine infusions.[90]

[90] R. Warnock and A. Zumkeller, eds., *Der Traktat Heinrichs von Freimar uber die Unterscheidung der Geister* (Würzburg, 1977), 158. The text dates from the first quarter of the fourteenth century.

Keep your soul's container open above and closed below. In this way you may . . . open your heart to your God, so that the balsam of his grace and consolation might deign to infuse there.[91]

These snippets of advice from Henry of Freimar and Venturino of Bergamo show a convergence between the themes of the previous chapter and this one. The rhetorics of open versus closed physiology, and of the heart as the seat of divine possession, were brought together in the "proto-discernment" treatises of these two authors: *The Four Inspirations*, by Henry of Freimar, and *Treatise on the Holy Spirit* and *Remedies for Spiritual Temptations*, by Venturino of Bergamo. I designate these works "proto-discernment" texts both because they are rather sketchy in their approach to the issue and because they are couched as advice to the pious rather than as guidelines for observers wishing to decipher the possessed behaviors of others. It was left for a later generation of authors to adduce more systematic guidelines for the exterior judgment of spirits. Nevertheless, these early-fourteenth-century texts advanced the debate over discernment in important ways. First, these authors synthesized the various physiological factors that had been discussed in relation to spirit possession and discernment. Second, they expressed a valuation of physical calmness and serenity as preeminent means of attracting divinity into the heart. Third, they initiated a backlash against outward, physical signs of asceticism. This latter theme, in turn, was to have significant repercussions in a reevaluation of how to read possessed behaviors that occurred in the decades surrounding the turn of the fifteenth century.

Thus I end this chapter with a group of writings that were poised between a slowly atrophying set of ideas about spirit possession (the naturalized model, which had reached its fullest development by the late thirteenth century) and new discernment guidelines adduced in the late fourteenth century. These texts look both backward and forward; they synthesize and in some respects anticipate. Yet they do not coalesce: their authors were unaware of each other's writings, and the works themselves did not initiate a broader discourse or debate about the testing of spirits. They crystallize a moment in the history of the testing of spirits but cannot be said significantly to have influenced the development of discernment ideas within their lifetimes.

Henry of Freimar's lengthy text, likely composed sometime in the first quarter of the fourteenth century, treated the four inspirations in turn: divine, angelic, diabolic, and natural. Henry clearly was familiar with the lat-

---

[91] G. Clementi, ed., *Un Santo patriota: Venturino da Bergamo dell' Ordine de' Predicatori (1304–1346): Storie e documenti*, 3 vols. (Rome, 1909), 3:74–75.

est thinking on the primacy of the heart within human anatomy: he explicitly refers to this organ as the "principle of human life,"[92] and he used the heart as the main organizing principle of the sections devoted to the divine and diabolic inspirations. Indeed, Henry's comments on divine inspiration constitute an extended meditation on how to manipulate the porosity or openness of the heart in order to receive divine infusions. The segment on diabolic inspiration, conversely, centers on the notion that the devil can distance his victims from their own hearts, such that they are unable to experience the desire to have God enter therein. Henry thus counseled a vigilant guarding of the heart and one's interior disposition and senses. Filling out the text are sections on angelic inspiration, which is quite brief; and natural inspiration, which focuses on the pitfalls of pride and intellectual subtlety.

Henry was strikingly insistent on the fact that the main way to open one's heart to interior union with the divine is through calmness and abstraction from all "tumult":

> For mildness, as we have seen, opens the heart and mind with its sweetness, and therefore arranges the soul so that God may freely enter. . . . For experience proves that, to the degree that someone is more self-contained and exists in close contact with one's heart, so is that one stronger in repelling temptations. It is established, then, that divine inspiration always calls one away from the exterior tumult of the world, and attracts one to the simplicity and the unity and the closeness of one's heart. . . . Therefore, one should go toward the most secret and intimate place in one's heart, so that there one may hide away from all the tumult and anxiety of the world, and then one will be exalted into God himself, through a plentiful influx of divine piety.[93]

Henry was here advancing the germ of a notion that was to become steadily more influential in the discernment of spirits: divine possession is associated with calmness, serenity, and stasis. Just as the heart manufactures and disperses the human spirit throughout the body in rarefied and subtle manner, so, too, is divine possession a rarefied and subtle process. The best preparation for the divine infusion is a withdrawal of energy and attention to the calm, quiet center of the heart. This, in turn, enables openness to the Holy Spirit. Thus Henry conjoins the language of the spiritual system with images of open versus sealed anatomy. The unwritten corollary to this view is that

[92] Warnock and Zumkeller, *Der Traktat Heinrichs von Freimar*, 23, 192.
[93] Ibid., 158–62.

tumultuous, extreme behaviors—rigid trances, swellings, convulsions, spiritual pregnancies, or uncontrolled shouting and sobbing—should not be perceived as valid indications of divine possession. These are not "mild," "calm," or "gentle" behaviors, to use the terminology favored by Henry. Thus with *The Four Inspirations* we see the complex of possessed behaviors beginning to have a more constrained range of interpretations.

The diabolic spirit, explained Henry, alienates one from one's own heart and soul. In so doing, the devil "severs one from the divine presence, so that one cannot perceive it." Henry went on to cite Alcher of Clairvaux's foundational work on the human spirit, erroneously attributing it to Augustine (as did everyone except Aquinas):

> For according to Augustine, God is more fully inside the soul than the soul itself. It follows that the closer one is to one's heart, the nearer one is to God, and in consequence one perceives His presence more easily and more acutely. Therefore the devil strives to distance one from the heart through the exertion of his malice, so that the taste and sweetness of the divine presence is lost. Therefore Christ said to Peter, in Luke 22, "Behold, Satan has asked for you, to sift you like wheat." That is, he seeks to turn you about like a piece of grain, to sift you so that you are more alienated from your heart. And thus you may be weakened in resisting his machinations.[94]

These machinations may include sensual delights. Henry later exhorted his audience to avoid consorting with women, "no matter how religious and devout they may seem. . . . 'often, lustful loins are hidden under an appearance of religiosity.'"[95] The best defense against diabolic inspiration is to guard one's heart at all times. "Above all, from this it is evident that it is highly useful and necessary for a person to diligently guard one's heart and to diligently focus one's interior disposition."[96] In this way, one can render the heart open to divine infusions and closed off from diabolic influences. Henry thus extended the implications of the physiology of the human spirit, begun with Alcher, to their logical conclusions by conjoining this discussion to a treatment of possession and discernment.

Venturino's two epistolary treatises were addressed to unnamed correspondents who had requested compositions from him on these topics. *The*

[94] Ibid., 182.
[95] Ibid., 194. Henry attributes the last line to Augustine, but the text is pseudo-Augustinian; cf. 195 nn. q, s.
[96] Ibid., 184.

Holy Spirit was sent to a specifically female audience: his "dear daughter in Christ . . . and the other nuns." In fact, Venturino maintained a lively transalpine correspondence with various Rhenish religious women, as well as with female conventual communities in Provence having Dominican affiliations. What is most striking about both treatises is their interest in domesticating and disciplining the body so as to purify the heart. Venturino, like Henry, believed in a strict custody or guarding of the soul, and he employed quite forceful, even violent, images to communicate this need. In order to attract the Holy Spirit, Venturino recommended that his correspondent should "shackle the vessel of your soul well, that is, constrain it strongly with hoops . . . and these hoops should be knotted up like wicker work. This is done for the careful guarding of all the body's senses." Later, he expanded on the custody of the tongue: "If you want your heart to be inflamed by the fire of divine love, you must close your mouth. Pronounce few words, ones that are that are rational and well thought out, and with a timid voice."[97] In order to keep the heart open to God, one must keep the body and its senses closed off and guarded. In this sentiment, Venturino was much in accord with Henry of Freimar's discussion of divine inspiration.

The *Remedies for Spiritual Temptations* is the more interesting of Venturino's texts for our purposes, as it devotes more space to the discernment of spirits. Indeed, Venturino begins with a lament that spiritual temptations have increased of late and, in a refrain that will recur throughout the treatise, attributes this new level of demonic activity to the imminent arrival of the Antichrist. Venturino goes on to present a rather damning indictment of supernatural gifts and visions. The foremost means of avoiding demonic snares, according to Venturino, is actively to avoid trances and other supernatural gifts.

> The foremost remedy against the spiritual temptations of recent times . . . is that you should not aspire to visions, revelations, or experiences that are supernatural or beyond the common ken of those who love and fear God. For those desires cannot exist without a root and foundation of pride and hubris, or without the voyeurism of a vain curiosity about God's mysteries, or without a fragility and defect of faith. The justice of God departs from the soul of those who have such desires, and so such a person can enter into the illusions and deceptions of the devil. This is how the devil spreads the greater part of the spiritual temptations of the current times, and plants them in the hearts of those who are heralds of

[97] Clementi, *Venturino da Bergamo*, 3:73, 74, 78.

the Antichrist. . . . You also ought to know that true revelations and spiritual experiences of God's mysteries do not come from such desire, or through any undertaking or enthusiasm that the soul can accomplish on its own. Such things come only through the pure goodness of God inside the soul. . . .

The second remedy is that, in your prayer and contemplation, you should not maintain any great or little consolation in your soul. . . . God, through his just judgment, grants the devil the power of accelerating such consolation, and through this means he imprints totally false and extremely dangerous experiences and other illusions onto the soul. Because of the consolations, the soul thus imprinted believes and thinks these things to be true revelations. Alas! God knows for sure how many people have been deceived in this way. Therefore, know for certain that the greater part of the raptures of the raving heralds of the Antichrist come and proceed through this means.[98]

Venturino was very careful with his language. The devil can tempt the heart or imprint something upon the soul, but he is never said to be inside the soul in the way that God may be. Rather, the devil relies upon the individual's cooperative measure of hubris and self-love in order to accomplish his desires: one who wishes for supernatural graces is readily convinced of having received them. Indeed Venturino went on, later in the text, to warn against those who "have a great esteem for their own visions as well as for their trance experiences," again emphasizing that the visionary may be an unwitting collaborator in her own deception. Such an individual may become a herald of the Antichrist precisely through aspiration for knowledge of God's mysteries, through an overly keen thirst for spiritual graces, and through supernatural gifts. Thenceforth, according to Venturino, "they defend their errors and imperfections, or rather their imperfections and inanities, their dishonesties and their dangerous ways of living, by expounding holy scripture according to their own whims, justifying the excesses and idiosyncrasies with which they exhaust themselves."[99]

Interestingly, Venturino's skeptical attitude about the discernment of spirits was derived from direct personal experience. He recounted a personal brush with diabolic deception in sheep's clothing, in a 1340 letter directed to Egenolf von Ehenheim, vicar of Unterlinden. The missive was in response to a letter of Egenolf's, now lost, which requested advice in judging the vi-

[98] Ibid., 137.
[99] Ibid., 140.

sions of a woman—perhaps a nun at the convent of Unterlinden, a foundation known for its visionary inhabitants. Venturino's letter counsels that the "safest route" is skepticism: "If you really wish to know what I think about this case," he warns, "I say that I believe a diabolic illusion has been at work." Venturino's letter relates how some eight years earlier he was himself deceived by a young laywoman claiming visions of the Archangel Gabriel. Impressed by the girl's simplicity and innocence, Venturino initially believed her visions to be genuine. With the passage of time, veneration for the girl spread, and admirers went so far as to send her saints' relics and an icon of the Virgin adorned with precious stones. Meanwhile, her parents set up a reclusorium for her in their home. Two years later, however, Venturino returned and "found that girl in a different state,"[100] an elliptical statement that presumably refers either to her loss of an air of purity or perhaps, more literally, to her loss of virginity and renunciation of the recluse's life. Whatever the case, Venturino now recognized beyond doubt that her earlier visionary pretensions had been diabolic in character. Since then, he had adopted an attitude of intense suspicion in regard to all visionary claims. He was not to be the last author on the discernment of spirits to draw upon personal experience in defense of a skeptical attitude.

Venturino's comments also bear an interesting comparison with a brief paragraph in the *Treatise against Diviners and Dreamers*, composed by Agostino of Ancona in 1310 and directed to Pope Clement V. Agostino's polemic covers a broad territory, censuring everything from the Spiritual Franciscans to the use of amulets and incantations fashioned by silly women.[101] A short portion of this portmanteau treatise deals with the testing of spirits, and here Agostino, too, condemns extremism in behavior and lifestyle. Noting that God bestows his gifts freely, Agostino harshly rejects those who "practice deprivations and fasts and who offer good words. It is firmly to be believed that all these things are received by the devil, who transfigures himself into an angel of light, as a pact and confederation between himself and those who seek knowledge in this way."[102] The notion that asceticism, fasts, extended prayer, and spiritual consolations are signs of demonic status, rather than of sincere piety and devotion, accords with Venturino's parallel hostility toward trances and the thirst for visionary revelations. Presumably this disdain derives from the fact that women and laity increasingly were engaged

---

[100] Ibid., 2:85, 86.
[101] P. Giglioni, "Il 'Tractatus contra divinatores et sompniatores' di Agostino d'Ancona: Introduzione e edizione del testo," *Analecta Augustiniana* 48 (1985): 7–111.
[102] Ibid., 94.

in these practices, which hitherto had been the preserve of elite religious specialists.

If Henry of Freimar's treatise promoted calm and mildness as primary indicators of divine inspiration, Venturino of Bergamo's (and Agostino of Ancona's) approach provided a complementary rhetoric of mistrust for supernatural behaviors, gifts, and visions. Together, these authors present a restrictive interpretation of possessed behaviors. Until this point, those who lived surrounded by a tumultuous aura of the supernatural were seen as ciphers in need of interpretation as either divinely or demonically possessed. Henry and Venturino argued, by contrast, that such tumult was demonic, while divinity was manifested in stasis and serenity. The presence of God inside the heart led to meekness and a deep centering; the presence of the Evil One led to a disordered self-love, inflamed sensory impulses, and false raptures portending the advent of the Antichrist.

It would require another half-century or more before Henry's and Venturino's ideas came into a position of influence. Indeed, Venturino's letters seem not to have been known to the later, more influential generation of discernment authors, and Henry's text, while possibly known, was not directly cited.[103] Yet though these two authors were not to have an immediate influence upon their own contemporaries, they represent a particular interpretive moment, an escalation of discernment anxiety and a turning of attention toward the body and its comportment as a means of telling apart the divinely and the demonically possessed. Both rooted their ideals in a deep understanding of human spiritual physiology, centered in the heart, and both began the process of translating the interior disposition of a person to a readable exterior. Although the full ramifications of this interpretive turn were not to be realized for some time, in some senses the discernment of spirits began with Henry's and Venturino's generation.

[103] For Henry of Langenstein's relationship to Henry of Freimar, see the introduction to *DS*, 38.

PART III

DISCERNMENT AND DISCIPLINE

CHAPTER FIVE
EXORCIZING DEMONIC DISORDER

Grant . . . that the ears of this, your maidservant N., might be open
without any blockage from Satan and that she may be freed, with the
evil of demons cast out from her, and might receive your words with
honor and praise to you.
— EXORCISTS' MANUAL

B etween 1470 and 1480 an artist now known as the "Master of San Severin" painted an altarpiece, one panel of which depicts the exorcism of a young woman (fig. 21). This painting provides a useful starting point for an exploration of exorcism in the fifteenth century, when its functions and processes were entirely reconfigured from earlier practice. Exorcism was formalized into a scripted liturgy designed to serve the ideological needs of a Church beset by a crisis of authority from above (the Great Schism and its aftermath) and continual critiques from below (increasingly insistent reform movements). The expulsion of demons, which earlier had been left to the informal realm of saintly tomb miracles, now was actively appropriated by the ecclesiastical hierarchy as a means to demonstrate the might of the clergy over demons, and thus the priestly figuration of God in the battle against demonic disorder of all kinds. The new liturgical exorcisms that resulted enact a performative convergence between the divine, the masculine, and the clerical, on the one hand, and the demonic, the feminine, and the lay, on the other.

Consider the painting. A priest, dressed in a white alb and crossed stole, holds an open book in his left hand and raises his right hand in a stern gesture of chastisement. The object of his admonition is a young woman who convulsively collapses, her head thrown back and hair flowing down, into the arms of a richly dressed young man. A nun dressed in black looks on from behind the priest-exorcist, and in the center a monk holds a candle, protecting its flame. The purpose of the candle was to demonstrate the departure of

Figure 21. Saint Severin exorcizing a demoniac with a manual of exorcism. The exorcism, spoken by the priest, calls Saint Severin into action. The priest lunges forward as he reads the conjuration, while the woman demoniac, as if responding to his forward momentum, collapses into the arms of a stylishly dressed young man. Predella to a disassembled altarpiece, by the "Master of Saint Severin," c. 1470–80. Florence: Horne Museum. Photo courtesy of Scala/Art Resource.

all unclean spirits, the last of which would be adjured to extinguish the flame as a proof that it had left the demoniac's body. The still-lit candle here suggests that more demons lurk within the flailing girl's form.

Above the heads of these figures a much smaller drama is enacted: this is the unseen, supernatural level of the exorcism, made manifest by the artist. At the viewer's left, a small bat-winged imp flies away above the heads of the victim and her kin. Above the head of the priest, the tiny, haloed spirit of Saint Severin emerges from a floating cloud. His right arm is raised in a gesture of rebuke that precisely parallels the comportment of the priest below him. Thus the priest and Saint Severin exorcize the demoniac in tandem.

This painting forms an intriguing contrast with earlier representations of exorcism, which traditionally show a saint's tomb or bier accomplishing the expulsion through saintly *virtus* alone, without the aid of priest, book, or candle. Exorcism, in this earlier model, was entirely a supernatural battle of unseen spirits. For example, a woman who had a vision of Verdiana of Castelfiorentino exorcizing her child described the struggle between the spirit of the dead saint and the unclean spirit as an invisible tug-of-war: "She saw her son, and he was gripped by the feet by a demon and dragged down some stairs; and on the other side, he was held back by Saint Verdiana. Each was straining at it with great exertion, until finally the saint made the sign of the cross on the child, and since the demon fled from it, the boy remained safe and sound."[1] Upon the battlefields of the spirits, the saint and the fallen angel contend over their human quarry. The vision, like the predella, unveils this unseen clash of spirits. Unlike the altarpiece, however, Verdiana's exorcism of the child requires neither clerical aid nor liturgical intervention.

Indeed, the Master of Saint Severin has placed enormous emphasis on the figure of the clerical exorcist. His gleaming white robes and tense posture draw the viewer's eye more quickly than the small black figure of Saint Severin drifting out from a cloud above his head. The priest holds his bright red manual of exorcisms at the base of a V formed by his crossed stole, which effectively points to the book. Furthermore, the exact parallelism between the saint's and the exorcist's gestures—right hand raised in rebuke, index finger extended, left hand somewhat lower—makes it appear as though the saint is the puppet of the priest, drawn into action by the gestures and actions of the larger figure. This altarpiece, in short, depicts a new model of exorcism, one in which the sacred power of the saints is mobilized through the clerical performance of a written liturgy. Whereas, earlier, exorcism had demonstrated the power of the saints, increasingly throughout the course of the fifteenth century it came to embody the power of the institutional Church.

In the following pages I inquire into three aspects of the late medieval liturgy of exorcism and its relationship to the discernment of spirits. First, I attempt to reconstruct the history of these rites by laying out their evolution from earlier kinds of informal exorcism and from other clamors and conjurations. Second, I discuss the ritual "scripts" themselves, understood as didactic texts that aim to authorize and regularize a particular set of ideas about spirit possession, sin, demonic activity, and ecclesiastical authority. Since these texts have not been widely studied in the past, I examine them in some detail. I argue that these scripts are designed to function as transparent, self-interpreting performances. By this I mean that they express a particular vi-

---

[1] *Vita Verdianae Virginis, AASS,* February 1:264.

sion of Church authority and aim to impose that singular vision upon participants and witnesses to the exorcism, while narrowing, as far as possible, the latitude for alternative interpretations. While complete transparency of this kind was impossible to achieve, the texts clearly are designed with a flair for didactic drama. Third, circling back to the testing of spirits, the chapter asks: How do the rituals' representations of demonic possession and its cure contribute to the task of distinguishing diabolic from divine possession?

CHRISTIANITY AND THE RISE OF EXORCISM

Possession and exorcism figured prominently in the early Church as the main arena through which the cosmic battle between good and evil was played out, a quotidian enactment of Christian eschatology and soteriology.[2] Invocation of Christ's name as a means of driving out demons from human bodies was one element in the growth of Christian prestige in the first two centuries after Christ's death. The Book of Acts includes several incidents: the case of the slave girl with a spirit of divination whom Paul heals in 16:16; the gathering of the sick and possessed in Jerusalem for Peter to heal by allowing his shadow to fall upon them (5:16); Philip's healings in Samaria (8:7); and Paul's exorcisms through the distribution of handkerchiefs impregnated with his special *virtus*, or healing power (19:11–12). Especially noteworthy is a description of some Jewish exorcists in Ephesus who attempt to exorcize demons in Jesus' name, albeit without success (Acts 19:13–16). Indeed, exorcism was the miracle of choice for early Christian proselytizers, and it featured as a persuasive element in the winning of Christian converts (Acts 19:17, 20). As a showy display of the power of Christ's name, exorcism was a guaranteed crowd pleaser, "for every demon, when exorcised in the name of this very Son of God . . . is overcome and subdued."[3] Indeed, so closely were Christian ascetics associated with exorcism that when a little girl in fourth-century Syria wished to parody a monk, she did so by pretending solemnly to exorcize her friends.[4] Exorcism also was a competitive skill in which Chris-

---

[2] Reginald Wooley, *Exorcism and the Healing of the Sick* (London, 1932); Henry Kelly, *The Devil, Demonology, and Witchcraft: The Development of Christian Beliefs in Evil Spirits* (New York, 1974); Traugott Oesterreich, *Possession, Demoniacal and Other, among Primitive Races, in Antiquity, the Middle Ages, and Modern Times* (New York, 1930).

[3] Justin Martyr, *Dialogue with Trypho*, in A. Roberts and J. Donaldson, trans. and eds., *Ante-Nicene Fathers*, 10 vols. (Peabody, Mass., 1999), 1:241.

[4] Peter Brown, *Society and the Holy in Late Antiquity* (Berkeley, 1982), 123.

tians claimed to triumph over rival healers; it flourished in the Late Roman demimonde and widely was perceived as a form of supernatural healing power akin to sorcery.[5]

As Christians increasingly came to regard the world around them as infested with demons and unclean forces, the Church began to require the cleansing of converts before they could be integrated into the Christian community. There thus arose an order of exorcists charged with the ritual purification of converts at their baptism. The earliest reference to this formal order of exorcists derives from a letter from Pope Cornelius (251–53), which was partly incorporated by Eusebius into his *Ecclesiastical History*. Cornelius enumerates the entire Church hierarchy: forty-six priests, seven deacons, seven subdeacons, forty-two acolytes, and fifty-two exorcists, readers, and doorkeepers.[6] The title of exorcist was a humble one, however. Sulpitius Severus notes in his *Life of Saint Martin* that while Martin initially refused all higher orders, he accepted the office of exorcist lest he appear too proud to accept a lowly position.[7] The fourth Council of Carthage (398), in its seventh canon, is the earliest to prescribe the rite of ordination for an exorcist, in a passage that was retained throughout subsequent centuries.

> When an Exorcist is Ordained: Let him accept from the hand of the priest the little book in which the exorcisms are written, and let the priest say to him, "Take this and memorize it, and may you have the power of laying-on hands upon an energumen, whether baptized or a catechumen."[8]

This rite was retained for centuries, with only minor revisions. A tenth-century pontifical elaborates the above ceremony, adding the following elements:

---

[5] Peter Brown, "Sorcery, Demons, and the Rise of Christianity," in M. Douglas, ed., *Witchcraft Confessions and Accusations* (London, 1970), 17–45. See also idem, "The Rise and Function of the Holy Man in Late Antiquity" and "Town, Village and Holy Man: The Case of Syria," in *Society and the Holy*, 103–52, 153–65; Oesterreich, *Possession*, 159–68.

[6] Eusebius, *Church History*, in P. Schaff and H. Wace, trans. and eds., *Nicene and Post-Nicene Fathers*, 12 vols. (Peabody, Mass., 1999), 1:288.

[7] Sulpitius Severus, *Vita Sancti Martini*, in *PL*, 20:163.

[8] Exorcista cum ordinatur: Accipiat de manu episcopi libellum in quo scripti sunt exorcismi dicente sibi episcopo: Accipe et commenda et habeto potestatem imponendi manum super inergumenum sive baptizatum sive catechuminum. BV ms. Vat. Lat. 7701, IV (tenth-century pontifical). The canons of the Council of Carthage may be found in *PL*, vol. 84. This formula also is present in the Gelasian Sacramentary (*PL*, vol. 74), the *Panormia* of Ivo of Charteres (*PL*, vol. 161), and Gratian's *Decretum* (*PL*, vol. 187), among other places.

Prayer for the Exorcist: Lord Father Omnipotent, we humbly pray that this, your servant N., might be worthy to be blessed in the office of Exorcist, so that he may be a spiritual commander for the purpose of ejecting demons from the bodies of the possessed, along with all their multiform evils.

Blessing of the Exorcist: Holy Lord Father omnipotent, Eternal Master, deign to bless this, your servant name N., in the office of Exorcist, for the laying-on of hands and of the mouth. Deign to give him this office so that he may have command of the unclean spirits . . . let this man be a fully confirmed doctor in the ecclesiastical grace of curing.[9]

Yet by the time this tenth-century manuscript was produced, the order of exorcists already was in decline. The function of baptizing catechumens and infants gradually had passed into the care of the higher clergy. While ordination as an exorcist remained a nominal step on the ecclesiastical *cursus honorum* up to the modern day, in practice it appears to have been subsumed within other ranks of the hierarchy. The order of exorcists was a vestigial trace. Such exorcistic rituals as existed at this time period were intended primarily for the baptism of catechumens; the demonic possession of a baptized adult was considered an anomaly.[10] For example, an exorcism in a later, possibly eleventh-century hand, bound into the same manuscript as the tenth-century rite quoted above, presents demonic harassment, not possession, as the norm: "I adjure you, angel of iniquity, ancient serpent . . . to leave without any harm to body or soul. For you are given the power of tempting and not of possessing."[11] This text is unusual in including a relatively complex exorcism apparently intended for demoniacs, rather than for catechumens. More often, exorcisms of this period are abbreviated. Thus a twelfth-century set of exorcisms in Munich's Bäyerische Staatsbibliothek gives several short exorcisms "for energumens," one "for baptized energumens," and one "for

---

[9] Prex Exorciste: Dominum patrem omnipotentem supplices deprecamur ut hunc famulum suum N. benedici dignetur in officium exorciste ut sit spiritualis imperator ad abiciendos demones de corporibus obsessis cum omni nequitia eorum multiformi. Benedictio Exorciste: Domine sancte pater omnipotens eterne dominator benedicere digneris famulum tuum hunc nomen N. in officium exorciste per impositiones manuum et oris; officium eum eligere digneris ut imperium habeat spirituum immundorum . . . sit medicus ecclesiastice gracie curationum vir tute confirmatus. BV ms. Vat. Lat. 7701, 1v–2r.

[10] E. Whitaker, *Documents of the Baptismal Liturgy* (London, 1960); Henry Ansgar Kelly, *The Devil at Baptism: Ritual, Theology, and Drama* (Ithaca, N.Y.: 1985).

[11] Adiuro te angelus iniquitatis, serpens antiquus . . . exeas sine lesione corporis et anime. Data est enim tibi potestas temptandi et non possidendi. BV ms. Vat. Lat. 7701, 80v.

an infant vexed by the devil" all in the space of barely three folio leaves.[12] These texts are little more than traditional baptismal exorcisms divorced from the remainder of the baptismal rite, along with biblical readings and a prayer or two. Little effort has been put into elaborating these formulae into independent ceremonies. Minor variations on basic exorcistic formulae were also put to other uses: to consecrate the elements used in an ordeal, to bless houses and wells, to protect against bad weather, to keep bees from swarming, to protect horses against worm infections, and for manifold other practical matters.[13] Exorcism in these centuries is domesticated: its very ubiquity undermines any fearful or awesome qualities it might otherwise possess.

THE RISE OF DEMONS AND IMPROVISED EXORCISM

In the twelfth through fourteenth centuries, the difficulties inherent in dealing with the proliferating numbers of the demonically possessed were compounded by the lack of a clear course of action. The evidence about the diagnosis and cure of demoniac adults frequently betrays a sense of collective improvisation. Kin and neighbors of the possessed are portrayed as perplexed, lacking any indication of how, precisely, to define the possession or how to cure it. Seldom did a community possess a normative procedure to be employed on such occasions.

A good example is provided by the vita of Hildegard of Bingen. The hagiography describes at great length the puzzlement of bystanders when faced with a case of a woman diagnosed as demonically possessed. For three months the inhabitants of her town "labored in many ways" over the possessed woman, all in vain. Finally the demon itself mentioned that he "was not going to leave his little vessel, except through the advice and aid of a cer-

[12] BS ms. Clm. 3909, 250r–53r.
[13] For consecrating ritual objects see Karl Hampe, "Formeln fur Gottesurteile aus Karolingischer Zeit," *Reise nach Frankreich und Belgien im Frujahr 1897. Neues Archiv fur Altere Deutsche Geschichtskunde* 23 (1897): 380–84; Edmond Martène, *De antiquis ecclesiae ritibus*, 4 vols. (Hildesheim, 1967), 2:898–1002. For blessings of houses and wells and protection against bad weather, see BV ms. Ottob. Lat. 313, 159r–v. For stopping bees from swarming, see Stephanus Baluzius, *Capitularia Regum Francorum* (Venice, 1773), 2:441–60. For protecting horses against infections, see Federico Patetta, "Un Esorcismo del secolo decimoquarto," *Atti della Accademia delle scienze di Torino. Classi di scienze morali, storiche, e filologiche* 65 (1930): 401–8. See also Adolph Franz, *Die Kirchlichen Benediktionen im Mittelalter* 2 vols. (Freiburg-im-Breisgau, 1909), which includes a dizzying number of examples.

tain little old woman from the area of the upper Rhine . . . and he made fun of her name, twisting it around and calling her 'Scrumplegard.'" A local abbot recognized Hildegard in this description and wrote to her for advice. The confusion of the community demonstrates the lack of a commonly agreed-upon cure for demonic possession. Moreover, Hildegard's instructions for curing the woman seem to be largely her own innovations. Among other things, she prescribes the intervention of seven men representing Old Testament patriarchs, one of whom is to hold a staff representing the rod of Moses. These men are to fast and pray over the woman, and should blow in her face in a figural reminder of the breath of God. Finally, the saint sent along with her letter a copy of her own *Scivias*, "in order that they might be recited over her, humbly."[14] The community followed Hildegard's advice, and after a lengthy series of temporary cures and relapses, the woman finally expelled the demon.

Hildegard's letter mentions that both the cross and relics had been shown to the demoniac to no avail:[15] these actions remained popular improvisational means of exorcising energumens through the late fourteenth century. The thirteenth-century *Liber exemplorum* describes an attempt at exorcism through the application of holy objects, the inherent *virtus* of which was expected to expel the indwelling demons: "The demon was accustomed to appear inside the demoniac through certain swellings and disturbances of the parts that it possessed. As soon as the gospel or relics of the saints were placed upon a swelling in the throat, it descended to the side, and from there, when [the relics] were applied, it went to the lower parts of the groin. But when they were applied there, it surged back again to the upper parts [of the body]."[16]

The sense of bewilderment as to how to deal effectively with demonic possession is highlighted in this tale, which was retold in other exempla compilations and chronicles as well.[17] In another commonly attempted cure, demoniacs sometimes were given the Eucharist in an apparent attempt to have God and the demon battle it out within the human body. This recourse was usually thought to be ineffective because, as we have seen, the demon was believed to live within the physical spaces of the body, while the sacrament entered directly into the soul. Such improvised exorcisms seldom were

---

[14] *Vita S. Hildegardis Virginis, AASS*, September 5:693, 694.

[15] Ibid., 694.

[16] A. Little, *Liber exemplorum ad usum praedicantium* (Aberdeen, 1907), 9.

[17] *De Ap.* 2.36.4, 386–87; Gerald of Wales, *Journey through Wales*, trans. L. Thorpe (New York, 1978), 152.

successful, yet the authoritative force of a normative ritual was lacking in most communities.

Caesarius of Heisterbach offered a more hopeful example of an improvisational exorcism, but it was only after a lengthy process of trial and error that the demon was subdued:[18]

> One time a possessed man was led to the monastery in the hopes of a cure. . . . No remedy was able to heal him, not the relics of the saints, not the prayers of the monks. . . . [The abbot] read over him some prayers and chants that he had about Our Lady, and showed him holy pictures, through which he adjured all the demons to leave. Then one day he put the psalter over the head of the possessed man, with him screaming and frothing . . . and after an hour he came to his senses . . . crying out that he had been liberated from the devil.[18]

Gerald of Wales used the trope of books as exorcistic objects to humorous effect in describing how the unclean spirits possessing a man would fly away when the Gospel of John was placed on his lap, but when Geoffrey of Monmouth's *History of the Kings of Britain* was placed there instead, "just to see what would happen," the demons returned in greater numbers and harassed the victim even more bitterly.[19]

Another possible remedy was a regimen of prolonged prayer and fasting. In her letter regarding the possession case, Hildegard remarked that "this kind of demon you are asking about . . . does not greatly fear even the Lord's cross or the relics of the saints. . . . It will be ejected only through fasts, mortifications, prayers, almsgiving, and the direct order of God."[20] Self-mortification before God was considered a viable means of gaining his direct intervention in cases of possession: after all, Jesus himself had noted that certain demons could be expelled only through prayer and fasting (Matt. 17:15, 20; Mark 9:27–28; Luke 9:40). In accordance with this idea, some of the brief early exorcistic texts are mainly occupied with prescribing prayers and a strict diet for the victim, with few formulae or invocations. Thus a tenth-century text advises fifteen days of fasting in which only bread and blessed salt, along with occasional fish and beans, may be eaten by the demoniac. Additional dietary advice is given for the remainder of the year as well as lesser indictions

---

[18] *DM*, 2:52–53.
[19] Gerald of Wales, *Journey through Wales*, 117.
[20] *Vita Hildegardis*, 694.

for the rest of the victim's life.[21] A twelfth-century manuscript advises that "the priest should give him water blessed with holy salt to drink, mixed with a little absinthe, until he vomits."[22] Once this purging was complete, the demoniac was to observe a fast for forty days and nights, and to bathe only in holy water. The focus of these texts is practical activity rather than liturgical utterances and gestures.

In other cases baptismal exorcisms were employed to cure adult demoniacs. For example, when the friends of Christina of Stommeln wished to exorcize her of demons sometime in the 1270s, they consulted with one another about what course of action to take. Eventually, they decided to try the baptismal rite.

> Friar Wipert said to the Lord Parish Priest, "Dear friend, don't you know any adjurations through which our adversary might be expelled?" And he said, "I only know the one by which children are exorcised: 'Therefore, cursed Devil, accept your sentence,' and so forth." And he said, "You read it, and I will repeat it after you carefully so that we may put to flight this unclean spirit."[23]

This incident represents a transitional moment, in which the exorcism of an adult is improvised by using the baptismal liturgy. The passage is significant in demonstrating the increasing need for exorcistic solutions as well as the general lack of consensus about what to do in such a situation. The decision to fall back upon baptismal formulae of exorcism is one that would eventually be adopted in the fifteenth century, when such formulae were greatly amplified and inscribed within a new canon of scripted exorcistic liturgies targeted specifically at adult energumens.

The most important sources of exorcistic cures in the period before the fifteenth century, however, were saints and their relics. Indeed, the lack of a reliable antidote for possession could lead to a situation such as that described in the vita of the twelfth-century Cistercian monk and theologian Bernard of Clairvaux. During a trip to Italy the saint was besieged by friends and families of demoniacs requesting help, as it had became known that he had particular expertise in expelling demons. His hagiographer comments that he was celebrated throughout Italy as a powerful exorcist,[24] and his healings

---

[21] Franz, *Kirchlichen Benediktionen*, 2:562–63.

[22] Quoted in ibid., 563.

[23] Peter of Dacia, *Vita Christinae Stumblensis*, ed. Johannes Paulson (Göteborg, 1896; reprint, Frankfurt am Main, 1985), 44–45.

[24] *Vita Bernardi de Clarevallis*, *AASS*, August 4:282.

there were indeed numerous. The impression given is of a proliferating number of demoniacs for whom no cure could be devised; Bernard's special *virtus* in this arena rendered him much in demand.

These dramatic expulsions of demons construct exorcism as a public spectacle. Indeed, exorcisms rarely are painted without a group of onlookers looming in the background, expressions of astonishment on their faces; and textual accounts invariably mention of crowds or bystanders watching the proceedings with intense interest. Clearly, in a culture with low rates of literacy, relatively few media of communication, and infrequent formal entertainment, the prospect of a good exorcism—that is, a good supernatural battle with much gnashing of teeth—would be occasion for some excitement. Furthermore, the meaning and import of this healing event was open to broad interpretations, occurring as it did outside the bounds of established texts and normative explanations. Thus, saintly exorcisms ideally functioned to undergird local popular notions about possession and spirits, as well as beliefs about the degree of holiness (or lack thereof) of local patron saints. The reintegration of demoniacs into the community took place at a local level, with the community debating and interpreting the episode from start to finish. The crowds rushing to the main church or town square to witness the healing decided how the possession must have come about and whether the exorcism was proceeding well; they suggested new techniques, commented on the victim's background and behavior, and debated whether the victim was healed and whether the exorcist was saintly or not. However, it also seems likely that the interpretation of these events frequently was contentious. We should beware of reflexively falling into a functionalist, consensus model in analyzing saintly exorcism. Evaluations of exorcism, like interpretations of spirit possession, could oscillate among various interpretations arranged along the axes of power, proximity, and public fame. Though rooted in the local community, saintly exorcism was ambiguous enough to permit wide latitude for interpretation and debate.

FROM RELICS TO TEXTS

By the fifteenth century exorcisms at saints' shrines were in sharp decline. According to a statistical study of the October volumes of the *Acta Sanctorum* performed by André Goddu, miracle collections appended to hagiographies reflect an exponential increase in the need for exorcisms in the thirteenth century, a slight decline from this peak in the fourteenth, followed by a precipitous drop in activity in the fifteenth century. The graphs that accompany Goddu's article show a veritable Everest centered over the thirteenth and fourteenth centuries, with sheer sides dropping off before and after that time.[25] Goddu interpreted this data as an indication that belief in the efficacy of exorcism was slowly being eroded by a more general lack of confidence in the sacraments at the end of the Middle Ages, and by an increase in medical diagnostic skills. It would be incautious, however, to accept the conclusions of this study, based as it is upon a limited sampling of one type of record, without examining other types of sources as well.[26] And indeed, Goddu's argument is flawed in a crucial respect. While he convincingly demonstrates that exorcisms connected to saints, and reported in the *Acta Sanctorum* (or at least in its October volumes), declined dramatically in the fifteenth century, this does not mean that all methods of exorcism disappeared. Because Goddu consulted only one type of source and a limited sampling of that type, he failed to understand that exorcism not only persisted but flourished. Indeed, it is precisely in the fifteenth century, the period Goddu posits as a nadir of exorcistic activity, that exorcisms suddenly achieved a striking visibility in other documents in European archives. Manuals of exorcism, produced for the first time in large numbers in the fifteenth century as portable pocket books, demonstrate that exorcism had not become a "failure" at all. It had simply mutated, ceased to be an improvised public spectacle at a saint's tomb, and instead become a liturgical performance. Thus the absence of exorcisms in the fifteenth-century saints' lives that Goddu examined may be accounted for by the fact that a different model of exorcism had become dominant at that time. These new exorcisms were scripted liturgies, rather than spontaneous healings: hieratic in tone, repetitive in form, and eschatological in doctrinal scope.

Not surprisingly, these liturgical forms privilege the ideological goals of the fifteenth-century Church, which found itself in a somewhat precarious situation. The laity's confidence in the ecclesiastical hierarchy had been shaken by recent historical developments such as the Great Schism and the anticlerical preaching of various reformist movements. The schism, which lasted for the forty years between 1378 and 1417, obfuscated the lines of re-

---

[25] André Goddu, "The Failure of Exorcism in the Middle Ages," in A. Zimmermann, *Soziale Ordnungen im Selbstverständnis des Mittelalters* (Berlin, 1980), esp. 552–57. The graph is plotted as follows: number of exorcisms in the *Acta Sanctorum* for the month of October in the tenth century, 2; eleventh century, 7; twelfth century, 12; thirteenth century, 30; fourteenth century, 23; fifteenth century, 4.

[26] A point well taken by Erik Midelfort in *A History of Madness in Early Modern Germany* (Palo Alto, 1999), 59–60.

ligious authority as two rival pontiffs each claimed the right to the throne of Peter. Since the ecclesiastical hierarchy was viewed in emanationist terms—that is, with each rung of the hierarchy deriving its authority from the rungs above, all the way up to the pope—the schism threatened to destabilize clerical status at all levels. At the same time, reform movements questioning the preeminence of the clergy over the laity gained great popularity in certain parts of Europe, most notably the Hussites in Bohemia, the Lollards and Wycliffites in England, and the so-called "free spirits" in France, Belgium, and the Rhineland. These reformist movements spurred a cautious strategy of containment and counterattack on the part of ecclesiastical authorities, an effort to reinscribe the authority of the ecclesiastical hierarchy on the daily life of the parish. Seemingly as part of this new mood, exorcism was appropriated from the realm of saints' cults and transformed into a discourse of clerical authority and power.

There is little evidence as to precisely how the change in exorcistic practice came about, but it occurred within a restricted time span and over a broad area. This would seem to indicate a coordinated effort to distribute rituals of exorcism throughout the dioceses of Europe. The sudden proliferation of the manuals is indeed striking. Most exorcisms listed in manuscript archives for the period before the fifteenth century are simple salt-and-water exorcisms, used since the time of the primitive Church to purify these elements for liturgical uses, as well as for sprinkling around houses for general protection against demonic influences.[27] Other exorcisms from this period are rather abbreviated and, surprisingly often, intended for mundane uses. A fourteenth-century Latin manuscript of an exorcism from Spain is only two folio pages;[28] another fourteenth-century text turns out to be an amulet intended for the protection of horses against worms;[29] a third contains a series of amuletic charms against general tribulation and snakebite.[30] In fact, these uses continued into the fifteenth century as well: a benedictional from 1420 specifies the goal of exorcisms as protecting fields and animals from disease;[31] another contains exorcisms for purifying bells, wax, and palm leaves

---

[27] Salt-and-water exorcisms are found throughout the Middle Ages and change little: BV ms. Ottob. Lat. 313, 158r–v (ninth century); BV ms. Vat. Lat. 12990, 122r–24r (thirteenth century); BV ms. Ottob. Lat. 356, 277v–78v (c. 1400); BV ms. Ottob. Lat. 672, 88v–91v (1452); BV ms. Vat. Lat. 6244, 307v (fifteenth century); BV ms. Pal. Lat. 488, 1r–2r (fifteenth century); BV ms. Vat. Lat. 5768, 125v (fifteenth century).

[28] BN ms. Lat. 3576, 122r–23v.

[29] Patetta, "Esorcismo."

[30] BS ms. Clm. 23374, 16v–17v.

[31] BS ms. Clm. 23645, 1r–2v, 10v–19v.

(the latter for use in religious processions).[32] Catherine Chène recently has documented the extensive employment of exorcisms against vermin, insects, and parasites in the area of Lausanne over the course of the fifteenth century.[33] These texts, while fascinating, are only marginally related to the history of the change I am exploring.

The first lengthy, independent exorcists' manuals aimed at the cure of adult energumens date from the fifteenth century. They all have similar basic structures, were aware of one another's existence, and assumed the ready availability of other such manuals. When, for example, a scribe found that part of the exorcism manual he was copying had been lost, he simply directed the reader to find another one, apparently assuming that this would not be difficult: "in the example . . . there are two folios missing, concerning which go look in other expulsions."[34] Thus a certain degree of conventionality was assumed to exist among exorcisms, a fact that also is attested by references to repressing illicit exorcistic practices. In the early fifteenth century, for example, Henry Gorichem wrote a "Tract on Ejecting Demons: Whether the Means of Ejecting Demons from Men That Is Used by Some Priests Is Licit and Approved."[35] Similarly, in 1384 a local Florentine sorcerer was prosecuted by the podesta for performing unauthorized exorcisms.[36] His procedure was suitably elaborate:

After [performing] other incantations and ceremonies, he took the girl by the hair, laid her on the ground upon a rug, and spoke into her ear certain magical words, which could not be heard by others, except a certain diabolical song which began: "Tanta muructa? Tiri? etc." Then, placing her upon her feet, he drew out the spirits so that they left her, and during this expulsion he extinguished a candle . . . which he had caused to be placed at a short distance from the girl. And this was done,

[32] BV ms. Pal. Lat. 484, 56v, 2r, 18v.

[33] Catherine Chène, *Juger les vers· Exorcismes et procès d'animaux dans le diocèse de Lausanne (XVe–XVIe s.)* (Lausanne, 1995). An appendix contains original texts in Latin along with French translations.

[34] In exemplari . . . est defectus duorum foliorum, de quo vide et quere in aliis expulsionibus. BV ms. Pal. Lat. 794, 78r. The scribe, in general a rather disorganized fellow, later found the missing pages and placed the deleted section at the end.

[35] Cited in Franz, *Kirchlichen Benediktionen*, 2:559.

[36] The case is discussed in Gene Brucker, "Sorcery in Renaissance Florence," *Studies in the Renaissance* 10 (1963): 7–24. The text is reprinted in Brucker, ed. and trans., *The Society of Renaissance Florence: A Documentary Study* (New York, 1971). For another case of an unauthorized, popular exorcist, see Giovanni Levi, *Inheriting Power: The Story of an Exorcist*, trans. L. Cochrane (Chicago, 1988).

and the girl remained free [from spirits], although she was in a weak state.[37]

Yet, as late as the 1480s the *Malleus maleficarum* was still proscribing popular exorcisms, including those of old women who made exorcistic rhymes or songs:

> The Blessed Virgin crossed the Jordan
> And Saint Stephen met her walking
> Then he asked her . . . [38]

The attempt to suppress these practices as illicit points to a conscious decision on the part of Church authorities to regularize exorcism and to condemn competitive healers of demonic maladies.

Manuals of exorcisms usually were produced as octavo volumes, a pocketbook size. They are not particularly fancy, with limited rubrication and no ornamentation. Most such manuals are compilations, with each book including several slightly different texts. One book even has an extra exorcism squeezed into the margins of its pages, as if the owner came upon a new exorcistic script and decided to include it in an already-bound copy. Three to four lines are given on the upper and lower margins of each leaf, with a system of asterisks and other symbols directing the reader to the continuation of the text (fig. 22). This same manual also has another extra exorcism bound with the main text, but on smaller pages.[39] This impulse to collect exorcisms is occasionally referred to in other texts. Thus in a 1491 case concerning a monastery of possessed nuns, the local bishop and a deacon performed exorcisms and "collected remedies from all over."[40]

These observations about the physical characteristics of the manuals as pocket- or handbooks suggest that they may have been intended as portable objects to be carried by itinerant representatives of the ecclesiastical hierarchy. Similarly, the squeezing-in of additional exorcisms in the margins testifies to a kind of mobile opportunism when a variant was encountered. These facts give us some clues about the identity of the users of these manuals. The compact size of the manuals would seem to be an attribute attractive to itin-

[37] Brucker, "Sorcery," 16.

[38] Henry Kramer and Jacob Sprenger, *Malleus maleficarum* (Lyons 1669), 195.

[39] BV ms. Pal. Lat 794, 68r–71v, has the marginal exorcism; 74r–76r are the smaller pages. Unfortunately, some of the marginal lines were lost when the manuscript was later trimmed and re-bound.

[40] From the Chronicle of Massaeo, excepted in *CJ*, 1:323–24.

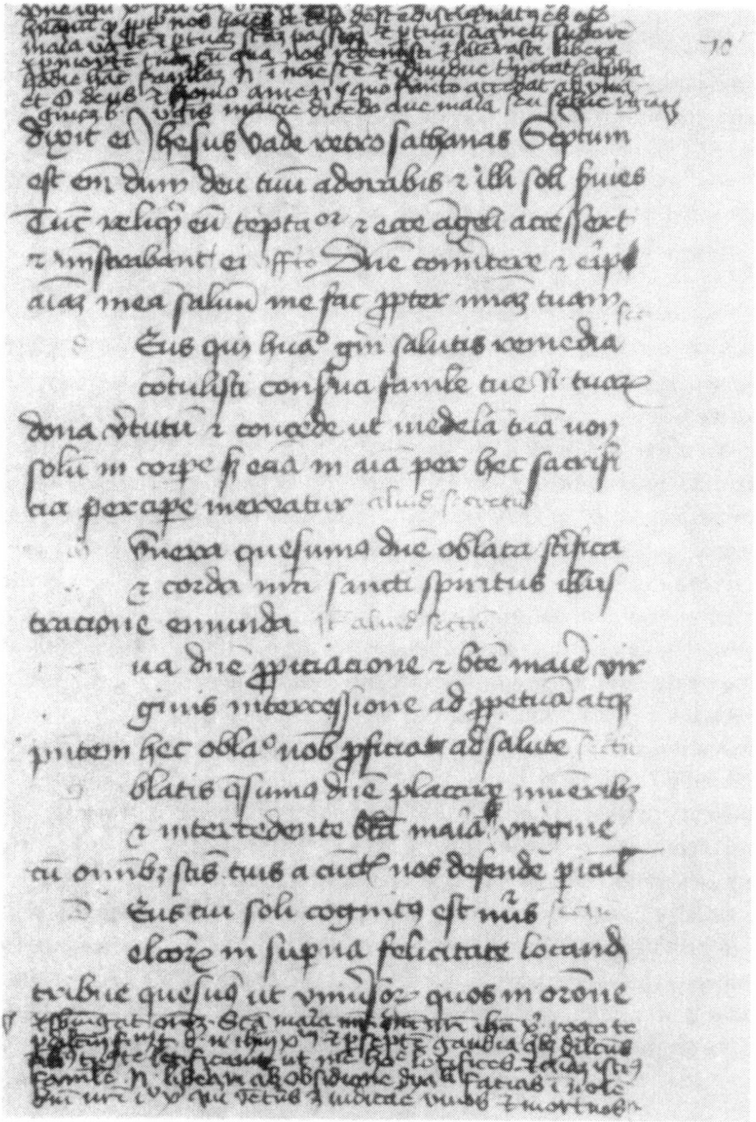

Figure 22. A clever use of manuscript margins. The neat scribe who copied this manual of exorcisms came upon a new formula and decided to add it in to the margins of his existing manuscript. Small triangles, one at the end of the top set of lines and another at the beginning of the bottom set, direct the reader to the continuation of the text. These pages were later trimmed and parts of the marginal text were lost. Manuscript folio, fifteenth century. Vatican City: Biblioteca Vaticana ms. Pal. Lat. 794, f. 68r. Photo courtesy of the Vatican Libraries.

erant preachers such as members of the mendicant orders. Certainly by the sixteenth century, the most prominent exorcists were Franciscans like Buonaventura Farinerio and Girolamo Menghi, both well-known exorcists and writers on the topic.[41] And although the composition of the fifteenth-century exorcists' manuals remains unknown, a group of writers from that period discussed the problem of exorcism at length: namely, mendicant inquisitors such as Johannes Nider, Silvestro Priero, or Henry Kramer.[42] Lastly, some anecdotal evidence shows mendicants acting in this role. The vita of Columba of Rieti, for instance, mentions an inquisitor-exorcist, a member of the Order of Preachers, who was traveling to Rome for consultation with Pope Alexander VI about a monastery of possessed nuns in France. Observing Columba's ecstasies, he accused her, too, of being possessed by the devil.[43]

It also seems likely, however, that many such manuals were owned by local priests or monks for use within their own communities. Most manuscript exorcisms assume that the officiant is a priest; discussions of exorcism in the *Malleus maleficarum* and Nider's *Formicarius* do so as well.[44] We have evidence that manuals of exorcism were commonly to be found in neighborhood churches, as in this testimony from the worried father of a possessed girl: "Thinking about [my daughter's strange behavior], and turning it about often my mind, it occurred to me that this was the work of the devil, and having first sent for . . . the priest who was in charge of the church near the house, I recounted everything to him openly. Immediately, he somberly ordered a clerk to fetch holy water and the book of conjurations."[45] Other manuals were owned by monasteries, such as the Vallambrosan foundation dedicated

---

[41] See Buonaventura Farinerio, *Exorcismo mirabile da disfare ogni sorte de malefici et da cacciare i demoni* (Venice, 1567); Girolamo Menghi, *Compendio dell'arte essorcistica* (Bologna, 1584); idem, *Flagellum daemonum* (Bologna, 1644). On Menghi, see Giancarlo Volpato, "Girolamo Menghi o l'arte essorcistica," *Lares* 57, 3 (1991): 381–97; Giovanni Romeo, *Inquisitori, esorcisti, e streghe nell'Italia della Controriforma* (Florence, 1990); Armando Maggi, *Satan's Rhetoric: A Study of Renaissance Demonology* (Chicago, 2001).

[42] On these authors see Maggi, *Satan's Rhetoric*; Walter Stephens, *Demon Lovers: Witchcraft, Sex, and the Crisis of Belief* (Chicago, 2002); Michael Bailey, "From Sorcery to Witchcraft: Clerical Conceptions of Magic in the Later Middle Ages," *Speculum* 76, 4 (2001): 960–90; idem, *Battling Demons: Witchcraft, Heresy, and Reform in the Late Middle Ages* (University Park, P.A., 2003); Martine Ostorero, Agostino Paravicini Bagliaini and Kathrin Utz Tremp, *L'imaginaire du sabbat: Edition critique des textes les plus anciens (1430 c.–1440 c.)* (Lausanne, 1999). I believe Catherine Chène is working on a complete edition of Nider's *Formicarius*.

[43] *Vita B. Columbae Reatinae*, *AASS*, May 5:180.

[44] BV ms. Vat. Lat. 10812, 226v; BV ms. Pal. Lat. 794, 72v. F 5.6, 78r–80r; Kramer and Sprenger, *Malleus maleficarum*, 184–86; 189–203.

[45] *Miraculi S. Joannis Gualberti abbatis*, *AASS*, July 2:441.

to John Gualbert in Florence. A remarkable series of exorcisms recorded by this monastery in the fifteenth century shows how the saint's arm relic was utilized in combination with the newer exorcistic technology of a scripted text.[46] It appears that the business of exorcism rotated among the monks, for one anecdote notes that a possessed woman was assigned to "one of the monks who had the office of conjuring demons, it being his turn in order."[47] He approached her girded with the cross, holy water and blessed salt, and "holy words"—presumably from an exorcists' manual.

The possibility that non-ordained persons might utilize a book of exorcisms is explicitly raised in one manuscript, which advises that certain actions may be taken "if the exorcist is a priest."[48] The same text also advises that the exorcist will have no success unless he is completely chaste; if this proves too difficult, however, he should refrain from fornication for a minimum of nine days prior to the conjuration. Yet this script later calls for the officiant "or another" to wrap the stole, a distinctively clerical accessory, around the victim.[49] These fragments of information are difficult to interpret: do they indicate that laity had access to this particular book? It is impossible to be certain, but it seems unlikely. Of course, one could be a monk or friar and not be in orders, and these may be the non-priests the author had in mind. It would be unusual, however, for a layman to be entrusted with so powerful a set of words—particularly since conjurations of a very similar kind were associated with forbidden magical invocations.[50]

The actual scripts or texts of exorcisms are difficult to characterize. In essence they are a species of *clamor* with similarities to other such liturgies, such as excommunications, humiliations, and maledictions.[51] And as we have seen, the earliest roots of such exorcisms sprout from the baptismal liturgy; with basic elements such as the blessing of salt and water derived from the ancient practice of this rite. However, many exorcisms are hybrid compositions; incorporating gospel readings alongside formulae in "demonic lan-

---

[46] Ibid., 417.

[47] Ibid., 397.

[48] "Exorcista si est sacerdos." BS ms. Clm. 10085, 3r.

[49] BS ms. Clm. 10085, 2r, 3v.

[50] Richard Kieckhefer, *Forbidden Rites: A Necromancer's Manual of the Fifteenth Century* (University Park, Pa., 1997). See also idem, *Magic in the Middle Ages* (Cambridge, 1990).

[51] Elisabeth Vodola, *Excommunication in the Middle Ages* (Berkeley, 1986); Patrick Geary, "Humiliation of Saints," in *Living with the Dead in the Middle Ages* (Ithaca, N.Y., 1994), 95–115; Lester K. Little, *Benedictine Maledictions: Liturgical Cursing in Romanesque France* (Ithaca, N.Y., 1993); On clamors used as a form of political discourse, see Geoffrey Koziol, *Begging Pardon and Favor: Ritual and Political Order in Early Medieval France* (Ithaca, N.Y., 1992). See also the texts of clamors, malediction, excommunications, and exorcisms in Martène, *De antiquis ecclesiae ritibus*, 2:898–1002.

guage" alternately cajoling and commanding the demon to leave. Kabbalistic and magical elements occasionally appear, and the structure of some exorcisms is quite similar to the "experiments" included in a rare surviving necromantic manual in Munich.[52]

Nevertheless, the inherently conservative nature of the medieval textual tradition tended toward a certain uniformity among exorcists' manuals. As in the example cited earlier, if pages were missing from one text it was expected that one could fill in the lacuna from another manuscript. And despite local variations, the manuals as a group have much in common. Most invoke events from the life of Jesus, list the names of God, call upon the aid of the saints and angels, and imagine vivid apocalyptic scenarios of demonic defeat and eternal torment. Each recipe for exorcism utilizes the same basic ingredients, though in slightly different proportions recombined like biblical pericopes. Moreover, the individual elements of the texts contained in the manuals often had deep historical roots. The innovation of the manuals was to collect, amplify, and extend already existing exorcistic elements rather than to fashion a new liturgical form from whole cloth.

This recombinant structure was not random, however. These texts represent finely crafted compositions directing the clerical officiant to demonstrate mastery over the demoniac in various ways. Thus liturgical exorcisms compile a vast storehouse of images of cosmic hierarchy extending from the zenith of heaven, descending through the body of the demoniac on earth, and on down into the abyss of hell. The strategic deployment of these images is self-referential, positioning the clerical exorcist as a transcendent axis of divine control over the forces of demonic disorder immanent within the demoniac body. The texts thus encode, and seek to communicate, a particular ideology of the Church Triumphant and of clerical preeminence. Furthermore, these liturgies aim to be self-interpreting, in the sense that they attempt to foreclose speculation about the meanings of particular gestures, prayers, and conjurations by constantly providing approved commentaries within the body of the text itself. Whether this attempt to craft a self-interpreting ritual form was successful, however, remains an open question. Since we possess few sources describing actual enactments of liturgical exorcism and responses to them, our analysis remains limited mainly to the prescriptive level of the exorcistic script itself.

---

[52] The text of the manual has recently been translated and analyzed in Kieckhefer, *Forbidden Rites.*

The first goal of an exorcism was discernment of the possessing spirits. Though exorcisms were by definition concerned with the demonically possessed, the texts nevertheless recommend gaining independent confirmation of this fact before proceeding to the conjurations. One could not simply assume that a person exhibiting possessed behaviors had been invaded by an unclean spirit. The behavioral and physiological disorder of the presumed demoniac must verifiably be linked to the presence of a demon. Fifteenth-century exorcists' manuals were the first medieval texts of any kind to include specific tests for determining whether an individual was truly possessed and, if so, by what kind of spirit.[53] There existed a few common methods, usually placed at the beginning of the rite:

> Here begin the expulsions of devils, et cetera. As soon as the possessed person comes to the church, let the body of the Lord along with the pyx be placed secretly on his head. If he is perturbed by this, or says he has pain, then ask him what he has on his head. If he tells the truth, the body of the Lord, then you know that he is possessed. But if you cannot tell this way, then secretly say this verse to the possessed person in the left ear: "You have relinquished the God who made you, and have forgotten the Lord your Creator." If this sends him into a fury then he is possessed.[54]

This proof, derived from Deuteronomy 32:18, has earlier medieval antecedents: the recommended verse is found as early as the thirteenth century in a tale told by Thomas of Cantimpré in his *On Bees*.[55]

A variation on this test found in an exorcism squeezed into the margins of one manual, is the recommendation to show the demoniac a picture of Saint Jerome, "which no demoniac can look at without pain."[56] This version also

---

[53] Franz, *Kirchlichen Benediktionen*, 2:560.

[54] Incipit expulsiones dyabulorum, et cetera. Statim cum obsessus venerit ad ecclesiam, corpus Domini ponatur, cum pixide, furtive super caput ipsius. Et si de hoc commovebitur, vel dicet se dolere, tunc interrogas eum quid habeat super caput. Si tunc dicet tibi veritatem, de corpore Domini, noveris [sic] eum obsessum esse; vel si sic non poteris considerare, dic hunc versum obsesso in aurem sinistram occulte: Deum, qui te genuit, dereliquisti, et oblitus es Domini creatoris tui. Si ex hoc in furore capitur, tunc est obsessus. BV ms. Pal. Lat. 794, 68r. Also see BS ms. Clm. 23325, 3r.

[55] *De Ap.* 2.57.67, 591.

[56] Quam nullus daemoniacus sine dolore aspicere potest. BV ms. Pal. Lat. 794, 68r, part of the marginal exorcism squeezed in at the top.

recommends blowing and spitting into the demoniac's mouth, then waiting to see whether the patient bites his or her tongue, or puckers the lips. Finally, the exorcist should lift up the victim's eyelids, stare into the sockets, and recite the gospel account of the Annunciation to Mary. A true energumen will begin throbbing violently at the temples in response; his or her eyes will turn red and roll back into the head, and other terrible physical symptoms will occur.[57] It is possible that the reason this exorcism was so compelling to the owner of this book—such that he took pains to copy it into the margins of his other exorcisms—was precisely because of the detailed and useful direction it gives in this regard.

A second kind of test consists of addressing the demon directly in its own language. This test was popular enough to be found in several manuscripts, with minor variations on the demonic words:

> If you want to know whether a person is possessed or not, write these verses on a card or sheet:
>
> AGLA ✠ LAY ✠ ELEYTH ✠
>
> Along with the four verses that are called "the devil's verses," because he composed those verses himself:
>
>> Omimara chentazirim post hossita lossita lux
>> Ebulus lepolpes mala raphamius allilous
>> Helmo starius sed poli polisque
>> Lux capit horrontis latet vertice montis
>
> [The following sentence is in German:] This proof should be placed in his hand. [The Latin resumes:] If he takes it in his hand, then he is not possessed; if he does not, then he is possessed.[58]

Amazingly enough, tucked into this manuscript was a slip of paper, of similar appearance to the pages of the text, with the exact formula carefully inscribed upon it. Quite similar verses are given in other manuscripts:

---

[57] BV ms. Pal. Lat. 794, 68r, part of the marginal exorcism squeezed in at the bottom and at the top of 68v.

[58] Si vis scire utrum homo sit obsessus an non, scribe ista versa [sic] in una carta vel littera: AGLA ✠ LAY ✠ ELEYTH ✠ et illos quatuor versus que vocantur versus dyaboli quia per se fecit illos versus: Omimara chentazirim post hossita lossita lux / Ebulus lepolpes mala raphamius allilous / Helmo starius sed poli polisque / Lux capit horrontis latet vertice montis. Dissen prieff solman in sein hand lege. Recipit autem in manu, tunc non est obsessus; si autem non, tunc est obsessus. BS ms. Clm. 23325, 32v.

If you wish to know whether a person is possessed, then write these names on a scroll:

✠ AGLA ✠ LAII ✠ GLAYCH ✠

And use the verses:

> Ammara choncha tyri post hostica lostica lyri
> Ebulus hepulpes mala, riphanus albanus abileus
> Helmo monstrarius sed poli polisque buarras(?)
> Lux capit horrontis latet in vertice montis

Let this scroll be placed in the hand of the possessed person: if he has taken the scroll, then you may believe it is a possession; if not, then the possession is doubtful. Then, take wormwood and push it into his [clothes?] so that it touches the skin. Then the demon himself will respond who it is, and from whence it came.[59]

Here, the diagnostic advice is opposite to that prescribed above: accepting a scroll with the demonic verses is an indicator of true possession.

A third exorcism simply has the following fragment written in the bottom margin: "Test: Ammara tuncta tyre post hostica lustica lyri."[60] There are no directions for how to apply or interpret this proof. A German magical manuscript composed in the vernacular recommends whispering a similar conglomeration of syllables into a demoniac's ear: "Amara Tonta Tyra post hos firabis ficaliri Elypolis starras poly polyque lique linarras buccabor uel barton vel Titram celi massis Metumbor o priczoni Jordan Ciriacus Valentinus."[61]

Another Latin manual recommends that the exorcist place his thumb in the demoniac's mouth and pronounce a demonic formula, though the purpose of this step is unclear. We also might recall the "diabolical song" used by the Florentine sorcerer-exorcist prosecuted by the podesta. While the

---

[59] Si scire vis an homo sit obsessus, tunc scribe hec nomina ad cedulam unam: ✠ AGLA ✠ LAII ✠ GLAYCH ✠ et habes versus: Ammara choncha tyri post hostica lostica lyri / Ebulus hepulpes mala, riphanus albanus abileus / Helmo monstrarius sed poli polisque buarras(?) / Lux capit horrontis latet in vertice montis. Ista cedula ponatur ad manum obsessi: si recepit cedulam, tunc credatur eius obsessio; si non recipit, dubitetur de obsessione eius. Et tunc recipe arthemisiam et trude in [unclear] eius ut tangat cutem eius; tunc respondebit quis ipse demon sit, et unde venit. BV ms. Pal. Lat. 794, 83v.

[60] Probatio: BV ms. Pal. Lat. 794, 74r.

[61] Quoted in Kieckhefer, *Magic in the Middle Ages*, 4.

devil's language does not appear in every exorcism, it is a widespread and well-established element of the exorcist's arsenal.[62]

Given that the demonic language is not an isolated motif, we must take it seriously as part of the conceptual apparatus of the ritual, rather than dismissing it as a mistake or a vulgarization.[63] Rather, the demonic tongue is an intentional ordering device that graphically represents—and thereby subordinates—demonic disorder. Unclean power is thus controlled and hierarchically defined in relation to the exorcist who literally wields it, reified into written form. Yet the potency of the demonic discourse depends on the fact that it is not entirely foreign but rather a twisting of legitimate language, which it turns inside out, as it were. As Stanley Tambiah has remarked in relation to a similar Sinhalese exorcistic *mantra*, "The language stratification is indicative of the hierarchical positions of gods and demons. The 'demon language' is consciously constructed to connote power, and though largely unintelligible is nevertheless based on the theory of language that the demons can understand. Thus far from being nonsensical and indiscriminately concocted, the spells show a sophisticated logic."[64] This logic flows through the structure and sound of the words and their endings: the demonic verses mimic Latin, even incorporating some true Latin words, without actually having any particular meaning. Rather than being the result of popular or folkloric influence, the verse is a highly "elite" notion. It is constructed to serve the interests of the learned exorcist, existing as a sophisticated illustration of demonic fallacies and striving after divine institutions, an inversion of the Word. The suggestion that this verse be written onto a scroll or slip of paper and then offered to the demoniac makes of this strange language a material representation of demonic fealty and exorcistic domination. In a recursive game of control and strategy, the demonic language is inscribed within the exorcist's own liturgical script, and thus appropriated to clerical ends.

[62] For more on the concept of demonic language as elementary disorder, see Maggi, *Satan's Rhetoric*, 21–53.

[63] Lester Little notes similar functions in cursing formulae, which often followed the word *anathema* with the Aramaic word *maranatha*. Though the word has no meaning in Latin, its reduplicating quality adds a measure of solemnity to the proceedings. Little, *Benedictine Maledictions*, 33–34.

[64] Stanley Tambiah, "The Magical Power of Words," in *Culture, Thought, and Social Action* (Cambridge, Mass., 1985), 20–21. An analysis of a medieval invented language is found in Jeffrey Schnapp, "Virgin Words: Hildegard of Bingen's *Lingua Ignota* and the Development of Imaginary Languages, Ancient to Modern," *Exemplaria* 3, 2 (1991): 267–98. For other parallels, see Harvey Alper, ed., *Understanding Mantras* (Delhi, 1991).

Within the script of the exorcism, the demonic language functions as a performative utterance that instantiates the radical alterity of the demoniac. Up until this point, the demoniac would have been regarded as human individual afflicted by terrible spiritual disturbances. To use demonic language against the demoniac is to adopt words of unknown properties but of evident power: the alliterative, rhyming quality of the verses seems intentionally designed to evoke a mysterious, illicit potency. The deployment of this language drains the demoniac of her humanity, reducing—or magnifying?—her to become the physical image of the language itself: unintelligible yet filled with menace. The demoniac henceforth will be increasingly emptied of her human identity until she becomes a mere husk, a human body controlled by an unimaginable entity of sinister might.

The exorcist's mastery of demonic language is only one means of giving him the exclusive power to set the demon back within its proper cosmological order. Thus following upon the test for possession, one should conjure the demon into the victim's tongue and constrain it to answer questions about its origin, status, and reasons for possessing the particular individual involved. Suggested questions include: Is it is a devil or a fantasm? A succubus, incubus, or dragon? What is the name of its master? What is its rank? In what form, at what time, and on account of what sin did it enter the victim?[65] The exorcist must first determine precisely what he is dealing with before proceeding to the actual expulsions. These procedures are nicely collapsed in a manual now located in Munich:

Take the head of the possessed person in your left hand and place your right thumb in the possessed person's mouth, saying the following words in both ears: ABRE MONTE ABRYA ABREMONTE CONSACRAMENTARIA SYPAR YPAR YTUMBA OPOTE ALACENT ALAPHIE. Then hold him firmly and say these conjurations: I conjure you, evil spirits, by the terrible name of God Agla . . . I also conjure you by the great name Pneumaton and by the name Ysiton, that you ascend to the tongue and give me a laugh. If they do not respond, then know that they are mute spirits. The exorcist should diligently discover and require whether it is incubi, or succubi, or even dragons that possess the obsessed person; whether they are attendants of Pluto, or servants of Satan, or disciples of Astaroth; if they

[65] A fantasm: see BS ms. Clm. 23325, 3r; a dragon: BS ms. Clm. 10085, 2v–3r; its master's name: BS ms. Clm. 10085, 2v; its rank: BS ms. Clm. 23325, 3r; when and why it entered: BS ms. Clm. 23325, 32v. See also the similar questions mentioned by Franz, *Kirchlichen Benediktionen*, 2:569 n. 1.

are from the east or the west, from noonday or evening, from the air, earth, water, fire, or whatever kind of spirit.[66]

Use of the demonic language thus establishes the exorcist's authority to inquire into the status and origin of the unclean spirit. The more information the exorcist can amass, the greater will be his control over the spirit. He is then empowered to remind the spirit of the true divine order of the universe—and the demon's lowly place within it. As a speaker of divine discourse—the names of God pronounced in God's name—the exorcist embodies the authority of the Omnipotent set up against the rebel angels, whose own language he likewise masters.

The *Miracles of John Gualbert* gives a rare observer's description of a book of conjurations being used to conjure a spirit and assess its nature and desires. The victim is a girl who was possessed by a spirit whom she first saw in the form of an old woman lying on a bed:

> When [the book of conjurations and holy water] were brought, we boldly (after making the sign of the cross) entered the chamber, which immediately was sprinkled by the priest with exorcized water, salt, and prayers. Then in proper order we approached the bed. "I conjure you," said the priest, "in the name of the Father, and of the Son, and of the Holy Spirit. If an evil spirit is living in this room, reveal to me what it is you want, what you are seeking." Scarcely had the priest finished when we immediately heard a whining voice.[67]

Thus the first order of business is to establish the name, rank, and serial number, so to speak, of the indwelling spirit; what it wants and how it can best be compelled to depart. If the demon is uncooperative and will not answer these

---

[66] Recipe caput obsessi in sinistra manu et pone pollicem dextere manus in os obsessi dicendo sibi verba sequentia ad ambas aures: ABRE MONTE ABRYA ABREMONTE CONSACRAMENTARIA SYPAR YPAR YTUMBA OPOTE ALACENT ALAPHIE. Et tunc tenes eum firmiter et dic illas coniurationes: Coniuro vos maledicti spiritus per terribile nomen Dei Agla. . . . Item coniuro vos per illud magnum nomen Pneumaton et per nomen Ysiton ut ascendatis in lingwam et detis michi risum. Et si non respondent tunc cognosce quod ibi spiritus muti. Debet etiam exorcista cognoscere et diligenter indigare utrum incubi, vel succubi, vel etiam dracones possident obsessum; sive sint satellites Plutonis, sive subditi Sathane, sive discipuli Astaroth; sive sint ab oriente sive ab occidente; sive a meridie sive a septentrione; sive de aere, sive de terra, sive de aqua, sive de igne, sive qualescumque spiritus. BS ms. Clm. 10085, 2v–3r.

[67] *Miraculi Joannis Gualberti*, 441.

questions, one should move on to more aggressive threats, as the following passage from a manual demonstrates:

Nor may you hide yourself, Satan: pain hangs over you, torments hang over you, the Day of Judgment hangs over you, the day of supplications, the never-ending Day that will come like a burning furnace. On that day will come the eternal annihilation prepared for you and the whole of your angels. Therefore, damned and to-be-damned one, give honor to the true, living God. . . . Whoever you are or wherever you are from, unclean spirit, whether from hell or from the air, or from a grave, or from caves, or from swamps, or from wet places, or from ruined places, or from the highways, or from woods, or from low places, or from high places, or from a flame of fire, or from cracks in a rock. . . . Behold ✠ the cross! Behold ✠ the cross! Behold ✠ the cross of the Lord! Flee, hostile powers! The lion from the tribe of Judah vanquishes: Allelujah! Repel, we beg, Lord, from this maidservant of God, N., all infestations of the enemy. . . . He commands you, who decreed that you be cast down from the zenith of the heavens to the center of the earth.[68]

On the one hand, this text includes specific indexical "stage directions": use of the symbol ✠, indicating that the exorcist ought to sign the victim with the cross at that moment; the abbreviation "N.," for *nomen*, meaning to insert the demoniac's name; and the gender-specific formulation "maidservant" (*famula*), a point to which I will return soon. These gestural indices give clues

---

[68] Nec te lateat, Sathana. Inminere tibi pena, inminere tibi tormenta, inminere tibi dies iudicii, dies supplicii, sempiterne dies qui venturus est velud clybanus ardens. In quo tibi atque universis angelis tuis preparatus eternus veniet interitus. Proinde dampnate atque dampnande, da honorem Deo vivo et vero. . . . Quocumque es, aut undecumque es, inmunde spiritus, sive de inferno, sive de aere, sive de monumento, sive de spelunca, sive de paludibus, sive de locis aquosis, sive de ruinis, sive de viis, sive de silvis, sive de infimis, sive de summis, sive de ignis incendio, sive de cavernis petrarum . . . Ecce ✠ crucem! Ecce ✠ crucem! Ecce ✠ crucem Domini! Fugite partes adverse! Vincit leo de tribu Iuda, Alleluia! Repelle, quaesumus, Domine, ab hac famula Dei N. omnem infestationem inimici. . . . Ipse tibi imperat qui te de supernis celorum inferiore terre demergi precepit. BS ms. Clm. 23325, 9v–13r. See BV ms. Pal. Lat. 794, 73r and BS ms. Clm. 10085, 25r for similar lists. Portions of this invocation also may be found in the 1367 miracle book of Anthony of Padua. The story concerns a woman deceived by the devil transfigured into Christ: she is told that she can redeem her sins only by committing suicide. In her despair, she has a dream-vision of Anthony of Padua, who gives her a parchment amulet to hang on her neck, inscribed with the formula in golden letters: "Behold the cross of Christ! Flee, hostile powers! The lion from the tribe of Judah and root of David vanquishes! Hallelujah! Hallelujah!" Waking, she finds the actual scroll around her neck. *De sancto Antonio Patavii liber miraculorum, AASS*, June 3:736.

to the performative reality of the exorcism within a scripted setting. They construct the body of the demoniac as female, as named, and as Christian. On the other hand, the insistent references to Satan's primordial sin and future defeat simultaneously make the body of the demoniac a cosmological battleground between the forces of good and evil, between history and eschatology, between the Divine Word and the Ancient Enemy of the Human Race. Possession is an intermediate stage in the gigantic span of demonic history, crowded by greater transgressions and punishments and figurally representative of them all. And wielding these cosmic forces and powers through language is the servant of the exalted, the clerical exorcist who casts out the rebel angels on God's behalf once again.

THE DEMONIC CONVERGENCE

Upon the heels of fallen angels follow fallen women. The ongoing war over human history is paralleled by a battle over the individual body of the demoniac—and that body is female. Indeed, it is noteworthy that as questions about spirit possession, exorcism, and discernment came to be articulated systematically in writing, the deep, underlying cultural association between women and possession increasingly came to be exposed on the very surface of the texts: their grammar. For I know of no group of medieval sources other than manuals of exorcism that commonly uses gender-inclusive pronouns.

As with most other languages, medieval Latin employed masculine pronouns and endings as a "gender-neutral" standard, and all the other major source groups for the period follow this pattern. Yet it is not unusual to discover exorcistic liturgies that take pains to include both masculine and feminine endings in their formulae: thus gender-specific words such as *famula* or *famulus* (the female and male forms of the word "servant") sometimes are presented with both endings in smaller lettering, stacked atop one another.[69] Even more strikingly, many texts that begin inclusively, or with masculine pronouns, switch to *exclusively* feminine usage as the script progresses.[70] If

[69] BN ms. Lat. 3501; BS ms. Clm. 23325; BS ms. Clm. 10085. BV ms. Vat. Lat. 10812 uses the masculine pronoun, as does the short formula in BS ms. Clm. 24932.

[70] BS ms. Clm. 10085 sometimes refers to a *famula Christi*, sometimes to a *famulus*; on 23r the text speaks of a *possessa*. The usage here seems to suggest a compiler or scribe who wished to retain the masculine neutral, but continually caught himself backsliding into feminine endings. BS ms. Clm. 23325 makes the transition to feminine endings on folio

the impulse to add feminine endings to the traditional, "neutral" masculine endings expresses a broad association between women and demonic possession, the slippage into entirely feminine usage hints at a latent inability to envision the body of the demoniac as other than female. Some manuals utilize feminine pronouns with only the most passing pretension at including men as the possible targets of exorcism. Thus an exorcism from the Vatican libraries consistently refers to the victim as a "maidservant" of God (*famula Dei*) and uses "she" and "her" after a brief prologue.[71] Others direct the exorcist to make accommodation for the sex of the victim as the first priority: "The order for helping people vexed by a demon. At first, when a sick person who is vexed by a demon comes to the priest, let the priest lead him to the church, before the altar, and let the person, whether male or female, be diligently questioned about why and how this suffering came upon the person." "As soon as the possessed person comes to the church, [the victim] should be led before the altar and it should be considered whether it is a man or a woman. And find out when or how this affliction happened to the person."[72] A fourteenth-century exorcism from Spain not only uses feminine endings but includes a meditation upon women's place within both the Fall and salvation history:

Death was first introduced into the world by a woman, for the Lord willed that the first, worst action should be brought to men through women, and not to women through men. However, the Lord did not wish this to be held . . . as a mark against the feminine sex. Thus just as

12v and retains this usage throughout the rest of the manual. BN ms. Lat. 3576 uses feminine endings only. BN ms. Lat. 3501 begins with double endings stacked on top of one another, uses the masculine ending alone on folio 131v, then switches to the feminine *eam* on folio 132v and for the remainder. BV ms. Pal. Lat. 794 uses the masculine *obsessus* on the recto side of the first folio (68), but this is the only instance of a masculine ending: the verso of 68 begins referring to a *famula Christi* and retains feminine endings for the remainder. The exorcism squeezed into the top and bottom margins of BV ms. Pal. Lat. 794 likewise uses feminine endings. BV Vat. Lat. ms. 10812 uses masculine endings only, though it does make special accommodation for the sex of the victim (see note 72 below). An exorcists' manual from Schlägl Praemonstratensian Institute, Plaga, Austria, ms. Lat. 194, uses feminine endings. Cited in Adolph Franz, *Die Kirchlichen Benediktionen im Mittelalter*, 2 vols. (Freiburg-im-Breisgau, 1909; reprint, Graz, 1960), 1:571 n. 4.

[71] BV ms. Pal. Lat. 794.

[72] Ordo ad succurrendum homines qui a demonio vexantur. In primis quando infirmus qui a demonio venerit vexatur ad sacerdotem, ducat eum sacerdos ad ecclesiam ante altarem et diligenter inquiratur ab eo sive sit masculus sive femina, quomodo aut qualiter illi eadem passio venerit. BV ms. Vat. Lat. 10812, 224r; Statim cum possessus venerit ad ecclesiam, ante altarem ducatur et consideretur utrum masculus sit vel femina. Et queratur quando vel quoniam hic passio illi contingerit. BS ms. Clm. 10085, 18r–v.

she gave death to men, she also was given the task of announcing life to men.... From a woman's hand, you, O sons of Adam, accepted the draught of death, and so from the mouth of the feminine sex, accept the joy of the resurrection.[73]

I have suggested above that the fifteenth-century model of scripted exorcism includes important didactic elements, as particular theological notions and authorizing discourses are communicated to the attending crowd by the presiding exorcist. Clearly, an additional power dynamic underlies the sexual roles played by the victim and the exorcist. The latter may be seen as advancing particular claims of priority for his sex (male), his status (clerical), and his power source (divine); at the same time, the exorcism is designed to emphasize the salutary subordination of the female, lay, demon-filled being that is conjured. The victim's inferior position reflects cosmic as well as social hierarchies, for not only is she physically conjoined with the demon, she is symbolically and grammatically identified with it as well. The "you" of an exorcistic conjuration always refers to the unclean spirit; yet before the eyes of the crowd there stands only a priest and another human figure, most likely a laywoman. In short, throughout the performance of the exorcism the woman consistently is addressed as a demon. The discursive construction of the exorcism's object conflates woman and demon into a single opponent: the second-person singular pronoun "means" the demon, but in performance it indexically addresses a human woman. The demoniac is thus both self and Other, a hybrid entity. She is indeed, to revive the popular aphorism of Tertullian, the Devil's Gateway, a conduit into this world for unclean and sinister forces.

When the demoniac is addressed in the peculiar accents of the demonic language, she is thereby displayed to the attending crowd as an embodiment of demonic alterity and of mysterious, literally unintelligible power. Furthermore, after this address the demoniac is expected to respond to inquiries about the rank and status of her possessing spirit by adopting a demonic persona and speaking in the demon's voice. Addressed as a demon, the demoniac must respond as one in order for the exorcism to move forward. Indeed, the whole structure of the conjuration is designed to achieve a full convergence between the demon and the woman before the two can be disentan-

---

[73] Per mulierem fuerat mors primum ad nunciatam mundo ergo voluit dominus primum pessimum accionem [sic] nunciare viris per mulieres et non per viros mulieribus. Quare non voluit dominus ne haberetur . . . in opprobrium siquidem feminei sexus. Et sicut dederat mortem hominibus itaque datur nunciando vitam hominibus . . . De manu femine accepistis vos, o fili Adae, potum mortis, et de ore femine accipite gaudia resurrectionum. BN ms. Lat. 3597, 122v.

gled. She must collude, must confess her demonic status, before she can be designated as healed and go home. A demoniac who refuses to acknowledge her demon nature cannot be restored to her human nature and social identity. This requirement functions as part of the legitimizing drama of the performance. Once the demon confesses its name and character through the woman's mouth, the authority of the exorcist is affirmed and the ideology of the exorcistic text—its view of reality as a hierarchically ordered chain of being—is ratified. Conversely, all potential alternate interpretations concerning the status of the demoniac (could she be ill? divinely possessed?), the nature of her possessing spirits (spirits of the dead? angels?), or the authority of the clergy (is this working? is there a better form of healing?) are discredited. Moreover, insofar as exorcism liturgies strive to be self-interpreting, they attempt to force spectators to attend to the pronouncements of the exorcist, while minimizing the potential for alternative interpretations of the event. Thus the crowd should be warned about demonic lies, and the demoniac should (in advance) be scrutinized in order to prevent possible disruptions: "The possessed should be carefully guarded when led to the sacrifice. . . . If the possessed sings and shouts in church during the mass, nobody will be cured. The exhortation on behalf of the possessed should be before the whole community . . . but warn the people that if the possessed person says many things to the exorcists, they should not believe all of it."[74]

Exorcisms thus script the main dramatis personae of the event into precise roles from which there can be no deviation. If the demoniac attempts to disregard this role, and to present an alternate, competing version of reality, the crowd is instructed to disregard her. The advance warning to the crowd acts to restrict the range of acceptable understandings of the event.

Significantly, the manifold insults and rebukes addressed to the demoniac are suitably bivalent, functioning as terms of opprobrium for both the demon and the woman. Admonishments such as "enemy of the faith," "tempter of the human race," "inventor of death," "root of evils," "kindler of sins," and "seducer of men" were classic evocations not just of demonic but also of feminine disorder.[75] These phrases place the accent upon woman's and demon's shared status as primordial first sinners, who both fell from grace before the beginning of time, dragging others with them. The application of precisely this kind of discourse to women would have been familiar to a medieval audience from preaching, popular fabliaux, and the misogynistic literature of

---

[74] Fifteenth-century exorcists' manual quoted in Franz, *Kirchlichen Benediktionen*, 2: 572 n. 2.
[75] Inimicus fidei, generis humani proditor, mortis actor . . . malorum radix, fomes vitiorum, seductor hominum. BN ms. Lat. 3501, 131r; see also BV ms. Vat. Lat. 10812, 226v.

female avoidance. In short, witnesses to the exorcism would observe a great deal of verbal abuse directed by the male exorcist against the female demoniac, with little means of discriminating between demon and woman as the intended recipient. Additionally, a number of gestures included in the stage directions for an exorcism require the exorcist to display physical mastery over the demoniac, involving minor elements of violence and compulsion. The language of one exorcistic liturgy, for example, directs the officiant to compel the demoniac to kneel, to forcibly turn the energumen's head toward the Eucharist, and later to place his thumb in the victim's mouth while proceeding with various conjurations, muffling any attempts on the part of the energumen to speak.[76] Again, we must note that the dramatic enactment of domination and submission involved in these directives represents a forceful appropriation of hierarchical prerogatives: divine over demonic, male over female, clergy over laity.

Another memorable moment in the liturgy is the purification of the victim's clothing, described as follows:

> Then let the priest say the mass written below as devoutly as possible. When he is finished let him approach the possessed woman confidently and entirely without fear, and have her led to the right corner of the altar. He should have her undress her completely, and have her shameful parts covered with some linen. Then, taking some blessed water, let him pour it in the shape of a cross over the head of the possessed woman, and let her clothing be sprinkled with blessed water, and then they may be put on again by the possessed woman.[77]

The forced public stripping of an individual—particularly of a woman—may be viewed from several different perspectives. Humiliation is only the most obvious level of understanding, though its impact should not be underestimated. Though the woman's "shameful parts" remained covered, this was a society in which women's arms and legs, to say nothing of the belly and chest, were normally kept concealed. Such exposure likely would have carried a significant degree of social shame in a society that, like medieval Europe, de-

---

[76] BS ms. Clm. 10085, 33v.

[77] Deinde dicat sacerdos missam suprascriptam quanto devotius possit; qua dicta, accedat securus et omnino interritus, et faciat obsessam ducere ad dextrum cornum altaris, et ipsam totaliter exuat, et verenda eius faciat tegere aliquo lyntheo. Et tollens aquam benedictam fundat in modum crucis super capud obsessae; vestimenta eius aqua benedicta aspergantur, et obsesse reinduantur. BV ms. Pal. Lat. 794, 72v. See also BS ms. Clm. 23325, 7v, 24r.

manded high levels of modesty from its women. Beyond this most accessible interpretation, however, lie other valences. For clothing was, of course, the most important and visible indicator of social status in the Middle Ages, transmitting a complex set of cues about wealth, ancestry, marital status, religious status, and geographic origin.[78] Stripping the possessed woman of her clothing thus temporarily stripped her of the marks of her social rank and position, symbolically severing her from her social identity. At this high point of the ceremony, the demoniac could no longer be considered an independent individual as understood in medieval society—that is, as a body situated by ties to various communities and corporate entities such as family, class, neighborhood, and so forth. She was simply a highly sexualized, fallen woman inhabited by a fallen angel, a potent hybrid emblem of sin and disorder: Eve and the serpent combined.

REORDERING THE DISORDERED BODY

At this point, the attention of the exorcistic liturgy shifts to the physical shell of the demoniac. The body itself is envisaged in the texts as a battleground between the divine power deployed by the exorcist and the unclean power of the indwelling spirit. Thus the demoniac body is represented as a microcosmic figura of an ancient, macrocosmic conflict between God and the devil. These comparisons are explicit in the text. Typically, liturgical exorcisms are composed of series of conjurations that consistently return to this macrocosmic level. They present lists of doctrinal elements, of Christ's deeds on earth, of angelic hierarchies, of human saints, of the names of God, and of insults for the demon. In short, the whole of Christian history and its cosmological hierarchy is patiently invoked and placed in the service of reclaiming the physical territory of the demoniac body, bit by contested bit.

Holy Lord Father Omnipotent, eternal God, expel the devil from this person: from the head, from the hair and crown of the head, from the brain, from the forehead, from the eyes, from the ears, from the nostrils,

[78] Diane Owen Hughes, "Distinguishing Signs: Ear-Rings, Jews, and Franciscan Rhetoric in the Italian Renaissance City," *Past and Present* 112 (1986): 3–59; idem, "Le Mode femminile e il loro controllo," in C. Klapisch-Zuber, ed., *Storia delle donne: Il Medioevo* (Rome, 1990); idem, "Sumptuary Law and Social Relations in Renaissance Italy," in J. Bossy, ed., *Disputes and Settlements: Law and Human Relations in the West* (Cambridge, 1983).

from the mouth, from the tongue, from under the tongue, from the throat, from the neck, from the chest, from the heart, from the whole body, from all its members, from all its ancillary members inside and outside, from the bones and nerves, from the blood, from the senses, from the thoughts, from her speech and all her actions, from her youthfulness and from all her interactions, now and in the future, so that the power of Christ the Son of the living God for all time may work within this person, Amen.

Adjuration: I exorcize you, unclean spirit! I do not command you, nor my sins, but the immaculate lamb Christ, God and Son of God, commands you! The angels and the archangels urge you! The patriarchs and the prophets urge you! The apostles and the evangelists urge you! The martyrs and the confessors urge you! The virgins and all of God's elect urge you, in order that the arts of the devil might begone day and night, in this month and in this hour and in this moment. Give back strength to her members! Give back health to her soul! You will not tempt her, nor betray her to death! You will not appear in food nor in drink, neither in these places nor in any future places, neither while she is sleeping nor waking; nor may you move her mind, nor be an obstacle to this person seeking eternal life. Through he who is coming in the Holy Spirit to judge the quick and the dead and the world by fire, Amen.

Go out, therefore, most unclean spirit, from this manservant[79] of God just as God the Father omnipotent separated the heavens from the earth, the light from shadows, the truth from lies, good from evil, the sweet from the bitter. So you will be separated from him by the power with which Christ vanquishes you, which casts you forth, nor are you able to come in! May Our Lord Jesus Christ triumph and deliver you over, damned one, to eternal pains. Lord, may the grace of your piety descend upon us. ✠ I cross your head just as God crossed the sick in Canaan and Galilee! ✠ I cross your eyes in order that the devil might be expelled from them, he who wounds all your flesh! . . . Holy Lord Father Omnipotent, eternal God, through the imposition of our hands, may the devil our enemy flee from the head of this person, from the hair, from the eyes, from the nose, from the ears, from the lips, from the tongue, from the neck, from the chest, from the stomach/womb, from the intestines, from the flesh, from the feet, from the tendons, from the heels, from the whole group of body parts.[80]

---

[79] The text has just made this switch: a moment ago, the pronoun *eam* was used.

[80] Domine sancte Pater omnipotens eterne Deus, expelle dyabolum ab homine isto:

This sort of circling movement of the text, verbally assaulting the devil and casting it forth from each member through the frequent repetition of lists of body parts, is a refrain that is found in all manuals of exorcism. Indeed, this element of the genre goes back at least to the eleventh century and may be found in pontificals dating from that time.[81] However, the extensive length of such lists of body parts, and the number of times they recur in the texts, grew exponentially over time. In general, the increasing amount of attention paid to the body was a significant element in the development of the exorcistic genre, even within the course of the fifteenth century.[82] This momentum toward the body highlights the degree to which demonic possession was understood as a physical invasion and disordering of the body's individual members.

Indeed, some texts were explicitly informed by the differential physiology of possession and thus refer to the devil's influence over the soul from within some other part of the body: "Leave altogether, do not presume to stay within or move about inside this body, or to hide in it, or to rage against it or the spirit or the soul or the clothing."[83] This passage is reminiscent of the idea

---

de capite, de capillis et vertice, de cerebro, de fronte, de oculis, de auribus, de naribus, de ore, de lingua, de sublingua, de gutture, de collo, de pectore, de corde, de toto corpore, de omnibus membris, de compaginibus membrorum suorum intus et foris, de ossibus et nervis, de sanguine, de sensu, de cogitationibus, de verbis et omnibus operibus suis, de iuventute et de omni conversatione eius, hic et in futuro seculo, ut operetur in eo virtus Christi Filii Dei vivi in saecula saeculorum. Amen. Adiuratio: Exorciso te, immunde spiritus! Non ego tibi impero, neque peccata mea, sed imperat tibi agnus immaculatus Christus Deus et Dei Filius! Urgent te angeli et archangeli! Urgent te patriarche et prophete! Urgent te apostoli et evangeliste! Urgent te martires et confessores! Urgent te virgines et omnes electi Dei, ut defficiant artes dyaboli die ac nocte, in mense et in hora atque momento. Redde fortitudinem membris! Redde anime sanitatem! Non temptabis eam et morti non tradas! Non apparebis in esca nec in potu, nec in locis presentis nec superveniens; vigilanti neque dormienti, nec mentem eius moveas nec impedias querentem vitam eternam. Per eum qui venturus est in Spiritu Sancto iudicare vivos, et mortuos, et saeculum per ignem. Amen. . . . Recede ergo, immundissime spiritus, ab hoc famulo Dei, sicut separavit Deus Pater omnipotens celum a terra, lucem a tenebris, veritatem a mendacio, bonum a malo, dulce ab amaro: sic eris separatus ab eo per potentiam qua te Christus vincit, qua te separet, nec unirere potes, sed vincat te Dominus noster Ihesus Christus, teque dampnatum eternis penis mancipet. Descendat ad nos, Domine, gratia pietatis tue. (Signo caput tuum sicut signavit Deus infirmos in Chana Galilee. (Signo ocluos tuos ut ex ipsis expellatur dyabolus, qui ledit omnem carnem tuam. . . . Domine sancte Pater omnipotens eterne Deus, per impositionem manuum nostrarum, refugiat inimicus dyabolus a capite huius hominis, a capillis, ab oculis, a naribus, ab auribus, a labiis, a lingua, a collo, a pectore, a ventre, ab intestinis, a carnibus, a pedibus, a cataneis, a calcaneis, ab universis compagibus membrorum. BN ms. Lat. 3501, 132r–33v.

[81] BV ms. Vat. Lat. 7701, 76r–77r.

[82] Franz, *Kirchlichen Benediktionen*, 2:583.

[83] Exeas omnino, nec stare nec discurrere, nec latere nec sevire in corpore istius et spiritu et anima aut vestimento presumas. BV ms. Vat. Lat 10812, 228r.

of demonic possession as taking place within the "open spaces" or "caverns" of the body, without the possibility of entrance into the soul. The unclean spirit can only tempt or harass the besieged soul from outside. Yet despite the fact that theologians continued to assert, in the fifteenth century, that demonic spirits cannot enter the heart and soul, some exorcisms do include the heart in their lists of body parts to be cleansed. This inclusion may simply reflect the extraordinarily comprehensive character of such lists, or it may be an example of the kind of loose language that Vincent of Beauvais noted in his discussion of how various spirits are said to be inside the heart: "[the devil] can be said to enter into it on account of the operations it performs within it: that is, seducing it by means of images and suggestions."[84] This convergence between the different textual genres of natural theology and liturgy underscores how very disciplined was the approach to spirit possession adopted by the ecclesiastical elite.

One manual advises writing a conjuration of the body in these words:

The three hundred seventy veins have long been filled with you.
And so have all two hundred forty bones![85]

This formula, coming at the beginning of one ritual, neatly defines the possession as entrenched within the deepest physical support systems of the victim. Although this particular conjuration appears to be unique, all the rites agree in placing the demons within individual members of the body. Indeed, as the decades of the fifteenth century passed, some exorcisms began to expand their simple lists of body parts into special paragraphs of conjuration for particular members of the body. These individual exorcisms, which took place while the demoniac was undressed, were directly addressed to the appropriate part of the demoniac body. The exorcist was directed to frequently cross the body with holy water on the appropriate parts, thus drawing the crowd's attention to these features. The formulae begin with special conjurations for the head and forehead, then move on to the senses:

To the eyes, say: Lord Father omnipotent eternal God, who created everything and who, through your only begotten son Jesus Christ, made a blind man see in order to manifest your glory. For you daubed his eyes with muck made from your spit. Daub the eyes of your maidservant

[84] *Spec. Nat.* 26.69, 1881.
[85] Trecente vene septuaginta diu sunt tibi plene. Simul ossa tanta sunt quadraginta ducenta. BS ms. Clm. 10085, 2v.

N. . . . so that she may look at you with her exterior eyes and mind; and so that, once healed from the obsession of the devil and all his infestations, she may understand . . . and praise you alone, who are coming to judge the quick and the dead, and the world by fire.

To the nose: Lord, holy Lord, holy Father omnipotent eternal God, who bestowed five exterior senses to perceive your majesty . . . grant, we beg, through your goodness and mercy, that this your maidservant N. might perceive the scent of your sweetness and be healthy in mind and body, and let the wickedness of evil spirits be expelled so that she might serve you in full freedom. Through Our Lord Jesus Christ, your Son.

To the ears: Lord Father omnipotent eternal God. You gave ears to men for receiving the Word of your Son, Our Lord Jesus Christ . . . Grant, we beg, that the ears of this, your maidservant N., might be open without any blockage from Satan and that she may be freed, with the evil of demons cast out from her, and might receive your words with honor and praise to you . . . Through Our Lord Jesus Christ, your Son, who lives and reigns with you.

To the mouth and tongue: Lord God omnipotent Father, who through the wisdom of your Son and with the Holy Spirit founded the universe, and placed humanity, the last creature, first among all the other creatures, and gave him speech so that he might offer you praise, cleanse the mouth and tongue of this maidservant N., so that she may freely offer you praise without any hindrance from Satan. Through he who is coming to judge the quick and the dead, and the world by fire.

To the neck. . . .

To the chest say the prayer: Lord Jesus Christ, who is one with the Father and the Holy Spirit, and who, in memory of your Passion, willed that the chest of a Christian should be imprinted with a cross at baptism, sign with your grace the chest of this your maidservant N. . . . Through he who is coming to judge the quick and the dead, and the world by fire.

To the shoulders. . . . *To the arms.* . . .

To the womb: Lord Jesus Christ, who willed to be incarnated in the most holy virgin womb of your mother Mary for the purpose of redeeming us, grant the liberty of your mother's womb to this your maidservant N., so that, having been freed through the intercession of your mother, she might receive purity in mind and body, and might possess you alone. Who is coming to judge the quick and the dead, and the world by fire.

To the knees. . . . To the feet. . . .

When these things are finished, let the clothing be blessed, and when the verse *Si iniquitates* is reached, then make the sign of the cross on each part of the clothing with salt and water that has been blessed.[86]

The choice of which body parts were singled out for this special treatment is significant. The senses merit particular attention, as does the womb. The former emphasis may be related to contemporary ideas about spiritual physiology and demons' use of the senses for entrance points into the body and for sending forth temptations; the latter testifies to an association between

---

[86] *Ad oculos, dic:* Domine Pater omnipotens eterne Deus, qui cuncta creasti et per unigenitum filium tuum Dominum nostrum Ihesum Christum caecum illuminasti, ut tua manifestaretur gloria. Nam luto quod fecisti ex sputo tuo linisti oculos suos; lini oculos famule tue N. propter tuam magnam pietatem . . . ut te oculis exterioribus ac mentis possit intueri et ab obsidione dyaboli et cunctis infestationibus suis te solum intelligat . . . et te collaudat. Qui venturus est iudicare vivos, et mortuos, et saeculum per ignem. *Ad nares:* Domine sancte Domine sancte Pater omnipotens eterne Deus, qui per quinque sensus exteriores tuam dedisti percipere maiestatem. . . . da, quaesumus, propter ipsam benignitatem et misericordiam tuam ut haec famula tua N. odorem suavitatis tue sano percipiat corpore atque mente, et expulsa nequitia spirituum malignorum, tibi plena serviat libertate. Per Dominum nostrum Ihesum Christum Filium tuum. *Ad aures:* Domine sancte Pater omnipotens eterne Deus. Quia percipiendum verbum filii tui Domini nostri Ihesu Christi, aures hominibus dedisti . . . . Da, quaesumus, propter misericordiam maiestatis tue, ut huius famule tue N. sine impedimento Sathane aures sint aperte, et exclusa ab ipsa malignitate demonum, liberata percipiat verba tua in laudem et honorem . . . . Per Dominum nostrum Ihesum Christum Filium tuum. Qui tecum vivit et regnat. *Ad os et linguam:* Domine Deus omnipotens Pater, qui per sapientiam Filii tui cum Spiritu Sancto universam condidisti et hominem postremam creaturam inter alias creaturas proposuisti cui sermonem contulisti, ut tuam laudem proferet, emunda os et linguam huius famule N. ut libere laudem tuam proferre possit absque Sathane impedimento. Per eum qui venturus est iudicare vivos, et mortuos, et saeculum per ignem. *Ad collum . . Ad pectus dic oratio:* Domine Ihesu Christe qui unum est cum Patre et Spiritu Sancto, qui ad memoriam tue passionis pectus christianum hominis cruce ad baptismandum infigere voluisti, consigna tua gratia pectus famule N. tue, . . . Per eum qui venturus est iudicare vivos, et mortuos, et saeculum per ignem. *Ad humeros . . . Ad brachia . . . Ad ventrem:* Domine Ihesu Christe, qui pro nobis redimendis utero sacratissime matris tue virgine Maria incarnari voluisti, da huic famule tue N. libertatem ventris matris tue, ut ipsa liberata per intercessionem tue matris mentis et corporis capiat puritatem et te solum possideat. Qui venturus est iudicare vivos, et mortuos, et saeculum per ignem. *Ad genua . . . Ad pedes . . .* Quibus finitis, benedicantur vestes, et cum perventum fuerit ad illum versum, "Si iniquitates," tunc fiant cruces ad singulas partes vestimentorum cum sale et aqua benedicta. BS ms. Clm. 23325, 24r–25v. Similar specific conjurations may be found in a manuscript footnoted by Franz, *Kirchlichen Benediktionen*, 2:583 n. 6, continuing onto the bottom of page 584.

women and demonic possession that is so thoroughgoing that the structure of the individually exorcized body is, once again, gendered female. This composite entity is a peculiarly feminine hybrid.

THE CHURCH TRIUMPHANT

The scripts of exorcisms consistently move from the particular to the universal, from the microcosmic to the macrocosmic, from the indexical situation at hand to the broad compass of the divine plan. Thus a prayer to God for aid in expelling the demon slides into a series of insults and name-calling that emphasize the historical role of the devil as the Ancient Enemy of the human race, from the Garden of Eden onward. Such insults also, as noted above, emphasize the collusion of the feminine and the demonic in responsibility for primordial sin. Nevertheless, the demon must be cast out of its assumed body, even as Lucifer was cast out of Heaven.

I humbly beg that you deign to lend me some help against this most wicked enemy and unclean spirit, so that wherever it hides it will swiftly come out and depart once it hears your name. He commands you, devil, who decreed that you be cast down from the zenith of the heavens to the center of the earth. He commands you, who commanded you to get thee behind him. Hear, then, Satan, and have fear. Depart, vanquished and prostrate, in the name of our Lord Jesus Christ. You, then, most wicked Satan, enemy of faith, deceiver of the human race, inventor of death, avoider of justice, generator of wrath, root of evils, kindler of sins, seducer of men, traitor of peoples, inciter of envy, origin of avarice, cause of discord, arouser of sorrows, master of demons![87]

This figural series of associations spirals outward from the specific request for aid to a description of the enemy that names, and therefore controls him.

[87] Supplex exposco ut michi auxilium praestare digneris adversus hunc nequissimum inimicum et immundum spiritum, ut ubicumque latet, audito nomine tuo, velociter exeat et recedat. Ipse tibi imperat, dyabole, qui te de supernis celorum in inferiora terre demergi praecepit. Ipse tibi imperat, qui te retrorsum redire iussit. Audi, ergo, Sathana, et time, victus et prostratus abscede in nomine domini nostri Ihesu Christi. Tu, ergo, nequisssime Sathana, inimice fidei, deceptor generis humani, mortis repertor, iustitie declinator, ire artifex, malorum radix, fomes vitiorum, seductor homini, proditor gentium, incitator invidie, origo avaritie, causa discordie, excitator dolorum, demonum magister! BV ms. Vat. Lat. 10812, 226v. See also BN ms. Lat. 3501, 131r.

All of human history is bound up with the wickedness and deceptions of demons: the expulsion of the spirit is one small victory against the impressively malicious credentials of the unclean hosts. The irruption into the body of the demoniac is preceded by its irruptions into the course of human history throughout the passing of the centuries.

Another naming tactic present in some exorcisms exploits the language of poisonous and stinging animals. Here the invocations of the demon focus upon the noxious aspects of its aggression. Before God, "the serpent withers and the dragon flees; vipers are silent and toads suddenly are controlled; the scorpion is extinguished, and the asp is driven away. The cave has nothing harmful inside, and all poisonous and formerly rather fierce and upstart animals . . . are weakened."[88] The devil and his legions of "apostate angels"[89] are the origin of all sin and sorrow.

By contrast, an impressive array of allies may be invoked on the side of God and the exorcist: "Lord Jesus Christ, expel all infestation of the Enemy from this, your man or maidservant . . . God of the angels, God of the archangels, God of the prophets, God of the apostles, God of the martyrs, God of the confessors, God of the virgins . . . deign to bestow your aid upon us against this most wicked spirit, so that, wherever it is hiding, it may swiftly go out and leave after hearing your name."[90]

If by chance one encounters a particularly stubborn demon, one must be patient. A persistent exorcist can tire a demon out with conjurations and threats like these: "If you have not [obeyed], I will repeat thousands of conjurations. I will compel you to enter into the depths of the foulest shit, and there you will be bound with burning chains that are most strong and unbreakable. There you may await the day to be feared, the day of judgment, the dreadful day."[91] Another rite warns that the exorcist may need to persist

[88] Serpens inanivescit et draco fugit; silet vipera, rubetha statim compescitur; scorpius extingwitur; regulus minatur et spelongus nichil noxium aperature, et omnia venenata et adhuc ferociora et repentia animalia . . . inanivescunt. BS ms. Clm. 24932, 11r.

[89] BV ms. Pal. Lat. 794, 70v. The phrase is part of the exorcism that is written into the margins of the book, on the bottom few lines.

[90] Repelle, Domine Ihesu Christe, ab hoc famulo/la tuo/a, omnem infestationem inimici . . . Deus angelorum, Deus archangelorum, Deus prophetarum, Deus apostolorum, Deus martirum, Deus confessorum, Deus virginum . . . nobis auxilium tuum praestare digneris adversus nequissimum spiritum, ut ubicumque latet, audito nomine tuo, velociter exeat et recedat. BN ms. Lat 3501, 130v–31r. The text gives both male and female endings in a vertical arrangement at the end of gender-specific words; I have rendered this with a slash.

[91] Si non fueritis ego repetam millefies conjurationes et compellam vos intrare in vilissimam stercoris profunditatem, et ibi colligati cathenis igneis firmissimis et indissolubilibus, ibique diem metuendum, diem iudicii, diem tremendum, expectabitis. BS Clm ms. 10085, 8v.

in his task for seven days of constant ritual, with the victim in a state of fasting. If this is not sufficient the exorcist should continue for an additional twelve days, being sure that the victim eats only unleavened bread and fish, with blessed salt and water mixed with all food. She should be sure not to take anything that heats the spirits in the blood, like wine or beer; she should eat only once per day; and she should sleep in a place sprinkled with holy water. To prevent recurrences, for a year afterward she should not eat bread, and on Sundays should avoid fruit, freshly killed meat, or freshly fermented beer. Yet another exorcism in this collection advises that in extreme cases one might wish entirely to submerge the victim in exorcized water.[92]

Liturgical exorcisms are rife with apocalyptic themes. The imagery of demonic submission is drawn largely from the Revelation to John, and the contest over the demoniac body is framed by echoes of demonic victory in the past and assurances of divine victory in the future.

> This maidservant of God, N., is off limits to you and your companions and all your rebel angels, unclean spirit. I adjure you now, therefore, by the advent of our Lord Jesus Christ, that you cut yourself off and go out from all body parts of this maidservant of God, N.: from her head, from her hair, from her neck and upper back, from her shoulders, from her arms, from all her members, from the three hundred sixty body parts. . . . You are adjured and constrained by the power and the name him of whom John said in the Apocalypse: I saw a man sitting between two candelabra . . . Therefore, cursed devil, damned to eternal burning, what will you do when the king of eternal glory comes, terribly, in the clouds of the sky, with great power and majesty, with an army of angels and archangels and with the full power of the heavens? Then all the mountains will ignite like wax, the fields will flash, the heavens will expand, and all men will appear in the clarity of his gaze. Where will you flee from his face? Where will you conceal yourself? Where will you withdraw yourself, unclean spirit? Where then will you be able to hide, before the wrath of God when he comes to judge the quick and the dead?[93]

---

92 BS ms. Clm 10085, 23r, 34r.

93 Interdicitur tibi et sodolibus tuis et omnibus angelis tuis contrariis haec famula Dei omnipotentis N.: nunc ergo adiuro te, immunde spiritus, per adventum Domini nostri Ihesu Christi, ut talias te et exeas ab omnibus membris istius famule Dei N.: a capite, a capillis, a collo et humeris, a scapulis, a brachis, ab omnibus membris suis, a trecente sexaginta membris . . . Adiuratus atque constrinctus per virtutem et nomen eius, de quo Iohannes in Apokalipsi dixit: Vidi virum sedentem inter candelabra duo . . . Ergo, maledicte dyabole,

Indeed, the medieval mental construction of the demoniac as a category was intricately knotted up with the increasingly apocalyptic frame of mind of the Later Middle Ages. The perception that the number of demoniacs was expanding was understood to be an indication of the renewed power of Satan in this world, which in turn was a sign that the End Times were drawing near. Not only was demonic influence percolating throughout the whole world in a diffuse, insidious way, but the devil's minions increasingly were able to reach into the very physical structure of the Church and the body of its adherents. Manipulating the course of world affairs through the deception, torment, and possession of human individuals, the devil extended his influence as relentlessly as the sinuous approach of an autumn mist. Yet paradoxically, any extension of the devil's power also was held to signal his ultimate doom. His very triumph prefigures his undoing, for if the increased number of demoniacs were an indication that Judgment was drawing near, then so too was the final conflict—in which divine victory was certain. Thus exorcisms could well ask where Satan could hide himself before the face of He who would judge the quick and the dead: then, dissimulation and concealment within the bodies of believers will no longer be possible. The fulfillment of the End Times will be the devil's greatest humiliation as well as his greatest triumph.

For a community imbued with a Christian sense of history, these were powerfully evocative phrases. The Christian narrative of individual experience is situated within a grander narrative of salvific history which has a specific beginning (Creation), a central plot development (Christ's life: Incarnation, Passion, and Resurrection), and a definite end (Last Judgment).[94] The outline of the entire story is known in advance: it only remains for the plot to be fulfilled in this world. Thus an increase in demoniacs signifies a certain progress within this narrative, a measurable turning of the pages that brings history closer to the story's end. Yet the tale is also figural: retold on a reduced scale in the unfolding of many briefer events. The exorcism's invocation of cosmic war and apocalypse is echoed at a more pragmatic level in the struggle over the demoniac's body.

---

eterna combustione dampnatus, quid futurus eris quando ipse rex eterne glorie terribiliter veniet in nubibus celi, cum potestate magna et maiestate, cum exercitu angelorum et archangelorum et in omnibus virtutibus celorum? Tunc omnes montes ardebunt sicut cera, campi fulgurabunt, celum amplificabitur et omnes homines apparebunt in conspectu claritate eius. Quo fugies ante faciem eius? Ubi te celabis? Ubi te abscondes, immunde spiritus? Ubi tunc pateris latitare ante iracundiam Dei, cum venerit iudicare vivos et mortuos? BV ms. Pal. Lat. 794, 79v–80r.

94 Stephen Crites, "The Narrative Quality of Experience," *Journal of the American Academy of Religion* 39, 3 (1971): 291–311.

And now, may you be adjured by the providence of the Father's and the Holy Spirit's counsel. . . . By the mystery of the Incarnation of the son of God. By his obedience, by which he deigned to take on human nature, accepting the miserable form of a slave in order to redeem us. By his holy circumcision. By the offerings of the three wise men. I also conjure you by the baptism and fasting of the son of God. . . . By his seizure and his flagellation. By the crown of thorns pressed onto his most holy head. By the willing suffering which he underwent from the treacherous Jews on the yoke of the cross. By the humility through which he sustained on our behalf illusions, opprobrium, spit, nails. . . . By his giving up the spirit, the power of which split the veil of the temple, and the graves opened up. . . . By his most bitter death. . . . By the power through which he broke open the inferno, entering to liberate his elect from there, and left it to the possession of you demons.[95]

The demonic seizure, suffering, symbolic death and entombment of the energumen are countered through the retelling of Christ's own redemptive tribulations. And so, too, Christ's final triumph over death represents a symbolic resurrection of the demoniac from death and entombment within her body, as her identity is overwhelmed by the indwelling demon's control.

The passage goes on, of course, to prefigure the divine apocalyptic triumph to come:

By the power that sits at the right hand of God the Father omnipotent, and thence to come and judge the quick and the dead. Therefore I adjure you, cursed spirits, by the arcane words or names El, Elon, Agla, and by all celestial, terrestrial, and infernal schemes. . . . And by the fearful Day of Judgment. By the living God, who is coming to judge the quick and the dead and the world by fire.[96]

---

[95] Adhuc sitis adiurati per providentiam consilii patris et spiritus sancti . . . per misterium incarnationis filii Dei. Per obedientiam eius, qua pro nobis miseris formam servi accipiens et induere humanam naturam ad redimendum nos dignatus est. Per sanctam circumcisionem eius. Per trium magorum oblationem. Item coniuro vos per baptismum et ieiunnium filii dei. . . . Per comprehensionem et flagellationem eius. Per spineam coronam suo sacratissimo capiti impressam. Per spontaneam passionem eius quam pertulit a perfidiis Iudeis in crucis patibulo. Per humilitatem qua sustinuit pro nobis illusiones, obprobrias, sputam, clavos . . . Per emissionem spiritus eius, per virtutem qua velum templi scissum est, monumenta aperta sunt. . . . Per amarissimam mortem eius. . . . Per virtutem qua fregit infernum intrans, et electos suos inde liberavit, et vos demones in possessionibus reliquerit. BS ms. Clm. 10085, 7v–8r.

[96] Per virtutem qua sedet ad dexteram Dei Patris omnipotentis, inde venturus est iudicare vivos, et mortuos. Ergo adiuro vos maledicti spiritus, per archana verba vel nomina

Christ's final victory is inevitable within the narrative of Christian history, as well as within the contested body of the demoniac. The exorcism simultaneously tells the story of the past (Christ), the present (the demoniac's struggle), and the future (End Times).

IDEOLOGY AND LITURGY

Exorcisms orchestrate a highly disciplined, hieratic message of authority and subordination, which they both enact and explain. The design of these texts, as liturgical scripts, is in accord with the broader context of late medieval ecclesiastical attempts to impose a universal religious order upon clandestine, rebellious, or simply indifferent sectors of society. This movement toward seeking a greater uniformity and centralization within the Church took on added urgency over time, in response to the challenges of reform movements and the crisis of the Great Schism. Read against this background, the appearance of liturgical exorcisms in the fifteenth century takes on an added significance: these rites represented a repeated performative enactment of ecclesiastical triumph over alternative sources of power or authority.

How can we understand the strategic employment of these rituals? The question is complex, in part because theorists of ritual have difficulty distinguishing between ritual and nonritual acts, and historians remain divided over the utility of this category. While some works of medieval scholarship have employed the notion of ritual to illuminating effect, others regard it as a misleading category of analysis and advocate shunning the word altogether.[97] In any event, one cannot study medieval rituals in the same way that anthropologists can study living cultures. As Phillipe Buc points out in a critique of historians' use of the category of ritual, "there can be no anthro-

---

El, Elon, Agla, et per omnem machinam celestium, terrestrium, et infernorum. . . . Et per tremendum diem iudicii. Per Deum vivum, qui venturus est iudicare vivos, et mortuos, et seculum per ignem. BS ms. Clm 10085, 8r–v.

[97] See, among others, Richard Trexler, *Public Life in Renaissance Florence* (Ithaca, N.Y., 1980); Edward Muir, *Civic Ritual in Renaissance Venice* (Princeton, N.J., 1981); idem, *Ritual in Early Modern Europe* (Cambridge, 1997); Geoffrey Koziol, *Begging Pardon and Favor: Ritual and Political Order in Early Medieval France* (Ithaca, N.Y., 1992); Frederick Paxton, *Christianizing Death: The Creation of a Ritual Process in Early Medieval Europe* (Ithaca, N.Y., 1990). Prominent critiques of the notion of ritual have been advanced by Philippe Buc, "Political Ritual: Medieval and Modern Interpretations," in Hans-Werner Goetz, ed., *Die Aktualität des Mittelalters* (Bochum, 2000), 255–72; idem, *The Dangers of Ritual: Between Early Medieval Texts and Social Scientific Theory* (Princeton, N.J., 2001).

pological readings of rituals depicted in medieval texts. . . . only anthropological readings of (1) medieval textual practices or perhaps (2) medieval practices that the historian has reconstructed using texts, with full and *constant* sensitivity of their status as texts."[98]

Buc's stringent insistence upon the bare textuality that governs our apprehension of medieval ritual is a highly consequential reminder. It directs our attention to the evanescent character of ritual: we cannot witness the ritual performance but only peruse textual records of these events, flattened onto the manuscript page. In the case of liturgical exorcisms, our texts are ideal forms that dramatize a dream of timeless hierarchy. For, "authority or directive is *intrinsic* to liturgical order."[99] That is to say, the liturgical scripts for exorcisms are an inherently coercive textual form. On the one hand, such liturgies intend to bring about some change in the scope and fabric of reality, to force an alteration in the balance of social, natural, or supernatural forces. On the other hand, composed liturgies of this type seek to compel the collusion of observers as well as of the demoniac who is conjured. The script aims to impose a constricted range of interpretations of the event, while uniquely legitimizing the authority of the officiant and the institutional hierarchy he represents. The conflation of woman and demoniac, for example, that is inherent in the script is confirmed by the exorcism's compulsion of the demoniac to speak in the demon's voice, lest the event never progress. This requirement acts as a self-legitimating aspect of the performance, a validation of its precise premises, conclusions, and power structure. Liturgical rituals, then, move within the interstices between the real and the ideal, to mingle ideas from Roy Rappaport with those of Jonathan Z. Smith.[100] The finely honed scripts of such ritual forms attempt to arrange things as their composers believe things ought to be, in contrast to the way things are; their precise stage directions attempt to impose an ideal linear order upon the unruly and disordered fragments of social reality. Indeed, exorcisms consistently present the proper order that embraces the entire universe as preexistent and unchanging, needing only to be brought down to the level of everyday reality. Hence to attend a liturgical exorcism, to watch its dramatization of hierarchical order presided over by the clerical officiant, is to im-

[98] Buc, *Dangers of Ritual*, 4.

[99] Roy Rappaport, "The Obvious Aspects of Ritual," in *Ecology, Meaning, and Religion* (Berkeley, 1979), 131.

[100] The idea of transmitting messages derives from Rappaport, "Obvious Aspects"; Jonathan Z. Smith, *To Take Place: Toward Theory in Ritual* (Chicago, 1987), discusses the tensions between real and ideal present in ritual performances.

pose its authority upon oneself, if only temporarily. To cede attention is to legitimate the authority of the performance and its officiant.

These points are particularly evident when we compare the use of liturgical exorcisms in the fifteenth century with the form of exorcistic healing that predominated earlier: miracles at saints' shrines. In essence, this alteration in practice represents a change from a peripheral to a more centralized form of control; from the charismatic *virtus* of a local saint's cult to the power of office; and from an emergent and communal process of interpretation to a textually based ideal that seeks to micromanage the process of interpretation. At the same time, the removal of exorcistic miracles from the still largely ungovernable realm of saints' cults was a step toward greater control over these local cults of veneration. Communities were encouraged to obtain the imprimatur of the papal curia before proceeding to the veneration of local holy men or women, and now the miraculous activities of local relics and tombs was partially curbed by the textualization of exorcism into a liturgical form and its appropriation by a clerical cadre of officiants. Thus the shift to liturgical exorcism was bound up with the discernment of spirits in more than one way: it regulated divine possession by disciplining the cult of the saints, and it regulated demonic possession by submitting its cure to the realm of Church specialists.

Exorcisms invariably attracted crowds. However, the crowd present at a liturgical exorcism was not meant to derive entertainment from the event, but to witness it and learn from it in an atmosphere of controlled devotion. The extent to which the didactic, canonical message of the ritual is privileged is evident in the careful precautions taken that there be no distractions: "Everyone should be solemn when the possessed person is conjured: no one should laugh, and no one should be going in and out while the conjuration is happening in the church. The dogs, especially, should be shut out. The women should be on their best behavior."[101] This highly controlled atmosphere heightens the authority of the clerical exorcist and the awe of the liturgical miracle to be enacted. The solemn sacramental tone of the occasion enacts a disciplining of the social body that precedes the disciplining of the body of the demoniac, as both are rendered submissive to and collusive with the dramatic process envisioned in the exorcistic script. Of course, this level of high dignity may not often have been achieved: the injunction "Everyone should be solemn . . ." attests not only to the ideal atmosphere for an exorcism but also to the sloppier reality that often must have prevailed.

---

[101] Fifteenth-century exorcists' manual quoted in Franz, *Kirchlichen Benediktionen*, 2: 572 n. 2.

Would the crowd have understood the liturgy and its teaching? The exorcisms are, after all, written in Latin, the language of the clerical class. There is some indication, however, that in performance the rituals may have been partially translated. Ecclesiastical officiants, used to translating or paraphrasing exempla and gospel readings in their preaching, were probably quite adept at impromptu renderings of Latin into vernacular languages. Some manuals even include extensive vernacular conjurations, and one manual directs the exorcist to translate the Latin portions at his discretion: "Next are read the prayers and conjurations that begin, 'Lord Holy Father omnipotent,' either all or part in German, according to the will of the exorcist. . . . Then the exorcist should . . . say the German conjurations written at the end."[102] Even in cases where Latin was used extensively throughout the exorcism, however, it is possible that the audience may have understood a substantial part of the proceedings. Many of the vernaculars were not yet so remote from Latin as to be unintelligible. Indeed, there are many instances in medieval texts wherein a formally illiterate person exhibits full understanding of Latin speech. The common saints' miracle, in which an unlettered woman suddenly finds herself able to understand Latin, may not be quite as breathtaking as it seems. For example, Osanna of Mantua's father prevented her from becoming literate, maintaining that it was dangerous and indecent for a woman to acquire such skills, yet she learned how to read and understand Latin, supposedly under the tutelage of the Virgin Mary.[103] Similarly, Humiltà of Florence, when requested to read in Latin by the prioress of her foundation, found herself able to do so even though she technically was illiterate.[104] Ida of Louvain was said to have miraculously acquired the sudden ability to translate Latin into the vernacular.[105] And when Lutgard of Aywières prayed to understand the Psalter, she was soon able to comprehend both the words and the meaning.[106] Beneath these "miraculous" acquisitions of knowledge, however, one might discern a simpler trend: perhaps Latin was not so difficult to understand for those used to hearing it.

The passive understanding of Latin is explicitly referred to in one exemplum collected by an anonymous cleric in the thirteenth century. The cleric

---

[102] Deinde leguntur orationes et coniurationes que sic incipiunt: Domine sancte pater omnipotens, cum Theutunico totum vel medium, secundum arbitrium exorciste. . . . Tunc exorcista . . . dicendo coniurationes Theutonicas in fine scriptas. BS, ms. Clm. 10085, 33v. The word *dicendo* in the second sentence is in a dependent clause attached to a subjunctive verb (*ponat*): therefore I have kept the translation subjunctive: "should say."

[103] *Vita B. Osannae Mantuanae, AASS*, June 4:578.

[104] *Vita S. Humilitatis Abbatissae, AASS*, May 5:208.

[105] *Vita Venerabilis Idae Virginis, AASS*, April 2:188.

[106] *Vita S. Lutgartis Virginis, AASS*, June 4:193.

heard the tale from an *illiteratus,* who in turn had heard it in Latin from a *literatus:* "He heard the tale from a literate man, but he remembered it in the words of his mother tongue, for he could not remember the vocabulary of the other language."[107] This *illiteratus* understood the gist of the story well enough to remember and recount it in his own language. Even more apropos is an anecdote from the twelfth century concerning a layman's understanding of a baptismal exorcism:

> They called him Eudo . . . an illiterate and stupid man, so crazed by the teasings of demons that, since in the French pronunciation they called him "Eon," he believed that it referred to his own self, when in ecclesiastical exorcisms it is said, "Through him (*eum*) who is coming to judge the quick and the dead, and the world by fire." Thus he was plainly a fool, who couldn't tell the difference between *Eon* and *eum,* but in an unusually amazing blindness he thought himself to be the Lord and the judge of the living and the dead.[108]

Eon may have had some trouble with his pronouns, but he seems to have understood the rest of this liturgy rather well. A less grandiose listener might have had no trouble at all understanding an exorcism, particularly in combination with the various gestures and formulaic repetitions so characteristic of these texts. The verbal meanings would also have been underscored by expressive gestures: pointing to parts of the body, crossing the victim, sprinkling her with holy water, having her change clothes, and so forth. Through these media, the teaching of Church doctrines on possession is communicated: the nature of unclean spirits as fallen angels within an eschatological view of history; the sinfulness of humanity and the omnipotence of God; the association of possession with sin and with women; and the corporeality of possession as a physical invasion. Most importantly, the liturgy teaches a lesson about proper hierarchy and subordination: God over the devil, clergy over laity, men over women. At the same time, the exorcisms establish a conflation between the respective terms of each pair, linking divinity with male clergy and forcing a convergence between the laywoman and the demon.

A recurrent theme throughout this book has been the impossibility of testing spirits from the external vantage point of the observer: to discern spirits

---

[107] Quoted in Jean-Claude Schmitt, "Le tradizione folkloriche nella cultura medievale," in *Religione, folklore, e società nell'occidente medievale* (Rome, 1988), 41.

[108] William of Newburgh, *Historia rerum Anglicarum,* ed. Howlett, Rolls Series, vol. 25 (London, 1884–85), 1:19.

is ultimately to discern bodies. This fact gained implicit recognition in the processes of social discernment, through which communities and ecclesiastics attempted to test the spirits of the possessed by scrutinizing their behavior and comportment. Similarly, the elaboration of physiological models of possession initiated an attempt by elites to naturalize the process of spirit possession into the deep systems of the body. With the compilation and augmentation of exorcistic formulae and their dissemination in manuals, this process of discerning bodies reached the field of liturgy.

Liturgical exorcisms' insistent focus on the body in all its detail not only re-ordered the body of the demoniac, however, they simultaneously re-ordered cultural conceptions of the body's role as the vehicle and horizon for possession. The didactic and demonstrative character of the exorcisms had important repercussions in the broader semantic field of possession. For within these ritual scripts, demonic possession was ever more strongly and uniquely defined as that which is entrenched in convulsive bodily dis-order, extreme physical disarray. Moreover, the language of the manuals suggests that the demoniac body generally was envisioned as female, even as the indwelling spirit made of the demoniac a hybrid entity of conjoined, fallen natures. The demoniac body at war within itself required direct ecclesiastical intervention in order to be put right.

What, then, of divine possession and the extreme physical behaviors that also were associated with this category? In the light of the exorcistic liturgy, could there still exist a divine disorder? For the testing of spirits presupposes a tension between the two possession categories: divine and demonic possession had long been constructed as near-identical states in their public manifestations. Hence the discernment of spirits involved an interdependent evaluation of both categories, and adjustments in one dictated the horizon of possibility for its companion category. Thus as exorcisms increasingly came to privilege the disordered female body as the site of exorcism, they helped shift the interpretation of possessed behaviors away from the ambiguous center ground they previously had occupied, poised between divine and demonic possession. The new meanings that these exorcisms attached to the possessed body thus held significance for both categories of possession. Women who incorporated foreign spirits and exhibited strange physical transformations as a result, were very strongly identified as the demonically possessed objects of these rites. Over the course of the fifteenth century, the texts thus helped to engender a definition of the possessed female body as exclusively demonic, whereas the alternate pole of representation for possessed women—the divinely inspired visionary—increasingly was marginalized and questioned. Within the economy of competing interpretations about the origins of individual spirit possessions, the balance was shifting toward an emphasis upon the demonic character of the possessed body.

As the next chapter shows, new definitions of sanctity that were being set forth in contemporary discernment of spirits treatises were approaching an identical theoretical position from the opposite direction. These tracts increasingly defined sainthood as incorporeal, not incorporative, and forged a newly exclusive definition of sainthood that targeted the cultural idiom of the divinely-possessed holy woman for exclusion. It is to these texts that I now turn.

CHAPTER SIX
TESTING SPIRITS IN
THE EFFEMINATE AGE

This is indeed an effeminate age, as Hildegard foretold.
— *Malleus maleficarum*

Consecrated by Hildegard of Bingen, the "effeminate age" was consummated by Henry Kramer, author of the *Malleus maleficarum*. For Hildegard, who originated the image, it signified a decline in the natural moral leadership of men that had begun around 1100. In a sign of impending apocalypse, clerics and other male leaders had become effeminate, abdicating their virile duty to guide women and the laity. The latter groups were forced, against their nature, to guide themselves, and inevitably would fall prey to false inspirations and false prophets. However, Hildegard also foresaw an eventual return to a "virile" order, in which proper gender roles would be restored. Yet nearly four centuries after the effeminate age was said to have begun, Henry Kramer regarded this prediction of a return to manly rule as an unfulfilled hope, a fading mirage. Rather, the Dominican inquisitor viewed his own late-fifteenth-century culture as slipping ever deeper into feminine quintessence, his society as dominated by womanly weakness, perversity, and malice. Above all, Kramer lamented, the current state of social degradation was encapsulated by the surge of witchcraft, the female crime par excellence. Hildegard of Bingen lived on the cresting swell of the "women's religious movement"; Henry Kramer on the breaking wave of the witchcraft craze. Yet the two were pulled together by the tidal undertow of this image, their invocations of cultural effeminacy.

The effeminate age was more than a rhetorical trope: it was a shorthand designation for a complex set of notions about "natural" gender roles and their inversion or transgression. Medieval observers like Hildegard and

Kramer used it as an economical allusion to the declining spirit of their age: a cultural imbalance toward femininity that contrasted sharply with the "virility" of the apostolic age, when even women were upright and manly. The shift in the status of these two observers, however, and of the significance gave to this phrase, provides an apt overview of the changes traced in this book. That the image of a *muliebre tempus* should persist from the twelfth to the fifteenth century as a signifier for the spirit of the age; that its meaning should be transformed from a caveat about male weakness to a fearful signifier of feminine collusion with demonic perversity; that it should be invoked by a famed female prophetess at its origin, and an infamous inquisitor at its terminus—all testify to important cultural transformations that have been the subject of the preceding chapters. Indeed, Hildegard was a necessary forerunner to Kramer. The so-called feminization of sanctity was a precondition, even a precipitating factor, in the feminization of the demonic that characterized the very end of the Middle Ages. The effeminate age was Janus-faced, looking back toward an efflorescence of religious roles for women and forward to an apocalyptic senescence. As such, it provides an appropriately ambivalent refrain for this final chapter.

The testing of spirits had been a preoccupation of western European culture since the late twelfth century, but the issue was forced to a climax by the tumultuous circumstances of the Church between 1378 and 1417: the Great Schism. Many believed that this crisis, too, had been foretold by Hildegard: a widely circulating, thirteenth-century compilation of her prophecies noted that the effeminate age would persist from about 1100 "until the great schism, when the bishops and all the clergy will be expelled from their places and cities."[1] Hildegard's prophetic *oeuvre* gained prestige when this prediction of a schism was uncannily fulfilled. Yet Hildegard's words also suggested, ominously, that the disaster of the schism was the logical outgrowth of feminine rule. Indeed, as we shall see, many prominent ecclesiastics agreed that the intervention of women into men's affairs was directly responsible for the schism and the apocalyptic unfurling it portended. Paradoxically, the schism thus both ratified Hildegard's prophetic claims and called into question the prophetic leadership of the effeminate age, which had led things to this point.

In this taut atmosphere, a magnified level of scrutiny was brought to bear upon laywomen who had gained reputations as divinely possessed. For the

---

[1] *Speculum futurorum temporum*, in Joannes Baptista Pitra, ed., *Analecta Sanctae Hildegardis Opera Spicilegio Solesmensi Parata* (Montecassino, 1882), 8:485; André Vauchez, "Le prophétisme médiéval d'Hildegarde de Bingen à Savanarole," in *Saints, prophètes et visionnaires: Le pouvoir surnaturel au Moyen Age* (Paris, 1999), 114–33; Katherine Kerby-Fulton, "Hildegard of Bingen and Anti-Mendicant Propaganda," *Traditio* 43 (1987): 386–99.

central claim characteristic of this idiom—direct inhabitation by the Holy Spirit—bypassed Church authority structures entirely. At a time of troubled debate about who and how many should lead the Church, the exaltation of women to an inspired leadership role seemed absurd to many ecclesiastics, a destructive distraction from the serious business of reordering the Church and Christian society. Furthermore, the characteristic behavior patterns of this "new" female sanctity—lay, ecstatic, prophetic, and imbued with a quotidian sense of the supernatural—lacked the imprimatur of an antique tradition, a criterion that steadily was gaining ground in the evaluation of sanctity. Indeed, these claims and behaviors seemed too intensely feminine, a degraded form of histrionic religiosity that lacked the virile vigor of the early Church. In sum, for many leading thinkers of the day, the preeminent symbol of the Church's recent moral and regimental laxity was the uncritical veneration of laywomen claiming direct divine revelation and the inhabitation of the Holy Spirit.[2]

Against the background of the schism, these concerns about female religiosity gave rise to the first explicit discernment of spirits treatises. These works described visionary women as self-dramatizing delusives who had managed to lead astray foolish, unwary men. Certain discernment writers explicitly linked this situation to Hildegard's effeminate age. All shared the sense that the Church had succumbed to a malaise in which both sexes were debilitated by weakness and frivolity. The remedy for this divisive situation, they agreed, was a return to sober, virile leadership and to proper, divinely instituted hierarchies. In sum, the discourse of discerning spirits was in large part a meditation upon proper gender roles and the questions of leadership and subordination they involved.

The coevolution of spiritual discernment and bodily discipline that this book has traced ultimately culminated in a backlash against divine possession as a religious idiom and against the effeminate age within which it flourished.

---

[2] Several articles by André Vauchez are of interest here: "La sainteté mystique en Occident au temps des papes d'Avignon et du Grand Schisme" and "L'Église face au mysticisme et au prophétisme aux derniers siècles du Moyen Age," both in *Les laïcs au Moyen Age: Pratiques et expériences religieuses* (Paris, 1987), 251–58, 265–76; idem, "Les théologiens face aux prophéties à l'époque des papes d'Avignon et du Grand Schisme" and "La naissance du soupçon: Vrai et fausse sainteté aux derniers siècles du Moyen Age," both in *Saints, prophètes et visionnaires*, 199–207, 208–20. See also Renate Blumenfeld-Kosinski, "Constance de Rabastens: Politics and Visionary Experience in the Time of the Great Schism," *Mystics Quarterly* 25, 4 (1999): 147–68; Jo Ann McNamara, "The Rhetoric of Orthodoxy: Clerical Authority and Female Innovation in the Struggle with Heresy," in U. Weithaus, ed., *Maps of Flesh and Light: The Religious Experience of Medieval Women Mystics* (Syracuse, 1993), 9–27.

Extreme actions and behaviors came to be viewed exclusively as indicators of evil. (We already have seen part of this process unfold in the last chapter's analysis of liturgical exorcisms.) Prophetic and visionary claims to authority were rejected as the basis for lay, feminine leadership, which now was viewed as having wrought chaotic disorder within the Church. The supernatural and somatic elements of laywomen's religious careers were rejected as new definitions of valid sanctity emphasized the incorporeal character of the saints and rejected the incorporative elements associated with the idiom of divine possession. This rejection, in turn, laid the foundation for an exclusivist interpretation of women who displayed extreme behaviors as demonically motivated. From there, it was but a short step—both chronologically and conceptually—to the formation of the witchcraft stereotype.

THE EFFEMINATE AGE IN ACTION

The number of laywomen canonized in the Middle Ages is six. Of those six, four were contemporary or "new" saints who lived between the twelfth and the fifteenth centuries. Of those four, two were visionaries or inspired women. Of those two, one had to be canonized, then recanonized, and canonized yet a third time before her halo was set firmly in place.

Despite the expanding numbers of women claiming divine inspiration and prophetic prerogatives, Brigit of Sweden and Catherine of Siena were the only such women to be sainted in the Middle Ages.[3] Thus the ideal of feminine leadership through divine prophecy can hardly be said to have received the imprimatur of the Church. Indeed, Brigit and Catherine provoked significant hostility from highly placed ecclesiastics who, questioning their suitability as models for the faithful, continually attempted to impede their canonization.

The fact that both women intervened in the sphere of ecclesiastical politics by urging the Avignon popes to return to Rome was a central point of contention. On the one hand, their familiarity with popes and other highly placed ecclesiastics granted Brigit and Catherine a prestige seldom known to women visionaries. On the other hand, the fact that the papal return to Rome ultimately led to the Great Schism was troubling to many observers. These events seemed to fulfill Hildegard's prediction of effeminate leadership resulting in a schism. At the same time, the schism raised questions about the

---

[3] André Vauchez, *Sainthood in the Middle Ages*, trans. J. Birrell (Cambridge, 1997), 369.

source of Brigit's and Catherine's visionary claims: would the inspiration of the divine spirit lead to the confusion of Christendom? Was it not more likely that the Ancient Adversary was once again using the frail sex as an agent of disorder? Would the End Times soon follow?

Not surprisingly, the language that Brigit's and Catherine's opponents employed in their attacks was the rhetoric of discernment. The Swedish widow and the Italian tertiary frequently recur as examples fueling the debate over the testing of spirits as it entered its most vigorous phase of textual production, in the late fourteenth and early fifteenth centuries. A brief sketch of the careers of these two women will lend depth to the discussion to follow.

On July 23, 1373, Brigit of Sweden died in Rome. This wealthy, aristocratic widow and mother, whose ecstatic trances led her to convey hellfire-and-brimstone prophecies about the debased state of the Avignon Papacy, inspired a scalding controversy that persisted for five decades after her death.[4] Indeed, so very divisive was her cause, Brigit was canonized no less than three times, in 1391, 1415, and 1419, by three separate pontiffs.[5] In effect, Brigit became the first test case for the discernment of spirits, for her death initiated an intensive debate at the highest levels of ecclesiastical culture over whether she was a true saint who prophesied in God's voice or a herald of the Antichrist possessed by the devil—and how one might tell the difference.

Brigit was the first laywoman even to be considered for canonization whose claims to sanctity were primarily visionary in character.[6] Indeed, her vivid prophecies already had been examined for demonic influence during

---

[4] An important starting point for the controversies over Brigit after her death is Eric Colledge, "*Epistola Solitarii ad Reges*: Alphonse of Pecha as Organizer of Birgittine and Urbanist Propaganda," *Mediaeval Studies* 18 (1956): 19–49.

[5] Vauchez, *Sainthood*, 255.

[6] Earlier advocacy for representatives of the new feminine, incorporative idiom of sanctity, such as the cause of Margaret of Cortona, brought before the Holy See in 1325 by the commune of Cortona, had not even resulted in a local enquiry. André Vauchez and Joanna Cannon, *Margherita of Cortona and the Lorenzetti: Sienese Art and the Cult of a Holy Woman in Medieval Tuscany* (University Park, Pa., 1999), 30–31. Recent successful canonizations of laywomen included Elizabeth of Thuringia and Hedwig of Silesia, but both were royal figures noted for their aristocratic charity rather than their visionary gifts. This emphasis upon a *beata stirps* was characteristic of Central European patterns of female sanctity. Gábor Klaniczay, "I Modelli di santità femminile tra i secoli XIII e XIV in Europa Centrale e in Italia," in S. Graciotti and C. Vasoli, eds., *Spiritualità e lettere nella cultura Italiana e Ungherese de basso Medioevo* (Florence, 1995), 75–109; idem, "Miraculum and Maleficium: Reflections concerning Late Medieval Female Sainthood," in R. Po-Chia Hsia and R. Scribner, eds., *Problems in the Historical Anthropology of Early Modern Europe* (Harrassowitz, 1997), 49–73; Vauchez, *Sainthood*, 253–55. Brigit's cause, too, was aided by her noble background, yet the question of her inspiration remained controversial because of her possessed behaviors, that is, her ecstatic, visionary, and prophetic qualities.

her lifetime by a panel composed of the archbishop of Uppsala, along with three other bishops, a master theologian, and an abbot.[7] Eventually, an apologetic treatise written by the theologian Master Matthias became solidly wedded to Brigit's book, appearing in the earliest redaction of her materials compiled with a view toward canonization and in all Latin editions, both manuscript and printed, since then.[8] In it, Matthias defends Brigit's truthfulness (she is not possessed by a "spirit of untruth"), humility (she is not seeking glory), and divine inspiration despite her female sex.[9] Thus a pattern of anxiety that Brigit might be a false prophetess and minion of the devil, rather than an inspired prophetess of God, was underway long before the real possibility of her canonization could arise. Indeed, Brigit herself engaged in a great deal of auto-discernment of her visions and revelations, frequently expressing concern that she might have fallen into a deceptive snare of the evil one disguised as an angel of light. She was said to have feared that the foreign movements she sensed in her heart—and which her spiritual director claimed to be able to see from outside her body—were a diabolic illusion, but eventually she accepted them as indicative of the interior incorporation of Christ.[10]

Such self-doubts did not, however, impede Brigit from arrogating to herself a leadership role in the affairs of Christendom. In an exemplary fulfillment of Hildegard's prophecy of an effeminate age, Brigit persistently complained about a lack of leadership and strength on the part of the ecclesiastical hierarchy. Her intense dissatisfaction with the leadership of the Church from Avignon rather than from Rome led her to engage in a protracted campaign—extending through the papal reigns of Clement VI, Urban V, and Gregory XI—for the return of the papal curia to the Eternal City. Brigit's interference in this matter rested on her claims to direct celestial visions and revelations, which she believed exalted her, though a woman, to a position of influence. Speaking directly in God's voice, Brigit acidly complained to Clement VI that he had abdicated his proper pastoral role and instead become a "killer of souls" and "worse than Lucifer."[11] When Urban V

---

[7] Carl-Gustaf Undhagen, ed., *Sancta Birgitta Revelaciones Book I, with Magister Mathias' Prologue*, Samlingat Utgivna an Svenska Fornskriftsallskapet, ser. 2, Latinska Skrifter (Uppsala, 1978), 7:1, 47.

[8] Carl-Gustaf Undhagen, "Special Introduction," in Isak Collijn, ed., *Acta et Processus Canonizationis Beate Birgitte*, Samlingar Utgivna av Svenska Fornskriftsallskapet, ser. 2, Latinska Skrifter (Upsalla, 1924–31), 1:38.

[9] Collijn, *Acta Canonizationis Birgitte*, 1:231, 232, 234.

[10] Arne Jönsson, *Alfonso of Jaén: His Life and Works, with Critical Editions of the* Epistola Solitarii, *the* Informaciones *and the* Epistola Servi Christi (Lund, 1989), 137.

[11] The Latin is excerpted in Colledge, "*Epistola Solitarii,*" 22.

was elected Clement's successor, Brigit continued her campaign, on one occasion transmitting a revelation so wrathful that Cardinal Beaufort, her messenger, dared not deliver it, once he had perused its contents. Urban finally did return the curia to Rome, but only for three years, a fact that must have frustrated the Swedish prophetess. She met with Urban twice during his Italian sojourn, hoping to persuade him to make the move permanent. When Urban finally departed for Avignon, she predicted a painful death for the pontiff, a prophecy that swiftly was realized. However, Brigit may have been encouraged that the new pope, who took the name Gregory XI, was none other than Cardinal Beaufort, who had been so awestruck with her earlier prophecies. She corresponded with him in the last year of her life, but she did not live to see Gregory's permanent return of the curia to the Eternal City.

Brigit was not the only woman visionary to attempt to force a return of the papal court to Rome. The virgin recluse Catherine of Siena, who died of self-imposed starvation in 1380, claimed to be fully possessed by the spirit of God. She recounted to supporters her vision of mystical marriage to Jesus, in which she became joined with him in one spirit as human spouses were joined in one flesh. Her heart, too, was "made one heart" with his. As a result of this deep and intimate union with God, Catherine also claimed to bear Christ's stigmata and wedding band on her body, though these marks remained invisible to all eyes but her own.[12] In addition, Catherine exhibited many classic possessed behaviors, engaging in the harshest possible fasts, entering prolonged trance states, prophesying, complaining of demonic harassment, and weeping frequently. She also, like Brigit, claimed the right to a feminine leadership role that extended to the counseling of popes through prophetic revelation.

Like Brigit, Catherine was a fulcrum for debates and dissent during her lifetime: her hagiography is brimming with defenses of her spiritual gifts against detractors who murmured that she was a simulator of sanctity if not demonically possessed.[13] In 1374 she was examined for signs of demonic possession or of false sanctity by a panel of Dominican theologians at the General Chapter meeting in Florence.[14] Yet rumors about Catherine continued to be rampant, so much so that on a trip to the papal curia in Avignon during the summer of 1376, three highly placed prelates came to examine her.

[12] *VCS*, 908.

[13] *VCS*, 933–43 is a particularly sustained defense, but the issue is present throughout the vita.

[14] Vauchez, "L'Église face au mysticisme," 267.

Their hostility was provoked not only by Catherine's possessed behaviors but by her continual insistence that God had revealed to her that Gregory XI must return to Rome. They observed that Gregory granted Catherine several audiences, during which he listened to her closely. Their visit thus was designed to limit Catherine's feminine influence in the virile world of papal politics. As a witness later described their interrogation of Catherine,

> They said, "You are but a worthless little female (*vilis femella*), yet you presume to discuss such subjects with our Lord Pope. . . ." They asked her very many terribly difficult questions, in particular about those trances of hers and about her unique way of life. In addition they asked, since the Apostle says that an angel of Satan can transfigure himself into an angel of light, how could she recognize if she were deceived by the devil? And they said many other things and posed other questions. In sum, there was a protracted disputation.[15]

When on 17 January 1377 Gregory XI did return to Rome, Catherine widely was credited as significant influence on his decision,[16] though Brigit too was viewed as having contributed to the move. Indeed, many of Catherine's letters to Gregory survive, some of which adopt quite a domineering tone. "I am begging you, I am *telling* you to come!" she writes in one missive. In another she demands, "This is His will, father. . . . Since he has given you authority and you have accepted it, you ought to be using the power and strength that is yours. If you don't intend to use it, it would be better and more to God's honor and the good of your soul to resign. . . . See to it, as you value your life, that you are not guilty of irresponsibility."[17] An iconographic motif developed of Catherine leading Gregory XI out from the city of Avignon and then into the city of Rome (fig. 23). In her Dominican robes, Catherine walks before the pope's white palfrey as he follows her and fulfills her prophetic urgings. In reality, Catherine did not travel with the pope's entourage, but the way she is depicted literally leading him suggests the role she played in the imaginations of some contemporaries.

Yet when Gregory died a scant fifteen months after the return, on 27 March 1378, the Great Schism was the immediate result. The selection of

[15] CPCS, 269.

[16] For background on the schism, see Walter Ullman, *The Origins of the Great Schism* (London, 1948); Richard Trexler, "Rome on the Eve of the Great Schism," *Speculum* 42, 3 (1967): 489–509. For contemporary testimonies on Catherine's role, see CPCS, 430 ff.

[17] Catherine of Siena, letters 63 and 71, in *The Letters of Catherine of Siena*, trans. S. Noffke (Binghamton, 1988), 202, 222.

Figure 23. Pope Gregory XI led by Catherine of Siena. On the right, we see Gregory XI leaving Avignon; to the left, he enters Rome to return the papal curia to the Eternal City. In both scenes Catherine of Siena, dressed in the typical Dominican garb of a black cloak over a white robe, leads the way. The painting thus depicts a moment that Catherine's supporters regarded as a triumph, but which others viewed as a prelude to the Great Schism. Panel painting by Girolamo di Benvenuto, late fifteenth century. Siena: Museo della Società di Esecuzioni di Pie Disposizioni. Photo courtesy of Scala/Art Resource.

Urban VI as Gregory's successor was contested three months after the fact by the college of cardinals, who now favored a different candidate. This second Pope took the name Clement VII and moved into the papal palace at Avignon. Since both candidates claimed the prerogatives of the papal tiara, they and their successors reigned simultaneously for nearly forty years (until 1417), the "Urbanist" faction from Rome and the "Clementine" party from Avignon. Catherine of Siena died two years after Gregory's return (still declaiming the legitimacy of Urban) and her posthumous reputation, along with Brigit's, was lastingly affected by these highly politicized events. Thus was fulfilled Hildegard's prophecy of an effeminate age leading to a great schism.

Devotees of Brigit and Catherine immediately began preemptive moves to vouchsafe the divine inspiration of their prophetesses, and by extension, of the Papacy's return to Rome and the legitimacy of the Urbanist obedience. Each woman had powerful supporters, as well as opponents. Brigit's spiritual director, Alphonse of Pecha, moved to Rome in order to devote himself to her canonization. He produced a treatise designed to cleanse Brigit's spotted reputation and thus to promote her cult. The *Letter of a Solitary to Kings* analyses the discernment of spirits in Brigit's case, concluding that she can only have been divinely inspired and thus that her prophetic interventions were guided by God. Not surprisingly, the *Letter* also has been termed a piece of "Urbanist propaganda" because of its attempt to rehabilitate Brigit's (and thereby Urban's) names, as both by now were regarded as precursors to the Great Schism.[18] Not surprisingly, it was a pope of the Roman obedience, Boniface IX, who canonized Brigit for the first time in 1391. Presciently, Alphonse complained of those who doubted Brigit of Sweden's divinely inspired leadership on the basis of her sex alone.

> Since . . . the theory and practice of discerning and rightly judging visions and spirits is (what a shame!) found in few people lately, therefore many, like blind men blundering along in this regard, would rather condemn simple and saintly persons out of hand (*ex arrupto*). . . . They especially condemn . . . the female sex as heedless and flighty both in capacity and in reputation, and therefore as unworthy of receiving divine visions or prophecies.[19]

These words were themselves prophetic, as we shall see. A similar defensive textual production made on behalf of Catherine of Siena appeared somewhat later within the schism period, in 1412. Penned by Catherine's ardent devotee Tomasso Caffarini, the *Little Supplementary Book to the Longer Legend of the Holy Virgin Catherine of Siena* defends Catherine's trance behaviors, extended fasting, prophecies, and stigmata as divine, rather than diabolic, in origin.[20] Indeed, Catherine's order, the Dominicans, was determined to procure her a halo so that they, like the Franciscans, might have a stigmatic saint. Though the Roman Pope Gregory XII ordered a canonization inquiry for Catherine, conducted between 1411 and 1416, she was not canonized until long after the schism was resolved, by the Sienese pope Pius II in 1461.

Those who were skeptical of Brigit and Catherine, by contrast, tended to regard the Urbanist wing as beholden to malign female leadership, which they placed at the origin of the schism. No more preeminent example of the

---

[18] Colledge, "*Epistola Solitarii*."

[19] Alphonse of Pecha, *Epistola Solitarii*, in Jönsson, *Alfonso of Jaén*, 119–20. For context, see Colledge, "*Epistola Solitarii*."

[20] Thomas Antonii de Senis Caffarini, *Libellus de supplemento legende prolixe Virginis beate Catharine de Senis*, ed. Iuliana Cavallini and Imelda Foralosso (Rome, 1974).

effeminate age could be imagined: men, having become weak and effeminate, had abdicated their responsibilities and instead turned to the leadership of weak laywomen who had raised themselves up through prophetic authority. The result of this role inversion was devastating disharmony that cried out for renewed vigilance in the discernment of spirits.

Not coincidentally, three leading thinkers on ecclesiastical politics during the schism produced the most significant treatises on the discernment of spirits in the forty years between 1383 and 1423. Henry of Langenstein, professor of theology at the University of Paris (and later the University of Vienna), published the earliest discernment text about five years into the schism, in 1383, when it had become clear that the situation would soon not be resolved. This was *On the Discernment of Spirits*.[21] Langenstein's works were widely read in the Parisian circles frequented by Pierre d'Ailly and his student Jean Gerson, who produced the remainder of the relevant treatises during this period. D'Ailly composed two subtly barbed tracts, both titled *On False Prophets*, one before 1395 and the other around 1410–13.[22] D'Ailly's student Jean Gerson made three main contributions: *On Distinguishing True Visions from False*, composed in 1401; *On the Testing of Spirits*, composed in 1415 at the Council of Constance as an analysis of Brigit of Sweden; and *On the Examination of Doctrines*, composed in 1423, five years after the end of the schism.[23]

---

[21] For more on Langenstein, see Anna Morisi Guerra, "Il silenzio di Dio e la voce dell'anima: Da Enrico di Langenstein a Gerson," *Cristianesimo nella storia* 17 (1966): 393–413; Vauchez, "Les théologiens face aux prophéties"; C. G. Heilig, "Kritische Studien zum Schriften der beiden Heinriche von Hessen," *Römische Quartalschrift* 40 (1932); F. W. E. Roth, "Zur Bibliographie des Heinricus Hembuche de Hassia," *Zentralblatt für Bibliothekswesen* (Leipzig, 1888); Lynn Thorndike, *A History of Magic and Experimental Science*, 5 vols. (New York, 1934), 3:473–510.

[22] The treatise now titled "Tractatus II" probably was the first in order of composition, dating from before 1395. See Laura Smoller, *History, Prophecy, and the Stars: The Christian Astrology of Pierre d'Ailly, 1350–1420* (Princeton, N.J., 1994), 100–101, 191 n. 92. Both treatises are published in Louis Ellies Dupin, ed., *Joannis Gersonii Opera Omnia*, 5 vols. (Antwerp, 1706), 1:497–604. A biographical sketch of d'Ailly is in Bernard Guenée, *Between Church and State: The Lives of Four French Prelates in the Late Middle Ages*, trans. A. Goldhammer (Chicago, 1991), 102–258.

[23] A chronology of Gerson's works may be found in Palemon Glorieux, "La vie et les oeuvres de Gerson: Essai chronologique," *Archives d'histoire doctrinale et littéraire du Moyen Age* 18 (1950–51): 149–92; and idem, *Introduction générale*, in Palemon Gloreieux, ed., *Jean Gerson: Oeuvres complètes*, 10 vols. (Paris, 1960–66), vol. 1. Paschal Boland, *The Concept of Discretio Spirituum in John Gerson's "De Probatione Spirituum" and "De Distinctione Verarum Visionum a Falsis"* (Washington, D.C., 1959), includes a translation of the two texts; however, the commentary that follows must be used with caution by the historian. For a biographical sketch and selected translations (including *DVVF*) see Brian McGuire, trans., *Jean Gerson: Early Works* (Mahwah, 1998). See also idem, "Late Medieval Care and Control of Women: Jean Gerson and His Sisters," *Revue d'histoire ecclésiastique* 92, 1 (1997): 4–

Gerson's writings have attracted the most attention, and with good reason. Gerson played a leading role in the debates at the Council of Constance, which met between 1414 and 1418 in an attempt to mend the schism. Moreover, Gerson's writing style was considerably more colorful than those of Langenstein or d'Ailly. When addressing the questions of discernment and the "new sanctity," Gerson adopted a lively—and, over time, increasingly polemical—tone that makes for vivid reading. He spiced his writing with contemporary examples of false saints, and these pungent anecdotes do much to clarify his concerns. Yet if Gerson's rhetoric was showy, his ideas were neither unique (he was influenced by both Langenstein and d'Ailly) nor particularly effective in molding the consensus of his own generation. If the discussion to follow highlights Gerson, it also emphasizes his indebtedness to d'Ailly and Langenstein, and the contributions of all three thinkers to elaborating a definitive discourse of discernment for the first time.

THE FRUITS OF EFFEMINACY

The Great Schism lasted so long that it began to seem like a permanent state of disarray rather than a temporary confusion. For medieval people, the obfuscation of the lines of ecclesiastical hierarchy and authority was frightening. Because all ecclesiastical authority emanated from the pope as vicar of Christ, the schism threatened to destabilize the whole clerical hierarchy. The "conciliarists" even argued that the Church should be led by councils, rather than by a monarchical pontiff.[24] Indeed, things declined further in 1409, when the Council of Pisa attempted to heal the split, but only resulted in the

---

37; Catherine Brown, *Pastor and Laity in the Theology of Jean Gerson* (Cambridge, 1987); John Morrall, *Jean Gerson and the Great Schism* (Manchester, 1960); Guerra, "Silenzio di Dio"; Brian Caiger, "Doctrine and Discipline in the Church of Jean Gerson," *Journal of Ecclesiastical History* 41, 3 (1990): 389–407; Dyan Elliott, "Seeing Double: John Gerson, the Discernment of Spirits, and Joan of Arc," *American Historical Review* 107, 1 (2002). I also am indebted to Nancy McLoughlin for sharing her unpublished essay "For the Sake of the University of Paris: The Targets of Gerson's Condemnations at Constance." Francis Oakley suggests a more complex relationship between Gerson and d'Ailly than a simple master-student bond in "Gerson and d'Ailly: An Admonition," *Speculum* 40, 1 (1965): 74–83. C. Roth, *Discretio spirituum: Kriterien geistlicher Unterscheidung bei Johannes Gerson* (Wurzburg, 2001), came to my attention too late for me to take into account.

[24] Francis Oakley, "Natural Law, the Corpus Mysticum, and Consent in Conciliar Thought from John of Paris to Matthias Ugonius," *Speculum* 56, 4 (1981): 786–810. For a contemporary defense of pontifical preeminence, see Heiko Oberman et. al., *Defensorum obedientiae apostolicae et alia documenta* (Cambridge, Mass., 1968).

debacle of three papal contenders. The Church, long viewed through the organic metaphor of a well-composed body, suddenly had become a bicephalous, and then a tricephalous monster, a classic image of demonic disorder. As one contemporary complained, "Innovations engender discords. . . . Thus we are witness to a hydra that is flourishing, and continually developing: at first it was two-headed, now it has become three-headed. . . . It is no longer one schism, but several stemming from one."[25]

Henry of Langenstein, too, was concerned about the deleterious effects of innovation. He connected the schism with the proliferation of new feast days, however. In 1382 Henry set down his thoughts on novelty and schism in a work titled *Advice for Peace: On the Union of the Church*. Arguing that canonizations of new saints ought to be curtailed, Henry asked several rhetorical questions about how the schism might be related to dangerous innovations: "Look, is it right for there to be such a number and variety of religious orders? . . . Is it right that Urban V, Brigit of Sweden, and Charles the Duke of Brittany should be canonized, notwithstanding the excessive multitude in the numbers of saints? Is it fitting that the feasts of such new saints be celebrated yearly just like those of the principal apostles?"[26] Surely, Henry mused, the leadership of individuals like Urban, Brigit, and Charles of Blois (a royal saint who died on the battlefield in 1364)[27] did not live up to the ancient exemplars of righteousness found in the apostolic age. Henry's thoughts culminated in an extravagant image of inversion, in which the wise cower under the tyranny of the weak, the fatuous, and the ignorant: "Again, think: is it all the same for fools to be on top, and the wise at the bottom? For the young to rule and elders to serve? For the ignorant to discuss complexities, while the knowledgeable dare not speak?"[28]

The proliferation of new saints and new religious observances was linked, in Henry's mind, with a lack of proper order, a reflection of the apocalyptic world turned upside-down. Though himself faithful to the Urbanist obedience, Henry nevertheless deplored the exaltation of Brigit and Urban as holy. The ascension of women to the pinnacle of Christian spirituality; the vener-

[25] Palemon Glorieux, "Moeurs de Chrétienté au temps de Jeanne d'Arc: Le traité *Contre l'institution de fêtes nouvelles* de Nicolas de Clémenges," *Mèlanges de science religieuse* 23, 1 (1966): 26. For background, Christopher Bellitto, "The Spirituality of Reform in the Late Medieval Church: The Example of Nicolas de Clamanges," *Church History* 68, 1 (1999): 1–13.
[26] Henry of Langenstein, *Consilium pacis de unione et reformatione ecclesiae in concilio universali quaerenda*, in Dupin, *Joannis Gersonii Opera*, 2:839.
[27] André Vauchez, "Le Duc Charles de Blois et le culte des saints rois Breton du haut Moyen Age," in *Saints, prophètes et visionnaires*, 151–61.
[28] Henry of Langenstein, *Consilium pacis*, 839.

ation of contemporaries above the ancient apostles, martyrs, and confessors; the granting of prestige and authority to the foolish and the laity, in detriment to the clerical elite—all struck him as alarming signals of innovation and therefore of decline. Above all, Henry's negative musings on Urban V and Brigit within this treatise devoted to the schism suggests that the idea of a pontiff showing deference to a woman struck him as a disturbing example of inverted leadership—Hildegard's effeminate age in action, so to speak.

Indeed, it is likely that Henry of Langenstein became familiar with Hildegard's prophecies right around this time. In late 1382 or 1383, Henry was staying at the monastery of Ebersbach, where the *Mirror of Future Times* had first been compiled.[29] In a letter composed in 1383, Henry extensively eulogized Hildegard as the "German Sibyl" who had prophesied the schismatic disorder in her apocalyptic vaticinations.[30] Giving a detailed précis of Hildegard's collected predictions, Henry emphasized that the effeminate age was a direct precursor to the appearance of the Antichrist. He observed that the age "is called effeminate because during it Christians have begun to be in an effeminately weak condition more than ever before, being light-minded, deceitful, sensual, petty, lovers of adornment, lustful, greedy, and vainglorious."[31] That very same year, Henry wrote *On the Discernment of Spirits*, which combined a discussion of the dangers of novelty with a description of the deceits of false saints who pursue extreme penitential practices and claim exalted leadership roles. This text constituted the first broadly theoretical discussion of discernment.

Other writers also were looking at Hildegard's prophecies and suggesting that the same false saints who had engendered the Great Schism might, perhaps even unknowingly, be evil heralds of the End Times. Pierre d'Ailly, in the earlier of his two treatises, *On False Prophets*, turned to the prophecies of Hildegard, noting that she had predicted that "the people [will be] seduced by the devil and his herald, who will come with a pale face and behaving with all sanctity."[32] These false prophets, suggests d'Ailly, would foment disruptions precisely like the Great Schism in order to seduce the Church away from the path of righteousness. "The art of recognizing hypocrites of this type . . . appears to be especially useful in modern times, since already there

[29] Guerra, "Il silenzio di Dio," 397.

[30] G. Sommerfeldt, "Die Prophetien der hl. Hildegard von Bingen in einem Schreiben des Magisters Heinrich von Langenstein (1383)," *Historisches Jahrbuch* 30 (1909): 46–61.

[31] Ibid., 54.

[32] Pierre d'Ailly, *De falsis prophetis II*, Louis Ellies Dupin, ed., *Joannis Gersonii Opera Omnia*, 5 vols. (Antwerp, 1706), 519. The quotation is originally from Hildegard's letter 48, in *PL*, 197:250. The letter also was included in the *Mirror of Future Times*, on which, see the first work listed in n. 1 of this chapter.

appears a decline of this kind within the Church: to wit, the division of the schism. This truly is to be feared, lest it be a preamble to the Antichrist."[33] Invoking Revelation 20:7–8 ("Satan will be freed and will seduce the peoples of the four corners of the earth, Gog and Magog"), d'Ailly continues:

> These peoples, that is, the aforesaid seducers who will be accepted by Gog and Magog, will first themselves be seduced by the devil under the appearance of sanctity, and then proceed to the other peoples. Using the same appearance of sanctity, simple Christians will be deceived by them, and thus through these seducers and those seduced by them, the people will be prepared for the coming Antichrist. . . . And it is no wonder if it is difficult for others to recognize the [underlying] cause of this [saintly] appearance, and the rebellion of these hypocrites, for indeed, they scarcely are recognized among themselves. . . . Many hypocrites consider themselves to be saints because of the immoderate human praise [they receive].[34]

D'Ailly's argument that the schism derived from hypocrites who consider themselves to be saints because of the incautious praise of others is very likely an oblique attack on Catherine and Brigit. (Indeed, resort to evocative obliquities, as we shall see, is a prime characteristic of d'Ailly's writing style.) For the interventions of these two women conformed closely to d'Ailly's conception of the sincere, yet deluded, false visionaries who sowed the schismatic seeds of the apocalypse. Indeed, he amplified Hildegard's description of the seeming sanctity of false prophets by depicting them as given to ostentatious penitential practices and immoderate possessed behaviors. Although some false saints may fast and "exteriorly macerate their flesh, sometimes even unto death" (as did Catherine, in fact), according to d'Ailly they do so for worldly rather than religious reasons. Similarly, such persons may engage in extended prayer vigils and exaggerated self-accusations in order to gain praise and respect, but really they specialize in "novelties and unusual things, inventing new superstitions under the appearance of religion."[35] The establishment of new forms of life or orders (like Brigit's Order of Vadstena) was

[33] D'Ailly, *De falsis prophetis II*, 517.
[34] Ibid., 522–23.
[35] Ibid., 519, 520. For an interesting letter condemning an innovation in religious life supposedly received by a woman through direct divine revelation, see Paul Schmidt, "*Amor transformat amantem in amatum*: Bernhard von Waging an Nicolaus Cusanus über die Vision einer Reformunwilligen Nonne," in John Marenbon, ed., *Poetry and Philosophy in the Middle Ages: A Festschrift for Peter Dronke* (Leiden, 2001), 197–215. My thanks to Barbara Newman for bringing this article to my attention.

an innovation to be resisted. Their simulated miracles are the ultimate hypocrisy: "they feign sanctity not only in their clothes and conversation, but even in their deeds."[36] Such demonstrations may seem impressive, but the wise man remains on guard against the seductive lure of exterior penitences.

More explicit on this subject was Jean Gerson, a pupil of d'Ailly's and an admirer of Langenstein. For Gerson, the uncritical veneration of new saints such as Brigit and Catherine was a symbol of the Church's recent effeminate degradation. Indeed, Gerson's *On the Testing of Spirits* was composed about Brigit of Sweden and the work adopts a frankly hostile tone. Gerson regarded the whole idiom of divine possession as too intensely feminine: self-dramatizing, histrionic, gossipy, deceptive, and futile. A recurring refrain of Gerson's discernment writings is a twinned critique of laywomen's pretensions to sanctity and of weak spiritual directors who foster the delusions of such women without appropriate discernment and scrutiny. "In the end," Gerson writes, "I think that the accumulation of greatest evils, which we are now enduring and experiencing with the schism, proceeds from this outbreak of lack of discernment."[37] Indeed, male assent to female leadership had wrought unparalleled devastation upon the Church, as Gerson writes in *On the Examination of Doctrines:*

Another warning follows on behalf of Superiors and especially for Doctors who are in charge of the lowly, particularly ignorant and illiterate silly women. They should be careful to whom such persons are given for oversight and example, lest [these directors] easily approve, by word or deed, the doctrines, miracles, or unusual visions of such women. . . . Gregory XI was a perceptive witness of this, though rather late. As he lay dying, holding the Body of Christ in his hands, he denounced such people in front of everyone. He told them to beware of those (either men or women) who speak about the visions of their heads under a pretense of religion. For he himself was led astray by some such and, dismissing the reasonable advice of his men, he dragged himself and the Church to the brink of an impending schism.[38]

When Gerson cautions against the doctrines or visions of "the lowly, particularly ignorant and illiterate silly women," and then mentions that some such persons led Gregory XI and the Church astray "to the brink of an impend-

---

[36] D'Ailly, *De falsis prophetis II,* 521.
[37] *DVVF,* 44.
[38] *ED,* 16.

ing schism," he is targeting Catherine of Siena and Brigit of Sweden.[39] "Dismissing the reasonable advice of his men," Gregory instead followed the unsound counsel of women. The schism was a consequence of male leaders' acquiescence to debased feminine frivolities, while scorning the sober advice of educated men.

These writers' insistence that women prophetesses like Brigit and Catherine were responsible for the schism fed into a classic discernment of spirits principle: Jesus' teaching that when false prophets arise in the End Times, "by their fruits shall you know them" (Matt. 7:16). This passage held the unequaled prestige of being Christ's own injunction in direct speech. All three discernment of spirits writers emphasized this point repeatedly: the fruits or results of a prophecy unveil its origins as either divine or demonic in character. Thus Henry of Langenstein counseled, "for inspirations whose origin is in doubt, let them be tested at their end point. Many times an outcome manifests what the origin hides. He who cannot judge his impulses at their origin, therefore, should investigate their end and fulfillment."[40] We may extrapolate from this passage some of the principles that underlay Henry's rejection, a year earlier, of Brigit and Urban V. Clearly the bicephalous Church was an avatar of destruction, disorder, and deception: this "end point" must have originated in demonic inspiration rather than divine illumination. To the degree that women like Brigit of Sweden exerted influence over the pontiffs involved in these events, they surely were acting as representatives of the devil. Similarly, Pierre d'Ailly explained that although "there is no art handed down in sacred scripture, through which one may sufficiently be able to know whether a prophecy was inspired by an evil spirit or by the Holy Spirit,"[41] yet "by their fruits shall you know them." And Gerson, too, highlighted the beneficent utility of visions and revelations as a primary means of judging their character. "If a miracle lacks any pious utility or necessity," he complained, "it should be suspected or rejected by that fact alone. . . . In our lifetime there has been a woman famed for such revelations, whom this sign, if I am not mistaken, shows to have been out of her mind."[42]

---

[39] Though this passage usually is associated with Catherine's name (see, for example, Brown, *Pastor and Laity*, 223), Colledge points out that Brigit could equally have been intended ("*Epistola Solitarii,*" 37 n. 108). Indeed, the Latin gives the plural form *tales* when discussing those who led astray Gregory, thus indicating that more than one person is at issue. The origin of the identification with Catherine is the Dupin edition of *ED*: Dupin, *Joannis Gersonii Opera*, 1:16.

[40] DS, 62.

[41] D'Ailly, *De falsis prophetis II*, 512.

[42] DVVF, 51.

The fact that the schism was so closely linked in these authors' minds to unregulated feminine prophecy was therefore a damning indictment. The principle of "investigating the fulfillment" of supernatural events demanded that prophecies resulting in the schism of Christendom be evaluated as diabolic. The outcome of Brigit's and Catherine's visionary interventions in world affairs was a patently demonic disorder. Hence feminine prophecy was proven to be false prophecy; the effeminate age, a demonic age.

THE TERMS OF THE CRITIQUE

While the discernment of spirits treatises produced during this period stemmed from concerns about the schism, they nevertheless took seriously the obstacles to an impartial judgment about spiritual inspiration. All three of the authors admitted that the project was fraught with complexities. Henry of Langenstein observed, "Since there exists such a multiplicity (*turba*) of spirits impelling man to his acts, it is rather difficult to discern which movements of the mind are from this or that spirit. Therefore blessed John well said, 'Do not believe every spirit, but test the spirits, to see whether they are of God.'"[43] Similarly, Pierre d'Ailly noted, "The Lord did not give us a doctrine by which to recognize [false prophets], that is, a doctrine that is particular, certain, and infallible. And this was for a rational cause. To wit: that in order to recognize them we must always be in battle against them, that is, in vigilance and watchfulness."[44] And even Jean Gerson conceded, in a classic tautology, "To test the spirits to see if they are of God, in a particular case, through a general and infallible rule or art, either cannot be done at all or can scarcely be done through human ability. This requires a gift from the Holy Spirit, which the Apostle called the discernment of spirits."[45]

These uniform confessions of fallibility help set an appropriate tone of humility. This was an important issue of bona fides for these authors, given that a critique of hubris was central to their message. Yet despite such protestations, Langenstein, d'Ailly, and Gerson did not shrink from identifying the precise characteristics of those whom they regarded as false prophets, false saints, and demonic heralds. They all agreed that certain claims and behaviors should raise red flags for vigilant testers of spirits.

[43] *DS*, 54.
[44] D'Ailly, *De falsis prophetis II*, 523.
[45] *PS*, 178.

To begin, demonic interference is particularly to be feared in cases where a person reports continual intimacy with the supernatural.

> A spiritual person is not to be quickly and easily believed, who continually labors at contemplating and fantasizing that every impulse, or any remotely unusual thing that happens, is the intervention of a supernatural spirit. Indeed, it seems that a person who has easy credulity in such things has a vain craving to be surrounded by supernatural revelation and miraculous motions. Moreover, there are some who can attain such gullibility and lack of judgment in this regard that every noise or tumult they hear around themselves or around others (something that often occurs from unseen dormice or cats or some such thing) they believe and immediately affirm to be the work of the devil.[46]

These caveats from Henry of Langenstein constitute one of the foremost complaints that skeptics of divine possession put forward: the very ubiquity of supernatural interventions into the lives of such individuals is inherently untrustworthy. Indeed, we have seen this identical grievance in the earlier letters of Venturino of Bergamo. To lay claim to constant temptation from demons is to regard oneself as an object of unusual cosmic concern. Conversely, to pray for constant revelations is to make presumptions about the divine willingness to intervene in one's life on an ongoing basis. In an amusing passage, Henry asserts that God is more likely to cherish a person who simply listens to his commands and fulfills them rather than one who "every hour pesters the ears of the Lord by interrogating Him about what he ought to do, and asking that He reveal this thing or that."[47] Obnoxiously insistent supplications for revelations are a form of hubris that tempt God.

Gerson grumbled with evident frustration that it was unseemly to believe that Brigit of Sweden "receives advice not only from angels but from God; and not only in cases of necessity, but almost constantly, in daily conversations."[48] In the introduction to *On the Testing of Spirits*, delivered before the Council of Constance, he noted that Brigit,

> claims commonly to receive visions from heaven, in which she is treated as a friend not only by angels but also by Christ and Mary, Agnes, and other saints, who talk with her as a bridegroom to his bride. Both alter-

---

[46] *DS,* 58–60.
[47] *DS,* 80.
[48] *PS,* 181.

natives—approval or rejection—are dangerous. To approve false and delusive and silly visions as true and solid revelations—what could be more unworthy, more foreign to this sacred Council? Yet, on the other hand, to condemn these things now, when they have been tested many times in varied ways by different nations (or so it is said), could produce no small scandal to the Christian religion, and a shock to the devotion of the people.[49]

Gerson's skeptical aside—"or so it is said"—reveals what he thinks of the so-called tests that have been applied to Brigit's continual "false and delusive and silly visions." Brigit's assertion of intimacy with Christ and the saints irked Gerson and struck him as unreasonable, much as it had bothered Henry of Langenstein some years earlier when he argued against her canonization. Indeed, Gerson went on to refer approvingly to Henry's call, in *Advice for Peace*, for the restriction of contemporary canonizations.[50] Since Henry had, in this text, explicitly counted Brigit among those whose sanctity he found doubtful, Gerson's reference must be viewed as another subtle way of expressing his own disapproval.

Indeed, Gerson wrote of the high likelihood of malign causes for visions in all his treatises. Gerson was conversant with the medical theories of his day, and he often pairs pathological with demonic causes as explanations for visionary phenomena, clearly preferring such mechanisms to a divine explanation. Thus in *On Distinguishing True Visions from False*, he writes, "One should attribute such visions to an injury of the imagination, and should worry about having some defect like the insane, maniacs, or melancholics. One should beware lest this has been given for a condemnation, because of the enormity of past sins, so that one may be led astray by delusions."[51] Alternately, in yet another text Gerson derided those who "excessively seek after spiritual consolations, and who murmur and get impatient in the absence of them," warning that such ingratitude can lead the soul to "whore itself away from God."[52] Lust for visions may easily end in demonic seduction.

A second area of contention that recurs throughout discernment of spirits treatises is a harsh indictment of extreme ascetic and penitential practices. Henry of Langenstein was the first to offer a warning against excessive asceticism, which in his mind was linked with the undisciplined fervor of those

[49] *PS*, 179.
[50] *PS*, 181. "Henry von Hessen" is another moniker for Henry of Langenstein.
[51] *DVVF*, 40.
[52] Jean Gerson, *De signis bonis et malis*, in Glorieux, *Jean Gerson: Oeuvres complètes*, 9: 164.

who are newly converted to the religious life. "They immediately desire to be the highest, and are impelled by a spirit of austerity that leads them into an excess of abstinence, vigils, hardships, contemplations, and prayers." Henry derides these people's claim to have left the secular world for the spiritual, for it is apparent that such persons lack the guidance of a rule and the structure of a broader community. Impelled toward extravagant asceticism, they are "perverted" by this "indiscreet and foolish, unremitting excess beyond the bounds of human capacity." Such persons, continues Henry, not only are mortal sinners, they are "quite hateful to God." To pursue such immoderate behavior is antithetical to human nature, which God endowed with reason precisely so that such repugnant excesses might be avoided. Indeed, Henry affirms that such individuals actually sin far more than those at the other end of the spectrum: people who are "religious only in name."[53] For not only does immoderate asceticism and contemplation drain physical strength, but its practitioners eventually lose all spiritual grounding and fall into a state of spiritual stupor. As a result, they follow only their own judgment, disregarding the better guidance of others; if not checked, they easily go insane or become enmeshed in demonic schemes.

Worst of all, since the austerity of these hypocrites impresses the common herd, they often achieve an undeserved reputation for sanctity that feeds their self-satisfaction. This in turn results in a tendency to be overly judgmental of others. Thus a vicious circle may form, in which a foolish person's lack of moderation receives positive reinforcement from the local community, which leads to an acceleration of the immoderate behaviors and the growth of hubris. At their worst, these people are characterized by smug pride and continual self-promotion: "they believe that because their life is inspired by God in all things, they are not permitted to err."[54] Such novelties, Henry asserts, add nothing to a true understanding of God, which is best found in the scriptures and in ancient exemplars of sanctity. The era of direct revelation is long over, and the false new saints should look to the old: "One can be aided in one's actions and understanding just fine by the things that God already has shown and bestowed upon humanity in the past. . . . It is not fitting—indeed, it is not necessary—that God should miraculously and recently interfere with his own handiwork, directing [his creation] with new revelations or the performance of new miracles."[55] Thus claims to direct revelations from

[53] *DS*, 66–68.

[54] The paragraph leading up to this was a paraphrase of *DS*, 70–72; the quotation is at 72. One wonders whether Marguerite Porete was in Henry's mind when he formulated this statement.

[55] *DS*, 78.

God are absurd, chiefly because they cannot add to the level of human understanding already gained by the ancient saints.

As we have seen, Pierre d'Ailly expressed similar misgivings about excessive vigils, fasting, prayers, and even miracles, for "false prophets can bring about false miracles through their magic arts, which are the same in appearance as true miracles wrought by true prophets through divine power." They "conduct fasts, superstitiously abstaining from certain common foods"; they "make up long, wordy prayers for the sake of human praise"; and (in ways that d'Ailly does not explain) they seek worldly riches through almsgiving. In addition, much of d'Ailly's second *False Prophets* treatise is taken up with warnings against facile credence in those who adopt a humble appearance and vile dress, comparing them to ravening wolves in sheep's clothing.[56] Such individuals may live in poverty, macerate their flesh, fast, pray, and give alms, all in an insidious imitation of divine sanctity.

Gerson followed his mentor and Langenstein in expressing identical sentiments, though with his characteristic flair for drama. Gerson illustrated the dangers of excessive penitential behavior with a picturesque exemplum drawn from his own experience, which merits quotation at some length:

> There are others who are pleased to follow their own feelings, and who walk within their own inventions. A most dangerous guide leads them; more accurately, their own opinion impels them. They torment themselves with excessive fasts; they protract their vigils; they disturb and weaken their brains with irrational amounts of tears. Meanwhile, they refuse to believe any warning and will not take any advice to behave more reasonably. They do not care to listen to or take counsel from learned men. . . . In respect to such persons, I say that they quickly fall for any demonic illusion. . . . Exercise special vigilance about anything they may announce to you about unusual revelations.
>
> A few months ago, while I was in Arras, I heard about a certain married woman with children who went without food—sometimes for two days, often for four days or more. Because of this she was admired by many people. . . . She was unable to offer any solid reason as to why she acted thus, except she said that she was unworthy to eat. She also admitted that she had not received this way of life from her confessor or anyone else. . . . I admit I was horrified and afraid. Nevertheless, hiding my feelings, I began to show her that these things were traps laid by

---

[56] D'Ailly, *De falsis prophetis I*, Louis Ellies Dupin, ed., *Joannis Gersonii Opera Omnia*, 5 vols. (Antwerp, 1706) 513, 519–20, 489–500.

demons, and that she was dangerously close to insanity. . . . Finally I urged her . . . to give up this foolish and stubborn fasting, and to do nothing unique without the advice of experienced men—especially since she was annoying her husband.[57]

For Gerson as for Langenstein and d'Ailly, penitential asceticism could be the beginning of a dark cycle spiraling toward excess, hubris, and insanity, especially if left unregulated by superiors. The woman of Arras, who neither submitted to a male confessor nor deferred to the wishes of her husband, the head of the household, was a tragic example of the fruits of a female arrogation of power. While she gained the respect of her peers, Gerson easily could see that she was enmeshed in a diabolic snare.

This leads to a final concern shared by these authors: the question of self-regulation. Among the novelties deplored by these authors was the attempt to regulate one's religious life by oneself. As Henry notes, most false saints, "altogether refusing to take the advice of good and more discreet men, or holding it of little account, remain incurable and totter from foolishness to foolishness until, finally, they go completely insane."[58] These individuals attain the height of irrationality in their stubborn insistence that they know best. Of course, this rhetoric thinly conceals a quite specific referent: these are expressions of distrust for lay religious movements, such as Beguines and Beghards, mendicant tertiaries, and recluses, above all. The woman of Arras exemplified this lay, domestic form of religious life, in which penitential excesses and possessed behaviors are pursued within the secular world. Monastic and clerical religious careers, by contrast, were structured so as to place individuals within a clear chain of command and *cursus honorum* for further advancement. The critique of self-guidance makes sense only when applied to lay religious movements and the numerous self-proclaimed visionaries they spawned. Indeed, we know that Gerson distrusted laywomen's religious movements in particular, precisely because they operated outside the sphere of clerical oversight: "the customs of Beguines and of other women living in little groups ought to be known, for among such women are found certain wicked doctrines and superstition."[59] While Gerson encouraged simple piety among the laity (like his sisters, who pursued a quasi-religious life in the

---

[57] *DVVF*, 42–43.

[58] *DS*, 70.

[59] Gerson, *Rememoratio agendorium durante subtractione*; the Latin is quoted in McGuire, "Care and Control of Women," 8 n. 14.

parental home), his vision of this lifestyle emphasized quiet contemplation under strict clerical scrutiny.[60]

Obedience to superiors was a theme of particular importance to Gerson, and he continually juxtaposed the poles of humble submission and stubborn pride. The proud person "relies on his own wisdom rather than being ready to submit to his superior's judgment, reason, and will."[61] Thus Gerson deftly transforms the question of discernment into one of obedience to the authority of the ecclesiastical hierarchy: failure to conform to the judgments of a superior is a sign of pride, and therefore of demonic delusion. In an echo of the lessons of the exorcistic liturgy, Gerson's works emphasize that the laity should be subject to the clergy, lower social strata to higher, wives to husbands, and women to men more generally.[62] We can further expand the thought with reference to Gerson's short 1415 tract titled *On Good and Evil Signs*. Despite its title, the text lists evil signs only; the work is likely Gerson's notes for *On the Testing of Spirits*. Here he identifies the foremost "evil sign" of false inspiration:

> One evil sign is to try to understand oneself on one's own, spurning the advice of others—as if one could understand oneself and one's actions better than anyone else! This sign is found among petty people, and it is all the worse when they seem to be humble. . . . Another sign similar to this is to neglect the evangelical rule of law and even of reason itself, and to attempt to guide oneself as if through miraculous inspirations and certain interior experiences.[63]

Those who abandon the ecclesiastical mandate for guidance can easily be persuaded by the delusion that their lives are directed by God through inaccessible visionary experiences. Gerson goes on to complain of those who, as a result of such self-regulation, exhibit an "unquiet fervor," "excessive scrupulousness," and "the presumption of divine aid," comparing these behaviors with the impurest of bodily effluvia: "fetid things like a menstrual rag or the little rags lepers use, which are made filthy through a continual flow of corrupt blood."[64] Gerson took the divinely instituted pastoral responsibilities of clergy seriously, and he expected that the laity would as well. Petty

[60] McGuire, "Care and Control of Women"; Brown, *Pastor and Laity*, 171–208.
[61] *DVVF*, 41–42.
[62] For Gerson's thoughts on hierarchy, see Brown, *Pastor and Laity*, 36–44.
[63] Jean Gerson, *De signis*, 162.
[64] Ibid., 163.

people who attempted to direct their own spiritual lives risked falling into the ultimate uncleanness of demonic ruses. Thus laypeople and other subordinates should not assume that they know what is best for themselves, but should comply with the directives of a clerical superior. Lacking obedience, even the performance of miracles is suspect, for, Gerson notes (in the spirit of d'Ailly, and with an alliterative rhetorical flourish), "Antichrist will be the most mendacious minister of miracles."[65]

CRITIQUING THE EFFEMINATE AGE

According to Langenstein, d'Ailly, and Gerson, certain characteristics of false saints and false prophets stand out above all others. The demonically inspired tend to be people who, in an inversion of proper hierarchical order, seek to exceed a lowly status by excelling in religious austerities and innovations that they design themselves in the absence of a strong clerical superior. They fast (sometimes unto death), they protract their vigils and prayers, they innovate, they revel in self-abasing acts of penitence, and they always seem to be crying. They allow their immoderate behaviors to escalate to the point that they fall prey to delusions of grandeur. At this stage, they feel themselves to be at the center of a swirl of portentous supernatural dramas: demons attack them, angels reassure them, the saints and even God himself console them as close friends. They receive visions and prophecies as ratification of their exalted status and do not hesitate to transmit these revelations to others. Indeed, they claim the right to counsel popes, to lead the leaders of Christendom.

This description is not gender-neutral. In fact, it describes in abundant detail precisely the kinds of possessed behaviors and leadership claims made by laywomen in this time period. Thus even when these texts leave aside Brigit and Catherine, and purport to adduce broad general guidelines for the testing of spirits, they read as gossamer-veiled indictments of women visionaries and the claims to inspired female leadership they represented. In short, discernment of spirits treatises are transparent critiques of feminine religiosity.

Perusing Langenstein's work, for example, one cannot avoid the conclusion that this author's rejection of immoderate asceticism as manifested in fasts, laments, and extended vigils, his dismissal of constant visions, and his

[65] *DVVF,* 42.

ridiculing of reports of continual demonic attack were crafted with women predominantly in mind. Henry's concern for inversions of social and religious hierarchies also clearly target women who attempt to lead others. *On the Discernment of Spirits* thus presents an exhaustive catalogue of possessed behaviors—the idiom of divine possession favored by women—as suspect signs in the testing of spirits.[66]

By contrast, when Henry presents positive signs in the discernment of spirits, the characteristics he finds most predictive of truly divine inspiration are weighted toward male clergy:

Just as the Lord gave human beings dominion and care over the animals, so he placed superior and more perfect people above the inferior and more imperfect people, so that they should care and provide for them, and direct them toward salvation in their actions and thoughts. . . . Therefore, if there is any doubt about whether someone's visions or miracles derive from a good spirit, one should look to the degree or level in the ecclesiastical hierarchy that they hold or held. In particular, consider whether he is a prelate, a bishop, or a doctor of the Church.[67]

If a cleric receives a vision or revelation, his reports are not to be dismissed lightly, for such individuals were placed by God at the forefront of the Christian community. Thus visions or miracles are likely to be genuine if they are received by an exalted individual such as a prelate, bishop, or doctor of the Church. Conversely, visions or miracles occurring among the "inferior and more imperfect people"—that is, the laity, including all women—are to be stringently examined and suspected. Implicit in Langenstein's formulation is the idea that for God to reveal secrets to the laity or to women would be to undermine His own hierarchy of perfection. Legitimately ordained clerics already are the chosen tools of God for the leadership of His worshipers; why, then, would God choose to work through a weaker vessel? The natural order instituted by God, suggests Henry, sustains the preeminence of the clergy

[66] Roughly a decade later in 1392, Henry composed a treatise refuting the apocalyptic prophecies of the hermit Telesphorus da Cosenza, who predicted a complex scenario of resolution for the schism involving war, three antipopes, and the ascent to the throne of Peter of an eventual "angelic pastor," who would initiate a thoroughgoing reform of the corruptions of the Church. Henry also denigrated the canonization claims of Pope Urban V. Thus although *On the Discernment of Spirits* must be read in part as a polemic against the possessed behaviors of women, Henry's overall concerns were broad in scope. Henry's treatise against Telesphorus is discussed in Vauchez, "Théologiens face au prophèties," 199–207.
[67] *DS*, 112–14.

in all religious enterprises, whether institutional or charismatic. All other declarations of authority must somehow justify their deviance from the divine distribution of power.

By contrast, Pierre d'Ailly may appear to be the most nonpolemical discernment writer to a modern reader. D'Ailly does not explicitly suggest, in either of his two *False Prophets* treatises, that one sex is more likely than the other to incarnate Antichrist's prophets. Yet d'Ailly clearly did suffer from fears about the effeminacy of his age, and worried both about the prominence of laywomen visionaries and of the weaklings who encouraged them. His indictment of extreme fasting, self-flagellation, and other penitential excesses suggests a particular concern with the religious conduct of laywomen and its apocalyptic repercussions in the form of the schism. However, if d'Ailly counted persons of both *sexes* among those being led astray by false prophets in these schismatic End Times, he identified only one *gender* for this faithless group: feminine.

Here we turn to an important passage in d'Ailly's later *False Prophets* treatise, dating from the second decade of the fifteenth century: "These false prophets, in order that their rapacity might be satisfied and that their malignity might not be perceived . . . travel around and run through different places. They are wanderers from place to place and they go from house to house. They especially go into the homes of silly women and of effeminate men."[68] This passage is dense with allusions that a modern reader easily may miss, but which contemporaries could not fail to understand. To begin, d'Ailly's words echo those of 2 Timothy 3:6–7, which counsels avoidance of proud and self-centered false prophets who, in the End Times, will "creep into homes and lead captive silly women burdened down with sins, women who are led by various lusts, always learning and yet never reaching true understanding." Thus d'Ailly's language, following scripture, invokes the project of discernment as part of the apocalyptic scenario, and places silly, sinful, lustful women at the forefront of those who abandon righteousness in order to follow false prophets. However, d'Ailly's paraphrase makes a noteworthy conceptual addition to 2 Timothy: the reference to "effeminate men," which does not appear in the biblical text. The inclusion of effeminate men ignites his apocalyptic image: not only do women follow false prophets (something to be expected of the weaker sex), but certain men, having lost their virile righteousness, meekly follow women into the train of the demonic herald.

D'Ailly goes on to offer several glosses on his revision of 2 Timothy. First, invoking traditional gender categories, he suggests that effeminate men are

[68] D'Ailly, *De falsis prophetis I*, 496.

analogous to silly women insofar as both are fundamentally "inconstant" or impressionable, and therefore easily seduced. Second, he speculates that effeminate men might more easily be led astray by women who are seduced by the Enemy directly, in a recapitulation of the Adam and Eve story. Finally, d'Ailly directly quotes Hildegard of Bingen denouncing the clergy's lack of pastoral care for the laity. The pronouncement foretells that this neglect and weakness on the part of effeminate men will force women to lead themselves, and that they will fall into demonic errors as a result. Here we are back to Hildegard's effeminate age, populated by emasculated men and independent women.

D'Ailly's language contains an additional clue that allows us to identify the silly women and effeminate men he had in mind even more precisely. The section of 2 Timothy he used—in particular the seemingly innocent phrase "those who go into homes (*penetrantes domos*)"—was commonly employed as a derogatory euphemism for the mendicant orders in the later Middle Ages.[69] The use of this phrase in such a way stemmed from the academic politics of the University of Paris in the mid-thirteenth century, torn by rivalry between seculars and mendicants. This competition coincided with a wave of apocalyptic speculation, and ultimately the two trends converged in a series of polemics penned by seculars against contemporary *pseudopraedicatores* ("false preachers") and *penetrantes domos*. These writings targeted the mendicant orders without explicitly naming them. As one scholar has pointed out, "considering their reputation as polemical attacks, the most startling feature of all these works is the almost total absence of any reference to the friars themselves."[70] Such a strategy permitted the authors of these texts (notably William of Saint-Amour, who pioneered the use of 2 Timothy in such a way) to criticize an accepted, even papally protected, group under the guise of historical exegesis. Over the subsequent centuries, the trope flourished in France and England, achieving its most famous incarnation in the corrupt figure of Sire *Penetrans Domos* in the apocalyptic vision of *Piers Plowman*.

There is no doubt that d'Ailly, himself a secular from the University of Paris, was familiar with this rhetorical tradition. Indeed, his treatise rather ostentatiously draws attention to the phrase *penetrantes domos* by embroidering upon it with additional images of vagrancy and wandering. (He also refers to this group as *gyrovagues*, another derogatory word for uncloistered reli-

[69] Penn Szittya, *The Antifraternal Tradition in Medieval Literature* (Princeton, N.J., 1986). I am much indebted to Nancy McLoughlin for bringing this reference to my attention. Kerby-Fulton, "Hildegard of Bingen"; Brown, *Pastor and Laity*, 73–78. See also below, n. 71.

[70] Szittya, *Antifraternal Tradition*, 18.

gious figures drawn from the Rule of Saint Benedict.) D'Ailly thus aligns apocalyptic false prophets with the mendicant orders: the itinerant "wolves in sheep's clothing" who appear saintly and self-abnegating but who secretly seek worldly honor. By extension, the "silly women burdened down with sins" whose homes these people go into can be identified as groups fostered by the mendicant orders in domestic settings: predominantly tertiaries and Beguines, who usually were placed under mendicant supervision.[71] Lastly, the "effeminate men" are those who ought to maintain a position of virile leadership, but who instead debase themselves to the level of silly women by following them into demonic error: men such as Gregory XI, who followed Brigit and Catherine into the apocalyptic disorder of the schism foretold by Hildegard. "The works of hypocrites," concludes d'Ailly, "are known by their fruits."[72]

We know that all three of Gerson's discernment treatises were composed as occasional pieces in response to specific cases of disputed inspiration among women. Gerson's best known work on discernment, *On the Testing of Spirits*, was presented on August 3, 1415, before the Council of Constance and was specifically concerned with Brigit of Sweden.[73] Earlier that year, Brigit's canonization had been defiantly reconfirmed by the latest pope of the Urbanist-Roman obedience, John XXIII. The delegates assembled at Constance, wishing to weigh in on all Church matters themselves, invited Gerson to address them on the subject of Brigit's visionary authority or lack thereof. Gerson was hostile to Brigit for several reasons beyond her implication in the start of the schism. For example, Brigit had favored the English side in the Hundred Years' War, a conflict that had touched Gerson personally. He would never return to Paris after Constance, for the Burgundians had deposed him of his chancellorship of the University and made it too dangerous for him ever to go home. In addition, Brigit's claims and behaviors fit all the characteristics of a delusive false prophet for Gerson: he viewed her

---

[71] Indeed, the association between mendicants and lay religious movements was so close that attacks on one often substituted for attacks on the other in the later Middle Ages. Jean-Claude Schmitt has argued that the polemic against Beguines in the Rhineland actually was a way of targeting the mendicant orders, and Nancy McLoughlin has pointed out that the arguments against lay visionaries in the discernment writings of Jean Gerson also functioned to undermine the mendicants. Jean-Claude Schmitt, *Mort d'une hérésie: L'Église et les clercs face aux béguines et aux béghards du Rhin supérieur du XIVe au XVe siècle* (Paris, 1978); Nancy McLoughlin, "For the Sake of the University of Paris." For documents restricting the connections between the two, see G. G. Meersseman, *Dossier de l'ordre de la pénitence au XIIIe siècle* (Fribourg, 1982).

[72] D'Ailly, *De falsis prophetis I*, 497.

[73] Glorieux, "Essai chronologique," 130.

as a spectacular instance of typically feminine overreaction. While Gerson did not explicitly call for Brigit's canonization to be blocked, he made his position abundantly clear from the outset, introducing the text with the skeptical rumination on Brigit's too-frequent visions of saints and angels, quoted above.

Gerson likely was selected to lead the discussion of Brigit at Constance because of his previous work on the testing of spirits. Some delegates may have been familiar with his *On Distinguishing True Visions from False*, composed in 1401 and also provoked by a laywoman's claim to visionary status. The case of Hermine of Reims, a widow who died of plague in 1396,[74] had been drawn to Gerson's attention by her spiritual director, Jean Morel, who had submitted her book of revelations to Gerson for judgment. These revelations, written down by Morel at Hermine's dictation, were dominated by the theme of unrelenting demonic temptation, with the hosts of Hell appearing in every guise imaginable, some sinister (flies, serpents), some appealing (kittens, a priest with a demonic Host). After what appears to have been a rather insistent correspondence from Morel, Gerson responded with a cautious letter sometime in 1401.[75] Confessing that he could find nothing manifestly unorthodox in Hermine's writings, Gerson nevertheless expressed unease and counseled Morel tightly to restrict the circulation of her text. The book, Gerson feared, could lead astray the simple masses. Gerson also indicated to Morel, in closing, that he might set down more extensive thoughts on the issues of discernment raised by Hermine's case. And indeed, Gerson soon composed *On Distinguishing True Visions from False*, partly in response to the issues raised by Hermine's case, as he explained in a later reminiscence: "Long ago, because of the accounts of certain men with a great reputation for merit, I was close to being led astray by a certain Hermine of Reims. I would have if, God willing, I hadn't moderated the tone of my own response. About that time I composed a brief text or single lecture, *On Distinguishing True Visions from False*."[76]

By this time, Gerson had come to regard Hermine's revelations as manifestly false, and he presented her case as an example of his own narrow escape from deception. Hermine's continual battles with demons who beat her, tempted her, and constantly tried to enter her body and possess her troubled Gerson and made him wonder whether the laity in general, and laywomen in particular, could be trusted to pursue a contemplative regimen, absent the

[74] Claude Arnaud-Gillet, ed., *Entre Dieu et Satan: Les visions d'Ermine de Reims (d. 1396)* (Paris, 1997), 21–27.
[75] For the Latin text, see ibid., 171–73; for the dating of the letter, 21–23.
[76] *ED*, 474. See also Arnaud-Gillet, *Entre Dieu et Satan*, 24–25.

strictures of a communal life, formal guidelines, and male oversight—all of which he recommended for his pious sisters.[77]

Gerson's final contribution to the discernment of spirits genre, 1423's *On the Examination of Doctrines*, cannot be linked with a specific woman's name, but as a reassertion and extension of his earlier thinking it too addresses the question of women visionaries explicitly. Brigit of Sweden had been canonized a third time, by the first post-schism Pope, Martin V, in 1419, a development that cannot have pleased Gerson given his muted, yet unmistakable hostility toward her in his Constance presentation. This final text links the schism to Brigit and Catherine's interventions into papal politics, in the rather grumpy complaint about Gregory XI quoted earlier.

It is striking how often Gerson returns to the theme of feminine debility and untrustworthiness. Indeed, this theme becomes significantly stronger over time. 1401's *On Distinguishing True Visions from False* entirely avoids systematic discussion of sex in the discernment of spirits—indeed, Gerson takes pains to include both Beguines *and* Beghards as the targets of his attack whenever he expresses his skepticism about lay religious groups. The best indication that Gerson already was concerned about women's claims to inspiration in particular is his use of anecdotal examples, like the fasting woman of Arras, which highlight female examples of false inspiration. Fourteen years later, in *On the Testing of Spirits*, distrust for self-proclaimed women visionaries is no mere subtext: it is a current that flows through the work with hydraulic force. Gerson now advances sex as an irreducible criterion of judgment in the testing of spirits. For example, a comment on the delusive extremism of the newly converted raises the specter of the fragile sex taking herself too seriously: "Find out if the person is a neophyte in their zeal for God, for the enthusiasm of a novice can quickly fall into deception if it lacks discipline—especially the young and women, whose passions are excessive, grasping, erratic, unrestrained, and therefore suspect."[78] Gerson goes on to complain truculently about those who secretly take pride in their own humiliations, penitential clothing, fasting, and virginity.

Even more interesting is a passage in which Gerson's sex-linked suspicions bubble to the surface of his self-consciously neutral prose. This is most evident in a section of the text that suddenly shifts, in a move reminiscent of contemporary exorcists' manuals, from the masculine pronoun *eum* (which he had employed earlier, as the neutral pronoun appropriate for a theoretical discussion), to the feminine *eam*.

[77] McGuire, "Care and Control of Women."
[78] *PS*, 180.

Be careful, whoever would act as a listener or an advisor to this kind of a person, not to applaud or praise *her* on this account, nor admire *her* as a saint worthy of revelations and miracles. Instead, be an obstacle! Challenge *her* sharply, reject *her* . . . so that it does not seem to *her* that *she* merits finding *her* salvation differently from the way other people do: through doctrine, the scriptures and the saints, and according to the dictates of natural reason.[79]

As in the case of the exorcists' manuals, the pronoun shift directs our attention to an important element of this debate: a reluctance to envision the dangerous, the delusive, or the demonic in terms other than female. Confessors and spiritual directors to women should harshly discourage their clients from aspiring to special graces, revelations, and consolations. Moreover, if she insists on describing such experiences, the conscientious male director will cut the conversation short, lest the devil be gratified by such a self-evident waste of time.

If the person is a woman, it is especially necessary to consider how she acts with her confessors and instructors, if she constantly breaks out in conversation, now under the pretext of frequent confession, now with extended narrations of her visions, now with some other topic of discussion. . . . If this preoccupation had no other detriment than an abundant waste of precious time, that still would be more than enough for the devil. Know, in addition, that a woman also has an incurable itching lust for looking and speaking, not to mention touching. . . . No one will be surprised if such people turn toward falsehoods and away from the truth, especially if these are women of the curious kind, about whom the Apostle says, "always learning yet never reaching the knowledge of truth." Where there is no truth, there necessarily is vanity and falsehood.[80]

Gerson here invokes the language of 2 Timothy, as d'Ailly had before him, but with greater boldness and specificity. This scourge of garrulous women claiming visions should not be fostered by male confessors, who thereby abdicate their divinely ordained, virile leadership role. Such encouragement only nurtures the women's false pretensions and delights the devil.

Yet Gerson was to become even more outspoken on this issue. His last

[79] *PS*, 181.
[80] *PS*, 184.

work on the discernment of spirits, *On the Examination of Doctrines*, is openly contemptuous of women. Gerson's jeremiad argues at one point that women are disqualified from divine revelations by virtue of their sex alone. He presents a formidable array of religious and social objections, as well as physiological arguments regarding the weakness of women's intellects and temperaments:

> The female sex was prohibited authority by the Apostle, lest they teach in public. . . . How, then, could it be suitable for this sex to walk in greatness, surrounded with miracles? To receive visions added to more visions daily? To consider injuries to the brain like epilepsy or catatonia (*congelatio*), or the symptoms of melancholy, to be a miracle? Finally, to speak entirely in God's place, without any mediating revelation? To call the priests of God, whom they ought to obey as superiors, their "sons"? The very sex where the devil was incarnated! . . . All the doctrines of women, especially those established in word or writing, must be considered suspect unless they have first been . . . carefully examined, and much more so than the doctrines of men. . . . Why? Because [women] are easier to seduce; because they are more pertinacious in seducing others; because it is not an established fact that they are knowers of divine wisdom![81]

Gerson perceived the plague of women visionaries as part of a broader abdication, on the part of men, of their duties of oversight. The comment concerning women visionaries who call their confessors their "sons" likely refers to Catherine of Siena, who did indeed address her confessors and devotees as sons, as they called her "mommy (*mamma*)."[82] On a broader level, however, the passage is an indictment of clergy who allow women to adopt the dominant role in their relationship and embrace a puerile and emasculated role for themselves.[83] To solve these problems, he suggests, male clerics must reassert their proper and natural authority—in part by seizing the initiative in the discernment of spirits.

---

[81] *ED*, 456.

[82] Vauchez, "La sainteté mystique," 252.

[83] For more on this trope, John Coakley, "Friars as Confidants of Holy Women in Medieval Dominican Hagiography," in R. Blumenfeld-Kosinski and T. Szell, eds., *Images of Sainthood in Medieval Europe* (Ithaca, N.Y., 1991), 222–46.

Langenstein bitterly lamented that fools, the young, and the ignorant ruled. For Pierre d'Ailly, too many men had become effeminate; for Jean Gerson, puerile. As a result of these dislocations of power, schismatic disorder reigned. The solution was, of course, for strong, mature men to seize their birthright as leaders and forcibly reestablish a virile age. Only in this way would the schism permanently be healed; only through masculine leadership could the Church regain her tarnished prestige; only through proper hierarchy could order be achieved.

Gerson had a unifying symbol of male dominance and power ready to propose. On September 8, 1416, a little more than one year after his presentation of *On the Testing of Spirits*, Gerson delivered an impassioned sermon to the Council of Constance on the feast of the Nativity of the Virgin. The main subject of his discourse, however, was Joseph, "Mary's husband, and thus her head, for the man is the head of the woman."[84] With this text, we may begin to explore Gerson's thoughts on masculinity. Gerson had long been interested in promoting a cult for the foster father of Jesus, and he argued that Joseph had been unfairly denied his rightful place in the regard of the faithful. His choice of Joseph as a role model is significant for several reasons. First, Gerson was exalting an alternate model of the exemplary lay saint in contradistinction to the form of lay sanctity that he rejected in his discernment works. Thus in opposition to the histrionic novelties of contemporary laywomen saints like Brigit and Catherine, Gerson offered the sober paragon of a lay male saint with apostolic credentials, whom he portrayed as a model of virile domination. He strenuously argued the case for a feast day in honor

---

[84] Jean Gerson, *In festo nativitatis B. Mariae Virginis*, in Glorieux, *Jean Gerson: Oeuvres complètes*, 5:344. For scholarly treatments of this text, see Rosemary Drage Hale, "Joseph as Mother: Adaptation and Appropriation in the Construction of Male Virtue," in J. C. Parson and B. Wheeler, eds., *Medieval Mothering* (New York, 1996), 101–16; Pamela Sheingorn, "'Illustris patriarcha Joseph': Jean Gerson, Representations of Saint Joseph, and Imagining Community among Churchmen in the Fifteenth Century," in N. Howe, *Visions of Community in the Pre-Modern World* (Notre-Dame, Ind., 2002), 75–108. I am much indebted to both of these scholars for their generosity in email correspondence. S. Melchior-Bonnet, "De Gerson à Montaigne, le pouvoir et l'amour," in J. Delumeau and D. Roche, eds., *Histoire des pères et de la paternité* (Paris, 1990), 55–70; Christiane Klapisch-Zuber, "Zacharias, or, The Ousted Father: Nuptial Rites in Tuscany between Giotto and the Council of Trent," in *Women, Family, and Ritual in Renaissance Italy*, trans. L. Cochraine (Chicago, 1985), 178–212.

of Joseph, though "not because we are in favor of a multiplication of feast days among the vulgar who live by manual labor—if only the number of such feast days among this type of people were lower!"[85] For Gerson, it was simply that Joseph, as an apostolic saint and the manly head of the Holy Family, merited a feast in a way that Brigit, for example, manifestly did not.

Moreover, Gerson's depiction of Joseph is, in itself, an interesting divergence from previous tradition. By the fifteenth century Joseph long had been portrayed as a divinely cuckolded, feeble old man entirely lacking in the vigorous qualities with which Gerson endowed him. Indeed, nativity plays and popular narratives such as the *Golden Legend* presented Joseph as comically emasculated, ineptly doing "women's work" such as feeding, bathing, or swaddling the child. In one popular drama, Joseph's incompetence in cooking porridge provokes a fistfight between him and the Christ child, which the infant Jesus quickly and decisively wins.[86] In response to this humiliating portrayal, Gerson attempted to remasculate Joseph as a righteous young male by emphasizing his virile leadership over his wife: "Joseph was the head of Mary, having therefore authority, preeminence, dominance, and rule over Mary."[87] In short, Gerson boldly was transforming a well-known example of an effeminate male into a virile one, and propounding this newly—and profoundly—masculine figure as an exemplar for his peers to emulate. If the "old" Joseph was the symbol of weak men in the effeminate age leading up to the schism, then Gerson's new, remasculated Joseph could provide a model for contemporaries to seize their neglected virility. Indeed, if feminine leadership lay at the origin of the schism, a collective turn to Joseph's manly model would, Gerson hoped, heal it. His sermon suggested that by instituting a feast in honor of Joseph, the Council might more swiftly gain its objective of Church unity and a return to the naturally hierarchical order of society: "Through the merits and intercession of so great a patron, of such a powerful and domineering man with respect to his wife . . . the Church may be reunited with her true and certain husband, a single pope who is her spouse and the vicar of Christ. Then finally, with your intervention, most glorious Joseph, and (if it is right to speak thus) with you laying down your law . . . we will be restored to the One God."[88] In the figure of Joseph the domineering *pater familias*, Gerson thus reestablished a male figure as the ultimate intercessory power. To honor Joseph in this masculine role would be

---

[85] Gerson, *In festo nativitatis*, 362.
[86] Hale, "Joseph as Mother," 106.
[87] Gerson, *In festo nativitatis*, 358.
[88] Ibid., 362.

the first step in the rebirth of the virile age, and hence the healing of the effeminate, schismatic disorder.

THE REJECTION OF DIVINE POSSESSION

Were the treatises on the discernment of spirits successful? When Langenstein, d'Ailly, and Gerson issued these dire warnings, was anybody listening? Did these texts have any practical effect? We must avoid the trap of assuming that an intellectual tradition necessarily influences practice, that merely because something is written down, it changes the way people think.

On the most restricted level of analysis, the answer to all three questions is no. To the degree that these discernment theorists singled out specific individuals for judgment, their counsel was a spectacular failure.[89] We know that Langenstein explicitly wrote against the canonization of Brigit, that Gerson derided Brigit and Catherine as silly women who led a pontiff into schism, and that d'Ailly likewise expressed concerns about the "false prophets" and their effeminate followers who initiated the rift in the Church. Yet Brigit wore a halo, and Catherine of Siena's canonization inquiry was underway. In short, precisely those people whom the discernment of spirits treatises aimed to prove vain and delusive were instead being canonized as divinely inspired visionaries. Brigit and Catherine were exemplars, for these writers, of the hubris of silly women who fell into the devil's oldest snare: believing events that were natural or demonic in origin to be marks of divine favor and individual merit. Yet the expert judgments of Langenstein, d'Ailly, and Gerson apparently carried little practical weight: the effeminate age persisted under feminine models of leadership.

Indeed, it is striking that every judgment about sanctity that Gerson proposed in his writings was ignored by his immediate contemporaries. This was so not only in regard to Brigit of Sweden and Catherine of Siena but also in terms of his saintly endorsements, which also failed to win the appreciation of his peers. He fervently urged the Council of Constance to institute a feast day in honor of a remasculated Joseph, but the suggestion was ignored in the short term: no cult for Joseph the *pater familias* was established in Gerson's lifetime. Indeed, Joseph continued to be depicted as an effeminate, feeble old

---

[89] I would like to thank André Vauchez for asking me about the failure of these writings in a conversation we had long ago at the Vatican Archives. His generosity in agreeing to have coffee with an excited graduate student is remembered fondly.

man in Gerson's generation. An additional counterexample is provided by the history of Joan of Arc—though her case is less about the discernment of spirits than about the political self-interests of those evaluating her. Gerson wrote in favor of Joan's holiness, a position that was informed as much by the precise form of her religiosity as by Gerson's own suffering at the hands of the Burgundian faction during the Hundred Years' War. Unlike Brigit, who had favored the English,[90] Joan was for Gerson a heaven-sent rallying symbol for France: "the celestial King chose this female standard-bearer for confounding the enemies of justice."[91]

More importantly, perhaps Joan's "virile" garments signified for Gerson a unique and positive gender transcendence, in which a woman had become miraculously masculine. Indeed, it is Joan's virile qualities above all that set her apart from Brigit and Catherine, whom Gerson viewed as excessively identified with femininity in all its immoderate fervor: garrulous, self-dramatizing, melancholic, hysterical, and easily deluded by demons. By contrast, Gerson likely saw in Joan a potential return to an age dominated by a masculine strength and righteousness that ideally should extend to both sexes. Women might again become like the virile virgins of the apostolic Church; men might (like Joseph) recover their domineering role, and thus both sexes would be removed from the vulgar pettiness of the late effeminate age. In this regard, it was highly significant for Gerson that Joan did not, like Brigit and Catherine, engage in histrionic penitential asceticism: Joan never entered altered states of consciousness in which she saw visions, nor did she claim direct intimacy with the Almighty, but only heard the voices of the virile virgin martyr-saints Margaret and Catherine.[92] Joan did not engage in extended fasts, vigils, prayers, or self-flagellation like the silly women of recent note. Most important, perhaps, she did not presume to disseminate written revelations or to offer religious interpretation of any kind. Joan thus avoided precisely those behaviors that Gerson had complained about in regard to Brigit and Catherine. However, in Joan's case as well, Gerson's individual judgment was diametrically opposed to the outcome of a formal inquiry, for Joan was burned as a heretic.[93]

[90] The effects of this choice are explored by André Vauchez, "La faible diffusion des *Révélations* de Sainte Brigitte de Suède dans l'espace français: Les causes d'un rejet," in *Les laïcs*, 162–74. For the English response to Brigit, see Nancy Warren, *Spiritual Economies: Female Monasticism in Later Medieval England* (Philadelphia, 2001).

[91] Jean Gerson, *De puella Aurelianensi*, in Glorieux, *Jean Gerson: Oeuvres complètes*, 9:661–65.

[92] For more on Joan's personal piety, see Étienne Delaruelle, "La spiritualité de Jeanne d'Arc," in *La piété populaire au Moyen Age* (Turin, 1980), 389–400.

[93] Of course, Joan's case also was complicated by political and military considerations, which nullified the religious evaluation of her career. For more on Joan, see Jules Qui-

Thus Gerson, for all his prominence at Constance and for all the aggressive bravado of his writings, was singularly ineffective in molding the opinions of his contemporaries on the topic of discernment: those whom he rejected as falsely inspired, typically "feminine" delusives were canonized, while those whom he exalted as uniquely "virile" lay saints were ignored or worse. In part, this situation was the result of Gerson's own obstreperousness. At the Council of Constance, for example, where Gerson led the French delegation,[94] he repeatedly turned the agenda of the council toward political considerations foreign to the main purpose of the meeting. Gerson's overzealous and repetitive denunciations of Jean Petit's defense of tyrannicide at this gathering devoted to religious affairs alienated many of his supporters, including some who ultimately were appointed as judges in the trial of Joan of Arc.[95] It is not difficult to imagine that Gerson's uncompromising character might have solidified opposition at Constance to some of his other positions as well.

However, to judge the influence of Gerson, Langenstein, and d'Ailly by this standard alone would be a limited purview. Despite these narrow failures, the discourse of discernment was to be extremely influential over the *longue durée*, though perhaps not in the ways imagined by its formulators. Although Gerson failed to impede the canonization of Brigit, his treatise dedicated to her case, *On the Testing of Spirits*, nonetheless survives in forty-eight manuscript copies.[96] Taken together with the less popular *On Distinguishing*

cherat, ed., *Procès de condamnation et de réhabilitation de Jeanne d'Arc, dite la Pucelle* (Paris, 1841; reprint, New York, 1965); Deborah Fraioli, *Joan of Arc: The Early Debate* (Suffolk, 2000); André Vauchez, "Jeanne d'Arc et le prophétisme féminin des XIVe et XVe siècles," in *Le laïcs*, 277–86. For the English response to Joan, see Warren, *Spiritual Economies*, 163–82.

[94] On the organization of the Council by nation, see Louise Loomis, "Nationality at the Council of Constance: An Anglo-French Dispute," *American Historical Review* 44, 3 (1939): 508–27.

[95] The details of the affair are complicated. Suffice it to say that Petit had composed a defense of tyrannicide in order to legitimate the murder of the duke of Orléans in 1407 by an agent of the duke of Burgundy. Although the latter originally had been a patron of Gerson's, he was outraged by the assassination and continually fulminated against Petit for the rest of his life, thereby losing the patronage of the duke.

Fraioli, *Joan of Arc*, 10–11, discusses how this debate galvanized opposition to Gerson among those who ultimately would be prosecutors in the Joan of Arc case. See also Sheingorn, "'Illustris patriarcha Joseph,'" which suggests that Gerson's promotion of Joseph was not immediately effective; Geneviève Hasenohr, "Religious Reading amongst the Laity in France in the Fifteenth Century," in P. Biller and A. Hudson, eds., *Heresy and Literacy, 1000–1530* (Cambridge, 1994), 205–21, showing that Gerson's guides for lay piety were not widely disseminated until closer to the end of the century.

[96] For this and other manuscript counts for Gerson's works, see Glorieux, "Introduction général," 39.

True Visions from False (eleven copies) and *On the Examination of Doctrines* (seven), Gerson's writings on the discernment of spirits can be described as moderately well disseminated before the introduction of print. I have been unable to find statistics on manuscripts of Pierre d'Ailly's works, but Henry of Langenstein's *On the Discernment of Spirits* outnumbered all of Gerson's treatises combined: a "non-exhaustive" survey lists seventy-nine versions of this text.[97] Thus while these treatises were not precisely medieval best sellers, neither were they ignored. Indeed, if we look to the next generation of thinkers, we can trace the broad cultural influence of these works clearly.

Taken collectively, this triad of authors succeeded in moving the debate over the testing of spirits to new ground, even as they humbly protested the difficulty of the undertaking. As Henry of Langenstein noted, one "cannot judge acts at their origin" but only "investigate their end and fulfillment." Combined with Henry's deep-seated suspicion of extreme behaviors and asceticism, this principle resulted in a discernment ideal that held bodily discipline and moderation to be the key elements of a sincere holiness. Histrionic possessed behaviors were not to be credited as indicators of divine indwelling. Pierre d'Ailly's concession that there is no "doctrine that is particular, certain, and infallible" was followed with an exhortation to be constantly vigilant and watchful against the excess asceticism of deceivers and false prophets, and the effeminate men they advised. Similarly, Gerson's caveat— "to test the spirits . . . through a general and infallible rule or art either cannot be done at all or can scarcely be done through human ability . . . [for] no one can recognize with infallible certainty those things which are done within the soul of another through individual experiential knowledge or an interior sentiment and perception"[98]—was juxtaposed with a perpetual stream of reminders to beware the overenthusiastic claims and behaviors of certain people: the young, the ignorant, and above all, women.

Here we arrive at the crux of the matter. Where Langenstein, d'Ailly, and Gerson succeeded was not in setting forth infallible guidelines for testing *spirits*, but in setting forth the criteria for testing *bodies*. The discernment of spirits was acknowledged to be impossible: visions and revelations are private, and hence unverifiable. One must rely upon the body alone: any effective practice of *discretio spirituum* was in fact a *discretio corporum*. This principle extended, of course, from bodily behaviors to bodily sex, with women singled out for particular attention.

[97] Thomas Hohmann, ed., *Heinrichs von Langenstein: "Unterscheidung der Geister," Lateinisch und Deutsch: Texte und Untersuchungen zu Übersetzungsliteratur aus der Wiener Schule* (Munich, 1977), 19–21.

[98] *PS*, 178.

To be sure, this emphasis upon the body was not a radical break with the past, for in some ways this standard was already in place. Communities scrutinized bodies and behaviors, because they could not verify visions. Intellectuals naturalized spirit possession, entrenching the operations of spirits within the deepest internal physiology of the body. Despite all the ink that had been spilled, it might seem that discernment of spirits had scarcely advanced beyond the words written by Innocent III in 1199: "It is not enough for someone to flatly assert that they have been sent by God, when that commission is internal and private, for any heretic can say as much."[99] What was new, however, was the precise hierarchy of values placed upon particular bodily behaviors. The fifteenth-century testing of spirits debate succeeded in prioritizing new ways of reading the body. Not surprisingly, the specific criteria our authors elaborated were charged with an electric significance for the history of the laity's and of women's claims to religious authority. The same behaviors that once had rendered possessed women ciphers, betokening either divine or demonic possession according to the interpretation of the audience, now were seen as clues to the indwelling of unclean spirits only. Acts of deep penitential asceticism, such as prolonged fasting, were redefined. Rather than indicating the possible presence of the Holy Spirit, such practices now were taken as likely indicators of hubris and demonic delusion, as in the woman of Arras. Trances and visions were relocated from the field of divine revelation to the terrain of the fatuous and the deluded. As Henry of Langenstein asserted, no new revelations were needed from God. For a lowly person to assert that she had received a revelation was an indication of either hubris or fantasy, and therefore a disqualification from holiness. The "gift of tears"—earlier seen as a miraculous capacity both for empathy with Christ's sufferings and for remorse for sin—was viewed by these authors as foolish and hysterical. Even the performance of miracles was of no value in judging visionaries, for "the Antichrist will be the most mendacious minister of miracles." Above all, the Great Schism demonstrated the disastrous lack of discernment that was characteristic of the leadership of the effeminate age. This proved how necessary it was to reorder the Church under properly virile authority, with women and the laity in subordinate positions. Even as Brigit and Catherine succeeded in becoming canonized, they initiated a debate that closed the ranks of the saints against other visionary women.

If we turn from the search to identify true visionaries and compare this rhetoric, for a moment, with texts dedicated to identifying and treating demoniacs, we see a striking convergence of values. For just as authors writing

[99] Innocent III, letter 46, in *PL*, 214:697.

on discernment saw women as unlikely to be the bearers of divine prerogatives, and the undisciplined body as a prime indicator of their falsity, so contemporary exorcisms identify women as the primary victims of demonic
possession and hold up the part-by-part disciplining of their bodies as the
main remedy for their condition. Similar, too, is the urgent eschatological
tone of the exorcisms, which present the irruption of possessing spirits into
the bodies of living human beings as a sign of the imminent End Times. Both
sources also were concerned with the reimposition of proper hierarchies:
men over women and clergy over laity. Lastly, the unwonted use in both genres of female pronouns—in one as a positive identification for demoniacs, in
the other as a negative identification of those unlikely to be saints—demonstrates yet another convergence of themes from both directions. A reading
of either group of texts leads to the following conclusion: as part of the early
End Times, many of the impressionable weaker sex will be led astray under
the inspirations of demons; they will display immoderate and extreme behaviors, for which the best cure is bodily discipline and the reordering of the
social body according to natural, divinely instituted hierarchies. Although
the textual genres are quite different, the broader cultural norms they express
are largely identical.

In sum, these texts together narrowed the scope of interpretation for possessed behaviors. Since the thirteenth century, a largely identical set of activities—trances, visions, convulsions, tears, frenzies, fasting—had been
ascribed both to the divinely possessed and to demoniacs. Thus the behaviors themselves were ambivalent, the individual displaying them was a cipher,
and the process of discernment depended upon the social negotiations of outside observers. The fifteenth century, however, saw a negative shift in the understanding of these behaviors, particularly when they were exhibited by
uncloistered, unmarried women. Now, immoderate possessed behaviors increasingly came to seem demonic in character.

The definition of sanctity that resulted from treatises on the testing of
spirits now had a new center of gravity. The incorporative religious idiom
preferred by laywomen since the thirteenth century was rejected, as sanctity
increasingly was defined in nonmaterialist, strictly metaphysical terms. The
saints embodied a more incorporeal, highly controlled state. Possessed behaviors and the attendant claims to have incorporated the Spirit of God were
simply too ambivalent, too close to manifestations of possession by unclean
spirits, to be sustained. The failed tradition of discerning spirits ultimately
engendered a discernment by body that was extremely effective. The elaboration of the idiom of divine possession in the thirteenth century helped

bring about a tighter, more exclusive connection between women and the demonic at the close of the Middle Ages.

EPILOGUE: FROM CONSTANCE TO BASEL AND BEYOND

In the next generation, the discourse of discernment reached its logical conclusion, like an overripe fruit that falls close to the tree that bore it. Henry of Langenstein, Pierre d'Ailly, and Jean Gerson all were dead by the time the Council of Basel convened in 1431. Yet their ideas were vividly present: at Basel, yet again, Brigit's revelations were publicly debated when the German theologian Mathias Döring attempted to have 123 propositions drawn from her writings condemned as heresy; the minutes note that "her revelations seemed superstitious to very many people there."[100] However, in these final pages let us direct our gaze to the work of another figure connected both with Constance and with Basel. The Dominican Johannes Nider, who attended both meetings, produced his famous dialogue between "Theologian" and "Mr. Lazy" while in attendance at Basel. This text, the *Formicarius* or *Ant Hill*, shows us the uses to which ideas about the discernment of spirits were being put in the generation after Constance. One of those uses was to set forth ideas about witchcraft.

Although some scholars have assumed a connection between the discernment of spirits and the formation of the witchcraft stereotype, no one has actually explored the substance or trajectory of this historical development.[101] In the present context I can only sketch a broad outline of this complex process, in which Nider's *Formicarius* constitutes an important hinge text. The work has long been known as a precursor and source for the *Malleus maleficarum:* its significance in this light continues to grow in recent scholarship on witchcraft.[102] At the same time, however, the *Formicarius* clearly

[100] Vauchez, "La faible diffusion des *Révélations*," 165. See also Gustav Beckmann, Rudolf Wackernagel, and Giulio Coggiola, eds., *Concilium Basiliense. Studien und Quellen zur Geschichte des Concils von Basel, Herausgegeben mit Unterstutzung der Historischen und Antiquarischen Gesellschaft von Basel*, 5 vols. (Basel, 1904), 5:123.

[101] I suggested this connection in Nancy Caciola, "Discerning Spirits: Sanctity and Possession in the Later Middle Ages" (PhD diss., University of Michigan, 1994). More recently, McGuire, "Care and Control of Women," 35; McNamara, "Rhetoric of Orthodoxy," 26; and Elliott, "Seeing Double," 54.

[102] For background on Nider, see Catherine Chène, "Johannes Nider, Formicarius,"

stems from the debate over the discernment of spirits and foregrounds consideration of true versus false visions. The text thus provides a mediating point between these two realms of discourse.

Nider's work has five books of twelve chapters each. These are their subject matters:

Book 1: On the rare examples and deeds of good people.
Book 2: On possibly good visions.
Book 3: On false and illusory visions.
Book 4: On the righteous works of the perfect.
Book 5: On witches and their deceptions.[103]

In short, the *Formicarius* is loosely structured around a double-binary discernment theme, prefaced by a warning and rife with skepticism. Book 1 stands alone as an analysis of the rarity of good deeds. But the remaining books clearly are matched together as mirror images of one another. Books 2 and 3, on possibly true and on clearly false revelations respectively, constitute a pair. So do books 4 and 5, on saints and witches. The whole work is initiated by a prologue that enjoins vigilant suspicion in evaluating all supernatural reports, but "especially those of women, unless they are tested, for I suspect that many of them are always delusive in such things."[104]

This statement sets a recurrent theme for the remainder of Nider's lengthy work. Indeed, though he acknowledges three diagnoses for false visions—simulation (for the sake of money), demonic possession, and demonic delusion—only in the first category do men dominate. When it comes to actual supernatural visions, women excel, a situation Nider described thus: "It probably ought to terrify us to no little extent that recently, in these days in which we find ourselves, as dangerous times approach, it is found that women, the sex that is weaker and more flighty of soul, have visions more frequently than men, by nature the stronger sex and more stable of mind." Nider here returns

---

in *L'Imaginaire du Sabbat: Editions critique des textes les plus anciens (1430 c.–1440 c.)*, Martine Ostorero, Agostino Paravacini Bagliani, and Kathrin Utz Tremp (Lausanne, 1999), 99–265. Michael Bailey, *Battling Demons: Witchcraft, Heresy, and Reform in the Late Middle Ages* (University Park, Penn., 2003); idem, "From Sorcery to Witchcraft: Clerical Conceptions of Magic in the Later Middle Ages," *Speculum* 76, 4 (2001): 960–90. Arno Borst, "The Origins of the Witch-Craze in the Alps," in *Medieval Worlds: Barbarians, Heretics, and Artists in the Middle Ages*, trans. E. Hansen (Chicago, 1991), 101–24; I also have benefited from the unpublished comments of Gábor Klaniczay in "Trance, Apparition, and Skepticism in Johannes Nider, *Formicarius*."

[103] *F*, prologus, unnumbered folio.
[104] Ibid.

to an old refrain: the predominance of visions among women rather than men is itself a sign of the Last Days, as demonic forces become ever stronger and debilitate Christian society. At one point Mr. Lazy interjects a note of skepticism toward the Theologian's teachings on women, however. He recalls that he once heard about a woman who complained to a scholar, "You men put down in writing many things that are excessively contrary to our weak sex. But if we, like you, had the ability to write and teach, we would in turn raise doubts about your faith." The Theologian assures Mr. Lazy that he does not object to women per se, only to their stupidity and malice. He goes on to teach that men are superior to women in five ways: their nature is closer to God, they are freer in body and soul, their complexions are warmer, their bodies are more elegant, and their social status is higher. In conclusion, he urges Mr. Lazy not to credit female reports of visions, complaining that one should not "quickly lend a believing ear to a silly women in their claims of visions . . . how easily the feminine sex errs if not regulated by the wise masculine sex."[105]

Nider illustrates his point with detailed descriptions of delusive female inspiration, a theme that dominates book 3. He mentions a recluse who proclaimed that she would publicly receive the stigmata on a particular day, but failed to become supernaturally wounded, and a woman named Magdalena who prophesied her own public death, only to live. Yet another woman wandered throughout the city of Regensburg preaching that she was filled with the spirit of God. Arrested and tortured, Nider himself visited her in prison and explained to her the necessity for the discernment of spirits. Nider's presentations of these case histories are structured so as to pass on an important lesson that he may well have learned at the Council of Constance from Gerson's presentation on Brigit: visionaries—especially when they are women—must be tested. Silly women's claims to divine intimacy, to oracular utterance, or to bodily miracles are inherently suspect. The stories Nider tells are plotted so as to demonstrate, incontrovertibly and pragmatically, the lessons of discernment treatises. Thus in one case, the woman herself was made to see her errors, in prison, by Nider. In the case of the stigmatic *manquée*, her unwounded hands and feet testify to the falsity of her delusions. Magdalena is examined by the personal doctor of the town council for signs of mortality, and it is this man's announcement that life persisted in her body that provides the public dénouement to the episode. In the *Formicarius*, women's inner spiritual inspiration is irrefutably proven false during their lifetimes, with definitive results and eyewitness testimony. Thus did Nider lend scientific verisimilitude to the skepticism enjoined by Gerson at Constance.

[105] *F* 2.1, 20v; 3.4, 43r; 3.8, 49v–50r.

If Nider's work exemplified a new, stringent external standard for the discernment of spirits, it also contributed to the formation of another emerging cultural idea: the witch. Indeed, the Council of Basel was an important site for the early exchange of ideas about witches and witchcraft, and Nider's *Formicarius* was at the forefront of this nascent stereotype.[106] The contents of book 5 outline the classic features of diabolic witchcraft, thus adding this new ingredient to the project of discernment. Significantly, witches, as Nider describes them, are embodiments of every dark force or negative idea that ever was raised in relation to the testing of spirits. These characteristics are reduced to their most extreme and primal form, and synthesized with ideas drawn from other persecutory traditions, such as charges of infanticide and infant cannibalism.[107] To begin, witches like the divinely and the demonically possessed, were for Nider mostly female. Like demoniacs, witches continually are surrounded by a cacophony of destructive demonic forces that invade their bodies and pervert their actions—but they freely yield to these forces of their own volition, paying homage to their "little master," the devil. Like false prophetesses, witches hubristically seek influence over others and engender the apocalyptic downfall of human institutions—but do so as part of a vast demonic conspiracy sealed by a drink made from liquefied infants. Like the divinely and the demonically possessed, witches can work miracles: walking on water, changing the weather, revealing secret thoughts, predicting the future, controlling fertility.

Indeed, witchcraft is an extreme but logical conclusion of the shifts in the interpretation of possessed behaviors engendered by the discernment of spirits. Thus when Mr. Lazy requests an example of a witch who deceived good men, the Theologian responds with the example of Joan of Arc, noting that many men of high estate "wondered by which spirit she was ruled, whether divine or diabolic." Yet the ultimate resolution Nider offers about Joan is not that she was possessed in some way, but that she was a witch: "At last she confessed that she had a familiar angel from God which, in the judgment of highly learned men was deemed to be an evil spirit, after many conclusions and tests. Through this spirit she was made into a witch."[108] With Nider's

---

[106] Martin Ostorero, *Folâtrer avec les démons: Sabbat et chasse aux sorciers à Vevey (1448)* (Lausanne, 1995), 27; see also the sources cited in note 102.

[107] The scholarship of witchcraft is vast. For treatments that focus mainly on the medieval roots of the learned stereotype, see Bailey, *Battling Demons;* Norman Cohn, *Europe's Inner Demons: An Enquiry Inspired by the Great Witch Hunt* (New York, 1975); Carlo Ginzburg, *Ecstasies: Deciphering the Witches' Sabbath* (New York, 1991); Richard Kieckhefer, *European Witch Trials: Their Foundations in Popular and Learned Culture, 1300–1500* (Berkeley, 1976).

[108] *F* 5.3, 74r–v; 5.4, 75v; 5.8, 81v; 5.8, 82r.

work we see the traditional twin categories of discernment expanding to include an additional choice: the witch. This third alternative, now available as part of the process of judgment, was to become an important new category on the horizon of the supernatural.

The most extensive medieval compilation of witchcraft ideas, the *Malleus maleficarum*, derived much of its basic description of witchcraft from Nider.[109] Indeed, its author, Henry Kramer, explicitly complained of the effeminate age as a corrosive epoch of witchcraft and went on to describe a vast feminine conspiracy against male prerogatives of every kind: social-hierarchical, sexual, and religious. The perception of an inversion of the natural order of the sexes, earlier deplored by Gerson and others, reached its acme in the *Malleus*.[110] Moreover, the works of all these authors—Gerson, Nider, and Kramer—frequently were printed together in compilations of anti-witchcraft materials.[111] Together, they helped to define the witchcraft stereotype for centuries. The effeminate age was taking on new life.

[109] Catherine Chène and Martine Ostorero, "Demonologie et misogynie: L'emergence d'un discours specifique sur la femme dans l'elaboration doctrinale du sabbat au XVe siècle," in A.-L. Head-Koenig and L. Mottu-Weber, eds., *Les femmes dans la societé europeenne* (Geneva, 2000), 171–96.

[110] Indeed, it is notable that just as the *Malleus* was first published in 1486, Jean Gerson's reputation underwent a dramatic revival of prestige. Gerson's collected works were published in no less than six printed editions between their first incunabula appearance in 1483 and the last in 1494. Glorieux, "Introduction général," 71–72; also see Hasenohr, "Religious Reading," which shows that Gerson's works for the laity were not widely disseminated until the end of the century.

[111] McGuire, "Care and Control of Women," 35; Henry Kramer and Jacob Sprenger, *Malleus maleficarum*, 2 vols. (Lyons 1669; reprint, Brussels, 1969), 2:45–51.

INDEX

CPSIA information can be obtained
at www.ICGtesting.com
Printed in the USA
LVOW12s2131191017
553037LV00004B/358/P